WHITE LADY, BLACK SONS

White Lady, Black Sons

a memoir of adoption, abuse and awakening

Lisa Richesson

DEDICATION

This book is lovingly dedicated to the following people, in order of appearance in my life:

Marcy Johnsen

Fred Larkins

John Boles

ACKNOWLEDGMENTS

I WOULD LIKE to acknowledge and thank the following folks for their invaluable and kind guidance as I wrote this book. Without them, I'd still be wondering why I can't write:

Kim Severn Denny
Janice Harper, PhD
Marcy Johnsen
Brian Knight

A special thanks to Allegra Berrian McFarland for the cover design and a very special thanks to Aurianna and Makenna Boles for the back cover art.

And deep gratitude to Ginny Larkins.

Many thanks to my Indiegogo contributors:

Louise Allen
Gayle Anderson
Anonymous
Kate Blessing
Vera Bryant
David Brubakken, PhD
Amy Bush
Catherine Carter

Dale Hitsman
Denise Johnsen
Marcy Johnsen
Laurel Johnson
Fred Larkins
Mona Nelson
Sherry and Shelby Peterson
Rick Polintan
and Pacita Buang

Kim Severn Denny
Beth DeRooy
Dick Hansen
Janice Harper, PhD

Bob and Pat Rudolph
Paula Sage
Karin Strand
Sandy Wojnowska and
Marion Saunders

TABLE OF CONTENTS

PROLOGUE

Summer 1988

I WOKE EARLY and tiptoed down the hallway to the living room. There they were, sprawled on the floor in front of a flickering TV, fast asleep. Scattered all around them were empty gum wrappers, stray popcorn and tattered comic books.

I held my breath as I stood looking at them. Fifteen year old John was so tall and thin he looked like a refugee. At eighteen, Isaiah was taller and fuller, but he looked like he could have been John's twin. I listened to their rhythmic breathing in sync with each other as my own breath began to follow. I wanted to imprint this scene on my mind and in my heart in case I never saw it again. As I memorized each twisted limb, two perfect mouths, long eyelashes brushing both their cheeks, and each gum wrapper and popcorn kernel scattered around them, a rush of wonder, anxiety and hope engulfed me. There, right next to my fifteen year old, lay his older brother. The boy I had so reluctantly given up for adoption eighteen years before was now snoring on my living room floor.

My mind went back in time. All those years ago, I never dreamed I would see my sons together. All the heartache, guilt and secrecy of the past eighteen years were wiped away. I felt as if I'd just walked out of a dark and damning prison, free at last.

Chapter 1

They're Surrounding the Building!

In August 1969, right after high school, I got my first job as a letter carrier. There weren't many female carriers at the time and I liked to think that I was a pioneer. It paid well, didn't require sitting in some stuffy office, and put me squarely and solidly on my own. My mother had been overjoyed, saying that as a civil servant, I would have this government job for the rest of my life, my financial future would be guaranteed, and a happy retirement would await me someday.

That might have been her idea of my future, but I had other plans: I would go to London where I would be poor and cold, suffer and lose weight, drink copious cups of hot tea and become a writer. I had longed to be in London for as long as I could remember. Perhaps it was the sense of history, or the literary lives that played out there over the centuries. I didn't know. It was just a pull of my heart and spirit to be there.

Inspired by John Lennon's *In His Own Write* I started writing poems at fourteen. I had no idea that writing could be so incredibly fulfilling. Poetry helped me build a world inside myself that was beautiful, replete with the joy of words. I had found my bliss quite early and fought hard over the years to retain it. I knew that London would inspire me to write great things, and I would soon earn enough money to move from my imagined garret in the East End to a posh flat in St. John's Wood. Those were *my* dreams, and *my* plans.

To get me started on my path to impoverished writing and literary fame, I got my first apartment. While it was sort of old-fashioned and dull, and nothing like the cozy book-lined studio I'd have in London, it was mine. I decorated it by hanging a poster from the Sgt. Pepper album on the wall, along with posters of Jean-Paul Belmondo, Marlon Brando, and Jimi Hendrix—rebels all. And my favorite dreamy troubadour, Donovan.

Every day began the same way. My alarm would go off at 4:30 and I would be up. It felt good to get up without my mom shouting at me to get my ass in gear. I was 18 years old and in my own apartment at last. The Murphy bed folded up into the wall; I closed the doors and voila – no one would know if I tucked in my sheets or not.

Things were going well in my new life. I had graduated from high school and was dancing to my own beat, working and spending my own money. But then one morning, after I'd showered and dressed and fixed breakfast, while the glorious morning sunshine poured through my kitchen window and the radio played a Stones song, I threw up my poached egg and toast. I'd never felt so nauseated. Avoiding the truth wasn't going to work anymore.

I was pregnant.

And the father was black.

And I'm white.

What the hell was I going to do?

The summer of 1969 was a time of extremes, and America was at a crossroads. I didn't realize it at the time, but I was at a crossroads as well.

There was a palpable feeling in the country that youth was wise and elders were not, that the inevitable revolution would result in an earthly utopia, and that absolutely anything was possible. But such good vibes, I supposed, had to come to an end.

As John Lennon said, the dream was over.

I was a junior at Rainier Beach High School in Seattle, a largely white school that found itself in 1968 at a crossroads in race relations. In an effort to integrate the school, the school board decided to bus black students in from nearby Garfield High School and no one was happy about it. White students resented the dark-skinned urban invasion, while the black students resented having to travel so far to a school filled with privileged white kids. It was a disaster in the making.

One day after school ended, a fight between two students, one white, the other black, broke out in the student parking lot. A large throng gathered to watch the fight. There must have been nearly two hundred kids watching and cheering them on. With shouts of "Kill the nigger," most of the students cheered on the white kid, as I watched from the periphery of the crowd.

Finally, a few white male teachers heard the shouting. They ran out of the school to the parking lot and broke up the fight. The black kid was badly beaten, bleeding from his mouth and nose and barely able to stand. The kids taunted and laughed at him, calling him a "pansy-assed nigger." No one, not even the teachers, bothered to see if the black kid was okay, while the crowd grew even wilder and more menacing. The writer in me was an observer, but I still had enough sense to leave a situation when it turned ugly. It was time to get out of there.

My car—a baby blue Mustang my mother originally bought for herself—was parked in the student lot and I walked to it, all the while watching the melee nearby. I saw students running toward the crowd as it grew in intensity and violence. I'd never seen anything like it. The situation was out of control. It had grown into a riot. I got in my car and quickly drove away. But I hadn't gone more than a few blocks, when a stream of squad cars roared by, their lights and sirens bright and blazing, heading toward the school. I drove home feeling guilty and furtive, but didn't know why.

The next day the story was all over the news—stories about racial wars and riots that only enflamed the already volatile situation. The black students were furious that the school was doing nothing to protect them. In no time at all, their concerns reached the ears of the Black Panthers and they decided to pay the school a visit.

The Black Panther Party had founded a chapter in Seattle just the year before. They believed that the non-violent approach to civil rights had failed and any promised changes via the 'traditional' civil rights movement would take too long. None of us knew what to make of the Panthers—on the one hand, they were calling for equal housing, education, employment and civil rights. They were feeding the poor and starting day care centers. On the other hand, they dressed in military garb, carried guns and kept women out of their ranks. Inevitably, most of the white kids were terrified of them, and most of the black kids saw them as heroes.

Someone in my class yelled, "They're surrounding the building!"

"They've got guns!"

"They're coming to get us!"

Everyone ducked under their desks but me. I wasn't scared; I was fascinated. Anything out of the norm intrigued me and that somehow provided me with protection. Not being fearful made me a neutral entity.

I went to the windows and sure enough, we were surrounded by Black Panthers, dressed in their black coats and black berets, rifles shouldered and aimed towards the sky. *Wow*, I thought, *these guys mean business!*

I gathered my books and purse and left the second floor classroom. As I descended the steps, I saw a few Panthers had already entered the building. I could hear their boots marching in the hallways. A few students who looked like they were trying to run out saw the Panthers and froze in their tracks. I stood at the bottom of the stairs and watched.

"Hey, kid!" one Panther called out to one of the white boys. "Where's the principal's office?"

The student, wide-eyed and speechless, had pressed himself against the walls. One of them pointed the way to the principals' office.

"Down this way," asked one of the Panthers, jerking his head towards the main hall. The students nodded in unison, their eyes wide with the white fright of having armed black men take over the school. I watched as the Panthers walked away. Their expressions were neutral, neither angry nor fearful. Their business was not with the students, but with the administration of the school.

I followed after them and saw the Panthers enter the principal's office. I walked out the door and faced the rest of the Panthers surrounding the school. There they stood like soldiers, rifles slung over their shoulders, looking straight ahead. Some of them noticed me as I walked toward them.

"Hello," I said, nodding politely.

"Hey," a tall, very dark man in his sexy beret replied. I got in my car and drove home.

After that incident, I began to think about race in a completely different way. I had no reason to think people of other races were scary, and never associated racial differences with violence. But suddenly, race was coming to mean a whole new thing. And violence was at the heart of it. A violence that would sweep into my life without my even knowing it.

CHAPTER 2

THE FALL FROM GRACE

I WAS ALWAYS told that I was the most wanted child in the world. I heard over and over that during the first nine years of their marriage, my mother endured many miscarriages and had at least one "therapeutic" abortion before I was brought to life. The miscarriages were brought on by a condition called pernicious anemia, which meant that whenever my mother became pregnant, she couldn't keep food down, became malnourished and anemic, and inevitably lost the baby.

I was the result of an experiment. My parents found a pediatrician, Dr. Culp, who wanted to treat my mom with massive vitamin B shots three times a week throughout the pregnancy. My mother thought he had an amazing medical mind, but a psychic once told me that my mother's father, who died when she was three, interceded on my behalf with the powers that be. Whatever the method, vitamins or divine intervention, I was born, the only child of Leo and Grace Ulrich.

After all her losses, she would never attempt another pregnancy. I was their one and only child.

The belief that an only child is spoiled and coddled was not true in my case. For me, it was a lonely existence made worse by the contentious relationship between my mother and father. I often wished I had a sibling, if for no other reason than to compare notes on our unbalanced parents.

For the near decade before my birth, my parents had a life that revolved around jazz, bohemians and parties. Together they haunted record shops and clubs, attended gatherings full of raucous music and drinking and lived in odd, artsy apartments on Queen Anne Hill, the kinds of places that are expensive condos today.

Both had a unique sense of style. My father Leo, was tall and thin, and combined tweeds, hound's-tooth checks, stripes and disparate colors to great effect. No one dressed quite like he did. My mother Grace, short and plump, always wore classy outfits with matching pumps and purses, and great big rhinestone brooches. They loved to dance and when they did, they glided across the floor like swans on a still pond.

Leo grew up in a series of small dusty towns in Nebraska, Wyoming and Montana. His mother, Nona, operated various restaurants in small towns, the kind of eateries with bare wood floors, a long soda fountain and plain food. She was married seven times and Leo had a succession of indifferent stepfathers, some of whom he barely knew and others he only knew by the back of their hands or their belts. In the few photos I have of him as a child, he looks sullen and unhappy. He grew into an angry young man, joined the Army in 1940 and spent most of the war in the Philippines, constructing railway tracks.

Grace was born in Helena, Montana into an impoverished family. She was the last of nine children. In 1920, when Grace was three, her father was electrocuted in an industrial accident, leaving her mother with no education, no income, no husband and nine mouths to feed. My mother grew up in absolute poverty, and by the time she was in the eighth grade, she had to leave school to find work. She got a job copying sheet music for the only piano teacher in town, Eileen. As Grace sat in Eileen's dining room, writing out musical notes for the students, she listened to the teacher's instructions through the dark burgundy velvet curtain that hung between the dining room and the small Victorian front parlor. Eavesdropping in this way, my mother taught herself to play piano.

At fifteen, she knew she needed to start working full time if she was going to survive. She figured she might get work playing the piano, but the only places that hired piano players were the local taverns. That didn't stop her; she merely lied about her age and began playing with whatever pick-up band happened to be passing through Helena at the time.

By the time she was eighteen, my mother was ready to get out of Montana. Some of her friends had already migrated to Seattle, so as soon as she'd saved enough money to get out of Helena, she moved there to join them. Compared to Helena, Seattle was vibrant and growing, green and mountainous. And while it was much bigger than Helena, Grace wasn't intimidated. She learned the city by riding bus lines to their final stops and back again. I'm sure I inherited her sense of fearless adventure. It wasn't long before she got a job as a bookkeeper at a bank. To save money, she lived in an apartment with her girlfriends. She met my father just before he left for the Army, and when he returned in 1942, she married him.

In the early Fifties, shortly after I was born, my parents were doing well financially. My dad was elected secretary-treasurer of the local AFL-CIO and left behind his pungent creosote-smelling work clothes for freshly laundered and pressed business shirts, suits and ties and the intriguing aroma of Old Spice. They bought a 1908 two story home on Queen Anne Hill and my mother filled it with things that were beautiful to her. Cranberry glass lamps on the maple end tables, flowers from the garden in milk glass vases, an original watercolor landscape above the sofa in the living room, a maple dining table and chairs upholstered in satiny green and taupe stripes. And her pride and joy—a shiny blank spinet piano. For my mother, who grew up so poor, this was heaven.

It was a Fifties dream. She didn't have to work then, so my mom stuck to a comforting regimen at home. Mondays were wash days, and that meant scrubbing clothes by hand and then feeding them through the wringer to press out as much moisture as possible. Then the clothes had to be hung to dry. If it was raining, there were wooden laundry racks in the basement. If it wasn't raining, she stood outside in the sun with a basket of wooden pegs, hanging the laundry on clothes lines. I would be outside with her, helping the clothes dry by running through them, creating a little breeze.

The wonderful fragrance of fresh linens would waft around me. I danced with arms outstretched with the sheer joy of a beautiful day and the warm smells of summer.

Tuesdays were ironing days. The dry laundry was brought in, sprinkled with water and folded until the proper dampness was achieved and the actual ironing could begin. Wednesday was vacuuming and dusting. Thursday was errands, like going to the dry cleaners to get my father's shirts. On Friday she did the grocery shopping.

Anytime the weather was cold, she went to the basement to throw coal in the burner. I hated those trips to the basement, but I had to go down with her because she didn't want me alone upstairs.

I'd cry and protest, "No mama, don't make me go down there!"

"Why ever not?" she'd ask.

"Because Hell is down there!" With the intense heat and raging fire, I thought the coal burner was the gateway to Hades.

"Oh, sweetie, that isn't Hell, it's just the coal burner. It's how we heat the house. You don't want to be cold, do you?"

I would cling to her red checkered apron and hide my face in the folds of her dress.

"It's okay, honey. I won't let anything bad happen to you."

Each morning, after breakfast, I sat on her lap and she would read to me. I loved *Rebecca of Sunnybrook Farm* and the *Heidi* stories, but my favorite was *Peter Pan*. I wanted to be Wendy and fly around Big Ben with Peter before heading to Neverland.

She always had the radio on or was at the piano and she taught me her favorite songs. Together we would sing *Peg O' My Heart, Side By Side, Sleepy Time Gal*. Patiently, she taught me how to harmonize on *You Are My Sunshine*. I liked to look at her sheet music, with lovely photos of the singer or composer on the front page—Patti Page, Jo Stafford, Rosemary Clooney, Perry Como, Duke Ellington, Ella Fitzgerald and Louis Armstrong. To me, it seemed that every day was summer—light, calm and happy.

But when I was five years old, the quiet, serene existence of our home was shattered in a single day when my father was arrested.

My father was having an affair with a red-headed waitress who thought my dad was the key to her future. In his position as secretary-treasurer of the local, my father worked long hours, managing all the dues and budgeting, but his own salary was too modest to support a mistress in style as well as his little innocent family. The waitress, eager to run away with my dad and live a life of luxury, persuaded him he deserved far more than what he was getting.

As an officer of the local, he didn't qualify for overtime, but the mistress urged him to write himself a check for the money she told him he deserved. And so he did, writing himself a check for $8,100, which would be around $64,000 in today's money— far more than his annual salary. He was caught standing in line at the bank, with the red-head on his arm, about to cash the check.

The next day, the news of his embezzlement was in the papers and over-night my parents lost every decent friend they had. At first, my mother insisted he was innocent, that he was set up by other union officers who were jealous of him, but everyone else knew he was guilty. They had to sell the lovely home on Queen Anne Hill and all of its contents to pay for lawyers. They even had to sell their prized collection of jazz records just to survive. Ultimately, a settlement agreement was made outside the courtroom that kept my dad out of jail. But he was stripped of his officer status and membership in the Seattle local and was told he couldn't work as a laborer in Seattle ever again. My parents had lost everything. My mother had to find a job and my halcyon days with her at home were ended.

Over the ensuing years, we moved from one rental house to another. For a time, we had no furniture and slept on lawn chairs. My mother went from being a vibrant happy woman to a desperately sad, bitter and angry harridan. She went from reading me stories to teaching me that keeping secrets and telling "white lies" was an honorable and necessary thing to do.

Soon her attitude towards me, my dad and the world itself was tainted with fury, betrayal and hatred. If she had ever wanted the best for me, she no longer did. Instead she focused her unhappiness on me. Even though I was young, I got the message that I was now responsible to provide her with any further happiness she might have in her life.

As for my father, he took his embarrassment, anger and humiliation out on both of us.

Prior to this incident my mother had joined a guild that raised money for a local children's hospital. She and the other ladies got together once a month to socialize and discuss fundraising ideas. After the incident, when the group came to our new rental house, my father did anything in his power to humiliate her.

She had just served her guests with cookies and tea when my dad walked purposefully into the living room. He looked surly and said, "Grace, when are these goddamn bitches going to leave? I'm tired of hearing their whiny voices."

My mom did her best to hide her embarrassment, but the ladies quickly found excuses to leave early and they never came back. She wept for the loss of her friends and bitterness began to creep into her heart.

But rather than confront my father, she turned her anger on me and would accuse me of something, anything, so that in her own mind she'd be justified for punishing me.

"Lisa, get up here," she yelled at the top of the stairs. I ran up and she grabbed my arm, pulling me into her bedroom. I was five at the time and scared beyond measure. Obviously she was angry with me, but I had no idea why.

She pointed to a round metallic box of powder that she kept on top of her dresser. "Have you been into my powder?" she demanded.

"No, mama."

"Don't lie to me! I know you've been in my powder."

"No, mama. I haven't been."

She took me over her knee and spanked me with the back of her large hair brush. It took a long time for me to stop crying, but when I did she told me how it was good to keep secrets.

"This will be our secret, okay?" she said. "We won't tell anyone. It's just between you and me. You will never tell secrets, will you?"

Fearing another spanking with her hairbrush, I said, "No mama. I will never tell.

I promise."

"I can trust you?"

"Yes, mama. You can trust me."

But my mother wasn't the only one to mete out undeserved punishment. My father also took his anger out on me.

I was outside, playing with my little friend Jeffrey, when my dad came out and said to us, "Did you know there is buried treasure under the porch?" Our eyes lit up with excitement.

"Really? Buried treasure?" Jeffrey and I were ecstatic with the prospect of finding gold.

"How far down is it, daddy?" I asked.

"Almost to China." Then he went back into the house. Wide eyed with excitement, Jeffrey and I looked at each other.

"Let's get some shovels!"

Off we flew to Jeffrey's house to grab two gardens trowels which, owing to our diminutive sizes, we mistook for shovels. We ran back to my porch and began to dig. We'd dug about a dozen trowels-full of dirt when my dad returned to the porch.

"What in hell are you doing?" His face looked like stone and he towered over us, looking like a menacing giant.

I could smell the meatloaf my mom had in the oven, but the safety of her kitchen seemed very far away.

Jeffrey and I looked up at him. Our little faces and hands were covered with dirt.

"We...we...are digging for the buried treasure you told us about."

"I didn't tell you about any goddamn buried treasure."

Jeffrey spoke up. "Yes you did, Mr. Ulrich. You just did. You said it was not as far as China." He was a stout little boy, with a blond crew-cut and saddle shoes and at that moment, he seemed very brave to me.

"You get your goddamn ass out of here." Jeffrey threw down his trowel and took off for home.

I was terrified. "But, daddy, you *did* tell us about buried treasure. Honest." He reached over the side of the porch to grab me, but I ran up the street. I hadn't gotten far when he caught me and began to beat me as he wrestled me down the sidewalk, up the porch, through the front door and into the house.

My mom ran up from the basement where she was folding laundry and demanded to know what was going on. He had me under his left arm while he hit me with his right hand.

"Your goddamn idiot daughter was trying to dig out the foundation."

"What on earth are you talking about?" My mother's face had gone red and her voice was cracking.

"She made up some story about buried treasure and convinced that little brat next door to start digging for it."

"Is that right?" my mom said. "You think it's possible for two little children to dig up the foundation of this miserable house?"

He got defensive. "Goddamn it, Grace. This house isn't ours. We can't afford any damage to it."

"And whose fault is that? Leo, are you out of your mind?" My mother's voice sounded furious but weary. As they fought, her angry words were gradually accompanied by the smell of something burning. She turned to glance at the oven and then looked back at my dad.

"Something is burning in the goddamn kitchen," he yelled, "Are you going to stand there like an idiot and let the house burn down?"

"You know what?" my mom said. "I don't give a shit. It can all go up in flames. I don't care."

Now I thought we were going to burn to death.

He still had hold of me and I had become hysterical, trying to wriggle my way out of his grip.

"I'm not the idiot," my mother said. "You are. You've never cared for anything or anybody but yourself. You're worthless. Even worse, you haven't got the sense god gave a goose. A moron is smarter than you."

His arm slackened and I fell to the floor. I got up, ran to my room and hid under the bed.

I could hear them arguing in the kitchen, on and on, until I finally cried myself to sleep.

Fortunately, I had an invisible sister, cleverly named Sis. She had been with me for as long as I could remember. She looked just like me, only she was a bit older. She wore the same dresses as I did and liked the same games. She was as real to me as the stars and sky.

I had told my mom about Sis and even though she couldn't see Sis like I could, my mom often encouraged her presence. She would even make Sis a little birthday cake because, when it was my birthday, it was hers as well.

Sis crawled under the bed, woke me up and asked if I was okay.

"I'm not sure." I glanced at my arms and noticed bruises. "Look at my arms. They've got big black spots on them and they hurt."

Sis told me that my daddy made up that buried treasure story just so he could spank me. She said that parents shouldn't hurt children, especially for somebody else's lies. That made me feel a lot better, and before she left, she promised me I was safe and that she would take me to the clouds where no one called each other names or fought or anything. I loved her for that, and for all the other times she came to be with me when my parents were fighting.

Without Sis, I didn't know what I would've done. Maybe I'd have had to go to the clouds on my own and look for her there. But, she was with me and that's all that mattered.

On the day that I started kindergarten, my mom asked me to introduce her to Sis.

"I can't. You can't see her. Only I can."

We were standing at the front door. My mom was buttoning my little grey coat and securing my matching hat.

"Oh, but I really want to be introduced. She's been with you for so long. I'd like to get to know her too." I sensed a hidden danger in my mom's request, as if she really wanted to destroy Sis rather than meet her.

Suddenly Sis appeared, standing next to me, violently shaking her head no. But my mother kept insisting until finally Sis looked at me, gave me a little smile and slowly disappeared. I never saw her again.

I think that had been my mom's intent. If I was starting kindergarten, she thought it was time I give up my invisible sister. Without Sis, I had no refuge from my parents' unhappiness and in order to survive, I aligned myself with my mother. War had been declared. It was my mom and me against my father, unwillingly engaged in hand-to-hand combat. The battleground was whatever house, apartment, boarding house or motel we lived in. The stakes were high but undefined. And as in real wars, there were no winners.

As the years went on, the chasm between the three of us widened, ultimately beyond any hope of repair. It was obvious, even to a young child, that my parents were deeply unhappy. The days of singing with my mom were over. Her spirit and joie de vivre had died and she disappeared into her misery.

My father became even more distant, controlling and mean. Although I had fewer unwarranted beatings, his cruelty moved into verbal abuse which in many ways is worse than being struck.

I could never understand why they stayed together. But I was young and didn't comprehend the complexities of adult life. I came to believe that all grown-ups were cruel to each other and to their children. I grew up with it and I expected it. Didn't everyone live that way?

CHAPTER 3

THE COLOR DOESN'T RUB OFF

SINCE MY PARENTS were jazz lovers, nearly all of their favorite musicians and vocalists were black. I grew up with the music of Ella Fitzgerald, Louie Armstrong, Art Tatum, Billie Holiday, Nat King Cole, The Ink Spots, and The Mills Brothers. Their styles ran the gamut—traditional, be-bop, piano jazz and sweet smooth vocals.

As far as I knew, my mother admired these black people. She didn't use any derogatory names for them like so many other white people did at the time, and told me that I wasn't to use those words.

That lesson was made clear to me, one day when I came home from kindergarten and told my mom I'd learned a new song.

"It goes like this: *eeny meeny miney moe catch a nigger by the …*"

"No, no, no!" my mother said. "Where did you learn that?"

"At school?" My lower lip was trembling. I thought I was in big trouble.

"Honey, that's a terrible word."

"What word?" I asked, as she sat down in her favorite rocking chair, pulling me onto her lap.

"The word that's starts with an "N."

"Oh, you mean nig…."

"Yes, that word. What you say is…'catch a *tiger* by the toe', okay?"

"Even if everybody else says the other word?"

"Yes, even though everyone else says it. You won't say it because now you know better. Right?"

"Right, mommy."

So when Yolanda moved into our neighborhood and became my best friend, I was completely unprepared for my parents' response.

We had just moved to Beacon Hill in Seattle—a neighborhood of Asian, Italian, Jewish and white families. I loved our new neighborhood and our new house; I had a big bedroom and there was an amazing monkey tree out front that I thought was so exotic. This would be where we'd stay forever, I just knew it. No more moving around. I was so tired of packing and unpacking all the time and having to move somewhere new.

One day, shortly after we'd settled in, a black family rented the house next to ours. Their little girl, Yolanda, and I became best friends. At five, she was a year younger than me and only in kindergarten. I was in the first grade and since I knew so much more of the world, I became her advisor in important things like how to ride a bike and play hopscotch. We loved music and dancing and watched *American Bandstand* every afternoon hoping to see Sam Cooke sing *You Send Me* or the Coasters sing *Searchin'* and the Jimenez sisters dance the calypso. We held hands and twirled around my living room, being careful not to break my mother's one remaining milk glass vase.

Yolanda was everything I wasn't. She was small and dainty; I was tall and clumsy. She had beautiful black curly hair that her mom put up in braids; I had limp brown hair that, despite barrettes and headbands, was constantly falling into my eyes. She had a buoyant disposition; I was often sick with asthma and had to limit my energetic bursts.

One time, sitting on the grass in my backyard, we did an experiment. It was spring. The cherry blossoms were starting to send out their pink blooms and we could smell that wonderful scent of brine and sea coming up from Elliott Bay. The grass was wet, as were the bottoms of our play pants, staining them bright green.

"Hey, Yolanda, look, the color of the grass comes right off!"

"Wow!" she said, "I wonder what other colors will come off."

We tried rubbing stones and sticks and dandelions on each other, giggling at our discoveries. Dandelions turned us yellow, but stones didn't do much at all.

"I know!" I said, a brilliant idea forming in my seven year old head, "How about if we rub our skin together? I'll bet you're pink underneath your skin, just like me!"

"And I'll bet you're brown underneath your skin, just like me!"

So we rubbed each other's arms to see if the color came off. When it didn't, it was a revelation to both of us.

The experiment ended when our moms called us in for dinner.

After I set the kitchen table, I told my mom about our experiment. "Mom, Yolanda's color doesn't rub off! Mine doesn't either!"

"Well of course it doesn't, silly. She's colored and you're white."

"What does that mean? She's colored? Aren't I colored too? There's a crayon in my box called 'flesh,' so that must mean my flesh is a color."

Just then my dad had come in to the kitchen and poured himself a cup of coffee.

"What are you two talking about?"

"I'm telling Lisa that a person's skin color doesn't rub off. Her little friend Yolanda next door is colored."

"Well, Jesus Christ, a nig..."

"Leo, I also told her not to use that word."

"I'll use whatever word I want," my father said, lighting a cigarette.

"No you won't. Not in front of our daughter."

It was clear to me, even at seven years old, that skin color was an issue. I thought about the musicians and singers my parents admired. Most of them were "colored." Why aren't white people called "not colored"? We certainly weren't white. We were beige, and that's a color. There seemed to be something mysterious and important about skin color that made people act angry or afraid. I thought it all very confusing.

After dinner that night, I asked my mom why a person's skin color seemed to be so important. I was standing next to her drying the dishes as she washed them. My dad was still at the table, reading the newspaper.

"Mommy, I still don't understand why skin color is so important. Everyone you listen to on the record player is colored, and you like them. Why does it matter?"

"Sweetie, there are a lot of things in the world that you're too young to understand now." I set the last dry plate on the counter for her to put in the cupboard since I wasn't tall enough to reach that high.

"When will I be old enough?"

My dad put the paper down and heaved a sigh. "Don't you have something better to talk about, you two? Lisa, go to your room or something."

I looked up at my mom. "Do I have to?"

"Yes, why don't you go to your room and play?" My room was right off the kitchen and as I closed the door, I heard my parents start to argue. My dad's voice was raised.

"What is she doing playing with a little nig….?"

"Leo, I've already told you not to use that word. Do I have to tell you again?"

"You don't tell me what I can say…"

I laid in my bed, hugging my sock monkey, and realized that I had ventured into a topic that in the adult world caused grown-ups to be nasty to each other.

And I had no idea what this had to do with Yolanda.

Then one night a group of neighbors came to visit my parents. There was a huge bunch of them, big, angry men with dark hats and mean faces. I only recognized a couple of them, our neighbor Mr. DiJulio and the school crossing guard, Mr. Stanley.

"Lisa, go to your room now," my mother said. I wanted to protest, but I could tell by her tone she meant business. Since being sent to my room when I hadn't done anything wrong signaled a big important adult thing was about to happen, I listened at the door.

I heard Mr. DiJulio's voice and couldn't believe what he said. "We're here to talk with you about your daughter's playmate."

"What do you mean?" my dad asked.

"Don't be coy, Ulrich. I think you know what we mean. Your daughter is to stop playing with that little pickaninny."

I listened to the men talking about Yolanda, saying she was a mongrel and that if God had intended the races to mix, he wouldn't have made white people the master race.

Voices were raised. I heard these strangers using curse words and the "N" word my mom said was so bad. I wondered why my parents weren't saying anything. As the rants of the neighbors got louder and louder, my parents remained silent.

I opened my door a little and saw the men standing above my parents who were sitting on the sofa. Several had their arms by their sides but their fists clenched and I got scared so I quietly shut my door completely.

Then I heard the front door close and they were gone.

"Lisa. Come here," my mother called to me, her voice stern, but shaky.

I opened my bedroom door, and went to the living room. My parents, sitting together on the sofa, looked stricken.

"Sweetie," my mom took my arm. "Sweetie, you can't play with Yolanda anymore." I was so confused. What did the visitation from the neighborhood men have to do with my friend?

"Why?" My lower lip began to tremble and tears formed in my eyes.

"Because," she said, as if that was an answer. "Don't ask questions." She was wringing her hands and her brow was furrowed. My dad sat next to her; the cigarette in his hand was shaking and I stared at it, waiting for the ashes to fall on the carpet.

"Just do as you're told. No more playing with Yolanda," he said from the couch. "Now go to your room!"

I stood there, defiant and confused, then turned around and stomped to my room, where I cried myself to sleep.

But Yolanda and I continued to play, surreptitiously, like little spies. We met up in my parents' garage, both of us feeling a bit frightened and bewildered.

I took her hand. "Did your mom and dad tell you we can't play together too?"

Her eyes were big with fear. "Yeah, they did. But I don't know why."

"Did some men come to your house?" She nodded. The neighbors had paid a visit to her parents, but they hadn't been quite as friendly. Yolanda's parents forbade her from playing with me as well.

"Yes, some men mommy and daddy didn't know. They threatened my daddy and my mommy cried."

"My mommy cried too. I just don't get it." We were conspirators in a battle for what we knew was fairness.

We were standing all the way in the back of the garage. A car smelling of burnt oil came down the alley and startled us. "Do you think we should sneak?" she asked me.

"Maybe we should run away!" I thought leaving home would show the grown-ups that we meant business.

"No, I think we should just sneak for now." Yolanda was obviously a cooler head even though her eyes were wide with fright.

So we ignored all the parental warnings and continued to play together, quietly and in hiding. Sometimes we played in the cellar steps of her parent's home, other times in my garage.

A week or so later, there was another knock on our door. They knocked and knocked, but my parents wouldn't answer.

"Open up, Mr. Ulrich. We know you're in there."

My dad got up reluctantly and opened the door.

In they came, a whole group of them, the same men as before but with some women as well. They all looked angry as they stood around the living room. My parents invited them to sit down, but none of them did.

"We won't be long here, Mr. Ulrich." This time their tone was much more strident and scary.

Hiding in the stairway to the attic, I heard everything.

Mr. DiJulio spoke again. "We advised you, Ulrich, to keep your daughter from playing with that nigger girl. You apparently didn't hear us."

Another man, Mr. Levine, said, "We don't want to get serious about this, but this mingling of your daughter with a mongrel child of evil must stop or there'll be consequences."

DiJulio added, "Perhaps you'll hear us now."

That's when my mother spoke up. "I see your point and assure you there won't be any more problems."

"I'm so glad you see the wisdom in our advice," Mr. Levine said. "So, we won't need to bother you again?"

"No, you won't have to bother us again," my mom said. "We see your point and will comply. Your knowledge about such things is far greater than ours, isn't that right Leo?"

"Ah…yes….absolutely right," my dad said, predictably. My dad either gave in to my mom or never mounted a defense at all. What he did do was gripe and complain about it afterwards.

Then the door closed and it was quiet.

Again, I was called to the living room and told not to play with Yolanda.

"But I don't understand," I cried. "Why not? What's wrong with her?"

Wham! My mother's palm stung as it hit my face but before I could grasp what she'd done, she burst into tears and I fled to my room.

Through my sobs, I could hear my parents arguing.

"What are we going to do?" my father asked. "Obviously we aren't getting through to Lisa."

"How can we? She doesn't understand what's happening," my mother responded. "But we have to do *something!*"

"Well I don't know what we can do other than lock her in her room until she's grown up," my father said, sounding exasperated.

"Then we'll move," my mother replied.

"Move? That's your answer to everything."

"Do I need to remind you why we move so much? Because I certainly can."

"Why don't you just shut up about that," my father said.

There was a long silence. I had no idea why we moved so much. I thought it was what all families did. And I couldn't imagine what my father had done to cause the moves.

I looked around my room—the yellow walls, the tall windows, my little play kitchen. I would have to move away from all this because my parents were afraid of the neighbors and of my friendship with Yolanda.

A week later, the U-Haul in front of our house was loaded and ready to go. Just as my mother was about to put me in the car, Yolanda ran up to her. Her eyes were wide with fright. She opened her small hand to reveal a coin.

"Mrs. Ulrich, if I give you this dime, can I please play with Lisa?" My mother shoved me in the car and slammed the door. "Just be quiet," she said to me. "And don't look back." But I did.

The last time I saw Yolanda, she was running after our car, crying, her arm outstretched with the proffered dime held in her open hand.

CHAPTER 4

GOING NATIVE

Although I didn't like their rifles, I sympathized with the Black Panther Party. I had seen the news coverage of Selma, Alabama, of Dr. King's *I Have a Dream* speech, of black people throughout the South being beaten and sometimes killed simply because they wanted a seat at the front of the bus. The huge divide between what I was seeing on the television news and reading in the papers, and what I lived in my own life, completely confused me. Although I lived in a segregated society, and had been forced to move because I had a black friend, "segregation" was still a word I barely understood, and I didn't grasp its' shameful origins. The history we'd been taught in school did not include what our country did to black people.

So when the Panthers came to my school that day in 1968, race hit my life in a way that not even my friendship with Yolanda had done. After the incident in the principal's office, police with guns and baton sticks hanging from their belts began patrolling the school and the grounds. Such an armed presence in schools in 1968 was unheard of and it scared everyone, white, black and everything in between. What if one of the cops whipped out a pistol and shot some unsuspecting freshman for smoking in the boys' room? What if there was another fight in the parking lot and the cops beat the kids with their sticks like we saw them do all the time to protestors on the news? What if they used tear gas on us next time there was a food fight in the cafeteria? These thoughts concerned me, but not enough to do much about it. At that point in my life, I was only interested in finishing school so I could buy that one way ticket to London.

Still, I became terrified of the police, but I was coming to admire the Panthers' guts, their organization, the food and medical care they provided to poor children, and their commitment to civil rights. And I found their dark skin, liquid eyes, and their slight sense of danger, seductive.

When my senior year arrived, I'd had enough of the police in the hallways and the tension that seemed to grow greater day by day. I hadn't made many friends at Rainier Beach, and felt no connection to what I was learning. I thought about dropping out of high school altogether, and heading straight for London to start my life as a writer, but I had sense enough to know that that wasn't a good idea. So I did the next best thing. Just as my parents had moved every time they faced a dilemma, so would I. I decided I would move to another school, and enrolled at nearby Chief Sealth High, a school named after a Native American that had no Native students.

Things were different at the new school. There was a mix of wealthy kids who lived in brick split level houses on the hill that overlooked Puget Sound and working class kids whose parents worked at the ship builders or steel factory and lived in clapboard ramblers. But I wasn't there long before I discovered that while the racial divisions weren't as distinct as they'd been at Rainier Beach, they persisted in palpable ways. Most of the kids were white, but there were some Asians and Hispanics and a smattering of blacks. Among them was a small clique of black chicks who showed up each day in Cadillacs, driven by their boyfriends. The rumor was that they were prostitutes and the boyfriends were their pimps. This was a new image of race I hadn't before encountered and rather than resolve my confusion, it only deepened it.

Society was changing all around me and I truly wanted to be part of the changes. So I decided, like a counter-culture anthropologist, to discover the real world I was living in, the culture and customs of other people and the dynamics of oppression and prejudice.

I knew there was something different about me, although I wasn't sure exactly what it was. But it made me feel closer to the marginalized in society than with the upstanding accepted white people around me.

Most of all, I wanted to know more about race. I asked the librarian at school to recommend some books.

"You want to understand about the colored race?" Her name was Mrs. McGill. She was dressed in a light pink twin-set and perched on her narrow white nose was a pair of glasses that made her look like a Siamese cat. The look on her face gave me the impression that I had just transformed from innocent student to rabid radical before her eyes.

"Yes," I said. "I do. What do you think I should read first?"

"I'm not sure. Let me ask Miss Jackson." She left the front desk and went back into the back room. Soon she returned with Miss Jackson who was as short, round and dark as Mrs. McGill was tall, skinny and pale.

"I understand you want to read about race," Miss Jackson said. She maneuvered around Mrs. McGill so that she could converse with me without Mrs. McGill hearing.

"Here," she said, pulling out a chair at one of the study tables. "Let's sit here and talk."

We sat next to each other and turned our chairs so that our knees nearly touched and our voices could be kept low. I felt as if she and I were creating a little cabal of radical idealism as we leaned towards each other and talked. "So, how is it that you're interested in black history?" she asked me.

I told her about the incidents at Rainier Beach and my friendship with Yolanda.

As I did, I could see her eyes soften and her shoulders relax. I had made a connection.

She leaned even closer and looked me in the eye.

"This is a large subject you want to explore, you know that, right? And you understand that the history lessons you've been getting at school are not truthful, or accurate, or honest?"

"Well, no. I didn't know my history class wasn't honest. Is Mr. Craig keeping things from us?"

"Heavens no! He's just teaching what the curriculum tells him to. But, if you are serious, I want you to realize that you will be walking down a path that will surprise you, shock you, and challenge what you've been taught to believe about your country."

"That's okay with me," I said. "I want to understand. I want to know the things that have been kept from me."

"Alright then, honey. Get out your pencil and paper and let's make a list."

As she spoke, I wrote down the names of authors I'd never heard of: James Baldwin, Ralph Ellison, Langston Hughes, Fredrick Douglass, and Richard Wright. Then I asked her about music.

"My parents have always listened to black musicians, but mostly Dixieland Jazz. Can you give me some suggestions about other musicians I should listen to?"

"Yes," she said. "And let me give you a little lesson to start with. The term 'Dixieland' is considered racially prejudiced. It harkens to the South, to slavery and lynching. Try using 'traditional jazz' from now on, okay?"

She had me write down the names of Miles Davis, John Coltrane, Charlie Byrd, Pharaoh Sanders, Sonny Terry and Brownie McGee, Muddy Waters, Leadbelly, Jack Johnson and Billie Holiday.

With list in hand, I set out to go native.

No one questioned the use of 'nigger' as a reference to someone with dark skin. I understood now that being called a nigger hurt peoples' feelings and didn't understand why people kept on using the word. But I wasn't really aware of the small changes that the civil rights movement was making.

But by reading, my understanding began to emerge and the anger of white and black folks around race began to make sense. The first three books on the list I'd made with Miss Jackson were Dick Gregory's *Nigger*, James Baldwin's *Notes of a Native Son* and Ralph Ellison's, *Invisible Man*.

And as I read the books, I was awed at the lives these men had lived. In so many ways, their lives were unlike anything I had ever known, and yet in other ways, I felt a deep connection to them, as if I, too, were somehow a stranger in my own land. I especially identified with Baldwin. I could see myself as an expatriate, living in London viewing my home country through the eyes of a disenchanted outsider.

I intrinsically knew that I couldn't read or listen my way into a culture, but it was a start. I began with the naïve notion that if I made some black friends at my new school, they would discuss their viewpoints about race with me. But after reading Richard Wright's *Native Son* about the social realities that kept us divided and in so many ways defined our different futures, I realized that it would never be that simple. And of course, I couldn't have known that in the near future, I would be experiencing race up close and personal.

The one book, and the one author that really chilled me, that truly opened my eyes to the rage that lived within many black men, was Eldridge Cleaver's *Soul On Ice*. It was a book I couldn't find in the library at school. I had to journey to a small leftist bookstore in the Pike Place Market to find a copy. Miss Jackson had said that if I was brave enough, I should read the book with an open mind, a mind ready to face the stark reality of one black man's experience in trying to right the wrongs of slavery, racism and ignorant hatred. Cleaver's description of stalking and raping The Ogre—white women— terrified me. I'd certainly never thought of myself as an ogre, but I could see his point: white women were the ideal but unattainable prize. Since he couldn't win the prize in the usual socially acceptable ways, he stalked and raped them.

It wasn't easy making friends at my new school, whether black or white. But that didn't bother me too much. After all, I already had plenty of wonderful friends outside of school, and since I was on my way to London as soon as I graduated, adding more would just get in the way of my future. But one day, I noticed some of the black guys noticing me. Then I noticed the black girls noticing them noticing me.

"Hey you little cracker-ass bitch," one of them yelled at me. "You think you can take one of our men?"

I felt like I'd just walked into the Twilight Zone. What on earth was she talking about?

I started to answer, but I stuttered and the girls laughed at me. One of them yelled, "Girl, I'll beat you down so low an ant can piss on you."

One of the boys approached me. I thought I was going to get slapped, but he put his arm around my shoulders and said to the girl, "Back off, bitch. This here's my girlfriend." The black girls scoffed and walked away.

"Thanks," I said. "I guess you saved me from a beating?"

"Maybe," he laughed. "Those girls just don't get it. Black guys are attracted to white girls because they don't swear and threaten us like black girls do."

Having just completed *Soul On Ice*, I said, "It's not that simple now, is it?"

"I guess not. I'm Darrin, by the way."

Always drawn to the forbidden and always a non-believer in rules, when Darrin asked me for a date several days later, I accepted.

CHAPTER 5

PIGS COMMITTING SUICIDE

ONE DAY, I was walking down the hall at school, head down, looking at the floor, when among the debris and litter, I saw a sheet of paper that blared in huge letters

"GET A JOB THAT WILL LAST YOUR LIFETIME!"

I had been thinking about life beyond high school and how I would get enough money to go to London. A job of some sort was inevitable, as there was no money saved for college or travel. A job that would last my lifetime sounded good—well maybe not my lifetime—but a good job could quickly provide me enough money to leave for London.

I picked up the paper, smoothed out the folds, and brushed off the dirt. It was about taking a civil service test to become a postal employee. The test was that upcoming weekend on the university campus. I didn't want to go alone, so I called my friend Megan, who we nicknamed Beethoven on account of her unruly hair.

"Hey Beethoven," I said, 'Wanna go take a test with me on Saturday?"

"No," she said, in a tone that implied I was nuts. I explained about the civil service exam and how much money we could make if we got jobs with the post office. That seemed to perk her up. "It'll be fun," I added. "Besides, it's an excuse to go to the University District. Maybe we'll score some weed from that guy who hangs out in front of the funeral home."

"Okay," she finally said. "I've got no plans for the weekend anyway. But didn't that guy at the funeral home get busted?"

"Don't know, but I guess we'll find out!"

The test was held in a lecture room in Kane Hall on the University of Washington campus. We took our seats and looked around at the large crowd who were also hoping for a lifetime job with the government. There were hippies, men in suits, women who looked like housewives seeking liberation from the kitchen, big people, small people and all sorts of people in between. I sensed something in the air, something I often felt during the Sixties and early Seventies that life was expanding beyond its previously known limits. I liked the feeling. It seemed there were endless and gentle explosions of enlightenment everywhere.

"God, Bay. I had no idea there would be so many people. I thought there'd only be a few. I mean, who in their right mind would want to work for the government?"

Beethoven said, "Well, we're here, aren't we?"

"Oh yeah, right. I guess that answers that question!"

The test involved putting addresses in numerical sequence, answering simple English grammar and multiple choice questions, identifying series of shapes, and alphabetizing. Other than the sequencing of addresses, the test had nothing to do with delivering mail. I scored 99 out of a hundred. Bay got 98. Afterwards, we had coffee and smoked cigarettes in the dark, dank cool of the Aeigervon coffee house. Our funeral home connection wasn't there. Perhaps he had indeed been busted.

I forgot all about the test until six weeks later, when I got an important and official government letter in the mail announcing I qualified for the civil service and asking when I could start. I called and said that I needed to graduate first before I could actually work. But they continued sending me announcements about carrier openings throughout the rest of the school year.

After graduating high school, I accepted a job as a letter carrier in the International Station, located in Seattle's Chinatown. I was thrilled, but at the same time, a bit frustrated. Here I was taking a government job, and what was to happen with my dreams of going to London? I told myself my dream would not die, that my job at the United States Postal Service would provide me with enough money to save up and leave within six months. That plan sounded acceptable and I clung to my dream of being a starving poet in London all the more.

There was one thing about the job that I wasn't looking forward to, and that was wearing a uniform. I had no desire to dress up in gray-blue gabardine slacks and matching shirt. Fortunately, new hires had to work for six months before getting postal uniforms. So on my first day of work, I looked through my closet, and found a paisley bell bottom pantsuit that would be just perfect with my purple high heels. Dressed like a professional hippie, I went to work, nervous but looking stylish.

After walking my first route with an experienced carrier, I returned to the station in pain. My supervisor suggested I might want to wear something more comfortable in the future and I couldn't argue with him as my feet were killing me. What was I thinking by wearing purple high heels on my first day as a letter carrier? So that evening, I went to the new mall, Southcenter, where I bought blue twill pants, a white shirt and comfortable suede Hush Puppies.

That was what I was wearing when I met Bob Jones on my second day of work.

I was perched on a stool and had just lit a cigarette when I heard a funny cracking and popping noise. Coming around the corner of my perch, Bob approached and introduced himself. His voice was a deep mesmerizing bass.

I was startled by how attractive he was. He was tall, muscular and quite handsome, his blue postal uniform nicely highlighting his smooth black skin. Although I had already dated a few black men, there was something smoky and dangerous in his eyes that I found alluring. I took a drag on my cigarette.

"Hi there," he said, looking me up and down. "I'm Bob and you are going to quit smoking for me."

"What?" I said. "Who in the hell do you think you are?"

We were off to a merry start. He pulled up a stool beside me and sat down. His initial haughtiness changed into a more congenial attitude. We chatted a bit more and as he walked away, I heard that cracking and popping again. Gads, I thought, it's coming from him.

I guess he saw me as a challenge and he bugged me until I agreed to a date. We went to a party and then ended the evening at his somewhat dilapidated house that he shared with other postal workers, and soon I was in his bed. He was sexually talented, making love in ways I'd never experienced. It was the Sixties and I adhered devoutly to the idea that if it feels good, do it. Tune in. Turn on. Drop out. Don't think about tomorrow. Have fun and die young.

But Bob was not exactly young. At twenty-nine, he was eleven years older than me. He had played football briefly and suffered a game-ending injury to his knees that resulted in the distinctive cracking and popping sound when he walked. He'd been in the Army in the early Sixties, stationed in Germany.

We began sitting in my car, talking, at the end of each work day. I asked him about his time in the Army. The Vietnam War was still raging and the idea of being in the military service was abhorrent to me. But he was in Germany in a non-combat role and therefore didn't see any of the tragedy and horror of Vietnam.

I asked him what it was like in Germany, remembering that the time the Beatles spent in Hamburg helped define their style.

"I had a German girlfriend named Schotzy," he told me. "Her parents really liked me and thought we should get married. You know how those blonde German ladies love black men."

"No, not really," I answered, flipping my bleached blonde hair with the back of my hand.

He laughed. "Of course, Schotzy's parents weren't too happy when I robbed two banks with a couple of guys from the base."

"What? Are you serious?"

"I'm dead serious."

"I don't believe you," I said. I felt surprised and scared, and a slight fluttering of anxiety in my chest. In my little hippie universe, everything was supposed to be all love and peace. But then again, weren't we rebels? Was he really a criminal, or was he perhaps a revolutionary?

"You didn't get caught?" I asked. After all, here he was right in front of me, not in any prison. But at the same time I had a picture in my mind of him twisting in handcuffs, cash spilling out of his pockets, accusing the cops of prejudice.

"We were way too clever for those Nazi cops," he said, a bit too confidently.

Then he told me he had a stable and I didn't know what that meant.

"Whores," he said. I'm a pimp."

How ridiculous. It made me laugh. "Oh sure," I said.

But he brought out a wad of money from his back pocket to convince me.

"Where'd you think I got of this cash?"

"Oh, I don't know. Working for a living?"

Stupidly, I was intrigued, and that was just what he wanted.

After a few dates, he told me more.

Bob was born and raised in Tampa, Florida, the 13th child of his birth mother. She gave him to another family to raise. There was speculation that the adoptive father was really his biological father. But, in the late Thirties and at the height of the Great Depression, in a poor black neighborhood, in a world of loose family ties and informal deal making, it didn't seem to matter much. He had half sisters and brothers everywhere and knew only a few of them.

He told me how much he loved his adopted mother, Jeanette, but he also told me harrowing tales of her cruelty which escalated after his father died of a stroke. His dad had been kinder to him, and with his absence, there was no one to intervene with Jeanette. She put knives to his throat or threw knives at him, tied and bound him and beat him with braided tree branches. He'd hide under his bed or under the house, but she would find him and beat him even harder.

Yet he said he would do anything for her. But all I could see was a little unwanted boy totally alone in the world, with a large family of people who didn't want him, left with a sadist for a mother and no one to protect him. He would do anything for her because he knew nothing else.

Maybe I felt sorry for him. Or maybe I was just recklessly attracted to him. Whatever it was, I agreed to another date.

He took me straight to his house and up to his room in the attic. I was expecting another romantic interlude. But once inside, he turned back to the door. He was doing something I couldn't see, but when I heard the lock turn, I got worried.

"What are you doing?" I backed away from him into the center of his room. The room had a pitched roof, small windows, clothes thrown everywhere, and a mussed bed. My heart began to pound and my stomach twisted with dread.

"You are not getting out of here tonight." His eyes had a strange flat look, as if he were staring at something just beyond me. His jaws were tight bundles of fury.

He moved towards me, and as he got closer I could smell the hot links that he'd had for dinner on his breath.

"You white bitch. Do you think you can belong to me if you are un-clean?" I saw madness in his intense brown eyes. He spit as he spoke as if too furious to swallow.

He circled around the room. "A woman is to leave her family and cleave to her husband. A wife is to obey her husband. There is no question of that! It's in the Bible. You read the Bible, don't you?"

I stammered. "I did…in school…at Holy Names…the New Testament mostly."

"Holy Names? What is Holy Names?" he demanded.

"Oh, it's just an all-girls Catholic school my parents had sent me to for my freshmen and sophomore years."

Then it seemed that he'd shifted into an alternate reality. He was staring at the ceiling, as if in a trance.

"God saw that there was an insane man and, taking mercy cast the evil spirits inhabiting his body into a herd of pigs. Do you know what the pigs did?"

He was now in my face. I could see the locked door only a few feet away, but he stood between me and the door. I was terrified of even looking at the door, afraid he might think I was trying to escape. Frantically I tried to project calm and assurance while thinking of a way to get out without him stopping and hurting me. I felt like I'd fallen into an episode of 'Outer Space.'

"Um…I don't remember that story. What did the pigs do?" I thought if I humored him, he'd calm down.

"They threw themselves off a cliff!"

"Pigs? Committed suicide?" Despite myself, I laughed out loud but immediately stopped when I saw the look in his eyes. If indeed evil existed in this world, I was looking at it in his face. The pounding in my chest moved to my throat and I could barely swallow.

"Any creature that is filled with evil must slaughter itself. Reprobates! Whores! Thieves! All must die by the merciful hand of Christ!"

He lunged at me, grabbing me by the throat. His hands squeezed tighter and tighter. Then he threw me. I hit the wall with a bang, pain searing through my neck and shoulders as I collapsed on the floor.

Then, with a sudden swiftness that defied logic, he changed. He fell on his knees, head in his hands, and sobbed like a little boy crying for a mother who was not there and may have never existed.

His entire demeanor switched to the Bob I thought I knew. But then he began to pace and talk to himself. I hoped he might have forgotten I was there.

I ran across the room, unlocked the door and fled to my car. I sped home. Once in my apartment, I turned out the lights and peeked out the windows to make sure he hadn't followed me, even though he had no car and no way of crossing town so quickly.

But I wasn't thinking logically; I was terrified.

For the rest of the weekend, I replayed the incident over and over in my head, and as I did, I found I was imbuing him with supernatural powers, powers that would follow me however far I tried to flee. He had swiftly destroyed my sense of what was real and what was imagined. My mind soon became a dangerous place, unwittingly distrusting my own sense of reality. Was I losing my sanity?

For that matter, had he lost his sanity? I'd run out of his house so fast that I wasn't sure what had really happened. I felt like a frightened child, desperate for protection. Had he really been trying to hurt me or teach me something I needed to know?

I was turning and twisting, lost in a conundrum. Was he for real, or just playing a game with me? Was I supposed to believe that in addition to being a bank robber and a pimp, he was a violent religious nut case? Or a romantic counter culture, black liberation rebel? How could he be so charming and attentive and then suddenly so violent and mean? I dreaded seeing him again, and began feeling as if he were right around the corner, following me, watching my every move.

I had no choice but to return to work on Monday, but the whole morning, I was so nervous I couldn't stop thinking of what I would do or say when I saw him again. I made it through mail casing without seeing him, and wondered if maybe he'd never come back. But by the end of the day, when I was standing at my work area, Bob came up behind me. I startled, turned and stared into his eyes, looking for some sort of clue to who this man was. Although I felt safe since we were at work, surrounded by other letter carriers, and the supervisors, I was trembling with fear. I knew everyone thought Bob was a great guy. He always listened to everyone's problems, offered them advice and they fell all over themselves to talk with him. They all called him "Big Bob" and there was no one who would believe me if I told them that he was, in fact, a monster.

But he was charming and suave and debonair, as if nothing unusual had happened.

Maybe if I pretended everything was normal, it would be. I didn't know what else to do. So I gathered up my courage and asked, as casually as if I was asking about the weather, "What was up with you last weekend? You seemed kinda crazy."

"Oh that," he said, "I was just playing with you."

"You were playing with me? You scared the shit out of me and you hurt me. It was like you became another person."

He looked into my eyes and said, "I just wanted to see how you would react. I wanted to see if I could scare you away. I wanted to see what sort of woman you really are."

His deep, soft voice was rhythmic and calming, almost hypnotic. I knew I should have turned and walked away, but instead, I found his words and demeanor were pulling me in.

And then the inevitable promise. "I'll never treat you that way again."

I believed him.

A few weeks and a few dates later, I threw up my breakfast.

CHAPTER 6

I AM EVERYWHERE

NOW MY LIFE took on the essence of a science fiction story. Bob and I had been seeing each other fairly regularly by this point, but I still didn't consider us a couple. So one weekend, shortly after I'd discovered I was pregnant, I didn't give it much thought when he asked me to come over that Saturday night. I said I might, but ended up hanging out with Mary, who was up from San Francisco.

The following Monday morning, I was walking down Sixth Avenue in Chinatown heading for work when all of a sudden a pair of hands grabbed my neck and squeezed hard. I had no idea where he'd come from, but I knew intuitively that it was Bob. It was as if he'd just materialized, forming himself from some sort of dark ether, traveling over the River Styx to take human form again.

This can't be happening, I thought, but there I was in front of a Chinese meat shop, people passing all around us as if nothing was wrong. I was barely able to breathe and looked about desperately. *Why won't someone help me?* But no one seemed to even notice that I was being strangled.

"Where *were* you?" he hissed into my face, squeezing even harder. "I waited for you all Saturday night and you didn't show up. Where were you? Huh? *Huh?*" People swirled past me, either ignoring the situation or unwilling to get between a man and his woman. Tears streamed down my face. I managed to croak out, "You wouldn't be treating me like this if you knew."

His hands stayed firmly around my throat. "Knew what? *Knew what?*" He drew me close to his deranged face, a face that looked more like an animal's than a man's. "Do you think I don't know that you're pregnant? Is that it? You thought I didn't know you're pregnant?"

I tried to shake my head but his grip had tightened so firmly I couldn't move it. I couldn't breathe and felt faint. I tried to scream and nothing came out. And still people walked by without offering help.

And then he let me go for a moment, raised his arms in the air and screamed at me, "I know everything and I am everywhere!"

Before I could run away, he took me again by the throat and dragged me to a filthy alleyway just a few yards away. Now I was so terrified that I began to hyperventilate, fearing that he might kill me, that my life was over before it had really begun.

My head was spinning and the alleyway seemed topsy-turvy. A unicorn could have galloped right past me and it wouldn't have been a surprise, the situation was that surreal. "In the future, when I tell you to be someplace, you'd better be there. *Do you understand?*" His hands fell from my neck and he pushed me into a brick wall. Then he began to pound his fists into my chest.

This is where I'm going to die, I realized, pregnant and alone amidst the stench of rotting food, beer, and urine, the eyes of a madman the last thing I'd see.

"How can you treat me like this if you know that I'm pregnant? Don't you care?" I began to sob, realizing that he was not only willing to kill me but worse, he was completely indifferent to the fact that I was pregnant with his child.

Then, inexplicably, the rage vanished from his face and in its place was a smirk, his contempt for me unmistakable. Then he dropped his fists.

"You were stupid enough to get pregnant," he said, his teeth bared. "Why should I care?"

"Because it's your baby."

"How do I know that? It could be anybody's."

I could hear the sounds of the street nearby. People passing, shop doors swinging, cars honking. Normal sounds that I would never have noticed otherwise, but I now suddenly craved. Let me in. Let me out. Let me go.

I realized that more than anything, I was insulted and furious. "How dare you insinuate that this could be someone else's baby?" I screamed at him.

He back-handed me across my face. Although I reeled and nearly fell, my paramount thought was to escape. My face stung and my neck was aching and bruised as I twisted past him and ran into the street. I saw the faces of people who might have been watching or listening to this little drama, and I knew what they were thinking. A white girl with a nigger. She's getting exactly what she deserves.

The fright stayed with me into the night, and into many nights. I startled at slight noises. I looked both ways up and down the hallway before I left the apartment and up and down the street before I stepped outside. *"I know everything. I am everywhere"* was embedded in my mind like a primitive stone carving, a twisted take on the omnipresence of the divine.

I barely slept, and when I did, I had terrible nightmares. Sometimes, wild animals menaced me. Grizzlies, cougars, tigers, and lions encircled me, driving me mad with the possibility of being torn alive by their giant jaws and teeth.

Sometimes, I dreamt that my body began to disintegrate and the first part to go was my hands. The terror of the wild animals and the physical decline almost made me want to be eaten alive or have my teeth fall on the ground rather than endure the menace and exquisite suspense that Bob had created.

How could a reasonably intelligent, independent, strong-willed person like me get into such a situation? I wondered. I thought about the shadowy world in which I grew up and couldn't believe it had come to this—pregnant, unmarried, and being strangled in the back alley behind a meat shop in Chinatown by the father of my child.

But finding myself lost and confused by love and sex was nothing new. When I was fourteen something had happened that changed the emotional landscape of my life, but also taught me how to carefully live a life of lies and subterfuge.

It was 1965. My parents had moved yet again. We rented a small white house near the beach that had a cozy fireplace and a little eating nook off the kitchen with a built-in corner cupboard. It was like a little doll-house with a peek-a-boo view of the water if you sat in just the right place in the nook. I was thrilled to be living so near the water and to have that lovely low tide briny smell greet me every day. At long last, we had a home that promised safety, security and joy. I had never been so happy, and the more magical and happy the home became, the more certain I was that my parents would never leave it. This is where we would stay, and this is where I could finally make friends I knew I would never have to leave.

It was spring and I was in eighth grade. I was in the girl's locker room, standing in front of my locker, when I heard the most incredible and infectious laugh. It was a rolling chortle that reached a raucous crescendo before settling into a giggle. I'd never heard such a beguiling laugh.

Who on earth could that be? I walked to the end of the aisle and looked toward the source of the laughter.

It was a girl. But she looked like a boy. She wore a plain skirt with an un-tucked man's sport shirt and what looked like a pair of men's Oxfords on her feet. Her brown hair was cut in a Beatles' style. She had one foot up on a bench and was surrounded by girls who were laughing with her, but it was her own laughter that stood out. I was instantly curious.

One of the girls with her, Maryanne, was someone I knew so I walked up to her. I took her aside and said, "Hey, Maryanne, do you know this girl? I've never seen her before."

"Oh yeah, she lives right next door to me. Let me introduce you. This is Lynne," Maryanne said. At first, Lynne ignored me. She was looking at another girl and whispering with her.

Then she looked toward me, extended her arm and shook my hand. "So you know Maryanne? Well, any friend of hers is a friend of mine." She smiled and I felt a strange tingling in my tummy.

"Wanna walk home with us after school?" she asked. "Us" included Maryanne, Liz, Bonnie, Gloria, and Lynne. And now it included me. Right there, right then, my life changed forever.

I had heard Lynne's name before. In fact, it was just about the first thing I heard when I started seventh grade at Madison Junior High School. On the first morning of the school year, the vice-principal, Mrs. Brewster, greeted me on the front steps of the school. She welcomed me and then pulled me aside.

"I would like to give a word to the wise," she said. "If you're smart, you'll stay away from Lynne McMillan." She said there were rumors about this girl and that I should heed them. She warned, "If you hear any dark whisperings that there's something wrong about her, there is. Let me warn you that any decent girl would stay miles away from her."

"Well, okay," I said. "This is my first day here and I don't know anybody. But if I should run into this person, I'll remember your warning." I smiled with as much charm as I could muster, thinking all the while that whoever or whatever this Lynne girl was, I was more interested in meeting her than avoiding her.

"Good," Mrs. Brewster said, satisfied by my response. She started to walk back up the stairs, but stopped and turned to look at me. "By the way," she said, 'don't you own anything pink?"

It was 1964 and I was pre-defining the Goth look. Everything I owned, down to my underwear, was black. I wouldn't have been caught dead in pink, but I assured Mrs. Brewster that I'd check my closet to see what I had, knowing full well that I wouldn't.

Having now met Lynne McMillan, I realized she was even more intriguing than the rumors had made her out to be.

I walked home with my new circle of friends that afternoon and every day from then on. I found Lynne inexplicably attractive; she was utterly fascinating and I couldn't stop thinking about her.

Liz had told me a little about Lynne; when she was little, Lynne had moved to Seattle from New Orleans with her mother and sister after her dad had abandoned them. A few years later her mother remarried a man named Ray, and now Lynne was having trouble getting along with him. But despite the rumors that had circulated around her, she had no trouble making friends. And now I was one of them.

There was something about her; she had an immense charm and charisma that was hard to pin down. I only knew she was amazing.

I didn't know what "gay" or "lesbian" or "queer" meant. I only knew that I couldn't get her out of my mind, and I didn't know what to make of that.

"What is wrong with me?" I asked Liz one day as we were walking home. "I feel jealous when Lynne walks with someone other than me. Sometimes she holds Bonnie's hand and that makes me really furious. I don't get it."

"You're in love with her, stupid," Liz said. "You can't help it. We're all in love with her, in one way or another. There's nobody else like her. It's like Beatlemania, only better."

"I'm *in love* with her? Are you serious?"

"I'm dead serious," Liz said. "But be careful. She could break your heart."

I had to think about it for a few days. The more I thought about it, the more confused I felt.

I remembered a person my mom and dad knew when I was ten years old. She was named Kay. She looked like a man, but her voice was like a woman's. She was small and wiry, with her hair cut short. She lived with a woman and I thought they were best friends. I'd never seen anyone quite like Kay.

I asked my mom if Kay were a woman or a man.

"She's a woman," my mom said.

"But she looks like a man. And she lives with Catherine."

"Well," my mom said. "This may not make sense to you just now, but maybe when you're older. Some people like to be with people just like them. Kay lives with Catherine because they love each other, like a man or a woman together. Kay and Catherine are lesbians."

"Oh, I see," I said. And that was that, I thought. But I sensed that Kay and Catherine were outcasts. They lived out in the country, up in a ravine that could only be gotten to by a dirt road. They rarely came out and I only saw them when my parents went for a visit. They never came to our house.

Now I thought of Kay in a different way. I realized that her life was not simple and that she lived with a certain amount of fear. I knew that some people said horrid things about Kay and now I wondered if I was just like her because of how I felt about Lynne.

No matter how I tried to rationalize my feelings, I realized that if I was in love, then love is not rational. It's just pure joy. Being in love with Lynne felt as natural as breathing, and as joyful as listening to The Beatles.

Several days later, I confided to Liz that she was right. "I am in love with her and that's just how it is."

"I'm in love with her too, but I haven't told my parents about it," Liz said.

"Why not?"

"They'd probably freak," Liz said. I left it at that.

Lynne and I began to see each other every day before school, between classes, at lunch and after school, and soon we were sharing all our secrets, hopes and dreams. She was the first person I'd ever met who got me. No one else understood who I was quite like Lynne did. She became the center of my thoughts and dreams and the occupier of my happy heart. When I closed my eyes at night, I saw her smiling face and heard her laughter as I fell asleep. In the daytime, I needed to be near her. Now that she was in my heart, I couldn't imagine life without her.

I'd never been in love before. I'd had crushes but this was different. It was the most extraordinary feeling of being alive. Suddenly the birds were singing for me, the sun shone for me, flowers bloomed and songs were sung for me. I could feel the sweet, soft salty air from the beach permeate my skin with the softness of a caress. I floated above the earth, happily infected with first love.

Liz became my friend and confidante. Her hair was short and blonde and she wore it in a bouffant as so many did at the time, reminding me of

Doris Day. And, like the Doris Day of the silver screen, Liz's outlook was always upbeat, sunny and optimistic. It seemed like she walked in sunshine, and in the gloom of Seattle and my teenage angst, that was exactly what I needed.

Liz had told Lynne that I was in love with her, and to my shock and delight, Lynne had told her that she felt the same—and it wasn't long before she was saying those words to me. "There's something different about you," she told me one evening as we strolled along the beach.

"What do you mean?"

"I'm not sure. I just know that I love your mind and your creativity. I feel very close to you in so many ways. I feel like you can do anything you want, that you're capable of whatever you set your mind to and that we relate on many different levels."

"Well," I said, "there's something definitely different about you!" She laughed that special laugh that drew me to her in the first place. She took my hand and held it, just like she'd done with Bonnie, though it felt far more intimate and private. We walked on until it got dark and we had to go home.

Over the next few months, my world revolved around Lynne. I kept a diary into which I poured my happy heart and joyous soul. I wrote copiously about how much I loved her. We exchanged letters declaring our never-ending love. We wrote poems to each other and quoted song lyrics. I even convinced her that running away to London with me was her future, as much as it was mine. Lynne was all for it, so together, we made plans for our future get-away to London.

Each Friday night, we went to the movies. Lynne always sat next to me and held my hand throughout the movie. Her hand was smaller than mine, but strong and powerful. She would lean toward me and whisper something silly that would make me giggle at inappropriate moments. We must have seen the Beatles' movie, "Help!" a dozen times that spring and it wasn't long before we were saying the lines in unison and giggling at our cleverness.

One evening, we were all sitting on huge logs at the beach. We laughed and smoked our stolen cigarettes, talking about the stupid teachers at school and how dumb our parents were, the sound of the waves a backdrop to our laughter. Yet for all our foolishness, there a sense of maturity within all of us. In one way or another, we'd all been forced to grow up quickly. I was the only child of two complex, needy adults; Liz's mother was very sick and so she had to raise her little sister and brother; and Lynne's parents had taken her to psychiatrists who said she needed shock therapy to make her more "girly."

Suddenly, as the tide moved in, Liz blurted out, "Lisa's never been kissed!"

"Liz! You can't say that!" I responded, feeling myself turning deep red.

Lynne looked at me. "Really? Well, now's a good time to fix that!" Her deep brown eyes focused on my face and when she leaned in toward me and her lips touched mine, I felt a bolt of electric shock race right through my body. It was the most astounding feeling I'd ever had—and it was addictive. I wanted it again and again. So did she. We snuck kisses wherever we could—in the park, at the beach, at home in her house or mine. Kissing her made me dizzy with joy and another feeling completely new to me—passion. And while I had become addicted to her kisses, I tried to act casual around her, not because I was embarrassed, but because if I didn't, I'd lock lips with her and never let her go. Not something you want to do in the corridors of junior high school or the rec room at home. But it was something we did the moment we got out of school.

Until one stunning day, giddy from holding hands on our walk home, I arrived home to find something was completely, utterly different.

CHAPTER 7

PAINT THE SKY ORANGE

I DIDN'T KNOW what it was but something felt odd. There was a stillness to the house I couldn't quite figure. I called for my mom, but there was no answer, which was no big deal, but for some reason it just didn't feel right. I went into my parent's bedroom, to see if my mom was in there, but the room was in disarray and no one was around. Then I looked up and saw that their closet had been left wide open, and half the clothes were gone. Looking closer, I realized it was my father's clothes that were missing.

My mother had once again kicked him out of the house. *He must be cheating on her again*, I thought. He was never very good about disguising his philandering and once more, my mother had had enough. Although I was somewhat accustomed to his sudden disappearances, this time I was ecstatic that he was gone. The house was quiet and calm. There was no fighting or arguing, no tension or slammed doors, no swearing and accusing. There was just a sense of peace that coupled with my new love for Lynne made the world seem just about perfect.

The next evening Lynne was visiting, clearly upset about something. We were standing in the kitchen talking with my mom, who really liked Lynne and noticed her distress.

"Hey, sweetie," she said, "What's wrong tonight? You seem agitated. Would you like a cup of coffee?"

"No thanks, Mrs. Ulrich." We sat at the kitchen table. "It's just that I've had another fight with my stepfather. I can't stand him and he's on me all the time about the way I look and act. I think he wants me outta there so he can have my mom all to himself. I try to stay away as much as I can."

My mom reached out and touched Lynne's hand. "We've got plenty of room here now. As long as it's alright with your mother, you're welcome to stay here anytime you want, and for as long as you want. Just remember that."

I nearly fell off my chair. I couldn't believe what I'd just heard. My mother was clearly enchanted with Lynne and I couldn't have been more pleased.

Lynne and I went into my room, shut the door and talked earnestly about how cool it would be if she moved into our house, at least until the school year was over. And with my dad gone, there was room for one more in the house. But I knew if he returned, all the tension and the darkness would return. Lynne or not, I didn't want my father coming back home.

While my mom and I washed the dinner dishes, I revealed my true feelings to her about my dad, something I'd never done before.

"Mom, please don't let him come back this time. Please. I'll do anything. I'll get a job. I'll help out in any way I can. Just please, please don't let him come back." She put her dish towel down and looked at me.

"Are you serious?"

"Yes. I'm completely serious. Mom, he's so mean and cruel. He hits me and treats us both like idiots."

My mom looked surprised; she had always turned a blind eye when he abused me, as if she didn't hear it or see it. But now that he was gone, there was no point in denying it any longer.

"C'mon mom, you know what he does."

She didn't answer me. She put the towel down, covered her face with her hands and cried.

The next day, everything changed.

I came home from school to find my father sitting at the table in the eating nook, and my mother sitting beside him. Both looked stern and disdainful. They told me to sit down across from them, as if they were judges and I was some lowly criminal facing charges.

I couldn't believe that she'd let him come back, especially after I'd given up my secret to her—that I couldn't stand him. How could she? I tried to search her face, but she wouldn't look directly at me.

I sat down as they had asked. Then she turned hardened eyes toward me, which bore straight through my heart. They both looked disgusted, as if they hated me. I couldn't imagine what was going on, other than the possibility that an unholy alliance had quickly developed between them, making me the enemy they came together to battle.

"What's the matter?" I asked them. A late spring storm was gathering outside. The clouds were low and the air felt close, sticky and ominous.

"That *friend* of yours," my mother said, her face pinched and ugly with hate, "Lynne." She spat out her name as if her mouth were full of venom, "You are *never* to see her again!"

I suddenly felt like I was back in first grade, being told I couldn't play with little Yolanda.

"Why not?" I asked. "Just yesterday you said she could live with us! I don't get it. What changed?"

My mother narrowed her eyes and said, "I think you know. We got a phone call from Mrs. Brewster at school. She said we should know who our daughter is associating with."

Then she reached under the table and pulled out the letters Lynne had written to me, notes passed in class, and my diary. I was horrified. I felt sickened and betrayed.

"You...you read my personal stuff?" I couldn't believe they had snooped in my things! How dare they?

"She is the scum of the earth, and she only wants you because you're so feminine," my mother declared.

"Feminine?" I burst out laughing. "I'm hardly feminine. Look at me. I only wear black. I've got a big nose and a big body. I'm always the tallest in my class and I'm a clod. That's hardly girly."

"Lisa, I think you know what I'm talking about. Girls like her prey on sweet things like you."

"What do you mean by 'girls like her'?" I thought back to Kay, and how friendly my parents had always been to her and her partner, and was completely confused. What was so bad about me and Lynne?

My father pounded his fist on the table and I nearly jumped out of my chair. "Do you hear your mother? Do you? *You* are the scum of the earth, just like your sick *friend.*" He, too, spit out the word as if they were a bitter seed in his mouth. "Now you've made your mother cry. Look at her."

My mother's mouth turned down and she began to weep, and soon her whole body was shaking in great convulsive sobs, so dramatic I wondered if she were faking the whole performance.

My father's face had turned red and he spat out at me, "Look what you've done to your mother! I could reach up your ass and turn you inside out!"

I found that odd, considering he never seemed to care about her happiness when he was cheating on her. *He* was the one who made her cry, not me, but I kept those thoughts to myself.

Suddenly my mom stood up, sniffled, and said, "I'm taking the dog for a walk." My mom never took our dog for a walk, but she attached a leash to the collar of our golden retriever, Honey, and left the house.

As soon as the door closed, my father grabbed me and threw me into the living room. I fell on the floor in front of the fireplace. He got my diary and letters from the kitchen and stood over me, randomly flipping through them, reading bits out loud.

"'Why don't we cast our fates to the wind and run away together?'" he read from a note Lynne had written in fifth period. "Well, isn't that just the goddamn sickest thing I've ever heard?"

He unfolded another letter.

"Oh, and how about this one? 'Your eyes are the color of sapphires. I see them when I close my eyes, just before I fall asleep.' Jesus Key-rist, that makes me want to vomit."

I looked from his sickening face to the rug on the floor. I counted the swirls in the red paisley pattern and then started obsessively doing long division in my head, something I'd learned to do as a child whenever the arguments began.

I didn't hear anything more as he continued to read on, mocking my love for Lynne and her love for me. All I heard were the numbers in my head, *a hundred and two thousand, three hundred, forty-five dived by twelve; six million, four hundred thousand and one divided by thirty-nine.* I made them as hard as I could, so I was forced to concentrate on the numbers, only the numbers and nothing else. When I looked back up at him, he was laughing derisively at me and I was ill with humiliation and rage.

Then he took all my letters and my diary and threw them into the fireplace. I watched helplessly as he struck a match and set it to the papers. There was a whoosh as it all burst into flames. The smell of burning words spread through the room. I saw the pages of my most important belongings curl and blacken as my love and my future went up in smoke.

My heart broke. Not only was he invading my privacy and deriding my love for Lynne, but he'd just destroyed my heart and soul, my writing— writing that I believed would take me to London.

He pulled me off the floor and began to beat me. He dragged me into my bedroom, threw me on the bed and got on top of me. What happened next is fuzzy in my memory. I know that I kicked at him and screamed, that my mother returned with the dog, that my dad suddenly got off me— and that my pants were unzipped.

The next morning, I got up and went to school as if nothing had happened. I met Lynne near our lockers. When she saw me, her face became alarmed. She reached out and touched my arm.

"What is it? What's wrong?"

"Lynne, you'll never believe what happened. My parents say I can't see you anymore and I don't know why."

Her brown eyes filled with tears.

"I know why. It's because I'm boy-ish and they're afraid I'm going to make you queer."

"Queer? Does it make me queer that I love you and that you love me too?" I wasn't even sure what queer meant. What did it matter who someone loved as long as they were happy and not hurting anyone?

That night, Lynne and I held hands as we walked home with our friends. Liz shook her head in disbelief and said, "I can't understand why they'd read your diary. I mean, that's just awful. I'd die if my parents read mine."

"I don't keep one for that very reason," Maryanne said.

"I guess you can't trust anyone," Lynne said. "Especially parents."

When we all parted to go to our separate homes, Lynne held me close and whispered in my ear, "They can't do this to us." Then she slipped a piece of paper in my hand. "Look at it later," she said. I took the paper and put it in my purse.

I remembered little Yolanda, and knew in my heart that they could and would do whatever they could to keep us apart, even if that meant moving.

"They will never keep me away from you. Never!" I said, determined that I wouldn't let them rip me from another friend.

In the days that followed, my life became a living nightmare. My mother told me that I was being followed and watched at school and that if I were even in the same room as Lynne, it would be reported to her. She emphasized that I couldn't "get away with anything."

The idea that I was being followed and watched freaked me out. Now that I knew that Mrs. Brewster was reporting to my parents, I didn't trust anyone at school, especially my teachers. I became furtive and anxious whatever I was doing. I couldn't sleep or eat and felt a vast emptiness playing around the edges of my heart.

But I refused to stop seeing Lynne. I had found my true love and wasn't about to let her go. But just as I feared, my parents did as they had done before. They packed up and moved. The tears fell from my face with every drawer I emptied, every poster I took down, and every box that I packed. Finally, when everything was in the U-Haul, I said goodbye to the little cottage I loved so much.

As we drove away, I quietly opened my little purse, took out the slip of paper that Lynne had slipped into my hand and read it. It was a little poem she'd written for me:

Paint the sky orange,
Paint the grass red,
Paint the white black,
Paint the black white,
Do it if you have to,
You above all others can,
Because you have the realization of life.
A gift God gives only few.

I folded the paper and put it in my wallet.

They put me in Holy Names, an all-girls Catholic high school and figured the incident was closed. But while they could remove me from our neighborhood and my school, they couldn't remove Lynne from my heart or stop the love I had for her. At least I didn't have to watch her chasing after my parents' offering a dime in her outstretched hand.

As my school years went on, I devised many devious ways to see Lynne and our friends, and once I had a car, there was absolutely no keeping me away. I told lie and after lie in order to be with her. I faked an interest in high school football games which allowed me to go downtown on Friday nights. But instead of attending the game, I got on a bus and headed over to the beach to be with Lynne, Liz and our other friends. Then I'd get back on the bus and arrive downtown just as the game ended. I'd quickly ask someone who had won the game so that when my mom arrived to pick me up, I would be ready to answer any questions she might ask. I learned to be good at pretending an interest in sports and in inventing all manner of subterfuge. I never got caught again.

But I did get the message: loving a girl was wrong. It made my mother unhappy. So I stuffed that integral part of me deep, deep down inside and tried to live the way my mother wanted and to be who she wanted me to be.

It didn't matter that I was living a lie. All that mattered was that I didn't make my mother unhappy by being honest about who I was. So I began dating boys.

I started with the box boy at the local grocery store who my mother thought would make a good beau. I couldn't stand him, but hanging out with him pleased my mom and that was all that mattered. If loving girls was wrong, pretending to love boys was right. I began amassing boyfriends like little girls amass Barbie dolls and in no time at all I was jumping into bed with one after another. My mother was practically ecstatic to have so many boys calling for me, but inside me, my heart was broken in pieces and Lynne remained stubbornly in each little shard.

Yet, despite all the guys, I didn't stop seeing her. As the years progressed from junior school to high school, I took every opportunity I could to see Lynne. And she didn't stop seeing me—until her parents took matters into their own hands and had her institutionalized for her sexual "deviance." By the time she got out, I'd graduated from high school and learned to put those feelings as far away as I could possibly stuff them—which meant that Lynne became as much a part of my past as pleasing my mother became my future.

CHAPTER 8

COMING UNDUN

A LTHOUGH ABORTION WAS illegal and it was six years away from the Roe v. Wade decision that would legalize it, one could be had for a lot of money. But the risk of back alley abortions was still high and many women died.

Bob offered to give me the money for an abortion, but as far as I was concerned, that wasn't an option for me. It was something I just couldn't do. I weighed my other options (such as friends and parents helping me) and came up empty-handed. All my friends were off living their lives—college, jobs, travelling—happily fulfilling their dreams. I didn't begrudge them that and knew that any help they might have offered wasn't available.

Having a baby without having a husband was bad enough; having a black man's baby was another story altogether.

The laws banning inter-racial marriage, called miscegenation, had been reversed only two years prior, in 1967. And although now legal, the "mixing of the races" was certainly not accepted or approved of in society. I was walking a thin line by dating black men, and bearing one's child was akin to practicing witchcraft.

I'd be on my own, not just during my pregnancy, but also in raising my child.

I had no siblings to take care of, nor did my mom let me babysit for pocket money. I had absolutely no experience with a baby.

All my friends had brothers and sisters and I knew that they often took care of their siblings. I asked them what it was like to care for an infant and without exception, they all said, "Ugh. I hate it. I'd rather be hanging out with friends."

Liz had a little brother and sometimes I'd watch as she gave him a bath or changed his diaper. It seemed to me that he was so little he might disappear down the drain. I was too scared to bathe him myself. I thought babies were as fragile as a box of loose crystals.

How on earth would I take care of my own baby? Would my ineptitude cause harm? And how would I deal with the certain hatred I would face as a white mother with a black child?

I realized that in terms of motherhood I was a potential danger to an innocent child. I knew in my heart that the child I was carrying would have a better chance at life with parents who were married, settled, financially comfortable and experienced—all things I was not. It didn't take me long to decide that the only reasonable thing was to give my baby up for adoption.

I made my decision sitting alone in the dark in my apartment. I was listening to *Undun*, by the Guess Who, on my portable record player, and realized that the song could have been written about me:

She's come undun
She climbed a mountain that was far too high
And when she found out she couldn't fly It was too late.

I was coming undone, and abject fear was unraveling any sense of self and strength I might have had.

Physically, the first few months of pregnancy were unbearable. With rampant nausea in the morning, I was barely able to stand while I cased my mail, and then trudged out to my route, hungry and tired. The hot summer days disappeared, replaced by rain, wind and bone chilling cold. My Hush Puppies fell apart in the mud.

Learning my route was tedious and slow. Some folks hid their mailboxes in odd places, like in the staircase down to a cellar. It took time and patience to find them. I was bitten in the ankle by a Doberman who had taken a distinct disliking to me. Each month, I was irritated by the arrival of Playboys (in their brown paper wrappers) and Vogues, not because of what they contained or represented, but simply because they were so heavy. I tumbled down a wet, slippery flight of stairs. I lost forty pounds, developed anemia and a bad case of bleak depression.

And I was all alone. My parents had moved to Hawaii because my dad had a construction job on Maui, so they wouldn't be around to help me. Bob had managed to disappear after he knew I was pregnant. I'd heard he had transferred to parcel post delivery and was glad to be rid of him.

I only told Lynne about it and she was mad at me for getting into this situation. Her anger hurt my heart and made me feel even more alone.

Eventually I just stopped going to work. I was just too exhausted and anemic to even get up and walk my route.

One morning there was a knock on my door. I opened it to find my supervisor. He stood in the darkness of the hallway, his hat in his hand.

"Mr. Lynch? What are you doing here?" I was completely rattled by his sudden appearance and didn't invite him in.

"I'm worried about you," he said. "Are you okay? Will you be coming back to work?"

"I'm . . . I'm . . . okay. But I'm not coming back to work. Sorry."

"Are you sure? You're doing the job well and have a future in the postal service."

I began to back away. *I don't want a future in the postal service, for heaven's sake. I want to go to London and be a writer.* "No . . . no . . . I have to go," and I shut the door. I walked away from the door, congratulating myself on speaking up and moving forward. Then I sat down on the couch and let the full realization of my act sink in.

What had I just done? Quit a good job because . . . because why? The thought of no food, no income, nowhere to live made me dizzy. I almost ran after Mr. Lynch, but I just didn't have the energy. Besides, it was too late anyway. I'd already closed that door.

I was never close to my parents and had never turned to them for help. But after four months of misery, weight loss, fatigue and tears, I called my mom in Maui and asked for help.

"Mom, I've got a problem." She didn't prompt me to continue, so I rushed into it without any other preface.

"Mom, I'm pregnant and the father is black. I'm not working, I'm broke, hungry and I'm about to be evicted."

There was silence, then she said, "Were you raped?"

"No."

There was another long pause on her end and then I heard the phone go dead. She'd hung up on me.

By December I no longer had an income and my landlord's threats to evict me had become downright menacing. My cupboards were bare and my hunger growing. My high school friend, Mary, was home for the holidays from university in San Francisco.

She called me soon after getting home. "Hey! How are you doing?" she said.

"Funny you should ask." I said. "Actually, I'm pregnant."

"You are not! God…who's the father?" I told her she didn't know him.

"Did you tell anyone from school?"

"Uh-uh."

"Well, your secret's safe with me." She invited me to her parents' church in Ballard where they spoke in tongues and prayed themselves into trances. I declined.

But she kept me fed with turkey sandwiches from her home, brought me little presents—a small hat, a magenta velvet handbag, an antique music box—and she gave me moral support without judging.

It was almost Christmas and almost my birthday. I felt so depressed I was barely able to rise out of bed in the morning. But only a few days after calling my mom, there was a knock on my door. It was the letter carrier, holding a small box with an Hawaiian post mark. It was from my mother. Perhaps it was a Christmas and birthday present. I couldn't imagine what she'd sent and I couldn't help but hope that the box was full of money. Maybe there'd be a loving letter of apology and some maternity clothes.

I brought the box in and set it on my little dining table. I tore it open and instead of seeing loose bills fly out of it, all I saw was a twelve ounce tin of macadamia nuts. I stared at the can, wondering what I had done to deserve such contempt. Then I started to cry, the sobs spilling out of me until there wasn't another tear left to shed. But rather than toss out the nuts, as I so desperately wanted to do, I slowly opened the can, wondering if a toy snake would spring at my face when I opened it, a giant "screw you," from my mother. But there was no humor in seeing the salty nuts nestled inside. It was the only food that I had. I was so hungry that I wolfed them down and then threw up.

Having not been in the care of a physician at that point, I didn't know if my nausea at five months along was normal. Surely devouring twelve ounces of macadamia nuts on an empty stomach would make anyone nauseated.

Christmas Day was dark and cold. Shards of frozen rain pelted the pavement. I drove over to Mary's house and she smuggled me into her parents' white brick home, afraid that they would see me, notice my small bump and throw me out. Hiding in the warm basement amidst the scents of Tide and Clorox, I could hear laughter coming from upstairs. Theirs was a big Catholic family. Her father said the blessing, but I could only hear parts echoing through the heating vents.

"Bless us our Lord and the food....receive....give thanks...blessings." I could hear fragments of their happy statements about what each of them was thankful for.

"...for the new ski boots..."

"Sister Eugenie gave me an "A"....."

I recognized her mother saying she was thankful "for the new wallpaper in the downstairs bathroom."

I longed to be part of Mary's family. I didn't know if they were happy or if they fought all the time. I just felt so warmed overhearing their reasons to be thankful on Christmas Day.

I was lying on the spare bunk bed near the washing machine when Mary appeared.

"Merry Christmas!" Mary said. She opened a paper bag that she'd brought with her. Inside there were little bundles of food wrapped in waxed paper. I stuck my nose in the bag and inhaled. The aroma was heavenly, like the wafting fragrance of a night blooming jasmine.

"I've got more turkey, cranberry sauce, potatoes, gravy and pumpkin pie," Mary said. In the past, I had never thought to be thankful at family gatherings, but I was grateful for the blessings Mary brought me that day.

The day after Christmas was my 19th birthday and I was feeling desperate. I knew I couldn't continue to live this way. So I phoned my mother again.

My dad answered the phone, and when I said hello, he wordlessly handed the phone to my mom. I heard her say, "Who is it, Leo?" I couldn't hear if he'd answered her but was sure she figured it out.

"Hello?" she said, her voice cold and hard.

"Hi," I said weakly.

"What do you want?"

"Mom, I really need your help. I don't have a job and my rent is due. I'm sick all the time. I don't know what to do."

After a long hesitation, she said "Well, I suppose you could come here for a while."

CHAPTER 9

AN HAWAIIAN KIDNEY INFECTION

MY MOM SENT me a ticket to Maui. I had a week to put my few things in storage, pack my clothes, and drop my car off at my cousins' for safe-keeping. While I didn't trust her or her motives, visions of papayas for breakfast and my mom's tuna casseroles for dinner danced in my head. I was fleeing the horrid winter of Seattle to restore myself in the sun of Lahaina.

I'll never forget the smell of gardenias in the air when I stepped off the plane. As I descended the stairs, looking all around at the tall, skinny palm trees, I saw my mother. Before I'd stepped off the last step and onto the tarmac, she reached up and grabbed my hand.

I looked around me, confused. She rarely ever touched me. Her grip disconcerted me. She hissed in my ear, "If anybody asks what's wrong with you, tell them you have a kidney infection."

"What?"

She brought her face close to mine. "You heard me."

"Let go of my hand."

She did but reluctantly, as if she were having second thoughts about letting me come there. I took the last step from the plane. "Who on earth is going to ask me what's wrong with me? I don't know anyone here but you guys."

"Nevertheless," she said, "just in case. You have a kidney infection."

And so it was, as far as my mother was concerned. The little baby inside me was...what...a kidney stone?

The drive into Lahaina was breathtaking. I'd never seen any place so beautiful. The water was clear and pure and so very blue. No, not blue. By turns azure, cobalt, sapphire and turquoise.

My parents had an apartment on Front Street, right on the ocean, with a long lanai looking over the beach and a swimming pool. I was to share one of the twin beds in the bedroom with my mother, while my dad and a member of his crew, Barry, slept on the sofa beds in the living room.

In 1970, there was only the beginning of land and resort development on Maui, but anyone with vision could see the trend coming. As a tourist attraction, it was a novel idea—to build a narrow gauge railway from Lahaina to Kaanapali. My father's construction company got the contract and off he and my mother went for a year in Hawaii.

It was called the Lahaina, Kaanapali and Pacific Railroad, a 6-mile narrow gauge rail line with open-air coaches to be pulled by vintage steam locomotives. During the construction, his crews faced heat, dust, torrential rains, scorpions and, understandably, some native hostility.

Hippies had discovered Maui only a few years before, realizing quickly that they had found paradise. Just down Front Street from our apartment was The Animal Farm, an old house owned by an old island family. To make extra money, they rented rooms to members of this new wave of relaxed invaders and it soon became a controversial eyesore. Someone put a porcelain bathtub in the front yard for cooling beverages or sleeping. Some of them were inspired botanists, working out back of the house on the development of Maui Wowie. Many of them walked around nude.

Further along on Front Street was the downtown area. The Pioneer Inn, a two story clapboard building painted deep green with white trim, was the only lodging for visitors in the town. And in Courthouse Square stood the symbol of the city—a huge banyan tree whose limbs, draped with moss, covered the entire square, creating a space of dappled sunlight and shadow.

My mother pointed these out to me as she slowed the car and turned into the apartments' outdoor garage. My father and Barry had not yet returned from work. Barry was my dad's protégée in the world of hard-hat construction. He was tall and gorgeous, a "black Irishman" as my mother used to say. Although he had a limited ability or interest in conversation (his usually response to anything was "Damn Skippy") and was an alcoholic, my parents wanted me to marry him. They voiced this wish many times and each time I asked why they'd want me to marry an inarticulate beer-drinking construction stiff their answer was "He makes a living and saves his money."

When they did get back from the fields, my dad and Barry's clothes were covered with red dust and spotted with salty sweat stains.

Seeing their state of dirtiness, my mother turned to me. "All I do around here is wash their clothes, feed them, clean for them and buy beer for them." Because my mother felt like an unpaid house servant during their time on Maui, she constantly said that she hated Hawaii.

I was exhausted and disoriented. Barry and my dad washed up and my mother announced that we were off for a wedding reception. One of the native guys on my dad's crew, Joe, was having a luau to celebrate his daughter's marriage. This was truly the miraculous result of air travel. In just one day, I went from hunger and cold in Seattle to poi and warm Cokes under palm trees on the island of Maui.

We left Lahaina and drove on the highway for a few miles, then turned onto a dirt road that wound up a hill through a field of pineapple trees. It was a warm evening, the soft breeze smelled of salt water and gardenias and the sky was sparkling with millions of stars.

Joe and several other native men greeted us with delight. They put leis made of *ti* leaves around our necks then led us to the party. We were introduced to the revelers by Joe saying *Aloha mai malihini*—Welcome newcomers! As we passed by, I noticed a pig roasting in an *imu*—the underground pit oven used to cook large animals. At the covered picnic area, Joe's family danced *hula* and sang Hawaiian songs, accompanied by a young man on ukulele.

On the tables, covered in red and white checked oilcloth, were bowls of *poi*— pounded taro root—and we were instructed how to eat it by cupping two fingers, scooping up the poi and putting in the mouth. It tasted like school glue and looked worse. Bowls of salted baby shrimp were eaten by the handful, like peanuts or potato chips.

Something unidentified was served in steaming banana leaves. I unwrapped layers of leaf after leaf, ultimately uncovering a mystery food item that I politely decline to eat. Everyone was getting drunk, including me. In fact, I brought a glass of liquor back to the apartment and went swimming in the pool with it, until irritable neighbors shouted at me to be quiet. I wondered if they were the ones I would need to explain my kidney infection to, but I later found out that my parents didn't know anyone in the building.

I soon settled into island life. I awoke to soft fragrant breezes that wafted through the slats in the bedroom window. I shed the coats, sweaters and heavy shoes of winter for muumuus and sandals. I ate the tuna noodle casseroles and papayas with gusto and soon began gaining weight.

We fell into a routine. My dad and Barry were up and out early, leaving my mom and me to linger over breakfast. Once a week, I accompanied her on her trip into Wailuku. While she signed in for her unemployment check and bought groceries, I went to the library on High Street. It was a wonderful 1920's era white stucco building with a red tile roof. I usually brought back two or three books to last me a week, preferring books of comedy like Auntie Mame and humorists like James Thurber.

But the kidney infection was growing bigger and bigger. I loved to sit on the lanai and watch the sun set; it was like a glimpse into heaven. The sound of the surf was the only thing I could hear, and its briny waves seemed familiar to me.

Then one night, I felt a strong movement in my belly. I had no idea what it was. I didn't know a thing about pregnancy at the time, and had no idea I would feel anything moving inside me. It didn't feel normal.

It frightened me and I went inside.

"Mom! Something is moving! Something is moving! What is it? Am I okay?" I was terrified I might be losing the baby or the baby was pushing my innards all around and I was going to die.

At first she feigned ignorance, which only made me more frightened.

"C'mon, mom. This is *not* a kidney infection. You know what it is. What is happening?"

Reluctantly, she told me that babies begin to move at about six months' gestation. They kick, get the hiccups, and roll around.

I was dumbfounded. "Is that normal?"

"Yes, it is," she replied. Then she turned away from me and picked up her Readers Digest.

My parents had bought an old 1951 Ford when they first arrived on the island. It was fine for short errands, but not much else. We tried to drive it up to Haleakala Crater but at 10,000 feet, the elevation was too much and the car vapor-locked. But my mom really wanted to see the crater.

For the next attempt to Haleakala, they rented a new car and we made it to the top. Barry and I sat in the back seat, joking and pushing each other.

The air was thin. I got dizzy from oxygen deprivation and had to visit a little station where oxygen tanks were available. It was then that I realized if my parents were going to bring me to such a place without any thought to what it would do to me and my baby, it was time to go. I had not once seen a doctor and realized that no one was going to take care of me but myself and besides, my bump was becoming evident even in my flowing muu-muus. Pretty soon, people would start wondering about my ever-growing "kidney infection."

The next morning, I told my mom I was leaving. I said, "I need to get back to Seattle so I can see a proper doctor. I'm getting kicked and my back is starting to hurt and you guys are not getting me the care I need in order to have a healthy baby."

She didn't argue and instead walked to the phone to call the airline. She looked irritated.

"Yes, that's right—just one ticket with no return. It's for my daughter and she'd like to leave as soon as possible." She wrote a few notes on a scratch pad and handed the note to me. She couldn't look me in the eyes. "Your plane leaves at 1:00 pm tomorrow afternoon." And then she looked relieved.

On my last evening in Hawaii, I went for a walk on the beach as the sun set. I waded into the warm water, interrupting the little white-capped waves coming to shore. The water was so clean that, as the waves broke, I could see little fish in the waves. Barry joined me as I got drunk on my father's Benedictine and went for a loopy swim in the pool. When I told him I'd see him again sometime, Barry said, "Right you are! You'll see me again. Damn Skippy!"

In the morning, I dutifully stood on the lanai with my father, while my mother took a picture from below. She dropped me at the airport with no comments, no keep-in-touch platitudes, just good-bye. Despite her denials about my condition, I was grateful to have spent some time with them on Maui. I was able to eat decent food, gain some weight and relax in the warmth of the Hawaiian winter.

It was mid-February when I returned to Seattle. Rain was drizzling as the plane landed. I looked out the window and turned to the lady next to me. With friendly irony, I said "Welcome to Paradise." She smiled wanly at me, no doubt thinking "flippant teenagers."

Within a week, I had signed up for welfare and moved into a small apartment with my high school friend Deego. It was an old church that had been chopped up into tiny apartments, perfect for students or poor high school grads like us. She slept on the Murphy bed and I got the sofa. It was filthy and on a noisy street in the University District but it was a roof over my head.

I had terrible insomnia, so I'd take off at night to visit anyone I could find who was still awake. Surprisingly, many were and soon I had a coterie of friends and acquaintances who welcomed me and even did what they could to help me. Mr. Walter, a hairdresser, gave me coffee and cigarettes which back then were not recognized as cancer causing and addictive. Jim, a physicist, provided me with the New York Times and lots of crackers to ease my nausea, which still hadn't subsided by my second trimester. Going from one friend to another to another, I could visit someone all hours of the day and night, spend my nervous energy and collapse on my little sofa bed around noon.

But eventually, it was time for the hardest part. Having made my decision, it was time to do something about it. I needed to find an adoption agency. I needed to find someone to help me give my baby away, as much as I wished it were different. I knew if I wavered on my decision that I would plunge into a deep hole of confusion so I steeled myself, accepted the wisdom of my decision and the inevitable sorrow at giving the little life within me to someone else to love.

CHAPTER 10

PANIC HOUR

IT DIDN'T START well. The receptionist at the Lutheran adoption agency, her hair pulled back in a tight bun making her look like a ferret, asked me to fill out a form while I waited in their reception area. Then a secretary in a mini-skirt took my information, without saying a word, into another room and closed the door. A few minutes later, she returned, looking stern and disapproving. Despite the fact that she was probably only a year or two older than me, she projected an adult sort of authority. She handed the forms back to me, then flipped her perfectly quaffed Vidal Sassoon bob with her hand.

"You need to leave please," she said. "Quietly. And do not return."

"Why?" I asked.

"I think you know why." She barely hid her disgust. "You're carrying the baby of a black man?"

"Yes," I said.

"Then we can't help you. Please leave. Now. And do not come back."

A week later, on a bitterly cold morning, I found a place to park on a slippery wet side street downtown. I walked carefully down the street to the Mercer Building on Columbia Street. It was an old brick building. The Catholic adoption agency was on the fourth floor and there was no elevator.

Panting with the effort of walking up so many stairs, I found their office and opened the door.

Within the dark unwelcoming reception room, a receptionist looked up from her typewriter. "Can I help you?" she asked.

"I'm here to talk with someone about relinquishing my baby."

"First we'll need you to fill out some forms," she said without looking at me.

"I've already filled them out and sent them in. I have an appointment." She looked up, as if noticing me for the first time.

"Your name?" I told her my name and she thumbed through her calendar. "Ah, yes, I see it right here. Have a seat and someone will be with you in a moment." I took a seat and waited, flipping through an old, beaten-up National Geographic and Ladies' Home Journal, until at long last I was invited into an office.

Sitting behind a massive wooden desk was a bird-like man. His scowling eyes were set close together and his ears were pointed. He wore a tweed jacket with suede patches on the elbows.

"Hello. I'm Dr. Bettemeyer." He stood and reached out to shake my hand. "I'm a psychiatrist and will be talking with you."

"Dr. Bettemeyer?" I laughed out loud. My patience had grown thin. The rejection, judgment, and self-righteousness I'd already experienced had worn me down. I began to lose what little vestige of acceptable behavior I could muster.

"What's so funny?" he asked, scowling even further. He looked like his eyebrows might engulf his nostrils. "Bettemeyer," I said. "Georgianna's father?" He nodded.

"I went to Holy Names with her. You're her dad? No wonders she's so screwed up."

I thought he'd throw me out but he didn't.

"I'd like to explore your comments," he said.

"You mean, like why I think your daughter is a mess?" I couldn't believe I had just said that. But I had and I couldn't take it back.

But still he didn't react.

"No. I want to know why you are so angry."

"Well, I might be angry because I'm pregnant and I want to relinquish my child and the father is black and you are bugging me." I was close to breaking down completely.

"When did you first become attracted to black men?" He made a tent of his fingers and posed them under his nose.

I tried to derail him. "I got asthma when I was four and almost died."

That got him. He leaned forward, fascinated. "Really? Why do think that happened?"

"I don't know. Are you going to help me or not?"

He sat back in his chair and placed his hands on his desk. "Oh no, we can't possibly help you with your...child...but I can help you with your emotional and anger issues."

I closed my eyes and thought that I'd just about had it. I said "Give my love to Georgianna" and left, stomping furiously out the door, down the steps and onto the rain soaked street.

I started to feel desperate. Would other adoption agencies also tell me to get lost? What was I going to do if no one wanted my baby? I had made my decision and there was no going back. But what if I couldn't find an adoption agency that would help me find a good home for my baby? I couldn't tolerate a moment of doubt or I'd drown in sorrow and regret.

But then I was told by the Protestant adoption agency (who also couldn't help me) that the Medina Children's Agency, in the Central District of Seattle might help. Progressive and liberal, the agency was funded by a federal grant specifically to place children of color and bi-racial children into good adoptive homes. Bingo!

I drove to their offices on an early spring day. The air had lost the crisp cold and the bone-chilling rain of winter and there was a barely discernible soft sweetness to the day.

I was taken into an office to meet with a matronly-looking woman. She stood as I entered and gave me her outstretched hand.

"Hello," she said. "I'm Mrs. Bell. If you'll have a seat, we can get started." She motioned to a comfortable looking upholstered chair in front of her desk. As I sat down, she began to explain the process.

"I understand you want to relinquish your baby for adoption. I also understand that your baby is bi-racial and I want you to know that placing bi-racial children in good homes is our sole purpose here."

I closed my eyes for a moment to savor the relief that was overtaking me. "I will need to know about you, the baby's father, your due date and where you will have your baby."

I gave her the information she wanted about myself and Bob, but couldn't answer the other questions. "I don't know what my due date is or where I'll have the baby."

"But you think you are seven months along?"

"Yes, I think so." She gave my large belly a professional glance and agreed saying she thought I looked to be only a few months from delivery.

"If you don't have a doctor yet, I recommend the Women, Infant and Children program at the University of Washington. I'll give you some phone numbers to call before you leave."

Mrs. Bell projected the warmth and caring that I had been missing. I felt my body relax for the first time in many months.

She explained how it would work. "On the third or fourth day after your baby's birth, we will come to the hospital with some papers for you to sign. You will not know who the adoptive parents will be. You understand that you will have no rights once the papers are signed?"

I nodded. The concept of open adoption was many years in the future.

"Our job is to find the best possible family for your baby. He or she may be in a foster home for a while until a family is found."

I nodded again, feeling my throat tighten. Tears stung my eyes as I attempted to maintain some semblance of composure and assuredness. Now the full gravity of my decision hit me and my sudden sense of relief was mingled with the seriousness of what I was about to do. I knew that if I let my emotions out, even slightly, I'd fall to pieces. Then indecision would enter my mind, and I couldn't tolerate that. My mind was made up. I must relinquish my baby and there could be no second thoughts about it.

Miss Bell recognized the conflict in my eyes and sought to reassure me. "You are doing a brave thing," she said. "This is a hard decision, but by relinquishing, you are providing a safe and secure life for your baby, a life that you cannot provide now. Perhaps you'll have another child who you will be prepared to raise."

I found small comfort in this. My gaze wandered out the window. Medina Children's Agency was in a new building of cedar planks and oddly sized windows.

Miss Bell's office looked out over a small stand of pine trees.

I imagined a small child climbing one of those trees, with a worried, but amused mother standing below, shouting admonishments to be careful and not to go any higher. I saw the child come down from the tree and run into its mother's arms. They both laughed. I imagined such a strong sense of ease and intimacy between this mother and child. My heart ached to have such feelings, to feel that close and loved by another human being. Then I heard Miss Bell's voice.

"...your baby is born."

"What?" Her words suddenly brought me back to reality and I listened to what she was telling me I had to do.

"I said to call us when the baby is born and we'll make the arrangements to get the baby into care. Are you alright?"

I could still see the mother and child frolicking among the trees, but let the vision fade. "Yeah...I'm okay"

"Good," she said as she walked me to the entrance. "We'll be in touch."

I left the building, not knowing that in the not-so-distant future, I'd be walking through that same door again, but for a very different reason.

My monthly welfare check of $60 didn't go far. Thirty dollars went to my share of the rent, the rest was supposed to cover gas and groceries, but it didn't. My all-hours of-the-day friends kept me fed. Sometimes after Deego got paid, we'd go to Clark's Around The Clock at 2:00 am and she'd treat me to fish and chips. We especially enjoyed watching the drag queens. Two in the morning was Panic Hour. The bars had closed and all the queens and dykes and fairies came to Clarks for a last ditch attempt at finding some company for the rest of the night. The queens screamed at each other, flaunting themselves up and down the aisles, their fastidious makeup starting to run and their carefully coifed wigs slipping to one side. The dykes lumbered into their booths, smoking, laughing, and patting each other on the back. They smelled of tobacco, leather and hair gloss.

Deego and I reveled in seeing a part of life we'd not known about when we were at Holy Names. It was a good laugh, a cheap fix for fish, and an added bonus was Deego's idea of economizing by stealing toilet paper from the ladies room.

I was admitted into the Women, Infant and Children program at the University of Washington medical center. There, as I entered my seventh month, I received my first prenatal care. Because it was a teaching hospital, each visit brought a new team of professors and interns, and I soon became accustomed to exposing myself to small groups of interested strangers. But while they checked my size of my belly, the dilation of my cervix and the position of the baby, they told me nothing about childbirth, what to expect, and that—oh, by the way—giving birth hurts. Inexplicable as it was, I had absolutely no idea that giving birth was going to feel like passing a watermelon through the eye of a needle.

In fact, it was a stranger at the cash register of a small downtown café who told me. She noticed I was pregnant and asked the due date.

"Sweetie, it won't last long. I mean, it's like the worst cramps you've ever had, but once the baby comes out, it's all over. My second kid came after four hours of labor! Can you imagine? Of course, my first one took 3 days...." Now I was not only worried but terrified.

But I did finally learn something about childbirth and babies at the University clinic. I was assigned a student nurse, Leeann, who proved a god-send. Leeann cared for me until the birth, and she became my teacher about all things having to do with being pregnant and having a baby.

"Expect labor pains," she told me. "When they come, start to count the minutes between each pain. When it gets to about four minutes between each pain, come to the Emergency Room."

"To the Emergency Room? Why?"

"Because your baby is coming."

We were sitting in a small exam room, she on a folding chair and me on the exam table, dressed in a hospital gown and swinging my legs back and forth. Perhaps it was the heightened sense I was having since becoming pregnant, but I loved the smell of rubbing alcohol that permeated the clinic.

"Of course, when your waters break, delivery will be imminent. So if that happens, get to the hospital as soon as possible."

"What waters?"

"The amniotic fluid, the stuff your baby is floating in."

"My baby is floating in water?"

Leeann shot me a look, as if to say, "Duh."

I was sitting on the sofa in our little studio reading *Siddhartha* when the pains started. I remembered what the lady in the restaurant said: "It's just like cramps." As the pains continued, I thought she must have been joking or referring to the worst cramps a woman could possibly have. Deego had just left for work, so I was all alone, and terrified of what was suddenly happening.

The pains were erratic at first but then became regular. Seven minutes apart, then six, five, and finally four. I called the hospital.

"Well young lady," a nurse on the maternity ward said, "it sounds like your baby is on the way. You should get someone to bring you in right away."

"But I'm alone," I told her.

"Call a cab. See you soon." I wrote a note to Deego telling her where I was, and taped it to the television. It was a safe bet she'd find it there.

Bent over with pain, I got in my car and drove myself to the Emergency Room.

I was having a baby.

Chapter 11

I Want to See My Baby

As I was unceremoniously readied for labor and delivery, it was clear from the beginning what the nurses thought of me. They'd obviously read my chart and were not the least compassionate. They barked orders at me.

"Get your clothes off and this on," one said as she threw a hospital gown at me. Then she marched me to a bathroom and handed me a bottle of Fleets.

"Use this now and return to your room when you've finished."

"But I don't have to go," I protested.

She shoved the bottle at me, "Drink this now, and believe me, you'll go."

In the small bathroom, I drunk the horrid liquid and waited, but nothing happened. There I sat, in a small, cold bathroom with a hospital gown open at the back, lonely and in pain, waiting for my bowels to empty.

After what I thought was an appropriate amount of time, I opened the door to find the nurse waiting outside.

"Everything okay?" she asked.

"Oh, yes, it worked perfectly," I lied

"What did I tell you?" She looked pleased in her smugness and I suspected that she enjoyed purging a wanton woman like me.

Back in the room, I endured more humiliations. I was shaved. A doctor came in and shoved his hand inside me. He poked and prodded, talked about effacement and dilation and left. He hadn't even said "Hello" to me.

When the pains became unbearable, I cursed. And cursed. No relief was offered. Instead, a nurse rushed into my room.

"You need to shut up! We can hear you up and down the hallway. You are spoiling the experience for the *married* ladies."

I cursed into my pillow. This was the worst pain I'd ever had. I would rather have chewed glass than endure this pain.

As day turned into night I wondered where Deego was. Surely she had seen my note. Where was she? I was panting in pain. It was early June and already hot. Beads of sweat ran down my face and neck. I wanted some ice and pressed my call button.

It took a long time for a nurse to respond and when she did merely poked her head into my room, clearly annoyed.

"What?"

"I wondered if I could get some ice."

She squinted at me, and slowly said, "We don't have any ice."

"But I saw you walking down the hallway earlier with a bucket of ice."

"We don't have any ice for *you*." She turned and walked out. At that moment, I felt as if I'd lost control of my muscles and my mind. I was trapped and powerless and nothing I could do would change that. I steeled myself to endure the thirst, the humiliation and the pain.

The pains were getting worse and closer together. Another doctor came in, looked at the progress and poked something sharp inside me. I felt warm liquid running down my legs.

"What did you just do?" I yelled at him.

"Broke your waters. It won't be long now."

I remembered hearing something about that before, then remembered the student nurse telling me to expect this. Only she didn't say anything about manually breaking the waters.

The pain was relentless. Now my whole body was covered in sweat. I looked around the bleak colorless room and longed to be home, only I wasn't sure where home was.

Then a crowd of nurses and doctors rushed in, put the head of my bed down, and pushed me into the corridor.

"Where are you taking me?"

The nurse said, "To the delivery room."

I looked at the gray ceiling and walls as they transported me.

Once there, I was transferred to a hard surgical table, where I laid flat on my back. The pain was intense and constant. I thought my back was going to explode.

"Sit up," a nurse said. With difficulty, I did, dangling my legs over the side of the table. They told me to be perfectly still, a rather odd challenge as my body spasmed with each contraction. I felt a sharp poke at the small of my back. They laid me back down and I watched incredulously as my legs were lifted and put into stirrups. I couldn't feel them at all.

I asked them what they had done to me.

"Epidural," a nurse said. "It deadens your lower half so you won't feel the pain anymore." As an after-thought, she said, "Although it does slow the process of birth."

But the baby came quickly after that. I heard them say "Push, push." As I lay on my back, looking at the bright ceiling lights of the delivery room, a mass of confused emotions gripped me. A little life was coming into the world that I would never know. It would be a birth and a farewell. I felt infinitely sad, but then I heard a baby cry.

"The doctor said, "It's a boy!"

"A boy?" I shouted. "A boy!"

But my elation ended. My new little baby was wrapped in a blanket and whisked away. I hadn't even seen his little face.

I was tired, so very tired and fell asleep on the delivery table.

I awoke in a room with three other women. Sitting beside my bed was Deego. She looked a bit disheveled, as if she'd just gotten out of bed.

"Where were you?" I asked.

"Well, I came home from work and you weren't there. I figured you were visiting one of your insomnia friends and I was tired so I went to sleep."

"You didn't see my note?"

"Oh, yeah," she said, "but I didn't see it until this morning."

"But I taped it to the television." I started to cry. I'd gone through this alone because Deego decided for the first night in her life not to watch TV. "But I'm here now!" she said brightly, clearly trying to stop me crying.

"Right. Here you are. So, you didn't want to catch *That Girl* before going to bed?"

"Re-run," she said. Despite ourselves, we laughed because we both knew we'd watched re-runs of *That Girl* over and over.

I looked out the window and saw a portion of Portage Bay and the roofs of a few houseboats. There's a world out there that knows nothing of me and my troubles, I thought. Nor do they care. And why should they? Everyone is living their own lives, and I need to live mine. I needed to be the one to care about myself and stop expecting it from others.

"What can I get for you?" Deego asked.

"A pack of cigarettes, please." I didn't know any better. Lots of pregnant women smoked back then, and it would be decades before the laws banning smoking in public places were enacted. She came back shortly with a pack of Winston 100's. I tore open the pack, took out a cigarette and lit up. I hadn't had one for over twenty-four hours.

Deego had one too. And together we said, "Ahhhh."

The door opened, a post-partum nurse entered and walked over to me to tell me the rules. She ignored Deego.

"You are to stay in this room with the other unwed mothers." My three roommates, who were sitting up reading or smoking like me, stared at their laps. They'd already heard this drill.

"Under no circumstances are you to go to the nursery. You may not see your baby. Don't ask to see him and don't try to sneak. We have the illegitimate infants at the back so even if you try, you won't find him."

Deego looked at me with anger in her eyes and then to the nurse. Even her shiny auburn hair seemed angry.

"My friend has every right to see her baby."

Uh ho, I thought. *Now she's done it. Gone and pissed Deego off.*

"No she doesn't," the nurse replied. "She's relinquishing him for adoption. She gave up her rights when she made that decision." I told Deego to let it go.

On my second day post-partum, I decided to call Bob. I hadn't seen him for nearly seven months and didn't even know if he still worked at the post office or lived in the same place. Why I wanted to call him I couldn't say. Perhaps I was looking for someone to be happy about the baby's birth. I dialed the last number I had for him. My voice was thin with fear and my hands shaking.

An unfamiliar voice answered the phone.

"Uh, hello. Is Bob there?"

"Bob?" said the stranger. "Bob who?"

"You don't know him? He worked for the post office, out of International Station?

"Oh yeah. That guy. He moved out a long time ago, before I moved in."

"Would you happen to know where he went?" I didn't know why I asked about his whereabouts and regretted it as soon as I spoke.

"Nope. No idea. But if for some reason he returns would you like to leave a message?"

"No. It's okay. Never mind." I said goodbye and hung up.

On my third day post -partum, my mother called from Hawaii. She'd first called the apartment and Deego told her where I was.

"I'm leaving Lahaina tomorrow," she said. "The job is over and we're coming back. I'm coming ahead to find an apartment and get the furniture out of storage."

"Oh, okay." Her imminent arrival was no cause for joy. But I did want her to know I'd had my baby.

"The baby was born two days ago," I said, "It was a boy!"

I swear she started to say, "What baby?" but she didn't. Instead, after a pause she said, "Yes, Deego told me."

"Well…so…you'll be back late tomorrow? I'll probably still be in the hospital. I'm in room 524 on the labor and delivery floor. So yeah, you know, yeah," I stuttered. "The baby was born, healthy and strong, so I'm told anyway."

Would she ask me how I was? I wanted to tell her what the whole experience was like, how frightened and alone I was, and to point out that she was actually a grandmother, if only briefly. But then I thought better of it. Maybe she really just didn't care.

But I ventured into those waters slightly. "I'm doing okay. A bit tired and sore."

She didn't respond and after a moment of silence she said, "I'll see you tomorrow," and then hung up.

Deego had left and it was getting late. As the sun set, shadows haunted the room. The other ladies in my room had been discharged and I was alone. The door was closed, but I could hear laughing and talking, bangs and thuds as Housekeeping moved their mops and pails up and down the floors. Suddenly, the door opened and a housekeeper came in with her mop. She took quick, wide swipes around the floor and then, without a word, left. Once again, the door was closed. I could hear only muffled noises and soon the sun had set and the room was completely dark.

The next day, I awoke to find two new ladies admitted to the room. They were both sleeping, snoring like trumpet swans.

Then two women from the adoption agency arrived, Mrs. Bell and Miss Hardy. I remembered Mrs. Bell. She was solid and self-assured and wearing a hat, a common accessory from the past that now was fading away.

But I had never met Miss Hardy. She didn't look much older than I. Her hair was straight and blonde. She wore a plain skirt and blouse and seemed earnest, but standing a few steps behind Mrs. Bell, she appeared timid and shy. I wondered how she would overcome her shyness if she was going to work in adoption and social service.

They pulled up two chairs to sit by my bedside.

"Good afternoon," said Mrs. Bell. "How are you?"

I could see by the earnestness in her face that she was trying to be bright and upbeat. Miss Hardy coughed into a dainty handkerchief she'd retrieved from her purse, looking uncomfortable.

Mrs. Bell took out a file from her briefcase and said, "Now, before we sign these papers, I want to talk a little bit."

"Sure." I tried to sound casual but inside I thought I might break into pieces that would shrink, fall and clatter around on the floor.

This is it, I thought. This is where it gets real serious. My palms were sweating and my hands began to shake. I closed my eyes and for a moment tried to visualize myself as a mother, holding my newborn in my arms, looking into his eyes, seeing myself in his face. What if I changed my mind? This is my last chance. Once I sign the papers there would be no going back.

Miss Hardy nodded in agreement as Mrs. Bell was saying, ". . .and there can be no turning back. We want to make sure you're firm with this decision." Right. No turning back.

I reached behind me to adjust the pillows so I could sit up straight. "I don't know what else to do. I don't have anywhere to live with a baby and I've never cared for one. What do I have to offer a child? I just....I just don't know what else to do." Oh damn, I thought, I'm going to start crying and if I do, I might never stop.

Miss Hardy looked alarmed, as if my sudden tears might drown her. She said, "I know dear, I know. Try not to cry. We just want to be sure your mind is made up. I can tell you a little bit about what will happen if you'd like."

The two new unwed mothers in the room had stopped snoring and I was sure they were listening. I asked Miss Hardy if she could close my curtains.

"Sure!" She jumped up to pull the curtain around us, seemingly glad to have something to do to be distracted from my impending sobs.

"We will come get the baby tomorrow afternoon. We don't have an adoptive family just yet, so he will go to a foster home." My eyebrows constricted into a deep frown.

"Don't worry. We always make sure our foster homes are more than acceptable. And it won't take long to place the baby, trust me. He will be treated with the best care."

Suddenly I didn't want to talk about it anymore. I didn't think I could endure another word. *My life is falling apart*, I thought. *I'm coming unhinged. My limbs are soon to amputate themselves and fall to the floor and I'll make a mess. The nurses will be mad and call Housekeeping to clean up after me and toss what's left of me into the garbage, which was maybe where I belonged. How can I do this? What am I doing?*

That moment of indecision felt like an eternity. I hesitated before answering, a slight hesitation that would forever affect the baby's life as well as my own. What if I *could* keep my child? I could do it, couldn't I? I'd figure it out.

As I struggled with these mixed emotions, it was if all the disapproving, judgmental faces I'd seen over the last nine months gathered in front of me, all jeering and shouting, "You can't raise a baby! You can't do anything! You don't have the sense God gave an idiot!" And the primary voice, the one up front and loudest, was my mother's.

"Give me the papers."

Miss Hardy was startled by my sudden demand and quickly handed me the papers and a pen.

I held the pen in my hand, hovering over the papers. Doubt crept into my mind once again, like rising damp in a London cellar. I looked about the room. There was no one with loving arms, holding my son with pride, cooing at him. There was no joy, no smiling familiar faces.

"Where do I sign?" Miss Hardy pointed out all the lines where my signature was needed.

I signed the papers. Mrs. Bell reached for them but I held fast. This was my absolute last chance to change my mind. Mrs. Bell gently pried the adoption papers from my hands and asked if I had something I'd like to say.

"Yeah," I bellowed as loud as I could. "*This is the shits!*" A nurse scuttled in, pulled my curtain open and told me to be quiet.

Mrs. Bell and Miss Hardy rose from their chairs. Miss Hardy brushed off her skirt and Mrs. Bell donned her hat. She said, "In time you will see that you have made the absolute right decision for your baby and yourself. You can go on to school, or find a good job, meet a really decent fellow, settle down and have a baby you can keep. You'll see!"

I thanked her for the encouragement, although I didn't believe a word of it. They departed and I was left alone in a room with two women in the same situation, both now snoring again.

I buried my head in my pillow and cried.

My mother appeared the next morning. I'd been moved to another room and she was a little put out that she'd had to go to the nurse's desk to ask where I was. She seemed flustered and started talking as if in mid-sentence as she sat in one of the side chairs.

She adjusted her dress, slipped her jacket off and fiddled with her clip-on earrings. They were my favorite, a circular array of autumn colored rhinestones. When I was younger and she was at work, I used to get into her jewelry box and wear those earrings until they either fell off or I took them off so that the circulation could return to my ear lobes.

"I had to catch a cab from the airport because, of course, you weren't able to pick me up. Fifteen dollars from SeaTac to here, not including tip. Can you believe it? What a bunch of shysters."

I waited for her to ask how I was, how the baby was, if the birth went okay, if I was holding up emotionally, but she didn't. I told her anyway.

"The baby is in the nursery. I'm not allowed to see him, but maybe you can, if you want."

She started to cry, her head in her hands and her shoulders lightly shaking.

"It's okay," I told her. "It's going to be alright. I promise."

She sat up, her face wet and her eyes red. She kept fiddling with her earrings.

"I've got to get going. I'll call you."

"Okay, but stop by the nursery to see the baby. He'll no doubt be the only dark little face in a sea of white ones."

She was shaking. "I can't. I can't. I've got to go."

"Honestly, mom, please don't cry. Everything will be alright. It's going to be fine, really. Please don't cry. Please."

In her wake she left the bright scents of her perfume, cigarettes and coffee, a familiar aroma that used to comfort me. When I was little, I would bury my face in her closet to inhale her scent, making me feel closer to her when she was gone to work or out on the town with my dad.

The next day I was readied for discharge. I was getting dressed in my now useless maternity dress when the nurse came in and handed me the discharge papers.

I suddenly felt emboldened, probably because I felt I'd nothing to lose, and said to the nurse, "I want to see my baby."

Her eyes widened, then narrowed. "That is against the rules, and I believe you've already been told so." The air smelled like baby powder and I could hear the bustle of happy families in the hallway. I swallowed hard. This was a formidable woman in her starched white uniform, her arms folded across her chest, a look of severe disapproval in her eyes.

"I don't care about the rules. I want to see my baby."

"And I'm telling you that it's against the rules!"

"And I'm telling you screw the rules. Bring my baby to me! Now!" I had lowered my voice to an alto growl and narrowed my eyes to a tiger's glare and it worked. I scared her right out of the room.

A minute later, she came in with my baby. He was asleep, wrapped in a little blanket.

"I want to hold him."

"You are going too far. How do I know you won't run out with him?" She held him tight to her chest.

"Now!" I demanded. "Give him to me. Now!"

Reluctantly she handed him over. It was the first time in my life that I'd held a baby. The nurse relaxed a little and told me how to prop his head and cradle him in my arms. Holding his little body, I was overcome with awe. I could barely breathe, looking at his sweet familiar face. I loved him instantly.

He looked like Bob, but I could see my features in his face too. Small loose black curls peeked out of the blanket. I had no idea a baby would feel like this, so warm and trusting, so little and helpless. I felt my heart start to melt.

But I had to let him go. I kissed him on the forehead and whispered, "I'll see you later." Then I handed him back to the nurse and left.

When the paperwork was all done, I was given a bottle of pain pills, a return appointment for six weeks hence and was told I could go. I walked slowly down the hallway, past the nursery, past the nurses' station and to the elevator.

I sensed folks gathering behind me, also waiting for the elevator. I turned and there were Mrs. Bell and Miss Hardy. Mrs. Bell was holding my baby, and would soon take him away to strangers in an unknown place. They immediately looked away and I stepped into the elevator with them, feeling uninvited but determined to hold my head high. We didn't look at each other, but the feeling of discomfort was palpable. As the elevator reached the lobby and the door opened, I turned to look at them and whispered, "Please take care of him." They nodded and then they were gone, and I was in a sea of people bustling around the hospital lobby. I saw patients arriving, patients leaving, white-capped nurses and doctors in lab coats, stethoscopes hanging around their necks, rushing to appointments, surgeries, teaching and learning.

Through this mass of accomplished people, I found the entrance and left.

CHAPTER 12

THE SWINGING PIANO

I RETURNED TO the sofa in the little apartment I shared with Deego. I didn't have much to say to her or to anyone. I sat all day on the sofa looking out the window at the parking lot next door. I watched people come and go. At the bus stop people waited, only to disappear when their bus arrived. Folks rushed to jobs or school. I could see that life was going on around me, but I didn't care. Where in this big busy city was my baby right now?

With each day, I became more depressed. I had unbidden thoughts of doom and dread as if the world had gone flat and colorless. At night, I had nightmares of babies torn from their mother's arms and thrown over a cliff. A grayness took over the world around me and slowly seeped into my heart. Soon I reached the point where I didn't want to go on living.

Deego, my pragmatic friend, grew worried and called my mother.

"Your daughter isn't doing very well. She won't eat, can't sleep and cries all the time. I think you need to come get her." Deego hung up and turned to me. "Your mom is coming for you."

She took charge and I let her. I was too exhausted to lift a finger to help. She packed my clothes and books, and then waited with me for my mother's arrival. My heart was too bleak to protest, although later I told her I understood why she had called my mom, even though it felt like she was tattling.

My mother had rented a one bedroom apartment in the nearby suburb of Kirkland while their house in Seattle was readied for re-occupancy. The new apartment sat on a pier over Lake Washington and was quite modern and luxurious. She came to get me and my things and took me home with her, where I could sleep on a more comfortable couch than the one I had with Deego.

Over the next six weeks, I rested. We never spoke about the baby and maybe that was good. I didn't think I could endure comforting her again as I did when she broke down at the hospital after the baby was born.

My dad and Barry returned from Hawaii shortly after I'd moved in, and no sooner did they get off the plane than they were put to work finishing up the move. My mother was very unhappy that the movers could not get her upright piano into the apartment and demanded that my dad and Barry figure it out. They tried to get the piano into the elevator and found, as the movers did, that it wouldn't fit in no matter how they tried. I heard my dad mumble under his breath, "God almighty. Don't I get a moment to rest after a year in Hawaii?"

He turned to Barry and said, "How in hell are we supposed to get that goddamn piano up stairs and into the apartment?" He was in his work clothes, sweating and with a cigarette hanging from his mouth. "Grace and her precious piano," he muttered, "I'd like to break it into little pieces and throw the goddamn thing in the lake."

"Hey, maybe we can lift it up over the balcony," Barry suggested. He looked distressed and seemed to hate my parents' fighting almost as much as I did.

"How do you think we can do that? Wave a goddamn magic wand and watch it levitate?"

"I've got an idea. We can use pulleys and rope to hoist it over the balcony."

"That's a damned good idea," my father said. "And if it doesn't work, it will fall into the lake and we can say that we tried our best."

Barry gave a small, tense laugh. "Damn Skippy!" he said.

They got tools from the truck, took some measurements then drove to a nearby hardware store for thick rope. Then they fashioned a pulley with the ropes over the balcony. By pushing the piano slowly and carefully on the edge of the pier they aligned it right under the balcony.

"Stay there," my dad yelled at Barry. I'll run up and fix the ropes." My mother was watching nervously from the kitchen window while I sat on the sofa, stifling giggles. Barry stayed with the piano while my dad ran up to the apartment and lowered the ropes. Back downstairs he joined Barry in looping the ropes around and under the piano.

"Grace!" my dad yelled, "send Lisa down here." He wanted me to keep an eye on the piano as he and Barry struggled to pull it up two stories to the balcony. I watched it swing like a giant pendulum and wondered what the folks in the apartment below thought as they watched a piano swinging to and fro in front of their window. Back and forth it swung, left right left as they slowly pulled and pulled.

"For god's sake, be careful," my mother hollered from the balcony, hands on her hips and her face fixed in a scowl. "That piano is an antique!" As they continued to hoist it up the pulley, she continued to holler out her demands.

"Watch it! If it keeps swinging like that it'll crash into one of the windows!"

"Why's it taking so long, goddamned it? I have food on the stove!"

"Careful! Don't scratch it!"

"Goddamned woman," my dad mumbled under his breath as he heaved and pulled.

Eventually, unbelievably, the piano was finally hoisted into the room. My mother immediately took off the ropes, rolled it into a corner of the living room, grabbed a dining chair and sat down. She was elated and banged out the Bessie Smith song *Gimme A Pig Foot And A Bottle Of Beer*.

Watching this scene I was filled with self-pity and anger, and tried my best to rise above it all since being jealous of a piano didn't seem to make much sense. But the truth was, I *was* jealous of that piano, as I longed for my parents to put as much care and concern into me. Didn't they see that I was about to crash at any moment?

Then as my dad and Barry finished unhooking the pulley and grabbed two Heidelbergs from the fridge, I realized how infantile I was being. I didn't need to be lovingly swung over a balcony or molly-coddled by my mother. I needed my own life, my own place in the world and my own future. I wanted to recover from this detour I'd taken and claim my life and dreams again.

While I was still frightened of Bob, I was ready to hold my head up and get back to the world. I didn't know where he lived or worked and he didn't know my whereabouts, so I allowed myself to feel safe and in control.

But first I needed a place to live, something small, cheap, furnished and convenient. I'd always thought living downtown would be cool, so I looked at places there and found a furnished studio in Olive Tower, an older fifteen story building next to the freeway.

I made an appointment to look at the apartment and when I arrived, I took in the old brass mail boxes, the worn lobby carpet and the smell of burnt cabbage. I found the manager's apartment and knocked on the door. The sound of heavy footsteps from within got closer and closer. "Coming. Coming." When the door opened, it was dark inside and I could only see a silhouette of her head. It looked like a tumbleweed had landed on her neck.

"Hello. I'm Mrs. Luger. You must be Lisa."

"I am. Nice to meet you," and I extended my hand. My eyes adjusted to the dark, and focused on the wild-haired woman covered in makeup standing in the doorway. Her lipstick extended about an inch beyond her lips, almost touching the end of her nose and extending halfway down her chin. She gave me one of those wan, nasty handshakes that involved a slight squeezing of the fingers, quickly releasing her feeble grip. I will never forget Mrs. Luger. She had thick, matted black hair and her narrow eyes were rimmed with thick black pencil, making her look half asleep. I wondered if I'd woke her up from a nap or if she was an aging beatnik who'd just stuck her tongue in a light socket. Either was plausible.

"Well," she said, looking me up and down, "aren't you statuesque?" The comment hit me like a brick; being "statuesque" was not a compliment for a woman. "Petite" was what I was supposed to be, not an Amazon. But before I could reply, Mrs. Luger continued. "The apartment for rent is right across the hall." She closed her door and stepped past me to the door opposite.

It was a first floor apartment with dirty windows facing Boren Avenue, a busy arterial that flowed with traffic. The apartment itself was small but clean, and best of all, it was furnished. But the noise of the traffic, along with the roar from the nearby freeway, was unrelenting. "Seems kind of noisy to me," I said to Mrs. Luger.

"Oh, you'll get used to it. After a while, it'll sound like ocean waves."

Remembering the beach on Maui, I thought it would take a monumental stretch of imagination to believe that correlation. But I wasn't looking for perfection. I just wanted to find an affordable apartment that wasn't crawling with fleas and had a working toilet.

After inspecting the little kitchen, the small dressing area and successfully test flushing the toilet, I told Mrs. Luger that I would take it.

She invited me into her apartment and motioned for me to sit on a maroon velvet covered Victorian settee. We briefly went over the lease: I would stay for six months and if I left before then, I would still owe rent until the lease was expired. No noise after 10:00 pm, no pets, no roommates or sub-letting. It sounded fine to me, so I signed it and she wished me luck.

Then I stepped out into the hallway and there, standing in front of the elevator with his arms full of groceries, was Bob.

An instant chill filled me, as a collision of attraction and horror rushed through me. *This can't be happening.* Of all the apartment buildings in Seattle, I unwittingly chose the one *he* lived in.

The coincidence shook me to the core. A line from Albert King's *Born Under A Bad Sign* ran through my mind: *If it weren't for bad luck, I'd have no luck at all.* I really didn't believe in luck. So if this wasn't luck, it had to be fate. I wanted to believe in fate, in the serendipitous turn of events that suddenly solves all problems and opens the door to the yellow brick road. But then again, look where the yellow brick road got Dorothy.

"What are you doing here?" I asked him. My voice cracked but I tried my best to hide my emotions. I thought how handsome and tall he was, how suave he looked and how deep his voice was.

"I live here," he replied. He lifted his arms a bit. "See? Grocery bags. For my kitchen. What are you doing here?"

"I...I...guess I live here too." Mrs. Luger stood in her doorway, listening.

Bob looked at my stomach and said, "So, you had the baby?"

But before I could answer, the elevator door opened and he stepped in. He gave me a wave and said, "See you," as the door closed.

I turned to Mrs. Luger. "How long has he lived here?" I asked.

"Oh, about a year." Her eyes were suddenly wide, bright and attentive. "You know him, it seems?" She had a barely perceptible smile fixed on her face, and it slowly slid into a smirk.

I looked down at the brown floral carpeting of the hallway and said, "Yes, we worked together for a while."

My hope for a new start on life began to diminish. Now, it seemed I was back where I'd started: looking down a hopeless abyss of terror and sorrow.

"Mrs. Luger," I said, "could I just sort of not have signed the lease? I've changed my mind."

But her eyes were wide with relish. "I'm afraid not, dear. It's a six month lease. I can't do anything about it."

"Why not? I haven't even moved in yet. Let's just tear up the lease and my check and pretend this didn't happen."

"Nope. Sorry. It's the rules."

Oh, sure I thought. I knew she could tear up the lease in the wink of a mascaraed eye. But clearly, she loved having the power to refuse. Her apartment was directly across the hall from mine and I had no doubt she'd enjoy any sort of exchange between me and Bob that she might overhear. I wanted to slit my throat.

With a feeling of dread, I moved in the next day. My possessions were few. The kitchen was small, but it did have a little table with two chairs. I had a glass Melitta drip coffee maker and a new coffee mug that had light and dark brown stripes. These familiar objects made me feel grown up. A small dressing room with closets and a small chest of drawers led into the bathroom, which was clad in small octagonal black and white tiles. In the main room there was a built-in corner unit, with a large end table and two bed-sized sofas jutting out on either side. The sofas had removable gold colored coverings and underneath were the mattresses. Most importantly, I still had my record player, records, posters and books to make the place feel like mine.

Despite the fright of discovering Bob was living in the very same building, I was determined to make the best of it. After all, having an apartment all my own again gave me a sense of having my life back. I was in control.

But for the next half year until my lease was over and I could move, each day would present a challenge. How could this happen? Of all the possible apartments in the city of Seattle, how could I end up in the same building as that crazy man whose baby I'd just carried, bore and gave away? Was the Universe teasing me? Was the Lord above playing a game of Truth or Dare with me? I remembered a little Robert Frost poem that I'd heard at Holy Names: *Forgive, O Lord, my little jokes on Thee, and I'll forgive Thy great big one on me.*

Whatever was happening, the obstacles before me only hardened my resolve. I told myself that this was an opportunity to build independence in the face of great opposition. Perhaps those harrowing stories about saints and martyrs at Catholic school would come in handy after all.

My welfare benefits were about to run out so I started to look for jobs. Thinking I'd go back to the post office and pick up where I left off, I called their personnel office. The clerk who answered the phone asked for my name and then put me on hold while she retrieved my file.

She returned to the phone. There was a bit of silence and I could hear paper rustling in the background. Then she asked in a puzzled tone, "Why would you want to come back to the post office?"

"Well, because I have experience and can do the work."

"Your records say you quit without notice and that you engaged in inappropriate behavior with a fellow carrier."

Inappropriate behavior? Was getting pregnant my "inappropriate behavior?" Or had Bob said something about me, told them some lie? I didn't know what to think, much less what to say.

Although I pleaded with her to listen as I explained the circumstances, shame overwhelmed me and I couldn't go on. I thanked her and hung up.

CHAPTER 13

WE DON'T HAVE ANY
OPENINGS RIGHT NOW

WHAT COULD I do if I couldn't return to being a letter carrier? Delivering mail was not a transferable skill. I hadn't worked for a year and couldn't provide an acceptable explanation to any prospective employer what I'd been doing the last twelve months. Studying abroad? Following a circus? Playing accordion in an oompah band? I wasn't a good liar when it came to pedestrian issues despite my mother teaching me that little white lies and secrets were okay.

I couldn't type, file, cut a mimeograph or gracefully answer phones. What were my options? Prostitution was out of the question. Dealing drugs was a bit dodgy and I wasn't good at sales anyway.

I turned to my friends. Deego had left the studio we shared to move back in with her parents. She'd decided to take more classes at the university. Mary was now living in Arizona and had just had a child herself. But Mona was still in town, working as "head girl" for the phone company and encouraged me to apply for a switchboard position.

I made an appointment for an interview, dressed in my old paisley pant-suit and went downtown to the Pacific Northwest Bell offices on Third and Union prepared to blow them away with my Catholic finishing school charm and wit.

A large man in a short-sleeved business shirt and clip-on bow tie introduced himself to me.

"I'm Arthur Peacock," he said, sweeping his hand to indicate some sort of possession of the large room, the switchboard and the staff.

"I'm the supervisor here," he said with pride. He invited me to sit down at his desk, as he took his seat and looked at my application. His eyebrows went up and down as he read. Then he pursed his lips. He looked up at me with disinterest and asked me how much I weighed.

It took a moment to overcome the shock of such an intrusive and irrelevant question. And having just given birth, the question really hit a nerve. "Pardon me?"

Clearly his bulk was on the problem end of an actuarial chart. He sat back and eyed me with contempt. "It's a requirement of the job to be at a sensible weight." He reached in his pocket for a handkerchief to wipe his brow. *Oh, here I am again*, I thought, *being denigrated for a switchboard job?* I felt my good behavior quickly dissolve.

Clearly my career would not start at the phone company. I thanked him for his time and walked out the door.

At the suggestion of my mother, I tried an employment agency owned by a woman she had worked with years before at Peoples National Bank. Elaine Kent had left the world of bookkeeping to run "Kent Employment: Temporary and Permanent Positions for the Young Professional."

The Kent Employment office was located in an old Art Deco office building downtown. I took the elevator to the tenth floor and found their office.

There was a small oak desk with a manual typewriter on top and a name plate that said Dory Stewart in front of it but Miss Stewart was nowhere to be seen. Green leather guest chairs lined the walls of the office. Opposite the desk was a door that said "Private." I took a seat in one of the guest chairs and picked up a magazine.

After waiting a half hour, the main office door opened. A young lady walked in and sat at the reception desk. She was thin and wore a white mini-skirt with a bright yellow top. Her hair was cut in a severe Vidal Sassoon bob and she perfumed the air with a heavy dose of the cheap dime-store cologne that everyone at the time thought was divine—Jean Nate.

I felt like a clod. I was bigger than Miss Stewart. My hair was short and curly. I wore layers of makeup in a Twiggy sort of look—fake eyelashes on my upper lids and long lashes drawn with an eyebrow pencil under my lower lids. On my lips, I wore a whitish-pink color that could have been called Dead Person Pale. If Mrs. Luger had looked like a clown, I resembled a harlequin. I thought I was rather fashionable until I saw Miss Stewart's clean, slender look.

"Hi, I'm Dory," she said, holding out a slender, perfectly manicured hand. "Are you Elaine's 1:00?"

"Yes I am. I'm Lisa Ulrich."

"She's running late, Lisa. I hope you don't mind waiting."

"Oh no, of course not." I took a deep breath and searched for patience. My mother had advised me to act as if they would be stupid not to find me a job, so trying to appear confident and self-assured, I feigned importance and flipped through Women's Day, as if I hadn't a care in the world.

At half past 1:00, the "Private" door opened and a young man with a briefcase walked out. He called over his shoulder, "See you soon." And then Elaine came out.

She looked at me and said, "Who are you?"

"She's your 1:00."

Elaine was tall and blond, her hair teased into a frizzled beehive. She wore bright orange lipstick and an over-sized rhinestone broach on the shoulder of her beige double knit dress.

She looked at me through squinty eyes. "Who are *you*?"

"I'm Lisa. Grace Ulrich's daughter? She said you'd help me find a job." I knew that I sounded much more confident than I felt.

"Grace? Grace Allstitch?"

"No, Grace *Ulrich*." I said diplomatically. "You worked with her at the bank."

Her eyes lit up with sudden recognition. "Gracie! Now I remember! We worked in bookkeeping until I got promoted. Yes. Yes. She wanted me to talk with you."

No one called my mother Gracie. It was not allowed; she was Grace, period. Clearly this woman didn't know my mom that well.

"And find me a job," I said as a way of helping her remember why I was there.

"Well, I've got to do a few things. It won't be long." She walked into her office and shut the door.

Dory avoided eye contact with me and tried to look busy. She must have known what Elaine often did to young inexperienced fools like me. A half hour went by then another and another. At three, Dory gathered her purse, slipped her shoes on and announced that she was done for the day. As she left, she said to me, "It shouldn't be long now."

"I hope not. I've already been here two hours."

"Oh, don't worry sweetie." She put her hand on my shoulder and patted me. Then she left.

I thought about knocking on Elaine's door but decided that doing so might appear aggressive. Maybe if I coughed really loud or accidently knocked over a chair, she'd come out and say "Oh gosh, Lisa. So sorry to keep Gracie's daughter waiting." But she didn't.

At four o'clock, she finally opened her door and without apologizing for the long wait, invited me in. I sat up straight on the hard chair in front of her desk, trying to appear eager and not the least bit annoyed that she'd kept me waiting for three hours.

She looked me up and down, her brow furrowed and her arms folded tightly across her ample chest.

"You're wearing too much makeup. Your hair is unkempt and that paisley pantsuit is garish. I want you looking like a lady, with less makeup, more style to your hair, a sober dress and then we'll talk about jobs. So for now, I want you to go home, adjust your look and then make another appointment."

I was thunderstruck. After all this waiting only to be told to come back another day looking more presentable made me burst into tears. I ran out of the office.

Furious, I called my mom from a pay phone down the street to tell her about what had happened.

"You'll just have to do what she wants. You're going to have to learn that you'll need to give up your pride and standards if you want to work."

"You want me to do her bidding and then return for more humiliation?"

"No. I'm saying that you need to conform a bit. That's all."

"Mom, why are you telling me to kowtow to such a hostile bitch?"

"Watch your mouth, young lady!"

"But she said I was unpresentable! She embarrassed me. I'm not going back there! And, she called you Gracie!"

A week later, I was sitting in the same reception room, dressed in a purple A-line dress with matching shoes. The night before, I'd put my hair up in curlers and in the morning, after a good teasing, I shellacked it with a heavy dose of Aqua Net hair spray. My only make-up was a tiny amount of rosy pink lipstick. It was a look that had impressed my mother, but I thought I looked like a ghoul.

As for Dory, she'd had her own makeover. She'd replaced her stylish Mod look with the Ali McGraw look. She was now dressed in a maxi-skirt and peasant blouse, as if she'd just seen *Love Story*.

This time, Elaine called me in right away. She looked me up and down.

"Oh, yes. You look much better this time." She paused for a moment, and then continued. "Unfortunately, we don't have any openings right now, but check in with us in a month or so. And say hi to Gracie for me."

Good grief. I wondered if I was being punished for some past life sin. If so, what in the world had I done in that life to deserve this one? Was office work that monumental that I needed to bend to everyone's expectations just to get a job filing letters and typing envelopes?

Chapter 14

Just Like Liz Taylor

FEELING DEFEATED I returned to the silence and safety of my apartment. What was wrong with me? Everyone I knew had a job, but everywhere I turned, the door slammed shut on me. I wasn't fit to be a mother, and I wasn't fit to be a civil servant. No one wanted me. No one would risk giving me a chance. It was as if I was invisible, untouchable, and inhuman. I sat on the couch, listening to the whirr of the freeway, its hypnotic roar lulling me into a deep, dark hole.

Someone was tapping at my door, rising me out of my pity party. I looked through the peep hole in the door to see who was knocking. There stood Bob. I backed away but heard him say, "Open up. I know you're in there. I just want to see how you're doing. Honest."

What is the definition of a fool? One who is deficient in judgment, sense, or understanding: The dentist said it wouldn't hurt. Or one who acts unwisely on a given occasion: Why did I quit my job without a new one lined up? Or maybe one who has been tricked or made to appear ridiculous. I opened the door to the abusive, psychotic father of the baby I'd given up and that made me a damned fool.

He peered over my shoulder and scanned the room then said, "Your apartment is just like mine, only I'm on the other side of the building on the 12th floor."

"That's nice."

"So, are you okay?" He looked earnest and caring. "What happened with the baby? Can I come in?"

"He was adopted."

"Oh, a boy!" He looked happy but in an instant his eyes narrowed and his face hardened.

"You gave away my son? *My* son? Who took him?" he hissed as he moved toward me.

I was scared witless and tried to close the door, but he stuck his foot in the doorway. "Tell me!" he demanded.

I stammered an explanation. "I used an adoption agency. They were nice ladies. They told me they were very successful in placing mixed-race babies. Honest. He's well taken care of."

As I anxiously tried to appease him with my words, I couldn't help but think at the same time what a hypocrite he was. First he had wondered if the baby was really his and now he's acting like I'd ripped his heart out? *My baby*, indeed.

Just as I was ready to kick his foot away and slam the door shut, he changed again, his face returned to normal. He suggested brightly, "Let's play cards. Do you know rummy?" I did know rummy and I was good at it. What the hell, I figured. If I close the door on him, what am I left with? Hours of loneliness and self-pity? The sound of the freeway to keep me company?

"I don't have any cards," I replied.

"That's okay," he said, "I brought some." Obviously, he'd planned this. Was I that easy? But since no one else was planning anything with me, a game of gin rummy was as good as it was going to get so I shrugged and opened the door wide, and let him come in.

We sat on the floor and he dealt. I won the first game, then the second. He started to get irritated, so I let him win the next game. I was really good at rummy and occasionally when I played with sore losers, I would let them win once in a while. But on the fourth game, he left himself wide open and I couldn't help but win.

"Ha!" I declared. "Shouldn't have put down that Jack of spades! It was just what I needed."

Instantly he threw the cards at me, stood up, grabbed my shoulders and pulled me to my feet. He put his face in mine and sneered "You bitch. You cheated! I *hate* cheats."

"I don't cheat. I never have and never will," I replied as calmly as I could, trying to pacify him. "It was just a run of luck. It could have been totally different. Some days you win, some days you lose."

He grabbed my throat and squeezed, then dropped his hands to his side and said, "You're not worth it." He turned and headed into the little hallway toward my door. I heard the door open and then bang shut.

I was absolutely shattered. Again he had managed to upset my already tenuous hold on reality. I looked about the room to anchor myself in the present. My books, records, posters, and coffee cup were still there. The roar of the freeway was still there. But I felt that I was losing my mind. I was confused and very angry. Under my breath I muttered, "You bastard!"

Out of the shadows near the door, I heard someone speak. "What did you say? *What did you say?*" His voice was coming from the entryway. Oh my god. He'd never left. He'd set me up.

From the corner of the little foyer where he been hiding, he charged back into the room, grabbed me and threw me against a wall. Then he picked me up and threw me against another wall. The third time he threw me, my head struck the wall and I collapsed on the floor, unconscious.

I don't remember crying or yelling for help or threatening to call the police. But when I came to he was gone, my door was open and Mrs. Luger was standing in my entryway, with her arms folded, looking at me.

"Takin' a little nap, are you?" she sneered.

I struggled to my feet and looked around me. My little apartment was a mess. He'd trashed it while I was unconscious. Playing cards, records, dishes, and clothes were tossed everywhere. "Get out!" I shouted at Mrs. Luger. She left, letting a little laugh float behind her. I slammed the door shut. Once again, I was coming undone.

Could things get any darker? How did I lose control over my life again, almost as soon as I thought I had it? It seemed I was always trying to please someone else or meet their unspoken expectations. I could have fought

Mrs. Luger over the lease, but instead I just gave up, defeated before I'd even begun. Abhorrent as it was to me, I could have had an abortion and that would have been the end of it. No one would even have known. Or I might have just disappeared somewhere, taking my problems and fear with me. But I did none of those things. I swallowed my dignity, steeled myself for more angst and got on with what I thought would make everyone pleased.

Fortunately, when I'd had my baby, I had been given a bottle of pain pills at discharge.

Now I sat with the bottle in my hands, my mind doing somersaults, trying to make sense of the mess I'd made of my life. How nice would it be to just go to sleep and never wake? I let my thoughts wander to the world beyond, a world where I mattered, and where I was surrounded by what mattered to me. Maybe I could have some laughs with Janis and Jimi, or debate existentialism with Sartre and Camus. I could have drinks with Jack Kerouac. I'd tell him how *On The Road* blew my mind. We could discuss his belief that the only people who interested him were the mad ones. I would tell him that I too was attracted to the mad ones. Was that the real reason I had let Bob into my life in the first place? Because I was drawn to his madness? No, that wasn't it, I figured. He was just plain old crazy. Still, I wondered what prompted such intensity and rage. What demons had Bob endured to turn him into such a troubled soul? Not that I cared. I'd never let him near me again.

I stared at the bottle of pills I held in my hand. I didn't really want to die but I couldn't see any other way out. I thought about what the nuns used to say. All people are born in God's grace and love, and all that other crap. *You guys are dead wrong*, I thought. God had completely abandoned me.

I didn't know anything back then about post-partum depression, and in fact, so little was known about depression at the time that I didn't clearly associate it with giving up my baby. All I knew was that I felt an overwhelming sense of fear and hopelessness. The fact that I had unwittingly moved into the building where Bob lived, and that I'd given away *his* baby left me feeling trapped and confused. And going out on a cloud of pain pills didn't seem so bad.

But I couldn't do it. I was afraid to die. *You've got a future to live for and you'd better figure out how to get beyond all this*, I told myself. I remembered a movie called *The Slender Thread* that was filmed in Seattle. It was about a woman played by Ann Bancroft, who tries to kill herself by swallowing a bottle of pills. She calls the Crisis Clinic and Sidney Poitier tries to keep her on the phone while others go into action to trace the call and save her.

That's what I'll do, I thought. I took the phone and dialed zero for the operator. "I need the Crisis Clinic," I said and was almost immediately dialed through.

Instead of Sidney Poitier's deep and comforting voice, a young woman answered. She had a sweet, gentle voice and asked my name and address, and then asked me to describe my problem.

"I've just had a baby and given it up for adoption. I feel horrible about it. I have a bottle of pain pills in my hand that I want to take. I'm so afraid. What should I do?"

She said, "You've done the right thing by calling us. You've given us your name and address and we're going to help you."

"How?"

"Someone will be at your apartment within minutes. Let them in and follow their instructions. Meanwhile, flush the pills down the toilet and try to relax."

I didn't flush the pills and I didn't relax. I thought those instructions were a bit lame. Why would I flush the pills until I knew for certain that I wouldn't need them? Instead I paced, and doing so made me feel better—a self-soothing rhythmic movement that was a calming physical response to my mental and emotional pain.

Soon there was a knock on my door. I looked through the peep hole and saw the face of a stranger. He said *sotto voce*, "I'm from the Crisis Clinic. Will you let me in?"

I opened the door to two strangers, a man and a woman. The man, tall and blond with a bandana tied around his head, introduced himself as Tom and his companion, shorter, brunette and dressed in shorts and a tank top, as Marcia.

I was now feeling ambivalent. Was this call for help just a ploy for attention and an easy way to get out of a tough situation? I knew I was coming close to the end of my rope, trapped, frightened and angry with myself for compromising my own dreams and needs to meet the demands or expectations of others. When my parents told me I couldn't love Lynne, I found a string of men to sleep with in order to please my mom and dad. When Elaine Kent disliked my clothes, I found a suit she would approve of. And I'd pleased my mother by giving away my baby instead of asking for help so I could keep him. And certainly I'd done what was expected of a wanton girl who took a terribly wrong turn in life by being ashamed and contrite.

But I remembered my manners. "Would you like to sit down?" and I pointed to one of the sofa beds.

They both sat and Tom opened a black case that he'd carried in with him. He saw I was still holding the bottle of pills. "Can you give those to me, please," he said, holding out his hand.

"I'm not sure I want to." I didn't know which way I wanted to go. If I kept the pills, then the option of taking them would still be there.

"You called us because you are scared, hurting and unhappy, right?" I nodded in agreement, but still held the bottle.

Softly and kindly looking into my eyes, he held out his hand and said, "Then, I'd like you to trust us. We're here to help and take care of you. But first, I need the bottle." Suddenly I was in turmoil. I didn't know which way to turn, what to say, who to be. Slowly, as Tom and Marcia sat patiently waiting for my response, I realized that taking a bottle of pills was not going to solve anything. Sometimes simply giving up is the wisest option.

"Here," I said, handing him the bottle. He took it and passed it off to Marcia. She asked where the bathroom was, I told her and she flushed the pills down the toilet. Tom asked me to pack a few clothes.

"What are you going to do?" I was a bit tremulous.

"We're going to take you to the Seattle Mental Health Institute up on 17th and Madison for a few days so you can relax, talk about what's happening and get you back on your feet."

"But I don't have any money. I can't pay for this." Tom told me not to worry, that it would be sorted out later.

"Right now," he said, "I just want you to concentrate on talking things out with a therapist and getting better." I felt mistrustful. Were they really that cavalier about money? It was hard to know. I'd never experienced this before. Was this the kind of "breakdown" that people whispered about? Was I in the same league as movie stars like Elizabeth Taylor and Vivien Leigh? I felt stupidly giddy and somehow important. I was embarking on the same journey of self-discovery as my favorite actresses.

I let Tom and Marcia guide me out of the apartment, out of the building, and into a white van. Was it my imagination or had Mrs. Luger peeked through her door? I imagined Bob watching me and that frightened me. Perhaps he had Mrs. Luger spying on me. I was flooded with contradictory emotions: fear of what would become of me if I stayed in the apartment feeling suicidal; fear that if I didn't do this now, I'd never move forward with my life; relief that someone was going to help me; happy that in time I would soon stand on my feet again.

I sat in the back of the van. Tom drove, and Marcia sat quietly looking out the window. I wondered what she was thinking. She seemed introspective. Perhaps she was mulling over a decision to end a relationship or start a new one. Maybe she was wishing she'd gone into another profession, thinking it wasn't too late to start again. Or she could have just been tired or bored.

I looked out the window as well, seeing familiar spots that now seemed strange and foreign: the ramp over the freeway, the little market on Olive where I bought milk and cigarettes, the B & O Espresso, the movie theater on the intersection of Broadway and John. They all looked different somehow. I was losing my sense of place, a sense of home and a sense of myself. I could only trust that Tom and Marcia would indeed help me.

Tom slowed the van and turned into a driveway, stopping at a large front veranda. He twisted around to look at me and said brightly, "We've arrived." I had been expecting some sort of cement block loony bin and was surprised that the Institute was in an old colonnaded two-story house with a semi-circular drive in front with manicured boxwoods lining the drive. Tom and Marcia helped me out of the van. Marcia took my little bag and Tom took my arm, guiding me with a certain strength that told me that my safety was important and he didn't want me running off, screaming down Madison Street.

Inside on the first floor, the formal rooms were now offices, counseling rooms and a reception area. Upstairs the original bedrooms were now inpatient rooms. In the wide hallway I saw a small nurse's station with a large nurse bending over the desk, talking on the phone in a hushed voice.

It was quiet within the Institute's walls. When she had finished her call, the nurse, wearing a white uniform and cap, admitted me. She introduced herself as Miss Silverstein and had me sign some forms. She said that I was now a patient of the Institute and asked if I needed anything in particular. I considered asking for a shot of Southern Comfort on the rocks, but thought better of it.

Miss Silverstein took me to my room. She gave me a pill saying, "This will help you sleep. We'll talk more in the morning after you wake up. For now, just rest. Oh, and by the way, you can call me Bobbie." Bobbie Silverstein? Just what I needed, another Bob.

She closed the door and I was alone. It was peacefully quiet. The room was simple, like the nuns' dorm at Holy Names, only less austere and more comfortable and homey. There were no crucifixes' or Bibles and for that I was grateful. I thought at last someone would take care of me. And then I felt very tired and remembered what the nurse had said, "For now, just rest."

I slipped between the sheets of the small bed and smoothed the pastel pink blanket, cuddled a pillow and curled into a ball. I fell asleep almost instantly.

CHAPTER 15

HOW DID YOU FIND ME?

SUN SHONE THROUGH my window, washing the little room in glorious light. It was August and wonderfully warm. I looked about me, momentarily confused, and then remembered where I was.   I got up and dressed in the jeans and tie-dyed top that I'd brought with me. Hearing me rustling about, the day nurse came in and introduced herself.

"Hi, I'm Christy. I'll take you downstairs to the dining room and then I'll go over your schedule for the day."

She seemed momentarily confused and started to worry the pooka shell necklace around her neck. "The first thing you'll do after breakfast will be to meet with Dr. Bob to map out a therapy program for you."

Dr. Bob? These little jokes can stop now, I thought. *Enough is enough!*

"Dr. Bob?" I asked. "Does he have a last name?"

"Of course he does, silly!" Christy giggled and then walked out.

The dining room faced south and sunshine glittered off the cutlery. Poached eggs and an English muffin, coffee and orange slices were a welcome change to my usual bowl of Grape Nuts. I savored the food and the quiet. Another nurse came in and asked how I was doing.

"Are you feeling a bit shaky? Because if you are, I can give you a pill for that." I nearly laughed. *A pill? Isn't that what got me here in the first place?*

"I'm OK for now. But I don't see anyone else around. Am I the only patient here?"

"Oh no! The others are in group right now. You were excused this morning as it's your first day and all. You'll meet the others later."

The "others" turned out to be two other inpatients, both girls about my age and sixteen outpatients who came in daily or weekly for group therapy. I'd never heard of "group therapy" before. But I would soon learn that it was a method of counseling that involves a bunch of folks spilling their secrets to a group of strangers. The therapy was called *transactional analysis* and was modeled on a best-selling book by Thomas Harris, MD called *I'm OK, You're OK*.

Only, I wasn't OK and I wasn't sure anyone else was either, which I was later to learn was a perfectly acceptable way to look at the world, according to Dr. Bob.

Since everyone was in group, I wandered around the Institute to see what kind of place I was in. It was apparent, with the high ceilings, the large crystal chandeliers, and the two large salons on either side of the entrance, that this house had once been grand.

Now there were offices with steel desks and file cabinets and large piles of papers and books on the floors. The kitchen in the back of the house had been remodeled, but still retained the original black and cream counter tiles. There were many bedrooms upstairs, each with one single bed, a nightstand, a lamp and a single chair. There were two large bathrooms upstairs, each with claw foot tubs and ivory colored fixtures. I could imagine soaking in one of those tubs, with bubble bath, rose-scented soaps and candles in brass holders.

As I was walking down the hall, Christy appeared from one of the bedrooms holding a light bulb. She saw me, threw the light bulb in a garbage can and said, "I've been looking for you! It's time to go to group, Lisa. I'll take you there."

She took my arm and guided me towards the stairs. I felt a mixture of tense anticipation and a strong desire to flee. What was I getting into?

As I entered the group therapy room, the patients turned around to look at me. They seemed somewhat irritated by my entrance. I felt as If I'd just walked into a secret Masonic meeting. I wanted to run out. But then I noticed a blonde man with a perm who looked familiar. I couldn't place him, but I knew that I knew him from somewhere. Then I recognized his sweater, the standard issue postal carrier's uniform. But I still couldn't remember who he was.

As I was staring at him, a large grinning man, with a head of thick brown hair and a thick beard to match, rose from his leather chair and walked towards me, his arms outstretched as if to give me a hug. He looked like a young Santa Claus in street clothes.

When I didn't respond to the offer of a hug, he took my hand instead and said, "Hi! I'm Dr. Bob! Welcome to group."

Then he waved his arm around the room indicating the others. "These are your co-conspirators in therapy," he said, winking at me.

If he was expecting me to laugh, I disappointed him. I was a patient in an asylum and had considered killing myself. I was in no mood for laughter. I wanted help, serious help.

Then he pointed to an empty chair. "You can sit here." I took the chair, and he returned to his. I noticed that only his chair was comfortable, the rest were folding chairs. Several patients had already abandoned their hard metal seat to sit on the carpeted floor.

"Where were we?" Dr. Bob said brightly. He looked around the room and then his face lit up. "Oh yes, Peggy was telling us about when her mother died. Peggy, do you want to continue?"

I looked to the woman he was speaking to, and saw a thin, stiff woman sitting rigidly upright. Her face was a study in fear and anger. She was dressed impeccably, in an expensive suit, pearls and polished pumps. All that was missing was a clutch purse and white gloves.

"Oh yes, I was sharing, but if someone else would like to share, I can wait. It's not that important anyway." Peggy flushed and began to wring her hands. Her face was set in a pinched expression, as if there were some powerful emotion she was trying to repress.

Dr. Bob looked around the room. "Does anyone want to share now or should we let Peggy continue?"

They all nodded and one said, "Peggy should share. She was just getting started." I felt like an intruder, as if my arrival had interrupted something very personal between them.

Peggy suddenly stopped wringing her hands and placed them neatly in her lap. Her voice was soft and low, and several people leaned forward to hear her better.

"Well, I was saying that the chauffeur brought me home from school and the house was empty and there was a sealed envelope on the table in the foyer with my name on it."

Dr. Bob looked pleased. "Yes...right, Peggy. Please continue, or would you all like to go around the room and introduce yourself to our new group member, uh...right...what is your name?"

Peggy, meek and acquiescing, immediately stopped talking.

Again everyone turned to look at me.

Quietly I said, "Lisa."

"I'm sorry. I couldn't hear you. Say it again, please," said Dr. Bob.

Loudly, I said, "Lisa. My name is Lisa."

"Ah, that's better. Everyone, meet Lisa. Let's start the introductions with this young man on my left."

I turned and saw a thin, red-headed freckled man with large horn-rimmed glasses. He introduced himself as Jim but before he could say anything more, Dr. Bob jumped in.

"Jim is a physicist at the university. He's in group because the police caught him trying to dump quite a bit of LSD into the water tower in Volunteer Park. He mixed up the acid in his lab at the U, isn't that right Jim?"

Jim demurely replied, "Yes, that's right." He looked about nervously, ducking his head as if he were dodging bullets. "I tried to turn on the whole of Seattle. But to add irony to my getting caught, I found out later that that water tower only serves Capitol Hill and most of those folks there are already stoned."

Everyone nodded in agreement and I heard a few voices saying, "Bummer. Bummer."

Apparently they all felt that trying to turn on the citizens of Capital Hill was a reasonable thing to do.

After Jim came Gloria, then Barbara, then Rasheed, then more. I couldn't keep track of their names, but would come to know their stories well. We exchanged introductions and smiles amidst a cloud of cigarette smoke.

I inhaled deeply, savoring the second-hand smoke. In my obedient rush to leave with the mental health workers, I hadn't thought to bring my cigarettes, and I was dying for one. But now that we were on a first name basis, I gathered up the courage to bum one from Barbara, a stout little woman with a bouffant hairdo.

"My pleasure," she said, with a curious smile. She held out the pack. Lucky Strikes. No filter and stronger than a cheap cigar. A horrid brand, I thought, but beggars can't be choosers.

Gloria was trying to decide if she should move to San Francisco and marry her wealthy boyfriend. Peggy was an only child, very wealthy and alone. Barbara was having a sexual identity crisis and Rasheed, the permed blonde in the post-office sweater, apparently thought he was black.

"His name is Michael," Dr. Bob said, "but we've agreed to call him Rasheed."

"In solidarity with my black brothers," Rasheed said, glancing at me with a knowing look. That's when I remembered who he was. He had started working as a letter carrier at the International Station just before I left. I remembered him telling me that he'd only gotten a job with the postal service so he could get the uniform sweater after his six months' probation. He had said at the time that he thought the sweater was really cool.

Dr. Bob said, "Rasheed is here because he had plans to assassinate the president. We are teaching him that deflected anger is not a good idea. He really wanted to shoot his mother, but his reason wouldn't let him do that, so Nixon became his target." Again, no one seemed upset by the notion that the president might be killed because Rasheed actually wanted to commit matricide. I was beginning to think that I could confess to just about anything and find unconditional love—but my own problems might have been so mundane that no one would love me.

As my thoughts started to wander, I looked up and saw that everyone was staring at me.

"So, Lisa," Dr. Bob asked, "What brings you here?"

Sensing that secrets and reticence were not allowed in group, I swallowed hard and said "I wanted to kill myself."

"Why?" asked Dr. Bob with a broad smile.

I hesitated. Is this where I admit to total strangers all my secret thoughts and what an ass I'd been? What do I say to them? That I met an insane yet alluring black guy, let him abuse me, got pregnant and gave the baby up for adoption? I decided to go with the condensed version.

"I met a man. He hurt me. He was nice one minute and then violent the next. I got pregnant by him and gave my baby up for adoption. Then I got depressed and wanted to die."

Everyone was nodding as if they understood my short history. Then I thought I'd put frosting on the cake and see how liberal they really were.

"Oh, and he's a big black guy."

I looked around, but they were just nodding.

"And he cracks his knees," I added.

Still, no one reacted, although several stared at the floor. Dr. Bob filled the silence.

"Well, we're very glad you're here," he said. Then everyone smiled at me and a few got up to walk over and offer a hug. I accepted them all. Barbara, the one struggling her sexual identity, hugged me extra tight and a little too long.

Once the introductions were over, Dr. Bob returned to Peggy. "Peggy was telling us about coming home to an empty house and finding an envelope addressed to her on the hallway table, right Peggy?"

Peggy nodded. She was still waiting to finish her story. Dr. Bob continued. "And what did the note say?"

Peggy started to cry. "It said that my mother had died and my father was at the hospital, my snack was in the fridge and I needed to get my homework done before any TV."

"And who wrote the note?" Dr. Bob asked.

"The maid."

"That's cold man. Really cold," Rasheed blurted out, as Peggy sobbed into a Kleenex.

How's this supposed to be therapeutic? I asked myself. I was dying for another cigarette and bummed a second Lucky Strike from Barbara.

It was 1970 and I still operated on the laidback attitude that everything and everyone was cool and there wasn't much to get to upset about. What the heck, I figured. I'm here and I'm entertained so why not just sit back and enjoy the show? I might learn something and I was certainly hearing some great stories I could use later on in my as-yet unnamed, unwritten and not-as-yet conceived book.

On my third day in group, just as Barbara started to talk about her attraction to women in high heels, the door opened. Christy poked her head in and said, "Lisa, you've got a visitor."

A visitor? Who on earth could it be? No one knew where I was, not even my parents. "Who is it?" I asked Christy.

"He didn't give his name. He's really tall and black and has a paper sack with him."

My blood ran cold. Slowly I got up and walked to the door. Dr. Bob said, "Lisa, are you okay?"

I turned back to him and said, "No, not really. Can someone come with me?" Rasheed volunteered.

As we walked toward the door, I pulled him aside.

"The man waiting to see me is probably the father of my baby," I said, and Rasheed smiled. "That's cool, man," he said, nodding.

"No, Rasheed, it's not cool at all. He's the abusive maniac I was talking about."

"Don't worry, baby, he gives you any shit and I'll take him out." I looked Rasheed up and down and imagined his skinny white ass up against Bob.

"Uh, that's okay, Rasheed. He'll be charming, I promise."

Then we walked out the door together.

"Big Bob!" Rasheed blurted the moment he saw Bob sitting there. "Wow! What are you doing here?" Of course he'd know Bob, it suddenly dawned on me. They had worked at the post office together.

Then Rasheed said, "So you're here to see Lisa?" Bob nodded. Rasheed whispered in my ear, "This is the guy you're scared of?"

I didn't respond, knowing he'd never believe me. Bob didn't respond either, and Rasheed stood there, as if waiting to be invited to join us.

"Well then," Rasheed said, giggling nervously. "I'll let you two catch up," and he returned to the group room.

I stood there before Bob, wishing to God it was just a nightmare and I could wake up. Was there nowhere I could go where he wouldn't find me? Not even a mental institution?

After an awkward silence, I asked, "How did you find me?"

Bob stood up, his knee cracking and popping, and came toward me. "I have my ways," he said, "Remember? I'm everywhere."

He wasn't smiling, and neither was I. His words sank into my mind and all I could do was imagine how impossible it was to escape him. Then he turned on the charm.

"The nurse said we could go outside and sit on the grass. I brought you some things," and he lifted the paper bag.

"I don't want to sit on the grass with you. I don't want to sit anywhere with you. I want you to leave. Right now."

Bob looked up at Christy, who was quietly writing up charts at the reception desk.

"See, I told you!" he said to her. Then to me he said, "I told her you'd get all fired up and not want to see me and I was right, huh. Christy?"

He had a big smile on his face and Christy giggled. "You sure were!" Her face was lit up with mirth.

"He said you'd have a fit, that you have a hard time accepting love." Apparently Christy didn't have a hard time accepting his love. She stared alluringly into Bob's eyes a little too long. One way or another, Bob was making sure he'd keep track of me.

Chapter 16

Warm and fuzzy

IT WAS BEAUTIFUL outside. The sun shone and birds sang. The hydrangea bushes that surrounded the front of the house were glorious with pink, lavender and white blooms. Bees buzzed by and I noticed a hummingbird hovering over one of the rhodies.

But as beautiful as it was, Bob brought a darkness with him.

I was so confused by him. Did he come to see me because he really cared, or did he want to hammer another nail into my coffin? In the absence of logical thought, I decided to believe Bob did indeed care and was just trying to show it. The alternative— that he didn't love me and wanted to hurt me—was, in the words of Dr. Bob, a buzz kill.

I was being too negative, too self-defeating, and too not okay.

Bob and I sat on the grass. The sun was in my eyes so I shifted so it would beat on my back. I thought of all the other times I'd sat with my friends on grassy places— Hippie Hill at the UW campus, a small meadow at Golden Gardens, or the sand at Alki Beach. Those were happy times, carefree, no worries and pure energy. Now, as I sat with Bob, it seemed that the sun dimmed and the birds fell silent.

I tried hard to be assertive and brave. I decided to come right out and say what was on my mind. "I want to know how you found me."

"Like I said, I have my ways." His eyes were penetrating, as if he were trying to look inside me and find my fears.

"No. I'm not going to accept that. You'd like me to think you're some sort of magician or wizard. But you aren't."

He just shook his head and laughed. "You don't know what I am."

"I know you're not Superman, that's for sure. Mrs. Luger was probably spying on me when I left. She must have seen me getting into the van or overheard us talking. There's no other way you'd know."

I needed to hear him tell me I was right—that he knew where I was simply because people gossiped. That was something I could handle. But until he told me that, all I could do was shiver—because no matter where I went or what I did, Bob would know. That's what his presence on the lawn was telling me—that I couldn't escape him.

He held up the paper bag and shook it. "Don't you want to know what I brought you?"

"No," I said. He opened the bag anyway and brought out a carton Winston 100's. My favorite cigarettes. I was aghast. "You brought me cigarettes? You, who on the day we met told me to quit smoking for you? I don't get it."

I was scared, but when I looked at Bob, his face wasn't at all scary; it was tender and caring and his beautiful liquid eyes gazed at me with love.

"I know that you're troubled right now, Babygirl, and I know that smoking is comforting or relaxing or something to you, so you just need to smoke right now and I want you to be happy."

"Babygirl?"

"Yeah, Babygirl. It's a term of endearment, like you are some kind of wonderful."

I couldn't have been more confused. First he's trying to kill me, then he's being kind and understanding. It didn't make sense. But maybe that was the point. The more confused I felt, the more in control he seemed to be. At least that's how I understand it now. Back then I just felt my heart grow warm and thought to myself, "He's not so bad; he really does care about me."

He reached into the bag again and brought out two sandwiches and two Cokes.

"I thought you might be hungry. Don't know what kind of food they serve in this place," he jerked his head toward the Institute.

I took a sandwich and began to eat. It was tuna on wheat bread that he'd gotten from a place called Barney Bagel and Susie Cream Cheese.

"Aren't you going to have the other sandwich?"

"Oh yes," he said, "but I just wanted to be sure you've got enough."

"Well, frankly, my appetite's not so good," I said, "but this is tasty."

We sat in the sun on the open front lawn. I opened a pack of cigarettes, lit one and sighed with pleasure as I blew out the smoke. I could do smoke rings, but he'd told me it wasn't lady-like. I lay on the grass and took a deep drag on my cigarette, feeling the nicotine rushing through my veins, bringing a sense of calm.

"You know," I said to Bob, blowing smoke rings into the soft warm air, "I think blowing smoke rings should be considered an art form."

"It's not ladylike," he said snatching the cigarette away from me.

"Then why did you bring me a carton?" I sat up and looked at my watch and noticed the time. Then I looked back at the building and saw Barbara peering through the curtains at us. "I've got to go back now. I'm missing group." He asked me what "group" was and I explained it to him.

"You don't talk about me in group, do you? I wouldn't be very happy about that."

I stood and headed for the front door. He stood too, and it seemed like his tall frame blotted out the sun.

"Don't come back, please," I told him. "They don't like visitors."

"You didn't answer my question. Do you talk about me?

I climbed the stairs and went inside.

Later, I told the group who my visitor was and that Bob didn't want me to speak about him and that I didn't tell him that I already had.

They all congratulated me. But deep inside I was terrified—what if he found out I had? He'd be furious. Then I told myself I was just being paranoid; no one was going to say a thing.

Everything in group was confidential.

Then I looked up and saw Rasheed. He just smiled.

Over the next few days I progressed in therapy and got to know the others in group and they got to know me. Little by little they became less like curious characters and more like friends going through some rough times. And little by little I felt more comfortable talking about my own demons. But I still stayed away from what had brought me to them—the subject of suicide.

But Dr. Bob asked me to talk more about why I'd been admitted to the Institute.

"Don't you already know?" I asked him. I still couldn't bring myself to openly discuss it.

"Yes, I do know, but you need to tell us in your own words."

"I'd really rather not," I said, "Can we just leave it at that?"

"No, I'm afraid not," Dr. Bob replied. "You need to disclose. It's the only therapeutic route to take if you want to get well. You must tell everything, even if it's painful or embarrassing. Especially if it's painful and embarrassing."

I hesitated but decided to go ahead and talk. But as I started to speak, I heard Bob's admonishment—*You're not talking about me, are you?* He'd found me at the Institute when nobody knew I was there. Maybe he really was magical or had superhuman powers, I thought. Then I realized how crazy that sounded. And while I was afraid that somehow he'd find out if I discussed him in group, I continued to share anyway.

"Remember I said I'd had a baby, the father is black and I gave it up for adoption?"

Barbara, piped up. "It wasn't that guy who visited you the other day? I saw you on the front grass with a black guy. Was that him? Why didn't you say something? I would have come over and protected you."

I took a deep breath. "Yes, that was him." There was a sudden silence in the room. My fellow group members might've liked to think they were hip and cool to that sort of thing but they weren't.

Dr. Bob caught the change in mood and interjected, "That must have been very hard to do, Lisa."

I looked directly at him and suddenly a torrent of anger and frustration burst out of me.

"Yes, it is hard. I feel so fucking defeated. All my friends and family have let me down and not a goddamn one of them was there for me when I needed them. Everyone I turned to for help, the social workers, the nurses, the employment agencies, all treated me like shit! And since they wouldn't help me, I gave away my baby for Christ's sake! And now everyone thinks I should just move on so yes, goddamnit, it is hard!"

Dr. Bob nodded and said, "Good, good, Lisa, you're breaking through!"

The others looked away, coughed or stared at their shoes. I imagined Rasheed rushing off to tell Bob what I'd just said, but he only picked at a thread in his sweater. Later, after group broke up, Dr. Bob asked me to stay behind.

He put his hands on my shoulders, looked into my eyes and said, "You were very brave in there. I hope you can continue to be as brave as the group progresses. Can I give you a hug?"

"I don't really want a hug just now."

"That's okay for now, but we are a warm and fuzzy group and we like to hug."

I took a step back, and asked, "How soon can I be discharged?"

He looked stricken. "Why do you ask about leaving just as you're starting to make headway?"

"Because he knows where I am. I need to leave before he comes back again. I'm afraid of him."

Dr. Bob could only respond with another attempt at a hug.

He had no idea why a woman could possibly be terrified of a man that she'd taken to bed. It just wasn't on his radar.

CHAPTER 17

KEYPUNCH IS THE FUTURE

I WAS DISCHARGED a few days later after promising to return for outpatient group at least once a week. But I couldn't go back to my apartment. Bob would be waiting, and after his appearance at the Institute, I knew that he would somehow, some way, try to use the situation to his best advantage. He might have acted concerned to the staff there, but I knew concern was the last thing he felt—he actually enjoyed my vulnerability—and returning to the Olive Towers would only give him the opportunity to exploit my recovery all the more. Once again I needed help, and once again I had no one to turn to but my parents.

They had moved from Kirkland and had rented a house in the Renton Highlands. I hadn't seen it but my mom had told me they had three bedrooms, so I knew there was room for me. Swallowing my pride, I took a chance and called my mother, asking to come home.

She was furious after I told her where I was and why. "There is nothing wrong with you. What do mean you wanted to die? You aren't depressed. You're just trying to get attention. I suppose you told your *group*," she said with heavy sarcasm on the word group, "that everything was my fault. Isn't that what you crazy people do, pretend there's something wrong and blame it on the parents?"

"Look, mom. I can't go back to my apartment."

"Why not?"

"Bob lives there, mom. I didn't know it at the time, but he lives there."

"Bob? Bob who?" Was there no end to her denial?

"Mom, please. You know who I'm talking about. Bob. The father of my baby? The man whose baby I had and gave away. I can't live there anymore. I'm afraid of him. Can I please come to your house until I figure all this out?"

After a long pause, my mother agreed to let me stay with them but only on certain conditions.

"You can come to the house, but your dad will not be happy about it. And there are conditions—you can only bring Deego and Mona to the house for visits. None of your other friends are welcome. As far as I'm concerned, most of them are just scum of the earth anyway. You're to help out around the house, do your own laundry and your own dishes. And you are not to date any black men while you're under our roof. Do you understand?"

So that was what their resentment was all about. She'd finally said it. It wasn't so much that I'd had a baby out of wedlock that had angered her, but that I'd dated a black man—I'd been shameful in crossing the racial divide. But I didn't feel like I had much choice. Here I was, nineteen years old and agreeing to follow my mother's rules so I could live under their roof. But doing so might be just what I needed to get my life back.

I thought about my cousin Laurel. She'd had a baby too and her mom forced her to marry the father. He left her soon after her son was born and now she was attending business school to learn keypunch. With that skill she hoped to have a career in the latest field of modern computing. Everyone was talking about it. Keypunch was the future. Maybe that was a way to get the money I needed to buy that one-way ticket to England, I thought. I may have given up my child, but I had not yet given up my dream—and maybe if I pursued being a writer, I might somehow, some way, heal the pain that was eating me up inside for losing my own child.

I agreed to her conditions but then I tentatively said that I, too, had one condition.

"Mom, you know how Laurel is in business school to learn keypunch?" "Yes," she said. "Aunt Jessie wants her to learn a skill so she can work and support that baby of hers." I winced at her words, realizing that had my baby been white like my cousin Laurel's, she'd want me to support that baby of mine. But I continued.

"Well, would you guys consider sending me to business school so I can get an office job and earn my own living again?"

"Let's talk about it later, after things are more settled." That sounded somewhat hopeful to me and I felt greatly cheered.

They came later that day to pick me up from the Institute and we went to my apartment. We quickly packed my few things. This was where my mother's constant need to move when I was growing up came in handy. She and I could pack up a household in less than two hours, move, then unpack in the new house, get curtains hung and the kitchen organized like pros.

My dad took my things to their car, grumbling under his breath, "How many times are we gonna have to move her? She needs to grow the hell up!"

Overhearing him, my mom snapped, "Leo, just leave it for now. Please."

"Well, she can just goddamn good and well live in a tent."

"Watch it, Leo, or you'll be the one out in the cold. Do I make myself clear?"

Before he could mumble an answer, my mom turned away from the car, and strode into the building with me close behind her.

My mother knocked on Mrs. Luger's door. I could hear her inside saying "Coming. Coming." She opened the door and stood there in her bathrobe, her hair up in curlers and her lipstick smeared across her face as if it had been applied with crayon. A burning cigarette dangled from her hands, and behind her was what appeared to be an avalanche of newspapers, dirty dishes, and old laundry piled high.

I heard my mother's barely concealed gasp of disdain.

Then she said, "My daughter is ill and can no longer stay here. We're taking her away. Her lease with you is null and void." Mrs. Luger's mouth dropped open as did mine. This was my mom? Standing up for me?

"Her lease is for six months and she's only been here six weeks," Mrs. Luger said.

"Did you not hear me?" my mom said. "She is ill and we are taking her home. The lease is over. Or do I need to call my lawyer?"

Lawyer? We don't have a lawyer, I thought. *Wow, she's really playing hard ball.*

"Forget it," Mrs. Luger said. "Just get out of here."

With some bravado, I took my mother's lead and said good-bye to Mrs. Luger and the Olive Towers. My parents drove to the Renton Highlands and I followed in my car, confident that I would never have to see or deal with Bob again. Here was another clean break for me and another step toward my dreams.

The house was a typical 1950's rambler on a cul-de-sac. One wall in the living room was paneled in some awful cheap imitation wood, a look that had unfortunately survived the Fifties into the new looks of the Seventies— popcorn ceilings and shag rugs. The kitchen had been remodeled and now sported the latest in kitchen design— avocado green Formica counters, a brown in-wall oven, harvest gold refrigerator and gold patterned linoleum. It was a house that could have been anywhere, lived in by any family, in any of the burgeoning cookie cutter suburbs in America.

But it felt like home.

My mom had hung her art pieces and put up her sheer Priscilla curtains in all the rooms, draping the windows in a fabric that seemed more suited to a wedding dress than a tasteful window treatment. She placed a large glass bowl on the Fisher stereo, and filled it with dozens of matchbooks— souvenirs she collected of every fancy restaurant, lounge or tourist attraction she'd been to. There was her green and white Chinese vase, with its chipped side turned toward the wall, on the mantle of the plain, unused fireplace. She had even managed to fit in her eight-foot sofa with the wild patterns of orange and yellow poppies that looked an awful lot like one of my pantsuits.

And there on the wall just inside the front door, was her piano. I wondered how in the world she had managed to get it out of the last place, but it didn't surprise me at all that she had. When it was something she wanted, my mother was indomitable. I could just imagine her cajoling Barry and my dad as they heaved the thing over the balcony of their apartment in a reverse playback of getting it in only a few months before.

There were two guest rooms and I chose the one that faced the back yard.

I brought in my bags and unpacked. Even though I'd never even seen this house before, it was as familiar as if I'd lived in it all my life. I put my albums out by the stereo, plugged in my radio and hung my clothes.

That night over dinner, I was on my best behavior, smiling and nodding and joining in the conversation as if I didn't have a care in the world. But all I could think about was whether or not they'd help me get into business school. My mother hadn't said another word about it to me since I brought it up on the phone, but I knew I needed to speak up and put it on the table for them to argue about. As I waited for the right moment to introduce the topic, I just listened to my parents talk for a while.

"That goddamn Dennine. He'll never stop harassing me." My dad took complaining about his boss to an Olympian level. "It wasn't enough to spend a whole year in goddamn Hawaii, now he wants me to go to goddamn Wyoming. For a year. I hate Wyoming!"

"So do I!" my mother agreed.

I looked up from my soup. "Have either of you guys been to Wyoming?" They both said no. "Then, how can you hate it?"

My mother said she didn't have to see Wyoming to hate it and my dad grumbled about "goddamn Dennine," while ignoring my question, but it settled them both down. After a bit more complaining they stopped, and then there was a prolonged silence. And it was just the time to gently wade into the waters with my own topic.

"I'm sorry Dennine wants to send you to Wyoming. I hope it doesn't happen since it seems neither of you want to have to leave again." They nodded assent.

"But to switch topics, I could use your advice," I said. My father looked up from his empty plate, as my mother shifted in her seat. "Would you mind if we talked a bit about maybe me possibly going to business school?" In answer, my father pushed his chair back, and got up and walked to the living room and sat in his recliner to read the paper. But I knew he could hear me so I kept on.

"Leo, your daughter wants to talk with you. You could at least give her the courtesy of staying at the table and listening."

"I can hear fine from here," he said, ruffling the sport section.

"And I'm saying that maybe Lisa should be given a bit of attention since she wants to talk about something I think might be important." My dad put his paper down and listened. I gathered up my courage.

"You know I need a job in order to get my own place, but I'm having a hard time finding anything. I could never afford an apartment. But if I could go to school and get a skill, I could get a good job." There. I'd given them my sales pitch. Now it was time to reel them in.

"Keypunch is the career of the future."

"I thought plastics were," my dad said.

"You're kidding, right?" I said, and he looked perplexed. I wasn't sure if he'd seen *The Graduate* but it sounded like he might have.

My mother stood up and began clearing the table. So I stood too, and walked back and forth between them, regaling them with all the wonders of this big new career path. Keypunch involved an operator sitting at a large machine using a standard keyboard to punch holes in envelope-sized cards, I explained. The cards were then read by and stored in huge computers as an information database. Looking back, it was a cumbersome, tedious job but in 1970 it was the wave of the future.

"I don't know, if you ask me it sounds like bullshit," my dad said into his paper. "Why don't you just get a job down at the grocery store? They're union. You'd get a good wage and benefits."

"Shut up for a minute, Leo," my mother called from the kitchen sink, "And let Lisa talk."

"Laurel says keypunch is the best skill to have. It opens up all kinds of job opportunities for you." I realized I was talking rapidly, as if the speed of my words would convince them to send me to business school. "And once I get a job and a paycheck, I can move out."

My dad looked alarmed. "And just how long will *that* take?"

"About a year, I think."

"A year? We have to put up with you for a goddamn year?" Clearly my dad was not thrilled. I wasn't thrilled either, but going to business school seemed like the only quick and realistic fix to my future.

"I'm happy to make myself scarce," I said. "I don't want to stay here any longer than you want me to." I had long ago learned to push the pain of his words from my heart, but still, he knew just how to hurt me.

I took a deep breath, and sat back down at the table, realizing my efforts to persuade him were not going well. I was all set to give up completely, when my mother, now sitting again at the table with her coffee, spoke.

"How much is the tuition?" she asked. Her elbows were on the table and she leaned a bit forward. I told her I didn't know. I knew that my cousin Laurel's tuition was paid by her dad's Social Security benefits.

"You find out the cost from the school and then we'll talk some more."

I agreed. Glancing over to my dad I saw him grimace into the sports page. And I knew it wasn't a football wager that he'd just lost. My mom was on my side.

I was afraid to feel hopeful yet I saw sunshine on the horizon. Maybe this would be the means to the end I wanted so badly. Not the end of being a keypunch operator, but of making enough money to get to London. And if being a keypunch operator was the fastest route there, that's what I'd do.

The next morning I called Peterson's School of Business, Laurel's alma mater, to ask about tuition costs for the keypunch program, but they wanted me to come in to discuss "educational options." I made an appointment for that afternoon, changed out of my jeans and t-shirt to my paisley pantsuit outfit and drove downtown.

The school was on Third Avenue between Virginia and Stewart Streets but I had to ask several people before I could finally figure out where to go. The school rambled over three floors in the Lowman Building and occupied two floors in the Bergman Luggage building across Third Avenue. It didn't resemble a school as much as it did a rambling corporate enterprise, which immediately made me suspicious.

I met with Miss Lindner in her second floor office. She was the school's career counselor. She was dressed impeccably in a bright yellow knit suit with practical but stunning black pumps. She was tall and slender, probably no more than a few years older than me. She reached out and shook my hand with a firm grip and gave me a pleasant smile.

I glanced around her office. The walls were painted orange, and above her desk was a poster of Golda Meir, who was the first woman prime minister of Israel. The large poster showed a black and white close-up of Mrs. Meir's face with the slogan *But Can She Type?* underneath. I thought that poster was particularly ironic in a school for secretaries, and immediately looked up to Miss Lindner.

She seemed to embody the new outlook that anything was possible; that the world was open to anyone with any interest in just about anything; that women no longer needed men to define their existence and could live just fine on their own. All in all, it was a very rosy future and Miss Lindner looked like she was fully in control of her life.

She motioned to a chair and asked me to sit, and then she stepped behind her massive desk and sat in her bulky leather executive chair—something obviously designed only for big men. Now she looked tiny, like Lily Tomlin's Edith Ann in her oversized rocking chair.

"So, you want a career in keypunch?"

I nodded yes, although deep inside I didn't. However, I was learning that hiding one's true feelings was the way of the world, especially if you wanted to climb to the top of a pile of papers.

"You've chosen a great career path, Lisa. Keypunch *is* the future. You will find doors opening wide after you've obtained your Keypunch Certificate. Are you as excited about this opportunity as I am?" Her eyes were bright with enthusiasm.

"Oh yes," I lied.

"Well then, let me show you around as I explain the curriculum to you. Are you ready for that?" I assured her I was and rose to follow her into the hall.

"First, we'll go across the street to our newest rooms in the Bergman Luggage building." It was a bright day but with a chill wind blowing up the street from the Sound just a few blocks away. We walked across Third Avenue, into the building and took the elevator up to the fourth floor. We passed classrooms where young women were pouring cups of tea.

Miss Lindner said, "One of your first prerequisites courses will be Business Etiquette." She waved her hand to indicate the young tea-pourers. "Here you will learn how to greet visitors, how to address them correctly, make and present tea, coffee and snacks, provide help for them and, of course, always appearing in your most professional clothes and shoes."

She said this as she looked me up and down. I could tell by the frown on her face that clearly my psychedelic outfit was not cutting it in the world of work and I vowed to never wear it again during daylight hours.

Then we went back to her office across the street. Once again we took our seats.

She arranged the things on her desk, aligning her pencil cup with her Rolodex and day-to-day desk calendar, seemingly lost in her task. Following her lead, I adjusted my top, patted my head of curly hair and twisted my lips to make sure my pale pink lipstick was spread sufficiently on my lips.

"There," she said, straightening a pile of papers perfectly before setting them back down. Then she looked up at me, just as I ran my tongue over my teeth to be sure there was no lipstick stuck to them. She looked bewildered for a moment, but went on. "Of course, after Business Etiquette, you'll take the other prerequisites: Spelling, Grammar, Pronunciation and Hyphenation," she said. "These requirements are important but will only partially prepare you for office work and ultimately, keypunch."

I felt a small lurch in my stomach.

"You will take three successive courses of typing, working on accuracy and speed. Once those are completed, you will learn shorthand and transcription. And then, after those courses have been successfully passed, you will receive your instruction in keypunch!"

I was overwhelmed with disappointment that I would need to take all these classes before learning keypunch. Why did I need to learn how to pour tea for some stiff suited businessman before I could learn how to punch cards?

Despite my misgivings, I felt the need to say something that sounded sincere. Besides, I figured, learning to type and even take shorthand would certainly serve me as a writer. I imagined myself a reporter, interviewing the Beatles and rapidly scribbling their every word into my stenographer's pad to be transcribed and analyzed for worldwide publication. I pictured myself like Jack Kerouac, hunched over a typewriter with a cigarette dangling from my mouth, hammering out my thoughts faster than I had them. And I pictured myself at the offices of *The New Yorker*, peering at the misspellings and grammatical errors of my underlings, as they handed in their copy for my keen-eyed editorial approval.

"Gosh," I said, realizing all the possibilities that such an education had to offer, "that sounds like a great program and I'd like to start real soon. But first, I have just one other question."

"Certainly," she answered, "You must be wondering about our dress code."

"Uh, yes, I am," I answered, glancing down at my once beloved tunic and bellbottomed pants, "but what I—"

"All the girls are expected to wear suitable dresses, pantyhose and pumps. No pantsuits, and," she looked me up and down again, clearly disapproving, "absolutely no dangling earrings. A pair of simple pearls is best."

"Good, yes, I understand," I said, wondering where in the world I would get the money for a pair of pearl earrings. "But what I was wondering was, what is the tuition?"

Miss Lindner looked a little disappointed. Perhaps she thought that I had asked a crass question too early in her presentation. But after all that was my reason for being there.

She turned to a grey metal file cabinet, pulled out a file, opened it and laid it on her desk. Muttering to herself, she ran a manicured finger down a sheet, wrote a few notes on her college-ruled pad of paper and then looked up at me, just as I stopped biting off a hangnail.

"We will need your transcripts from high school to start the admission process. Classes for the fall quarter start in three weeks, so you've chosen a great time to enter the program. The entire course is three quarters, so if all goes well, you'll graduate next spring." She appeared pleased with herself as she explained everything to me, except she didn't answer my question.

"Yes, indeed," I said, "that sounds real good. But, I do need to know what the tuition is."

She let out a little sigh. "It's around $100 per credit and you will need to earn eighteen credits to graduate."

"*Around* $100?"

Miss Lindner demurred. "Well, $159.32 to be exact."

I quickly did some mental multiplication, placing my index finger on my chin, hoping to look smart and skeptical. "So, that would be about $3,000. Does that sound right?"

Miss Lindner agreed that $3,000 sounded right but added, "And then there are the books, which you must purchase here."

"And those are…?"

I felt like I was trying to pull out one of her molars with a pair of tweezers. Was she incapable of giving a straight answer, or was this part of the "educational options" that they'd used to get me here rather than tell me over the phone?

"About another $500."

"Is there tax?"

"Some."

Her reticence was setting off alarms. "Would it be fair, Miss Lindner, to say that the total cost will be more like $4000?"

"Yes." Now she looked relieved, as if the worst part was over. But I was far from relieved. Four thousand dollars was a huge amount—in today's dollars, that would be nearly $25,000—far more than my parents could afford.

My instincts were also telling me that this seemed awfully shady and that I should leave. But instead of questioning her more directly, I politely told her I'd check with my parents and get back to her.

She walked me to the door and said, "I know you will make an excellent office worker and I'm so thrilled you want to go to school here."

I had a sudden thought and turned back to her. "Do you by any chance offer financial aid or scholarships?"

"Think of this as an investment in your future, a real career that will take you places!" I started to open my mouth but she cut me off. "But no, we don't have financial aid or scholarships."

"Sounds great, and like I said, I'll get back to you." I suddenly began to have doubts that being a keypunch operator would provide the funds I needed to ever get to London. I could end up paying for this education for the rest of my life, one pay check at a time. But I was willing to give it a go because so far my choices and haphazard approach to life had gotten me nowhere.

I drove back to Renton with my radio blaring out the latest tunes, feeling that this career path, however imperfect, was the right thing to do, even if the tactics of the career counselors at Peterson's School of Business were less than forthright. Yes indeed—a future in keypunch lay ahead for me. My only thought was: Will this future in keypunch actually take me to London? I trusted the answer was yes.

CHAPTER 18

TWO PATHS, ONE FUTURE

I F MY FATHER had ever wanted a child, he never let me know that. He remained a stranger to me throughout my life, and told me nothing about his past. My mother said that his own father had left when he was an infant, and his mother had brought a succession of other men into his life. In the few photographs I saw of him as a child, my father's head hung low, with his eyes fixed in a glare. My impression of my dad was that he'd found himself trapped in a life he didn't want and rather than take a risk and leave for a better life, he stayed in a gloomy existence. Perhaps he enjoyed being miserable.

It wasn't surprising that my father strenuously opposed my staying at their house and paying for my schooling, but my mother saw the wisdom of sending me to business school, getting a job and leaving.

My father could oppose and grumble as much as he wanted, but in the end my mother always won.

My mother and I were sitting at the kitchen table, having coffee and talking about the television show *Bewitched*. I had told her about the cost of tuition tentatively, fearing an explosion, but instead all I got a slightly raised left eyebrow.

She looked into her cup of coffee, pondering for a moment, and then looked at me with excitement. She'd had an idea.

"Do you think the school will accept a payment plan?" she asked.

"I think they'll accept any sort of payment arrangement, as long as they get it. I really don't know how to thank you for considering this. It means a lot to me."

From the living room, my father chimed in. "Well, you're not driving your car into town every day. That's way too much to spend on gas and parking, money that's coming out of my pocket. You can just take the bus."

I didn't know what to say to that. There were no buses from the Renton Highlands to downtown Seattle in 1970—a half hour drive by car, and I certainly wouldn't be able to walk it. I supposed he was just trying to get his two cents worth in the discussion, trying to assert himself.

I felt a strange mix of feelings. On the one hand, I was thrilled that I might actually get to go to business school, and gain some independence. On the other hand, my hope was mingled with a strong fear of conformity. Instead of a romantic future as a writer in London, I might end up like my dad, trapped in a life of severe mediocrity where my greatest achievement would be graduating from business school with the enviable skills of a key-punch operator and having Barry's baby whose first words would probably be "Damn Skippy."

I went to bed that night, tossing and turning, not knowing if I should be excited or resigned.

But the next day everything changed with a phone call.

When the phone rang, my mother told me not to answer it.

"I'll answer the phone while you're here," she said, "in case some black man tries to call you."

I just rolled my eyes.

"Hello. Yes, she's here. Who's calling?" I listened as the caller apparently explained who he was.

"Who is it, mom?" She pulled the phone from her ear and covered the receiver with her hand. In a whisper she said, "Dr. Bob? From SMHI?"

"Oh, gosh, that's my group therapist! I wonder what he wants."

"Well, here." She handed me the phone. "Why don't you find out?"

The phone had a long extension cord so I took it into the living room in order to have some semblance of privacy, although I knew that wherever I was, she'd be eavesdropping.

"Hi, Dr. Bob," I said, curious as to why he would call. After some polite greetings he got down to brass tacks.

"Lisa, I've been doing some research and I found out some information that I think could be very exciting for you."

My brow furrowed. "Oh really? What is it?"

"You were suicidal when you were admitted to the Institute, right?"

I thought that he should already know that, but I said "Yes, that's right."

"Excellent! So I've been poking around and I think I've found a very good benefit for you because you were admitted to inpatient care for thoughts of suicide."

I couldn't imagine what might be beneficial from that experience, but I let him go on. He sounded really excited, as if he were telling me he'd bought me my own airplane. But his news was more riveting than owning a 747.

"Have you ever wanted to go to school?" he asked.

Where was this conversation going? I wondered.

"Yes," I said, "I was just talking about it with my parents, in fact."

"Well, when you tried to kill yourself, you made yourself disabled!" He sounded happy about this questionable label, as if I, too, should be overjoyed.

"But I'm not disabled," I said, "And if I were, it would be even harder to get into school."

"That's just it," he said, his voice barely concealing his own excitement. "The Department of Vocational Rehabilitation will provide you a scholarship for four years at the University of Washington.

The phone fell to the floor and so did my mouth.

"What? I don't understand. What did you say?"

"I don't know how new this benefit might be, but the federal government is offering four year university scholarships for young people who might be considered mentally ill, like being admitted to an inpatient psychiatric facility. Maybe they're trying to reach out and educate kids who've had one too many bad acid trips. I don't know. But I thought of you immediately. You're so smart and bright. It would be wonderful for you to have a college education. And paid for by the government! What do you think?"

What did I think? I had never thought that going to college could be a reality for me.

When I was quite small, I had a big picture book about dinosaurs and decided I wanted to be an archeologist, but my mom assured me that I wouldn't like digging around in hot dusty places.

At twelve, under the influence of French café music, I wanted to be an *Apache* dancer and swirl around the Moulin Rouge in a striped French navy shirt and beret. But when I told my mother about it, she said that I couldn't learn to dance because I had asthma.

At fourteen, I read a bit of Freud and found that human behavior fascinated me. I was standing in the kitchen with my mother one day when I suggested I might be a psychiatrist. She laughed derisively and poured herself a cup of coffee.

"Do you know how long it takes to go to school to be a psychiatrist?" she asked, as if I was talking about going to the moon. "What on earth makes you think that you could be a psychiatrist? Your father and I never went to school past the eighth grade, and we turned out fine. I don't know why you think you need to be better than us."

At fifteen, I knew I wanted to be a writer. But a writer with a college education was beyond my imagination.

So now, out of the blue, I was being offered a four year university scholarship and asked what I thought. I was blown away!

I thought my mother would find some reason to kill a free education, but I wasn't going to let her succeed. Now that there was a means and a way, I wanted to go to college.

"What do I have to do?" I asked Dr. Bob.

"You go downtown to the Federal Building. The DVR is on the 14th floor. They're expecting you because I took the liberty to tell them you'd be there. Hope you don't mind."

I looked at my mother in the kitchen bent over the counter, chopping celery for soup. I pictured my father bent over in pouring rain pounding a spike into a rail track. I saw myself sitting in front of an enormous machine, punching holes in cards like a lobotomized Stepford wife.

"Oh no, I don't mind at all that you told them I'd be there. In fact, I think I'll head downtown right now."

Dr. Bob thought that was great and I promised to let him know what happened.

Without much thought, I decided not to tell my mother. I wanted to avoid one more fight until I had all the facts and could counter her arguments with a scholarship in my hand. Then the idea of a payment plan at business school would diminish and disappear from her radar. I grabbed my purse and jacket and called out, "Hey mom. I'm going to run an errand. Be back in a while."

"Okay. Can you stop at the store on the way home and get me a dozen eggs, some half-and-half and a can of coffee—Yuban, the dark kind?" She handed me some cash and I quickly wrote down what she wanted.

I found a place to park on the street only a block from the Federal Building. As I stood at the corner, waiting to cross Second Avenue, I found myself looking at strollers, noticing the mothers with their babies, and hoping that one of those babies might be mine. I searched their little faces for recognition, yearned that one might seem familiar, dreamed that I could stop a mom to casually talk about *her* baby, knowing that it was really mine. I knew that this behavior was a bit sick and that I might be some sort of baby stalker. But it was involuntary. All the babies whose faces I searched were not mine and had I actually seen a baby I thought was my little boy, what would I have done? Grab him and run? What if he turned out not to be mine? What then? Or worse, what if it turned out really *was* mine? What would I do? What *could* I do? Would I be kidnapping my own little boy? I could never get him out of my mind and my heart.

As the light changed and I started across the street, I told myself to get a grip, reminded myself I'd done the right thing and to move on. Yet, that constant looking for my baby was akin to seeking the face of a dead friend in every person that I passed. Neither effort would ever produce a satisfying result.

In 1970, one didn't have to go through a security check to enter a government building. I simply headed to the elevators and took one to the fourteenth floor. As the elevator doors opened, the office of the Department of Vocational Rehabilitation was just across the hall.

A young lady behind the reception desk asked if she could help me. Her name plaque said "Miss Harrison." She saw me noticing that and said, "You can call me Louise. How can I help you?"

"I think you might be expecting me. My name is Lisa Ulrich, and I was referred by SMHI to apply for a grant."

She brushed her long dark hair over her shoulder and peered at a small pile of phone messages. "Ahhh," she muttered, "here it is. Dr. Bob from Seattle Mental Health Institute called us about you."

I leaned forward towards her as if I could use my body to shield her words from anyone else who might have heard her. I didn't want her to broadcast why I was there.

Noticing my demeanor, she said, "Don't worry. I'm the only one who knows why you are here. Just take a seat and a counselor will be out with you shortly."

It was a typical government office. The walls were painted an indescribable slate grey-green adorned only by a large framed portrait of our president, Richard M. Nixon. Soon a young man came out, extended a hand and introduced himself as Robert. "If you come with me, we'll discuss your application."

I followed him through a maze of steel-framed desks, each with a manual typewriter and a typist, who all wore expressions of mortal ennui. We went into his office and sat down.

"Do you understand how this process works?" Robert asked.

Oh, great. Robert. Another Bob.

"I think I do, but first may I ask if you go by any sort of nickname?"

He looked a little startled. "Most people call me Robby. Why do you ask?"

"I was just curious. Do you mind if I call you Robby?"

"No, of course not." He had auburn hair that fell in small curls on his forehead, making him look like an eager Boy Scout, like someone I could trust.

Robby explained the paperwork, handed me a pen and a clipboard and set me to the task of filling out the forms and then took me out to the waiting room.

Most of the forms asked simple questions such as where I went to high school, whether I had siblings, what were my interests. The section on why I might qualify for a grant was mercifully short and included only check marks. 'Had I been hospitalized in the last year?' Yes. 'Was I given anti-depression medications?' No. 'Had I had thoughts of harming myself or someone else?' Yes. 'Had I been referred by a counselor or physician?' Yes.

I returned to Robby's office and handed him the clipboard. He took the forms from the clipboard and began to read them. As he did, he made a few notes for himself and occasionally said, "Hmm..."

When he was finished, he put the papers down and spread his palms on his desk. "Everything looks in order and I see no reason why you won't qualify for a grant. Have you thought about where you'd like to go?"

I closed my eyes and thought hard about the answer to this seemingly simple question. Finally I said, "I just don't know. Dr. Bob said maybe the University of Washington?"

"That's a good choice," Robby assured me. "It's right here in town so you'll have no need for a dormitory."

I bit my lip and looked up at the ceiling, trying to take all of this in.

"What would you like to study?" he asked, his pen poised to write down the answer.

"Uh, I don't really know," I said, "I haven't really thought about it. Will that be a problem?"

"No, not at all. You can always use the first two years of prerequisites to sample different areas of learning and see what feels right for you. The world, as they say, is your oyster."

I was stiff with excitement but tried not to show it for fear I might jinx this sudden bounty of good luck. As I stood to leave, I asked Robby how soon I would know if I'd gotten the grant.

Looking encouraging, Robby said, "Very soon. Maybe just a couple of days."

As I left the Federal Building, I felt pensive. Within just a few months, I had had a child and given it up, reencountered Bob and went to a mental Institute, moved back in with my parents, investigated business school and now this. I felt as if my world had just spun off its axis, leaving me to free float in space.

There was an elevated walkway to the ferry terminal in the next block that I loved to walk over. It took me under the Viaduct, where cars buzzed by overhead and ended at Colman Dock Ferry Terminal. There I could breathe in the smells of old Seattle, the Seattle that had been a wild and crazy port town. The smell of brine, seaweed and fish markets was enchanting to me. It was a good place to be pensive.

I took the walkway across to the ferry terminal and got a ten cent cup of tea from a vending machine. It was surprisingly good. Standing outside, I leaned on a rail, and watched the cargo ships, ferries and tug boats, and let the steam of the tea rise to my face. It was a slate grey day, so typical of Seattle.

There were now two paths that I could take to my future. One path would take a year, the other four years. One would give me immediate office skills and presumably a quick job. The other would enrich my soul, allow me to grow in ways I'd never thought of, and raise me out of the mire of a mediocre existence and—best of all—provide a pathway to London. My thoughts raced and my head was spinning with possibilities that hadn't even existed for me a few days before.

Chapter 19

There Will Be Consequences

On my way home, I drove right past a Thriftway, realized I forgotten my mom's grocery list, and made a quick turnaround. When I got home, my mother was still in the kitchen, pounding a cube steak and boiling potatoes.

"What took you so long?" she demanded.

"I said I had an errand to run and, well, it took longer than I expected. And I went to the store to get the things you'd asked for." I handed her the grocery bag and her change.

Her eyes narrowed and that special look of disdain that she used only for me took over her face. "Are you sure you weren't meeting some black man? Or *that* black man?"

"Yeah, I'm sure." I could feel a fight coming on. She lit a cigarette, leaned against the kitchen counter and blew out a cloud of smoke.

"I better not find that you're lying or sneaking around behind my back, because if I do, there *will* be consequences."

She was always threatening me with "consequences." Usually that meant taking the car away from me. But when the threats came, I would simply hand her the keys. I knew then, and I know now, what a difficult brat I could be.

But for my dad—who lied and snuck around behind her back all the time, with one mistress after another, "consequences" took on an entirely different meaning. Each time she caught him, the consequence came in the form of a tangible object. There was a new washer and dryer, a new stereo, refrigerator, or color TV. One time, she suddenly had a charge card to Fredrick and Nelson's Department Store, which was uncommon back then for a working class woman.

My dad almost did face some real "consequences." He was having an affair with a woman he'd met while working a job in Hermiston, Oregon. One day my mom got a call from the lady herself.

"Hello. Is this Mrs. Ulrich? I'm Doris. I live in Hermiston. I thought you should know that I've got your husband and you don't!" Doris taunted my mom, laughing at her, telling my mom that she just wasn't enough woman to keep my dad happy.

"He's living with me, you know. And he's being such a good father to my five kids."

For reasons I didn't understand, Doris actually told my mom exactly where she lived in Hermiston, which wasn't a big town at the time.

I think this might have been the last straw for my mom. I was in San Diego on vacation with Mona and her mom at the time. Had I been home, I would have prevented her from buying the gun.

She told me later that she got it at a downtown pawn shop and asked the pawnbroker for a brief lesson in how to use it. Then she drove four hours to Hermiston, found Doris's house, parked across the street and waited for my dad to show up.

I never heard what happened after that. All I know is that a week later, a big Sears truck pulled up to our house and unloaded a new refrigerator, one with a large freezer on the top.

It seemed the consequences of a cheating husband were appliances and charge cards.

"I know, Mom," I assured her, "I promise you I'm not sneaking around behind your back."

"I just don't want to see you getting mixed up with any more black men," she added, "I'm just trying to look out for you, you know."

"I know," I said.

"I just...I just...want to protect you, I guess." She sighed and sipped her coffee. "And if that black man does come around, you know I have a gun," she reminded me.

"Yes, Mom," I said, "I know you have a gun."

I put the groceries away as she started dinner. She put the steak in a frying pan, drained the potatoes and tore open a head of lettuce. The light outside was turning to dusk and I turned on the lamps in the living room.

There was a commotion outside. The noise of car engines and men laughing broke the relative silence of the cul-de-sac. It was my father, returning from work, with Barry, Johnny the Australian and old black Aaron, each in their pick-ups and all drunk as hoot owls.

"Oh look! The boys are home!" My mother opened the door of her recently acquired fridge and took out some cans of Rainier beer. She handed them to me and said, "Take these out to the boys."

"I think they've had enough already, don't you?"

"Just do what I've told you and do it snappy!" I knew my mother was still keen on hooking me up with Barry, or Australian Johnny—even though he could never return to Australia as there was some sort of warrant for his arrest. Johnny's criminal past and Barry's perpetual drunkenness didn't seem to bother my parents. I could see my mother shrugging her shoulders and saying, "At least they're white."

The men were falling over themselves, laughing and joking so incoherently they could have been yucking it up in Latin. Their three pick-up trucks were scattered on the front lawn making muddy tire tracks and knocking over several of my mother's petunia pots.

Barry called to me as I brought out the beers. "Hey Lise, come have a cold one with us!" He removed his baseball cap and rubbed his fingers through his jet black hair. My father and Aaron were stumbling about, their arms around each other's shoulders in a show of beery comradeship.

My dad always said nice things about Aaron—what a good worker he was, how helpful he was, and how he was a credit to his race. I always wondered if Aaron thought my dad was a credit to white people. I bet he did.

I handed out the cans of Rainier and said, "Thanks, but no thanks. I've got some work to do." But my mom came out, grabbed my arm and pulled me under the car port.

"Whatever 'work' you have to do can wait," she hissed in my ear. "Join the boys for a beer. Give Barry a chance." I tried to wriggle from her grip on my arm.

"A chance for what?"

"You know your dad and I think he'd make a good husband."

"He's a drunk."

"Yes, but he has a job and has saved up a lot of money. He told your dad that he's got over $200,000 in savings. And, he's good looking."

"Mom, I don't want to marry Barry. I don't want to marry anyone. Can you please stop bugging me about it? Please?"

"We'll see about that," she said.

She let go of my arm and shoved me out of the car port towards Barry and my dad.

"Hey, Lise! Have a beer, have a smoke." He offered me a cigarette and I accepted it. He handed me a beer and I opened it. I looked back to see my mother hovering in the car port, watching and listening. "So, how've you been, Barry?" I asked him.

"Damn Skippy! Got a good boss here," and he pointed to my dad, "a good friend" pointing to Aaron, "and a Damn Skippy pretty girl right in front of me. Can't get much better than that."

I went back into the house, my social obligations fulfilled, hoping that my mother would be satisfied that I'd had an exchange of smoke, beer and words with Barry. But I knew she wouldn't be happy until I got my hands on that $200,000.

Somehow Old Black Aaron got himself home. My mom was in the kitchen putting out a plate with the steaks. She asked Barry to stay for dinner. He thanked her for the invite and I set an extra plate at the table.

Johnny the Australian had disappeared, as if he simply conjured himself into and out of existence. A handy skill for someone running from the law.

Over a dinner of steak, potatoes and salad, my father and Barry complained about the day's work. They'd done this so many times before it was like a well-rehearsed baseball game.

My dad started first, throwing out an irresistible low ball to Barry. "Jesus Christ that goddam Dennine is going to drive us crazy."

Barry swung hard and batted the ball to left field. "I think we should just quit and start our own company." My dad nodded in agreement.

My mother called a time out. "How many times have you two said that and you've still done nothing? You two just like to complain. You'll never change anything." Her face took on the steely gaze and rock hard countenance of Mount Rushmore. She took the wind out of their sails and they withered under her contempt.

Barry asked me to pass the salt. I wondered if he wanted me to lob it or just hand it to him.

At that point, I decided to leave the ball park and go to my room to listen to Donovan sing *Isle of Islay* over and over again. I could hear them still in the dining room, bitching and laughing and getting drunker by the minute.

I had to admit that Barry was a good looking guy, really good looking. He was tall and usually tanned from working outdoors. He had the dark hair of the black Irish, and sort of lazy blue eyes that flashed when he laughed.

Definitely good looking. But he was an alcoholic and I was not going to spend my life enabling him, or making excuses for him, or giving up after years of nothingness and then leaving, just to please my parents.

Then Bob snuck into my mind. For a second, I wondered where he was. If I knew where he was, then I could avoid the area. Not knowing meant he could be anywhere and I didn't like that feeling.

Donovan sang in his fairy-like tremolo:

How well the sheep's bell music makes,
Roving the cliff when fancy takes
Felt like a tide left me here.

I thought of my baby and was gripped by a sudden panic. I wondered where he was and who had him. Was he okay? Was he even in Seattle? I rarely let thoughts about whether I had made the right decision enter my mind but sometimes I couldn't help it. When I did think about him, I felt anxiety rising in my chest. *What had I done?*

I could hear my parents and Barry laughing in the dining room. Did they know how much pain I was in? If I ran out of my room crying, would they know why I was so sad? Would they care?

Eventually I fell asleep listening to the sweet voice of Donovan.

When I awoke, Barry had left and my parents were asleep. I got up quietly, went to the living room, turned on the TV and watched The Dick Cavett Show with his special guest, Janis Joplin.

Several days later, with the sun still warm but the sure feel of autumn in the air, my mother retrieved the mail from the mailbox. When she came into the kitchen, she looked irrationally angry as she handed me an envelope from the Department of Vocational Rehabilitation.

"What is this about?" she demanded. I took the envelope and headed down the hall to my room. "Tell me what this is about! Now!"

I shut the door quietly and sat on my bed. I was shaking with anticipation, as if I were already holding an admission letter from a university. I opened the envelope, pulled out the letter and read that I had been accepted for a DVR grant to cover four years at a university of my choice. I was stunned speechless. I never thought this would happen. I was shaking with joy and couldn't wait to tell my mom. I opened my door and ran down the hall to the kitchen.

"Mom! Mom! You'll never guess what!" I waved the letter in my hand. She leaned against the kitchen counter and my heart sank. Her face had that familiar look of derision and disdain and I knew that whatever my news was, she would disapprove.

But I was overwhelmed with happiness and threw caution to the wind. Excited words tumbled from me. "Mom! You'll never guess! I've gotten a grant to attend a university! I think I'll go to the UW! But I can't think what to major in but I'll know after a few years doing pre-requisites. That's what they told me anyway." I babbled incomprehensibly as I tried to imagine all the possibilities before me.

"*Who* has told you this ridiculous idea?" She stood with her arms folded over her belly looking like a harpy that might devour me with her huge wings and sharp, ferocious talons.

I should have recognized her tone and expression but, overwhelmed with my excitement, I ignored it. I thought she would be as excited as I was. How could she not? After all, this was a life-changing opportunity.

"The Department of Vocational Rehabilitation."

She lit a cigarette and glared at me. "Why would they give you a grant to go to school?"

I suddenly felt the need to sit and took a seat at the kitchen table.

"Well, it's because I spent some time at the Seattle Mental Health Institute and was sort of…suicidal after I gave the baby up for adoption. Dr. Bob called me to say that I would probably qualify for a grant because of it and told me how to apply. That's why I had that errand to do last week."

With a sinking feeling in my stomach, I watched my mother's face turn from mild curiosity to frowning puzzlement, and finally, to scorn. The room seemed to shrink, pushing out all the oxygen. I felt a band tighten around my chest. Oh god, I thought, this was a mistake.

And that's when my mother exploded.

"You don't deserve a scholarship to a university! You did nothing to deserve it. You played up blaming me for everything, didn't you? After all, isn't that what you people do? Pretend to be crazy and then blame your mother? How can you even consider accepting a scholarship when you know you are taking it away from someone who *actually deserves* it?"

She rose from the kitchen chair, poured herself another cup of coffee, lit another cigarette and began to pace around the living room. My hands were shaking, but I lit a cigarette, as well. How could I reason with her? What appeal might work?

"I'm not taking this opportunity from anyone. Dr. Bob didn't say I was eligible because I blamed you for everything. I didn't. But I did have a baby, and I gave him away to strangers and I wanted to kill myself."

"Do I have to repeat myself?" She had that contemptuous sneer on her face that always made my stomach tie up in knots. I struggled with years of being held responsible for her happiness and wanting to achieve a happiness of my own. "And just what do you think you will be? A psychiatrist?" she said with a withering tone. "Do you think you are qualified for that now that you are officially crazy?"

I rose from the kitchen table and faced her. "Mom, I'm not crazy. I was depressed. It's no big thing. But I'm now being offered a chance to go to school. Why wouldn't you want that for me?"

She screamed at me, her face twisted with hatred, "Because you don't *deserve* it, that's why!"

On and on she went, beating me down with hateful, scornful words and contemptuous looks. She was good at this. After all, she'd been punishing me and my dad for years with this routine. She was unhappy, and I understood that, but why bring me down as well? And that begged the question—why hadn't she divorced my father years ago? Perhaps being a woman scorned seemed an advantage to her.

In the days that followed, she either yelled at me about what a cheat and a liar I was, or gave me the silent treatment. She shot me looks of disdain and contempt constantly. Her treatment left me so unsettled and desperate that, ultimately, I caved in. I did what I knew would make my mother happy. I ignored the letters and the opportunity for a four year degree.

I started business school that fall so I would be prepared for a lifetime of menial office jobs, just like the jobs she endured over the years. In a very twisted way, it was good to see her happy and to receive her approval which came so very infrequently.

I realized that making her happy was more important than my own future. I also understood in the bright light of day that I would have kept my baby if I'd had her support and her acknowledgement that I wasn't suffering from a kidney infection.

CHAPTER 20

AFTER ALL, THE BOSS IS A MAN

"**Y**OUNG LADIES! THAT is *not* how you sit!" She was looking directly at me.

Mrs. Trefzger's yelling unsettled me. She tried to rule her typing and transcription students as a nun would—with fear and humiliation. She reminded me of Sister Mary Claire Severina, who taught Spanish at Holy Names and once took me by the hair and slammed my head into the blackboard because I couldn't conjugate the Spanish verb for "to teach."

No doubt Mrs. Trefzger herself had been taught by nuns back in the Pleistocene era. By the time I met her she had been teaching typing and shorthand for decades. In place of a nun's wimple, she arranged her gray hair in braided buns over each ear, like earmuffs. And in lieu of a nun's black robes, Mrs. Trefzger wore black support hose beneath her brown serge skirts. She had a wattle neck like a turkey's and it vibrated when she yelled, and she yelled a lot. Her nose flared when she was angry, and she was angry a lot. Especially when it came to people who didn't respect authority. And that pretty much described me.

On my very first day at business school, I arrived wearing a 1940s bath robe in a pattern of red flowers on black background with shoulder pads and a wide belt that I'd gotten at Goodwill. I thought it was trend setting, taking the flowery peasant dresses of hippie girls to a new level of cool. It reached all the way down to my ankles, concealing my black orthopedic shoes that I loved to wear for comfort. Mrs. Trefzger hated my fashion sense.

"Don't you have anything else to wear?" she barked at me.

"No, I don't," I said.

"You're trying to provoke me, aren't you?" she accused. She scanned the class for their agreement, but saw none.

"No, I'm not trying to provoke you," I answered. "I can't really afford anything else just now. Besides, what does it matter?"

"If you dress like that when you're looking for a high-paid secretarial position, you'll never be hired!" That was her triumphant salvo. She was right and I would eventually conform by wearing business attire, but in those days, I was grateful that I no longer went to parochial school and didn't have to those wear hideous uniforms. As long as I looked stylish, as far as I was concerned, what mattered were my skills.

"Now everyone, *this* is how you sit!"

She perched on a green wooden stool at the front of the class and crossed her legs, holding the steno pad on her knee. Then she hiked up her brown skirt past her knees, dangerously close to revealing the terminus of her support hose and the beginning of her knickers. I stared in horror.

"It's fine to show a little leg," she said. "After all, the boss *is* a man. Offer him a little respite from the pressures of business by showing him a bit of your charm." Was this business school or a short course in the escort business?

She had the class mimic her preferred method of sitting and skirt hiking, and they all complied, except me.

"Lisa? Why aren't you hiking up your skirt?" she said, her tone cold and accusatory.

"I just don't think that hiking up my skirt has any place in a business setting."

I could tell by the look on her face that this was not an acceptable answer. It would be all downhill from there.

The classroom was long and rectangular. The walls were painted a military grey-green. There was row after row of tables, and at each seat was a typewriter. I took my seat in the very back row, where I felt safe and invisible.

I looked around and saw a room full of young, eager girls dressed in pencil skirts and sweater sets, their hair perfectly coiffed and their hands manicured. I felt completely out of place and wondered if I'd made the right decision in enrolling in business school. But the fact was I had enrolled, so there was nothing to do but learn what they had to teach me.

First, Mrs. Trefzger taught us typing.

"Typing is a skill that all girls should learn, and learn well," Mrs. T. announced, walking up and down the aisles. "After all, a man always needs someone to type for him so if you can type, you know you will always be able to find a good office job if you ever should need it."

Although I had no interest in devoting my career to typing for a man, I quickly realized that knowing how to type would help me as a writer so I applied myself with serious intent. We learned on Olympia manual typewriters back then. It was standard office equipment. By today's standards, however, they were clunky and stiff, but at the time, they were considered the latest in modern office equipment. I was so thrilled to be sitting at a typewriter, where I imagined myself writing great novels that I practiced and practiced until I finally was able to type up to 120 wpm without breaking my wrists, putting me straight at the top of the class.

Which so disappointed Mrs. Trefzger.

"Lisa, you're going too fast," she announced to the class, "you'll have too many mistakes typing that recklessly."

I pulled my paper out of the typewriter and scanned it for mistakes. There were none.

"Nope!" I said, proud of my work. "Not a one!" I smiled up at my teacher but she didn't smile back.

"Let me see that," she said, snatching the paper from my hand.

I watched as she perused it, her face as puckered and red as a baboon's behind. She was clearly unhappy with what she was seeing.

WHITE LADY, BLACK SONS

"Well," she finally declared, tossing it back at me. "You were lucky. But in the future, if you aren't more careful, you'll end up with a page full of typos and no businessman will be impressed."

Next we learned to take dictation which involved learning shorthand in order to speedily write down the words that tumbled from the mouths of our handsome male bosses.

We positioned ourselves at each typewriter, steno pad in hand ready to record the dictation from Mrs. Trefzger.

Every day she would dictate a letter, and with each day, her dictation got faster. After we took her dictation, she had us to read it back to her. Each time I started to read back, "Dear Sir, We are in receipt of your letter of September 12…" she would come unglued.

"That is *not* how you read back dictation!" The timbre of my voice was too low, she explained. She wanted me to raise my voice a few octaves and read out the dictation in a sing-song breathless way.

"This is how you do it. *Dear Sir, We are in receipt of your letter…tra la.*"

She would make me repeat it over and over again. I tried to raise my voice to her desired octave, but couldn't get there without going falsetto. With each repetition, she would interrupt me. "That's not it! Do it again!"

Transcription class mercifully ended before Mrs. Trefzger and I did each other bodily harm. She gave me an "A" because I earned it, but I'll bet doing so made her want to chew the legs off her desk.

The first semester completed, I was ready for the next one. It wasn't turning out so bad after all, I decided. I was actually doing well in class and the better I did the more confidence I had, no matter how much Mrs. Trefzger tried to deflate me.

The second semester proved to be equally successful. I took business etiquette, spelling and grammar and got straight A's. But by the third semester, my luck began to change. The crowning glory of my secretarial education would be the new keypunch class.

"Keypunch is going to be the wave of the future," she told us. "Any girl who wants a successful office career needs to learn it. It's only a matter of time before all offices are run with keypunch. With that skill, you can be assured you'll get a job in an instant!"

If that was the case, I was determined to master it. After all, it couldn't be any harder than learning typing or dictation, I figured.

The machines were deafening and the room stifling hot. Dressed in a pair of men's khaki pants and a maternity top I'd bought at Goodwill because I thought it looked real chic, I started to melt. The heat was unbearable and the noise was so loud it hurt my teeth.

I sat in front of a gigantic machine and watched as a conveyer belt of blank manila cards travelled through the leader and came to a stop in front of me. When the card was in position, I had to type words—names, addresses, phone numbers, whatever—and with each stroke of the key, the machine punched a hole in the card. Then when I hit the Enter button, the card disappeared, whisked away to the other side of the machine. Then came the next card, and the next, and the next. My eyes went from right to left each time a card came through until I felt car sick.

I lasted all of three days.

I ended up with a relentless migraine, my eyes felt permanently crossed and I thought I might never hear again.

I came home at the end of that third day and politely asked my mom if I could have a few words. She poured herself a cup of steaming Yuban, lit a Winston 100 and sat at the kitchen table with me.

"Mom, I can't do the keypunch class. It is mind-numbing. I would rather chew glass than make my living as a keypunch operator. I can type and take dictation and I'm sure I'll find a job quickly with those skills."

She took a drag on her cigarette and pondered this for a moment. Then her face lit up. "Can you get a refund?"

"Yes, I think I can."

"Then get the refund and start looking for a job." She got up and went to the refrigerator, took out some carrots to chop and a bunch of radishes to slice.

I watched her slowly prepare a salad. She looked tired. How many times had I seen her, exhausted and disappointed, fixing dinner for my dad and me after she had had a long day at work? I wondered how she did it, year after year. I saw myself sitting in an office, taking dictation and typing up letters, year after year in service to a man no smarter than me, and I quickly realized how much of my mother's own life had been devoted to that same end—giving up her own dreams for no better reason than she hadn't been born a white man.

"Here Mom," I said, taking the salad bowl from her hands. "Why don't I fix dinner?"

The next week, armed with my notebook of perfect transcription and swiftly typed letters, I went out to find employment. My mother had no trouble getting a refund—apparently they were thrilled to be rid of me. She gave me a bit of it to buy some professional clothes, so I exchanged the Goodwill robe for a mundane but acceptable A-line number in navy with white trim. It reminded me of my maternity clothes, but at least it made my mother smile.

I visited lawyers, insurance agents, car dealerships, and banks and was turned away at each place. Pretty soon it was clear—I couldn't get a job without experience and I couldn't get experience without a job—the age-old conundrum that the young and barely educated inevitably face. I began to despair of ever finding a job. I could see my mother getting restless and my father growing impatient.

"Why haven't you got a goddamn job?" He barked at dinner one night.

"I'm trying. I really am."

"You're trying, all right."

"She *is* trying!" my mom shot back.

"She's trying my ass!" he thundered. "The only thing she's trying is my patience!"

That was all it took for my mom to launch into a tirade of her own and as I had always done during their nightly dinner fights, I slipped away to my room to let them shout it out.

I had to get away from them. But I couldn't leave until I found a job and no one wanted to hire me. I was feeling desperate and was ready to give up on the idea of an office job altogether and just apply for a job at the new McDonald's when my friend Bobbey called.

I had known Bobbey since 7th grade when we were both infected with Beatlemania that lasted throughout junior high. When we'd outgrown our plans to marry Paul (her) and George (me), we began writing poetry. Our verses were mystical, somewhat romantic but more often depressing. Bobbey was born into a large Protestant Irish family. I envied her long lovely hair and she envied me for being an only child.

"Hey," she said. "I was thinking about you. Are you still looking for a job?"

"Oh yeah, I sure am. But it's so hard to find one without experience."

"Well, do you know that company I work for?"

"Yeah, so?"

"Cuz I've gotten a better job and I'm going to quit. If you're interested, I'll recommend you as my replacement. They really like me, so they'll like you."

"Am I interested? Are you kidding? Does Dolly Parton sleep on her back? Where is it? What is it? And how much does it pay?"

Bobbey gave me some basic information about the job and told me to call for an appointment with her supervisor, Dwane D. Dubbie.

I laughed. "Dwane D. Dubbie? That's a funny name!"

"Yeah it is. He's a little bit weird.

"Like how weird?"

"He takes me into the supply closet and gives me Crisscross." Crisscross was an amphetamine that had become a hot new drug among the younger crowd. I didn't want anything to do with speed, and I couldn't believe that Bobbey would take it.

"Okay. That's weird. Your boss peddles speed?"

"He doesn't peddle it. He just gives it to me."

"What else does he give you?"

"Do you want this job or not?"

"I do."

"Then quit belly-aching and write down his phone number." I did as she instructed.

Dwane D. Dubbie was the manager of Adams Acceptance Corporation. It didn't occur to me to ask what they did; I was just happy for the shot at an office job. I made an appointment with Mr. Dubbie for the very next day.

I arrived, prompt and eager. The office was on the top floor of an old brick two story building downtown. There was no attempt at decoration. In fact, I had the sense that they'd just unpacked and were ready to pack up again and get out at a moment's notice. I should have taken that as a sign that something was remiss right from the onset, but instead I figured I'd just disregard it. After all, I needed the job.

I took a seat in the reception area and waited for Mr. Dubbie. As I did so, I flipped through the notebook I'd brought along that included all my letters of recommendation and samples of my typing and dictation. While it had yet to get me a job, looking through all my achievements, I felt proud and confident.

"Ahh, so you must be Bobbey's friend," I heard and looked up to see Dwane D. Dubbie standing above me.

The moment I saw him, I understood what Bobbey meant by "weird." Mr. Dubbie had slicked back black hair, wore a black suit with a black tie and black patent leather brogues. He looked like Gomez, the patriarch of The Addams Family.

I instantly regretted giving up my black and red Goodwill robe. It would have been the perfect match to Mr. Dubbie's wardrobe. My conservative A-line navy dress with white trim made me look more out of place at Adams Acceptance Corporation than my Goodwill robe had ever done.

"Come into my office," he said with a creepy smile, escorting me through a door and into his barely furnished office. "Sit down, sit down."

I sat in front of his desk and handed him my notebook. "Here are samples of my work, and letters of recommendation," I said, smiling confidently.

But he just waved them away. "Yes, yes, I'm sure they're fine," he said, gesturing for me to take them away. "So, how do you know Bobbey? We really love her here."

I thought *I'll bet you do.* But I kept my mouth shut since I needed a job. "Oh, we met in 7th grade and have been friends ever since. That's about it."

"Oh?" he asked, curious. "So you know her well, it sounds like."

"Yes," I said, "I'm sure she can attest that I am responsible and reliable."

"Oh, yes, yes, I'm sure she can," he said, still smiling that creepy smile. "I wonder what she was like back then. Did she go out with a lot of boys?"

The question took me by surprise, and I sure wasn't about to answer it. "Oh, I really don't remember," I said, "but as I said, I'm sure she can tell you that I'm an excellent worker."

"Oh I'm sure she can. Bobbey's a good worker herself, and I am really going to miss her. Why do you think she's leaving?" he asked, even though he knew she'd found another job. "Does she have a boyfriend? Some guy she's trying to please?" The question floored me. And again, I wasn't about to answer it.

"If you're interested in hiring me, then offer me a job. Otherwise I'm outta here. I'm not comfortable answering anymore questions about Bobbey."

"Okay, okay," he said, holding up his hands in surrender. "I like your spunk. When can you start?"

"Monday?" I answered, so eager to take whatever job was offered I didn't think to ask what the job was or how much it would pay. I was afraid if I asked anything at all, he'd decide I didn't deserve it.

"Monday it is. See you then." I figured I would ask Bobbey for more information about the job and how much it paid later. Her last day was that following Friday, so she'd have time to give me an orientation.

Now, finally, I was ready to get started on a new life, hopeful that this time, everything would come together and I could walk down the path to writing and London.

Chapter 21

I'll See You Around

I WAS EXCITED about my last weekend before becoming a working girl. My parents had moved yet again, this time from their house in Renton to a huge house in the View Ridge neighborhood of Seattle. The house was a stylish fifties-era split level with a brick exterior giving it the look of a Frank Lloyd Wright knock-off. It was probably the nicest house they'd ever rented.

I had the lower level that was formerly a family room and turned it into my own studio. It was a long room with the cheap fake wood paneling that was so prevalent in those days. There was a fireplace and I found a sweet little chintz covered chair at Goodwill to place in front of it. I arranged my bed on the far north wall, my books and records that I played on a small portable record player. It was one of the best places I'd ever lived, and the space and privacy made me feel like I had my own apartment.

But it looked like we wouldn't be there long. My dad had been told by his boss that he had to go to Wyoming to work on some railroad track repair in the town of Sheridan. So there was no point in getting comfortable in this new and great place. In a matter of weeks, I'd have to find a new place to live.

And I wasn't alone in my despair. My mom was furious.

"I'm sick and tired of moving every goddamned time we get settled in!" she screamed. "And I sure don't want to pack up and move to Wyoming!"

She raged around the house, cursing my dad and his boss and the entire world for making her move yet again. My dad had turned sullen. His long thin face looked haggard and tanned like leather. I suddenly felt sorry for them both.

My mom was so mad she was sweating. The bobby pins that she used to hold back her hair were hanging from her temples like limp noodles. She lit one cigarette after another.

"Sheridan, Wyoming?" she screamed, yet again. "Why doesn't he just send you to Timbuktu? A year in Hawaii was one thing, but winter in Wyoming? Uh, uh."

My dad tried to reason with her. "You'll like Wyoming. It's...it's... pretty."

"No, it's not. I grew up in Montana, remember? I know what it looks like. And the only reason you want me to go is to have someone to cook and clean and launder your goddamned clothes and be your slave."

"That's not true."

"It's what I did in Lahaina, and it's what I'd end up doing in Wyoming. Besides, what about *my* job? Am I just supposed to quit it, like all the others? Has it ever occurred to you that if I hadn't had to quit my job every time you have to move, that I'd be making a pretty penny by now and we would own our own house?"

"Your stupid job would never pay for a house," my dad said and they battled on.

"Plus we just signed a year-long lease on this house," my mom added later that evening long after I thought the argument was over. "We can't get out of that." She was sitting on the couch at this point, absentmindedly pounding her cigarette into an ashtray.

Suddenly, I saw a ray of sunshine poke through their darkening clouds. The solution to my problem was right in front of me. I took up what I thought would look like a spot of authority by leaning on the kitchen door jamb.

"Hey, you guys! I have an idea!" They both stopped their tirades and turned to me. "You can go to Wyoming and I'll stay in the house and get a roommate and pay the rent with my new job and you won't have to break the lease!" I thought it was a brilliant idea.

My dad grunted and walked away. But my mother briefly stopped grinding her teeth. "What roommate? You aren't planning to have some black man move in, are you?"

I bit my tongue and ignored her. "I could ask Bobbey. She's good at keeping house and not making messes. We have always gotten on well. She just started a new job and we both want to save money to go to England. You know, two can live cheaper than one, right?"

My dad, totally frustrated went outside to pull weeds. My mom, still sitting on the sofa, calmed down. She took a long drag on her cigarette, gazed out the window with a thoughtful look, and said, "I don't like Bobbey."

"You don't like any of my friends."

She stood up and re-arranged her bobby pins. "I'll think about it." I knew that familiar response. It meant she would agree.

I ran downstairs to call Bobbey.

"Hey! I've got an idea. Tell me, are you still living on Capitol Hill?"

"Yup. And now Debbie and her boyfriend Paul, have moved a friend of theirs named Chico into the place and I can't stand him! Plays his music all night long and throws his underwear on the bathroom floor and doesn't flush the toilet. Why?"

"Because my parents are leaving soon for a job in Wyoming. You want to come live with me in this big house? You'd have a room of your own and much more privacy."

"Sure." She wasn't excited or surprised, she just took it like an offer of a second cup of coffee. Bobbey was casual that way. She didn't ask me anything about it. I told her what her share of the rent would be and that I'd let her know more about it soon and that was that.

I remember getting ready for my first day on my new job like it was yesterday. It was October. The sun was shining and the air was clear. I felt like I was standing on a mountain top, with an endless view into a clear sky. I felt like Marlo Thomas in *That Girl* getting my first job in the big city, with the world lying before me full of pristine promises and rainbows.

Adams Acceptance Corporation and Dwane D. Dubbie were waiting for me. I drove my baby blue Mustang downtown and made arrangements with the parking lot attendant for monthly parking.

Bobbey was waiting for me at the top of the stairs. She showed me around the small office and explained what I would be doing. I was to process contracts signed by desperate women who thought their husbands would love them more if they lost weight at Nu Yu Figure Salons. Nu Yu offered a "new and improved" way to lose weight. You went into the salon and lay down on a leather bed that vibrated for an hour. The shtick was that the vibrations would shake the fat away. Just lie down and relax your way to thinness, they were told. And thousands of unhappily plump women fell for it.

My job was to call the women who had signed up, and explain to them that Adams Acceptance Corporation had bought their contracts from Nu Yu. I was to explain the sale and confirm their agreement to the new terms of the contract, without calling too much attention to the fact that they would be paying a higher interest rate. I was to focus on the benefits and features of our company and the weight loss they'd surely enjoy, while minimizing the details.

What I didn't know was that Nu Yu and Adams Acceptance Corporation were owned by the same person, Mr. Adams. What I also didn't understand was that the set-up was illegal. I was just so very happy to have a job.

It was an easy job. I had my own desk and file cabinet and I felt quite mature. On the first day, Bobbey gave me a thorough orientation. I listened on an extension while she called the new "members" of Nu Yu and went through her spiel about agreements and payments, answering questions along the lines of: Will this really make me lose weight? How soon will I lose twenty pounds? Will my husband find out that I'm doing this, because he'll be furious if he finds out? Bobbey assured them that the weight loss would be significant but also individual. She told them that following a sensible diet would help too.

Then I tried a few calls with Bobbey listening. I was surprised they didn't seem very interested in the "details," which is to say, the higher interest rate. Their only concern was how much weight that they would lose and they wanted to be assured that now that we owned their contracts, it wouldn't affect their weight loss. Talking to them was a breeze.

"You did remarkably well!" Bobbey told me after my first few phone calls. "You're a natural at this!"

As for Dwane D. Dubbie, he stood by and merely watched. He added nothing to my first day, other than to tell Bobbey how much he'd miss her and how glad he was that I was there. I was glad to be there, too. Finally I had a job, and a job that I was good at. But by the end of my first day I was as exhausted as I was elated.

Practically skipping down the stairs, I reached the bottom, opened the door, and walked around the corner to the parking lot. I couldn't wait to get in my car and head home and sit in front of the fire. But no sooner did I see my car than my heart felt as if it had stopped. There, leaning against my car casually eating an apple, was Bob.

I gasped for air.

"Hi there," he said. "Got a new job, eh?"

I felt my blood turn to ice and I began to shake. Really shake. I thought with horror that I might pee myself. "How...how...do you know that?"

"Oh, I recognized your car and Jim here told me you'd gotten a job in this building. Jim's a great guy, ain't that right Jimbo?" He waved to the parking attendant who walked over to join in the happy reunion.

"That's right, Miss Lisa! Pretty cool he recognized your car and waited to see you." Jimbo had the crumbly yellow teeth of a long term speed freak, and lanky hair and beard that looked as if he hadn't seen a bath or a mirror in months.

Bob continued to munch on his apple. "Yeah, I told this guy that you had my baby and gave it away, but that I'd forgiven you."

Jimbo beamed. "Hey, this here is one great guy. We're going bowling tonight, me and Big Bob! Wanna come? Oh, I mean, if it's okay with the big man here."

"It's fine with me," Bob said, tossing the apple across the parking lot where it landed on someone's car. "And, oh by the way, I'm still at Olive Towers so we can have lunch every day. It's just a few blocks away."

I hadn't even realized it, but he was right. The office building where I now worked was just a few blocks away from where Bob lived.

I felt as if I would faint. What on earth was happening? *A bad dream. That's what it is. A bad dream. Pinch yourself. Pinch yourself. Wake the hell up.*

But it was no good denying it. Here, on my first day of my new life, was the seemingly omnipotent and omnipresent Bob, casually trying to re-enter my life as if nothing had ever happened.

When Jimbo left us to attend to a car, Bob grabbed my arm, pulled me close and hissed in my ear. "You will never ever get away from me. Wherever you go, I will find you. Anywhere, any time." His face was demonic. "You might as well give up."

I said nothing, but pressed myself back against the car as far as I could to distance myself from his grip.

Then he saw that Jimbo was returning and released my arm and smiled broadly.

"Lisa was just telling me how she'd love to go bowling tonight," Bob said to Jimbo.

"Actually, I wasn't. I'm really tired after my first day and all, so I'm going to head home." I moved towards my car, but Bob moved between me and it.

"I've always loved this car, you know," he said. "You should take me for a ride. Show me where you live. We could drive far out of town for an adventure. Oh, and I need your phone number."

I took a deep breath. "Please move. I'm tired and I want to go home."

"Well now, why should I do that? Looky here, I've found you again! We should celebrate."

"If you don't move away from my car now, I will scream bloody murder. I'll tell your new friend that you are the devil and that he needs to call the police."

Bob backed away but kept a big grin on his face. "You don't need to scream. You go ahead on home now. I'll be seeing you around."

I got into my car and sped away. A few blocks later, I pulled over, put on the brake, turned off the engine, beat the steering wheel and screamed.

CHAPTER 22

COWERING NEAR THE SCOTCH TAPE

MY DAD HAD already left for Sheridan and my mom was just finishing the last of the packing when I came home that day. She was busy and didn't notice that my face was marred by rivulets of mascara that had flowed down my face, slid off my chin and landed on the white trim of my navy dress.

She called out to me, "How was your first day?"

"It was great," I lied as I disappeared down the stairs to my room.

I sat in my chintz chair in front of the fireplace and stared. I stared into the black inner hearth of the fireplace. I looked around the room and it seemed the same as when I left it that morning. I stared at my hands. They were the same. I felt the chair holding me. I heard my mother moving around upstairs. I heard cars and children and the general hums that life produces outside of my room. Nothing seemed to have changed in the general world.

But my world had just spun right out into a black hole somewhere past the dark side of the moon. I had not seen Bob for over a year. I worked hard to expunge him from my life and my psyche. Yet, there he was—intruding into my life once again. Just as he'd found me in the mental institution, he'd found me in my new job. It seemed he was right. It didn't matter where I went; he would find me.

I placed my hands on the arms of the chair and slowly rose. A part of me wanted to give up, crawl into the fireplace and set myself on fire. But the other part of me said, "No more. No damn more. I will not let this person into my life again. I won't run or hide or be seized with paranoia and fear." I resolved to get through the second day of my new life, and the third, and the fourth and on from there. I'd hold my head up high, go to work, come home like anyone else and make Dwane D. Dubbie glad he hired me.

So in spite of strong trepidations, I went back to work the next day. Bob wasn't hanging around the entrance to the building or waiting to surprise me at the parking lot. He didn't appear during the rest of my first week, or the week after. In fact, he didn't appear the remainder of my first month. But rather than having a calming effect, it had the opposite. I found myself watching from the windows of the office, scanning the streets before I ran down the stairs to my car. I startled when I heard the door in the lobby downstairs open and shut because it might have been him. Even when the phone rang in the office, my heart started to beat fast.

I had no idea when or where he'd return, but I knew deep in my heart, that he would. He was playing with me, keeping me on edge, never knowing when he'd reappear.

Meanwhile, I was settling into my new job and learning to enjoy it. Bobbey had moved into the house and we spent our evenings playing cards or watching episodes of *Laugh-In*. It was working out well, being roommates. We got along, were saving money and in the not so distant future, we would be able to travel to England. As anxious as I was to get there, I knew that the only way to make such a move a success would be to stockpile some money to get there. But Bobbey couldn't wait to hit the road.

One day I came home to find her room empty and a note on the dining table. It said that she'd decided to hitch-hike around the country with Debbie, another friend from junior high. I wasn't expecting it, but I'd known Bobbey quite a long time and knew that everything Bobbey did, she did on a whim.

I was dumbstruck and tried to be understanding. But now I was alone, paying the bills by myself and feeling more and more vulnerable with each day. Now the house seemed too big and very empty. I had nightmares of Bob crawling into the basement like a werewolf, scratching and growling at my bedroom door. I took to wedging chairs under the front and back door knobs at night, keeping all the lights on and all the curtains drawn and pinned together, but I still couldn't sleep. I was too afraid of nightmares and too fearful of break-ins. I developed dark circles under my eyes and looked exhausted.

Dwane D. Dubbie noticed my state. "Are you getting enough sleep?" he asked me one day. "You look a bit tired."

I looked at him standing there and wondered the same of him. His suit was crumpled and his own eyes sagged like a basset hounds'. And his hair was so shiny with pomade that it reflected the ceiling lights and flashed me when he moved. He was so odd that I found him endearing.

"I'm okay, really," I told him. "It's just a little cough at night that keeps me awake." I thought that sounded believable since I still smoked.

"Well, you may know that I have something to help with that," he said.

I knew what he was talking about but feigned ignorance.

"I'm not at all sure what you're talking about."

"I think you do," he said moving in closer until I could smell the furniture polish he'd smeared on his head. "So, let me know when you are ready to feel better."

"No thanks," I said with a smile. "I'll manage."

After another week of sleepless nights and lost appetite, I gave in. I arrived at the office, put my purse in my desk drawer and stifled a yawn. I walked over to his desk.

"Ah…Mr. Dubbie…can I talk to you for a moment?"

He looked up expectantly at me and said, "Sure."

Feeling uncomfortable and looking at my feet, I mumbled "I think I want to take you up on your offer to help me not be so tired."

His face lit up and he said, "Come with me."

He escorted me to the supply closet and once inside, shut the door. He reached into his pants pocket and came out with a handful of the little white pills known as Crisscross. "How many would you like?"

"I don't know. Maybe just a few? I've never taken these before."

He cocked his head slightly and adopted a pitying look. "Well, I think you will enjoy these. They will make you feel energetic and happy. You should try one first thing in the morning and see how it goes."

With a mix of reluctance and resignation, I took several of the pills and promised to let him know how I was doing.

"You won't need to tell me how you're doing," he said. "I'll know as soon as I see you."

Crisscross certainly didn't help me sleep. It kept me awake instead. But I couldn't remember any time in my life when I felt so good, so elated and so extremely affectionate. Not in a sexual way, but just loving everyone. Speed allowed me to feel love and compassion for every living thing. I don't know if that was a common side effect of speed, but that's what it did for me. I found it relaxing, yet invigorating and I thought it was the answer to all my troubles. Just pop a little white pill and everything would be so fine, so wonderfully happily cosmically fine.

Then one day, as I was buzzing around the office masterfully doing three or four things at one time, I heard the lobby door open and close downstairs. I had been there nearly two months and was feeling pretty darned good about everything so I no longer startled at the sound of the door. Instead, I put on my professional smile and got ready to greet our visitor.

But as I listened to the footsteps climbing the stairs, I heard a distinctive cracking and popping that got louder with each step. No one else that I knew made those sounds when they walked besides Bob. It was the sound of his knees, his crappy football-injured knees.

I ran into the supply closet and popped another Crisscross, as if it would somehow magically protect me.

I heard Bob arrive in the small lobby and call out, "Anyone here?"

Then I heard Mr. Dubbie walk into the office and greet Bob.

"Hello," he said. "Can I help you?"

Bob's reply was muffled and I couldn't make it out. Then I heard Mr. Dubbie say, "Lisa? Oh she's here. I just saw her. Let me go look. Why don't you have a seat?"

I listened as Mr. Dubbie's footsteps came closer and closer to the supply closet where I was hiding.

Oh, shit, I thought. *I'm trapped in a room full of office supplies. How am I going to get myself out of this situation?* I felt like Lucy, about to be discovered by Ricky. With every step my heart beat faster, but I had nowhere to go. If Mr. Dubbie caught me in there he'd think I was insane. All I could do was hope and pray his footsteps were moving toward his office, and not toward me.

I was cowering near the Scotch tape when the door opened.

"Ah, there you are! You've got a visitor," he announced as if it were perfectly normal to find his secretary hiding under a closet shelf.

"I'll be right out," I whispered.

"Take your time," he said. Mr. Dubbie closed the door to the closet and soon I could hear him chatting with Bob. I heard Bob ask Mr. Dubbie if he liked to bowl. Mr. Dubbie said yes, but he hadn't done it for a while.

"Well you'll have to come bowling with me then. I can teach you how to be a winner and make lots of money!"

"You can, huh?" Mr. Dubbie sounded skeptical. "Are you a pro bowler?"

"I'm working on it," Bob declared.

I heard more chatter between the two of them but couldn't bring myself to move. And the longer I waited in there, the more absurd it would appear if and when I finally did step out of the closet. Instead of feeling braver as time went on, I only grew more embarrassed. Then, just as I was about to climb into one of the garbage bags and pretend to be a load of trash, the effect of the Crisscross spread across me and I was suddenly effervescent.

"Let me go find Lisa. I don't know what's keeping her," Mr. Dubbie said.

Once again I heard his footsteps coming towards the door and then he opened it.

"Here she is," Mr. Dubbie said, as I strolled out of the closet and sashayed to the little waiting area as if it were perfectly normal to spend twenty minutes in an office supply closet. But I no longer cared; with the

Crisscross pumping through my veins, I felt as if I were on top of the world, invincible and charming.

Bob was sitting there, dressed in a suit and tie, wearing his shiny black Stacy Adams Oxfords. In his large hands was a bouquet of flowers

"Hello there!" I chirped. "Haven't seen you for a while. Looks like you're dressed for church! What brings you here?" Love and affection for the whole wide world flowed through me like a rainbow and I could practically have hugged Bob and Mr. Dubbie in one rubbery embrace.

Bob rose from the chair and handed me the flowers. "I was hoping to take you to lunch."

"I already went!" I announced, like a proud toddler who'd just used her potty. I stared at Bob with what must have been an inexplicable smile, half happy, half stoned out of-my-gourd. He seemed a little taken back by my demeanor. I felt like I was having an out-of-body experience, prancing around on earth while at the same time floating above the room and watching my perky behavior in horror.

"Okay," he said, cautiously, "How about tomorrow?"

All of a sudden, a wave of paranoia hit me. I backed up a little and bumped into my desk. I reached behind me, searching the desk for my pack of cigarettes but couldn't find them. I realized I was still holding the flowers and the paranoia slipped away. Now I felt gleeful. I looked down at the bouquet, cradled them in my arms and imagined I'd just won a beauty contest. I heard my acceptance speech inside my head. *This is such a surprise! But I couldn't have won this without...Darn!...I said I wouldn't cry...*

And then I returned to the real world, refreshed and slightly jubilant.

"Tomorrow? Sure," I answered brightly. High as a kite, I was suddenly acting as if Bob was a perfectly normal gentleman, and I a nervous school girl.

"My lunch starts at noon and I have an hour."

"Good. I'll see you then. Start thinking of where you'd like to go.'" He looked a bit askance at me, as if he was not quite sure who I was. I saw the quizzical look on his face and fought the urge to say, *Hey, I'm the new Miss*

Olive Towers, crowned by Mrs. Luger. I thought, *What a great drag name! Olive Towers!*

Then I noticed the look on his face and realized I was a little overly whacky.

"Burgermaster is fine with me," I said, trying to calm down.

"No burgers," he said. "I'll think of somewhere. Maybe Black Angus."

An upscale steak house; not bad. No man had ever taken me to such an expensive restaurant.

"Oh, yeah, Black Angus," I said as if I ate there all the time. "Sounds yummy."

He turned and descended the stairs, and the sound of his knees cracking and popping receded.

Once I got home and the effects of the speed had worn off, the consequences hit me. I'd lost my mind. That was clear. Here I was letting Bob—the source of all my nightmares—back into my life, as casually as if we were old friends happy to run into each other. What was I going to do? I had no idea. But it seemed to me that the simple solution was obvious—*just take more speed.*

And so I did, as day after day he showed up to take me to lunch, and day after day I popped more speed. As soon as the speed would wear off, I'd be filled with shame and worry about what I was getting myself into. And as soon as I worried about what I was getting myself into, I'd be desperate to take more speed and no longer worry about a thing. It wasn't long before all I had to do was incline my head towards the supply closet and Mr. Dubbie would meet me there. He never asked for money; he just gave me speed as if it were a cup of coffee to make me a more productive worker.

Bob began taking me to lunch, at first once a week, then twice and ultimately every day. Each restaurant was even nicer than the one before and the lights got dimmer and dimmer while my mood grew brighter and brighter. I felt rather grown up going to fancy places for lunch and although Bob didn't drink, I sometimes would order a martini and feel even more elegant. I had no idea how he was paying for it given he had quit the Postal

Service to become a professional bowler, but as he told me more about the competitive world of bowling it became clear that he must have been making some decent money rolling those great big balls.

One day, over steak and lobster, he said, "I'm bringing you to these places so that you can grow up and mature. You need to move from burgers and a shake to this," and he gestured toward the crystal and white tablecloths that surrounded us.

I saw something new in his face. Was it concern? Caring? Loving? His eyes were soft and luminous and they smiled at me as if he were really sincere.

He slowly shook his head and looked me in the eye. "You haven't been raised very well, have you?"

"What do you mean?" I was insulted by his question.

"I mean that you have no common sense, no adult experience, and no insight about life."

"And how do you know this?" I sat up straight in my chair, assuming a haughty and insulted look.

"Your parents never let you be in the world. I can tell by how you behave. They sheltered you. Spoiled you. They never let you grow up, isn't that right?"

I was about to launch into an impassioned defense of my mom and dad but then I thought about what he said. I made a mental list. Did I know how to balance my checkbook? No. Have I started a savings account? No. Did I buy my car? No. Was I allowed to have baby-sitting jobs like my friends for pocket money? No. Is that what he was talking about?

For whatever reason—whether because I was an only child, or because my parents were too busy fighting to pay attention to me—what he said had the ring of truth.

"I'll finish raising you," he said taking my hand in his, "I'll teach you all the things that you need to know in order to succeed in the world. I'll make you a woman."

"I think I'm already a woman," I said somewhat defensively.

"How's that?" he said.

"Well, I've had a baby. That makes me a woman."

"No it doesn't. It just makes you careless."

I winced at the words, wondering what it made him.

"So, you think you know everything and I don't, is that right?" I asked him. In answer, he kissed my hand.

We had finished our lunch and he was waiting for the check. "I certainly know a whole lot more than you do," he finally said. "I'm eleven years older than you, if you remember. I grew up a poor black boy in the South. I've seen things and experienced things that you couldn't imagine. I've learned how to succeed in this life and I want to pass that knowledge on to you."

"Why?" I asked with some caution, not sure I really wanted to know the answer.

"Because I love you."

"No you don't!"

"See? You're so dumb that you don't even know what love is or what it means to love someone."

I was stunned. But he must have meant it, I figured, because you didn't just tell someone you loved them unless you really did, did you? But how could he possibly love me?

"Since when do you love me? You don't even know me"

"I'll tell you, and I'll show you, but later," he said, dangling the promise of something more to come.

"We'll see," I said, skeptical but at the same time, intrigued.

"Yes, we will," he said. "I don't just tell someone I love them. Believe me. If I say it, I mean it. I can make your life so much better than it is now. You don't even know. But trust me and you'll see. You'll be a fine woman someday if you let me be your daddy."

"My daddy? I don't want a daddy. Please. That's the last thing I need, or want for that matter."

"You're not listening to me. You don't know what you need or want, but I do. You have to trust me." He reached across the table and took my hand again. I looked first at his strong, brown hand and then up to his face. His smile was so inviting that I felt a rush of warmth overcome me.

"Look at me," he said. "This is the look of love."

In the dim light of the restaurant, his eyes shined sweetly at me. He lifted my hand to his face and kissed it. "You also need to learn how to let a man take care of you, starting right now." He got up and came around to me, pulling my chair out and helping me up. When we got to the car, he opened the door and helped me in. When we arrived back at the office, he got out of the car, ran over and held the building door open for me. Despite my misgivings, I felt just a tiny bit like a princess, like I really had been crowned Miss Olive Towers. And while the feminist movement was making headway and sneered at such things, I began to enjoy being doted on, treated like a lady and shown some respect. For the first time in my life, I felt special.

As our lunches turned habitual, I came to enjoy them. Bob seemed completely transformed; there was no longer anything the least bit threatening or scary about him. Instead, he seemed so sweet and caring that I soon forgot that he'd been such a monster. The memories of his abuse and fearsomeness started to disappear as I slipped into certainty that I was doing the right thing by going out with Bob and that he really loved me.

I had also slipped into the supply closet with Dwane D. Dubbie one too many times for my daily dose of Crisscross. I was high on speed most of the time I was with Bob and with that warm infusion of affection that I felt under the spell of the drugs, I decided I loved him, too. I didn't understand it, nor did I question it. If he loved me, then I loved him. Wasn't that how it worked?

Gradually he began keeping me out past my one-hour lunch. First it was just a few minutes late, then fifteen minutes, then thirty that turned into forty-five minutes and then an hour. When it got to that point, I felt frantic.

"I'll lose my job if you keep bringing me back late from lunch," I told him one day. We were having clam chowder at Ivar's.

'Who cares? You don't need that job anyway."

"Yes I do! Are you kidding? I've got rent and gas and groceries to buy."

He leaned forward to stare into my eyes. "I'm telling you that you don't need that job. You can do better. Much better. Those guys at Adams Acceptance Corporation and your boss are crooks. You'll go nowhere if you stay at this job."

"What do you mean by 'crooks'?"

"You can't see it, but trust me—they are crooks." He looked wise, like a kind, old grandfather might look.

"But how do you know?"

"I know. Period. I've been around a lot longer than you, and I know a crook when I see one."

I felt defensive and a little panicked. "You don't know how long I looked for a job, how long I went to school to learn to type and take dictation. This job is important to me."

"And I'm saying, you'll find a better job."

"I won't, you know that. Bobbey helped me get this job. Otherwise I'd still be looking."

Bob persuaded me to linger over lunch, while the discussion about crooks took different twists and turns, and by the time I looked at my watch and saw that it was three o'clock, I knew Mr. Dubbie would be furious.

And sure enough, after Bob delivered me back to my office three hours late, Dwane D. Dubbie fired me.

Several months later, Adams Acceptance Corporation was busted by the Feds. They were running a scheme that defrauded countless women. Mr. Dubbie and the rest of the staff were arrested.

The fact that Bob was right both reassured and frightened me. But I set my fright aside, and took comfort in his reassurance. Bob had saved me from possible prison. I'd be crazy not to trust him.

CHAPTER 23

SO, IS THIS GOODBYE?

I DROVE HOME that night in a complete stupor. My job and roommate were both gone and I was in shock. Bob's declaration of love at lunch was mysterious and unsettling. I couldn't imagine how he could love me. He didn't even know me—who I was, what I wanted in life, my childhood—all those things I thought you needed to know before you could love someone. And I didn't know who he was either other than a few things he'd told me about his mother and being in the Army. While I had fallen instantly in love with Lynne, that was different. That was the real thing. She was my first love; any subsequent affairs or liaisons would always be compared to my love for her and would undoubtedly be found lacking.

Days passed and I didn't hear from him. My confusion grew. You tell me you love me, get me fired and then disappear? I couldn't deal with it and became focused on finding a new job—and sleeping. The source of Crisscross gone, I was overwhelmed with exhaustion, and could barely keep my head up. I had never felt such crashing darkness descend. I was curled up in my bed going through withdrawal for a week.

By the end of the week, my habit was kicked, and I'd pushed thoughts about Bob out of my consciousness. I got out of bed and set out to find a new, and better, job.

I remembered Elaine Kent's employment agency that my mom had sent me to. Despite the fact that she had kept me waiting for so long and then criticized my clothes, she was at least a known quantity. Maybe now that I had a certificate from a business school, some work experience and, most importantly, a navy blue dress with white trim, she'd look at me differently. Maybe Elaine Kent would find me to be a most desirable employee now that I'd been transformed.

First thing the next morning I dug up her business card, called her agency and made an appointment. Dory Stewart, the young woman at the reception desk with the Ali McGraw look was still answering the phone. I instantly recognized her perky voice.

"Hi, I'm Lisa Ulrich. I was in about a year ago to get a job. Elaine sent me home to change my look..."

"Oh, yes, of course, I remember you," she said brightly.

"I'd like an appointment, please, to talk with Miss Kent about a job."

"She's not here anymore," Dory said. "She met some guy and moved to Florida with him. She sold the company."

My heart sank. I thought I'd need to start all over again. "Well, can I get an appointment with whoever now runs the agency?"

"That would be me!" Dory said. She told me that Elaine had given her a good deal on taking over the business and that she'd changed the name to Dory's Employment. "Simple is best, don't you think?'

"Simple is absolutely best. That's great! Congratulations! I'm really happy for you. So, can I come in to see you?" I asked.

"Absolutely. Want to come in today?"

"I'd love too. See you soon."

I put on my office attire, sensible shoes, toned-down my makeup and headed downtown.

The office was still in the same place. Since Dory had answered the phone herself, it occurred to me that she might need an assistant. But when I got there, I saw that Dory was still sitting at the reception desk. Her look was now quite professional.

She wore a beige suit with a white blouse underneath and white low-slung pumps. Her hair had grown long and hung to her shoulders.

We exchanged greetings and I took the chair next to her desk and looked around. The walls had been painted orange and the chair seats recovered in bright bold colorful fabric.

"I know what you're thinking," Dory said. "You're wondering why I haven't taken over Elaine's old office and am still sitting out here in the reception area."

"That's exactly what I was thinking."

Dory stood up and spread her arms. "It's a new day. All that corporate junk, that 'I'm better than you are' crap is over. This is a liberated agency. We're all equal in this struggle and we have to stick together!"

I wasn't quite sure what struggle she was referring to, as there were so many of them at the time. Civil rights, women's rights, gay liberation, the Black Panthers and the Gray Panthers were but a few. I assumed she meant women's rights and the budding feminist movement.

After expressing her new beliefs, she sat down and got down to business.

"Tell me about what you've been doing since the last time I saw you. It's been at least a year, right?"

"Yes, at least a year. I went to business school to become a professional secretary and got a job at Adams Acceptance Corporation, but after a few months, they let me go."

"They did?" she asked. "Why?"

I wasn't sure if I should tell the truth or make something up. I hadn't yet learned that sometimes in a business situation those little white lies my mother had told me about were appropriate to use. So I went for the truth.

"My ex-boyfriend kept coming to take me out to lunch and he wouldn't bring me back on time. I think he was trying to get me fired, but I can't imagine why."

"Sounds like a control thing to me," Dory said. "I'm learning in my consciousness raising group that men try many sick little ways to control women. If he got you fired, he probably hoped you'd turn to him for support and then wham, you're in his trap."

"Good heavens, I hadn't thought of it that way, but you're absolutely right."

"Of course I am! I could tell you stories about some of my boyfriends that would make your head spin. You're in the right place! I'll find you a decent job from an employer who will pay for your fee. A job where you will be treated with the dignity you deserve."

We stood and shook hands. I felt optimistic and enjoyed Dory's new sense of freedom and control of her own life, and I wanted to be just like her.

But I never got the chance to know her any better. The first interview she sent me on turned into a job.

The job was doing type-setting for a printing company. There were some really great things about the job and some not so good. The good part was that it paid well and offered a lot of overtime. The bad part was that it was in Kirkland which meant a commute of at least half an hour, over a toll bridge that spanned Lake Washington. But I took it for several reasons: It was far away from downtown Seattle and I would learn a new skill—typesetting—and a new industry.

The job was evening shift, starting at 4:00 pm and ending at midnight, unless there was overtime. I was delighted with the prospect of overtime which to me meant that I'd save more money faster for my one way ticket to London. I had a week before I needed to start.

I decided to use that week to totally reorganize my life, and started with the house. I cleaned it top to bottom. I emptied the kitchen cabinets, examined the contents, threw out what was not needed, washed the shelves and put the bottles of vinegar and cans of dog food back in place. I moved my bedroom upstairs, pulling the mattress up the stairs one step at a time. When I was done with everything, I was exhausted but satisfied. I made a pot of tea, settled on the sofa in front of the TV and watched an episode of the new British series, *Upstairs Downstairs*. I laughed and cried seeing myself as one of the servants downstairs, working her way up to a life of privilege upstairs. What could be more perfect?

Winter was coming. The days were short, dark and wet with that insidious Seattle rain that soaks into the bones and stays there until the next summer. It was the kind of weather that made me want to hole up with a blanket, book and pots of tea. But I knew that sort of existence wasn't going to pay the bills, so I tried to be jolly and, once out of the house and on my way to work, found it pleasant to think I'd meet new co-workers.

For the first three months of my new job, I worked fourteen hour days, seven days a week. I had to be to work by 5:00 am and usually didn't get back until it was dark. Then I ate some sort of dinner, showered, went to bed and started all over the next day. Working so many hours made the world suddenly shrink. I lost touch with the news, friends and reality. But it was not without its upside. Going back and forth twenty some miles from Seattle to Kirkland exhausted me, and I hadn't given Bob a thought other than to conclude that he was nuts and that, once again, I was well shod of him.

One Saturday, after my schedule had eased and I finally had a day off, the phone rang. I was in a good mood, having some time to myself and looking forward to catching up with old friends. I snatched up the receiver and plopped on the sofa, hoping it would be Bobbey, my long lost roommate who'd promised to call that weekend from wherever she had hitchhiked to.

"Hello," I said cheerily.

"What are you doing?" At first I didn't recognize the deep voice, and paused, confused. But then, in a rush it came to me. I sat straight up, my spine tingling. It was Bob. I could barely speak, but managed a faltering stutter.

"What am *I* doing?" I said. "What are *you* doing? How did you get my phone number?" A maelstrom of emotion swirled inside me as I felt a rush of excitement, tempered by Dory's warnings to be afraid.

But something Bob had once said came back to me in that moment. "Don't believe half of what you see, and none of what you hear." Perhaps Dory's warnings about men were one of those things I shouldn't believe for an instant.

"Your former boss, Dwane, kindly gave it to me when I told him how much I loved you and that I'd lost your number. Really nice guy, wouldn't you say?"

"No. He was a sleazy drug pusher," I said, my withdrawal from his speed having brought me to my senses. "What do you want?"

"I want to talk about our relationship." My eyes kept darting to the front door, making sure it was locked.

"What relationship?" I thought. *I wasn't in a relationship with Bob and didn't intend to be. What on earth was he talking about?*

"Well, my point exactly," he agreed. "I wanted you to know that I've been thinking and have come to the conclusion that you and I are not a good couple. I'm eleven years older than you. I'm black, you're white. We don't have the same interests and it would never work out."

What would never work out? I thought. I hadn't seen him in months. "I'm really not sure what you mean," I said. "I'm not aware that we are in a relationship but I guess that's what you think. So, I agree with you. I think you're right. You *are* older than me, a different race and we certainly have opposing interests. So, is this goodbye?" I felt terribly nervous, and not sure if it was fear or excitement but I tried to sound calm and in control.

There was a long silence on his end and then he said, "Yes. This is goodbye. I just wanted to wish you good luck and maybe I'll see you around."

I hope not, I thought. "Well, okay, fine. I think you'll be able to find someone way more suitable than me. So, I wish you good luck too."

He hung up and I relaxed back into the sofa. I was stunned—and relieved. But something about the conversation left me unsettled. Three months ago he said he loved me, then there's no communication at all, and then he calls out of the blue and says the "relationship" is over. It didn't make sense.

The house was silent, except for the sound of my breath. Everything looked the same—the pair of gold velvet chairs, the long floral-patterned sofa, the television with its rabbit ears cocked to the south—but my world had just righted itself after a long siege of fear and confusion. Bob was finally gone, once and for all.

"Wow," I said out loud. "Wow." I got up, went into the kitchen and put a kettle of water on the stove for another pot of tea.

Just before it started to steam, there was a knock on the door.

Thank goodness, I thought, *company—just what I need to get my mind off that call.* I opened the door and my heart froze. There stood Bob. He burst past me, then turned and slammed the door shut.

He grabbed me and pinned me against the wall, the shrill scream of the teakettle like an alarm going off unattended. His breath was hot and smelled of chewing tobacco.

"What are you doing here?" I could barely breathe.

"Oh, right," he said, laughing cruelly. "I forgot to mention. Dwane gave me your address too."

"But I don't understand why you're here after the phone call we just had." The tea kettle continued to scream in the background as if warning the outside world to come save me.

"You flunked the test!" he hissed. "I was testing you, to see if you really care about me. You should've argued, begged me to stay with you, but you didn't. Why didn't you?" His face was twisted in rage and the words that flew from his mouth were savage and crazed. *He must be out of his mind,* I realized. I'd never seen anyone look so demonic.

His hands gripped my throat tightly and I could hardly speak, but I knew words were my only defense. I tried to pry his hands from my neck but stopped after I saw the look in his eyes. I went limp and he loosened his grip.

"Um…because I thought you were right," I managed to squeak out, as his grip began to loosen. "You said that we don't make a good couple and that you should find someone your age and your race. I thought you were dumping me, so I said it to make you feel better." I was babbling, trying to say anything that would calm him down.

Instead, he exploded. He threw me to the floor and raised his foot above me. I winced in fear as he stomped it down on the floor right next to my head. I struggled to get up, but he lifted his foot and it came down again, this time on my shoulder, pinning me in place. He began to sweat and a small rivulet of drool dripped from his mouth. *He looks like an animal*, I thought. *A crazed, rabid panther just before the kill.*

"You are evil," he said, towering above me.

Was I? Was I Eldridge Cleaver's Ogre?

"You must confess your sins," he thundered, "admit to the sinful life you've been living and be reborn in the image of Christ. Beg to be saved!"

"What are you talking about?" I whispered from the floor.

"You haven't been saved in Jesus name. Admit your sins and be cleansed." I had only a moment to think, but I was suddenly seized by a hot flame burning inside me. It felt as if his fiery words had lit a fire inside of me—but it wasn't a fire of passion, it was a burning fear. Had he actually done something to me? If so, *how* had he done it? Was he putting a curse on me?

"Think!" he said. "Think about all the evil things you've done! Then ask Jesus to forgive you."

Sins? *My* sins? What had I done? But then I thought about how I treated my mother and father. I had been so disrespectful and demeaning to them. I had built a wall around me so high that no one could see in and I couldn't see out. If those were sins, then I was indeed sorry.

He picked me up and threw me against the living room wall again, punched me in the side of the head and I fell to the floor, unconscious.

When I came to, I was lying face down on the living room floor. I noticed fine dog hairs from our Heidi in the carpet. I could see a little oval brass plaque on the underside of the table. Hmm....Lane Furniture. I saw dust bunnies under the Fisher stereo, manufacturer's marks on the underside of the end tables. There was a small tear in the bottom skirting of one of the gold velvet chairs. I was seeing the world at the sight line of a bug and for some reason, it seemed calming. The mundane quality of dog hairs and ripped upholstery was somehow comforting.

I got up on my knees, dizzy and weak. When I stood, the room swirled for a moment and then righted itself. The house was quiet but I knew he could be hiding somewhere, about to burst out and clock me if I uttered a negative word about him just as he did in my apartment at the Olive Towers. I crept on tip toes from room to room, checking the bathroom, bedrooms, kitchen, and living area. It seemed clear, although I was too frightened to open the closets. What if he was hiding in one and burst out when I slid the closet door open? I was afraid I could have a heart attack and drop dead.

Then I cautiously went downstairs, moving as softly and silently as I could on the wooden stairs, and grimacing at every creak. I quietly checked the laundry room, the garage and my former bedroom.

No one was in the house but me, and I felt a wave of relief flood my throbbing body. But the notion he'd left me with—that I was a sinner and needed to be saved— remained. After years of Catholicism, I'd long ago laid the idea of sin aside. I didn't believe in sin, or guilt, or confession. But perhaps that was merely an excuse to not obey or accept the teachings of the Church. *God*, I thought, *what if he's right? It's the message, right? Not the messenger?*

I stood over the sink, gently pressing a wet cloth against my aching head. I squeezed the cloth and soaked it again under the water from the cold tap and held it against my chin and neck. Totally confused, thoughts of religion, original sin, purgatory, and limbo swirled randomly in my head like holy cards caught in a winter wind. I was seized with the unthinkable— that I'd been wrong all of my life, that I'd been wrong in eschewing the Church, mocking it and rejecting it's teachings like a used tissue. Did he indeed have a message and was I supposed to heed it?

The next day was Sunday. My head hurt terribly from Bob's punch, but at least I didn't have any visible wounds. His punch had landed on the side of my head, where my hair would conceal any bruising. My shoulder ached from his foot holding me down and I had developed double-vision. But at least he was gone.

I locked both the front and back doors and closed all the curtains. I made some tea and drank it as I paced back and forth across the room, listening for any sound of his return, but I didn't hear a thing. Every so often

I'd peak out the window, but it was obvious he was gone. Finally, I sat down on the sofa with Heidi and took comfort in her devotion. She licked my face, and I gave her a long, long hug.

The phone suddenly rang and I jumped as if I'd been hurled from a giant sling. I knew it might be my mother because she called every Sunday to check on things and gripe. I took my chances and answered the phone.

"What took you so long to answer?" my mom said.

"I was in the bath," I lied.

"Are you dripping water on the living room carpet?"

"I'm wrapped in a towel. So, tell me, how was your week?"

"This week? Your father expected me to provide an old-fashioned Sunday roast dinner for his entire crew. I told him to take the pot roast and shove it. But I did it anyway because it's easier to give in than fight. I'm tired of fighting."

I thought, *I would imagine you would be after all this time*, but I said, "Did you make Yorkshire Pudding with it, or dumplings?"

"The pudding. Barry said he'd never had it before and I told him with someone like you for a wife, he'd have all sorts of things he'd never had before."

"*Mom!* Enough already with the Barry thing, please!"

She asked me how I was doing. I told her things she'd want to hear which were, in fact, a bunch of lies – work was a breeze, I was happy, things were just peachy.

"Well, good. Be sure you pay the electric bill soon. I don't want the power shut off. Do you need money?"

"Already paid it," I lied again. "I'm fine. Really."

She said she'd call again the following Sunday and we rang off.

I let Heidi out to play in the fenced-in yard, and settled back on the sofa with another cup of tea and the movie section of the paper, when I heard a key in the front door. My blood turned to ice. The key turned nearly imperceptibly, back and forth, but there was no mistake. *Someone was unlocking my front door.* When the lock disengaged and the door opened, I screamed.

There was Bob, entering my house—with a key I hadn't given him. I reached for the phone to call the police.

"What are you doing?" He rushed at me, grabbed the phone and slammed it onto the receiver.

"Nothing. I'm doing nothing. Really." I was desperately afraid but stood up trying to be less vulnerable. But my body was shaking and I tried to back away, only to stumble on the sofa and momentarily lose my balance. I caught myself and felt angry and emboldened by the sheer craziness of the situation. I looked him straight in the eye and demanded, "How did you get a key to my house?"

His face broke into a wide demonic smile. His mouth grinned but his eyes had no humor or happiness in them. Instead they looked like two black holes boring directly to hell.

"I slipped the keys from your purse and had one made after I left the house yesterday. Now I'm returning them."

"You took the keys from my purse?" I said. "How could you do that?"

He walked over to me, his knees cracking and popping, and I instinctively protected my head with my arms, ducking into the sofa cushions.

"What's the matter?" he said softly.

"Get away from me. Now! Get away!" I drew my knees up to my chest and with my arms locked around my legs, began to rock back and forth. He moved closer. I screamed, "Go away. Now! Get out of here." He raised his hand above me. "Please, please don't hit me again."

I flinched, as he brought his hand down, to gently touch my shoulder.

"Oh, no," he said in a gentle voice, "I'm not going to do that. I made my point yesterday. I'm here to save you. Did you think about what I said? About confessing your sins? Wiping your slate clean so you can start all over again with me?"

"Ah…yeah…I did," I lied. I lowered my arms and looked directly into his eyes. Where only minutes before there had been evil, now his eyes were soft and liquid and sweet.

"Remember how I said you were not brought up well?" He sat next to me on the sofa and stroked my cheek with his huge hand.

"Yes, I remember. Why?" I tried to brush his hand away, but there was no point. He would always overpower me, always pop up, always stalk me.

"I want to be your daddy. I want to change you from the wild child you are right now to a strong, capable woman." He put his arms around me and hugged me tenderly. "Oh baby, I just want to take care of you, like your mama and daddy never did."

I burst into sobs. I cried because I was tired of fighting, tired of being frightened and wary. And because I knew he was right. I hadn't had a good upbringing. My mom and dad were flawed people but they did their best. It just wasn't enough.

My insecurity was overpowering. As the only child of unhappy parents I had no one to bounce things off of, no one who shared the same experiences as I did and who could verify if my mother and father were crazy or normal.

As I rocked in his arms I felt smaller and smaller, becoming a little girl once again. And oh, what awful times those little girl days once were. I was always sick with asthma or bronchitis or strep throat. Because of my constant illness, I missed a lot of classes and my grades fluctuated. I was always trying to catch up. And my parents' fights made it next to impossible to do so.

I couldn't sleep and I couldn't wake up. I developed insomnia. I'd pretend to be tired and go to bed early, but I'd keep my door open slightly so I could hear if that night's fight might result in an injury to one of my parents. After they went to bed and I felt safe, I'd get up, sit on the floor in front of the television and watch late night talk shows and movies with the sound turned down low and the flickering of the black and white screen the only light.

As I entered my teens, I felt lonely, unloved and unlovable. Meeting and loving Lynne was the best thing that had happened to me, but she was taken away and I hadn't seen her since we'd all graduated from high school. All that was left was confusion about who I was, who I could love and how I could balance that with pleasing my mother. If loving Lynne had been wrong when I knew she was so right, perhaps if I sought love in the wrong places, with the wrong people, and sometimes with dangerous people, someone might hear my cry for help. I just needed to be loved.

Deep within my being, I ached. I had fallen in love with another girl and let my parents take her away from me. I had be given a college scholarship, but my mother took it away from me. And I had given birth to a beautiful child and then let strangers take him away from me. I sometimes hurt so much that I wanted to run into a busy street and let some Volkswagen solve my problems.

My parents were in Wyoming and almost all of my friends were gone. I was overwhelmed with long work hours and exhaustion.

I thought I was strong and tough. I was proud that I'd made it this far without giving up completely. I wished I could be as self-assured and vivacious as Dory Stewart, twirling in her office with her future a bright golden road before her. While I was sure that my bravado made me look competent and confident all it did was make me seem vulnerable and easily duped.

For the next hour, I listened as Bob gently told me his plans to mold me into an assured, accomplished woman. With each word, his soft deep voice mesmerized me and put me under a spell. Slowly, I began to relax. And slowly, I came to see how overpowering my insecurity had been before Bob came along. When I was taking speed and working at Adams Acceptance Corporation, Bob had brought me confidence and security when I needed it most. And now in his comforting embrace, my security was slowly returning.

"We can't accomplish this project unless we are together all the time," Bob said as he held me close to him. "I know you will blossom into an amazing woman with my guidance. I know what I'm doing. I will make you successful and happy. But we must be together. Always."

Here is someone who is really interested in me, I thought. Someone who wants to spend time with me, teach me and devote himself to making me a better person. Maybe his methods were off, but he helped me to see that I would never progress in life unless I turned myself over to him, trusted him and let his wisdom guide me.

He held me at arm's length and smiled broadly. "Shall we get started?" he asked brightly. I looked around the room. My mother's framed prints hung above the sofa. The low walnut Fisher stereo was on the far wall near the kitchen. The piano was in the corner of the dining area. Everything was neat and tidy. Too tidy. Where was Heidi?

That's when I realized I'd left her outside, and in the intensity of our conversation, I hadn't even heard her whimpering and scratching at the back door. "You sit right there, Babygirl," Bob said, "I'll let her in." Bob went to the back door and let Heidi in. Soaking wet, she trotted over to him gladly and let him scratch under her neck, so instantly forgiving.

The tea in my cup had long gone cold. Outside the rain poured and a northerly wind kicked up. The heat came on warming the house. But inside I was cold. A feeling of desolation gripped my stomach. I could only see a grey hopeless world with nothing to offer but more loneliness and sorrow. I didn't want to spend my life alone.

"Okay," I said hesitantly. "Let's get started. I'm ready to change."

I agreed to move out of the house and into an apartment with him. The next day, I quit smoking, just as he had said I would the first moment we met at the Post Office so long ago.

Bob seduced me beyond just sex. He controlled me with constant switches— loving one moment, controlling the next, hugging me affectionately one moment and then hitting me the next. And yet, he was still a father figure to me, a man who offered comfort and affection when I needed it so badly.

I gave in completely and let him guide my way towards what I thought would be a bright new future.

Chapter 24

How to Manage Women

MY MOTHER WAS furious and I didn't blame her. I called her to tell her I was leaving the house, with almost all of her belongings in it, while she was stuck in Wyoming. I was even leaving Heidi, since Bob said she couldn't live with us. It would be up to my mom to come back or to find a home for her dog.

She said it was one of the worst things I'd ever done to her and I had to agree.

"I'm sorry, Mom. I really am. But this is something I need to do." And then I blurted out, "I think I love him, Mom."

That set her on a tirade.

"What do you mean you *think* you love him? Don't you know? Are you out of your mind?"

I could hear her light a cigarette and, like the practiced smoker that she was, she went on without even pausing to ignite it. "Are you trying to drive me crazy?"

"Of course not, Mom. I don't want to hurt you."

"But you *are* hurting me. Who is this guy anyway? Is he a pimp? Did he addict you to drugs?"

"Mom, he's just a regular sort of guy. He's not a pimp or a pusher. Honest." Bob was in the next room, playing solitaire, and could no doubt hear everything I was saying.

"I can never tell your father what you're doing," my mother continued. "He'll be furious. You don't know how he went on and on when I told him you were pregnant in the first place! How in the hell am I supposed to tell him you're going to shack up with the S.O.B. who got you knocked up in the first place?"

"I don't know, Mom. And I'm just so, so sorry. But I have to do this." I didn't say that I thought living with Bob, learning from him, and being cared for by him was my only road to happiness and fulfillment, but that was exactly what I thought at the time.

"Mom, can I call you a little later? I've got some things to do."

"Oh sure, why not? Call me later. Call me never. Up to you." And she hung up. I set the receiver back in its cradle and joined Bob at the table.

"So, you did it?"

"Yeah, I called my mom and told her," I assured him. "She wasn't happy."

"Did you expect her to be?"

"Well...no, but I feel terrible about what I just did. Now she's going to have to drive out here and get all her things and Heidi. Are you sure we can't take Heidi with us?"

"I told you that the landlady in the apartment building won't allow dogs."

"Right. But I'm still a little unclear about how you got an apartment on Capitol Hill without me. You were the landlady's mailman? I don't get it. You never delivered mail on The Hill."

For a brief moment, that evil flashed in his eyes. "Don't question me. I know the landlady and that's all you need to know."

"Okay, okay, you're right. I don't need to know. I'm sure it's a beautiful place and that the landlady is very nice." He had told me to regard everything he said to me, even if it was nasty, as a life lesson.

"I'm teaching you how to deal with life," he said, "because people will treat you like shit in this world, and you need to learn how to take it."

So, I guessed I was learning to trust his judgment and his motives.

My mom decided to use the opportunity of returning to Seattle to get out of Wyoming early. So she packed her bags and moved back home, where she would await my father's return.

But that still didn't mitigate the betrayal and selfishness of what I had done. She had left her home and dog in my care and trusted me to safeguard them, and I had just walked away.

I loved the apartment as soon as I saw it. The entire end of the living room wall was one big window that looked west toward the city, the Sound and the Olympic Mountains. We had very little furniture, so I became adept at bringing home orange crates I'd find at the back of grocery stores. I fashioned them into book cases, coffee tables and nightstands. Some neighbors who were moving gave us a small Danish modern sofa and chair and I found a blue upholstered rocking chair at Goodwill. What more did we need? I was embarking on a totally new and unexpected course in life. Possessions were superfluous. There was a certain romance in near-poverty. And the impoverished life of a writer was beyond romance. To my thinking it was downright necessary. I wasn't suffering; I was just paying my dues.

I continued to go to work at the printing plant while Bob worked as a delivery man for a moving company. When I wasn't working, I cut recipes from magazines, cleaned the apartment, did the laundry, bought groceries, cooked dinner, washed dishes—and doted on Bob.

Almost every evening after dinner, Bob went bowling. I often accompanied him if I wasn't too tired from a long day at work. I didn't like bowling, but he did and that was all that mattered. Besides, he explained that it could bring us in some income. He bowled in leagues that sometimes paid off, and to make more money, he taught bowling on the side, mostly to women who, he told me, were terrible bowlers.

I told myself over and over that I was happy making him happy and lucky to have a kind gentle man who was willing to "raise me," to see me grown and accomplished. My biggest job was to obey him, because he knew better than me. Day in and day out, he became the center of my universe and, as if I'd had a botched lobotomy, I allowed myself to disappear from my reality, my life and my friends and accept his idea of what my life should be.

The opportunity for a college education was already lost and I came to accept that that was okay. I would learn more through the one-on-one relationship with Bob.

"I never wasted my time in college," he'd say, "so why should you? When I was a teenager, I did had opportunity to go to an advanced school for black kids away from home, but my mom wouldn't let me go. I realized she was right. There isn't anything they'll teach you in a classroom that will help you get through life. I'll teach you what you really need to know."

And I believed him.

So I enrolled in The School of Bob and worked hard to excel at each lesson he gave me. Courses commenced soon after moving in with him.

My lessons fell into several areas. The first was Personal Appearance and Composure.

"Your footsteps are heavy and you walk like a cow," he told me. "I can hear you coming a mile away." While that hurt my feelings, once I paid attention I could see his point.

He showed me how to walk "like a lady." Toes down first, if I wanted to be really quiet, otherwise a purposeful, gentle walk with a straight back, head held high. I practiced The Walk in the apartment and out in the neighborhood, going to the store and the library and the drugstore. Soon I had mastered the art of carrying myself as if I were a queen demanding respect and admiration.

Bob's lessons were paying off.

"What would you do if someone made a pass at you?" he asked.

I quickly reviewed what he'd taught me so far. "I would quietly but firmly tell the guy to leave me alone, while maintaining my composure."

"Good. And if someone touched you?" His eyes opened a bit wider, as if he were about to pounce on my answer.

"I'd scream bloody murder?" I ventured.

"That might be needed in certain situations, but usually you'd just want to move away from him and then let me know. I'd take it from there." At that moment, he seemed like the big brother I never had, rising up to protect me, his little sister. I felt so secure and loved by his concern, though I hoped neither situation would ever happen. All the more reason to keep my head high and my gaze lowered and walk with purpose and determination, I concluded.

Next, I entered Physical Education. Because of my childhood asthma, I always had a doctor's note excusing me from sports and gym. But that didn't fly in The School of Bob.

"You are out of shape and fat," he said looking me up and down. I actually wasn't overweight at the time, but looking my body over closely, I had to agree. I was certainly not in shape.

"You will have a daily routine," he announced. I looked for kindness in his face and found a fleeting glimpse of one. But I knew that kindness wasn't what I needed. I needed discipline. I realized that he'd have to be a strict instructor since he was taking me into unknown territory.

"Except for riding my pink and white Schwinn bike, I've never exercised in my life," I said, a bit nervous about physical exertion bringing on an asthma attack.

"And it shows," he said.

I winced at that, but I couldn't argue. The truth was, no matter how thin I might be, it didn't matter. I only saw flab when I looked into the mirror.

He saw me wince and took me in his arms to comfort me. "That's not an insult. It's a challenge! And once you've mastered a challenge you will feel so good about yourself. Trust me."

He started me with floor exercises, a kind of Jack LaLanne routine combined with yoga, cross-pollinated with basic training.

I lay on the living room floor, dressed in sweatpants and t-shirt. He provided a beat: "One, two three, four," while he paced around, watching my progress, and encouraging me.

I thought I was going to rip my muscles. I moaned with each sit-up and groaned with every push up. But all he'd do was insist on more. "You can do this! Stretch harder! C'mon do it. Do it! One more! Just one more!"

I was horribly sore for days after starting. And while I could barely walk, he made me do more each day. He added jumping jacks, side bends, stretching, touching my toes, all with the accompaniment of The Spinners, The O'Jays, The ChiLites and Lou Rawls records on the stereo.

We moved on to weight lifting. We started with small hand weights and he taught me how to do curls. It felt good to feel muscles building, and with that my confidence and poise began to soar. And while I sometimes felt he was subjecting me to physical cruelty, as I gained more strength and less flab, I began to enjoy meeting the physical challenges.

On warm weekends, we walked down the hill to an old park near downtown. There we would play four square. As I was chasing the ball around, I realized that for the first time in my life, I was running outside and not having an asthma attack. What liberation!

Bob was changing my life.

After successfully completing Physical Education, we moved into classes on Workplace Success.

"The cardinal rule," he told me while we sat at the dining table and ate dinner, "is never, ever, ever gossip. Keep your opinions to yourself. Stay out of office politics and don't get drawn into anybody's battles."

"Boy, you are right about that," I acknowledged. "After all the craziness that I got involved in at Adams Acceptance Corporation, I'm happy to learn how to keep my head above the fray."

With time, I found that this one piece of advice served me well. I was viewed by all the folks at the printing plant as an honest, trustworthy person. While my coworkers tended to confide in me over lunch, they soon found that I kept their confidences and in no time I gained a certain stature at work—and I got a raise.

"Next," he said, "never give anyone a chance to say no."

"What do you mean?"

"Well, for instance, if you need to take time off, don't go in and say 'Can I have tomorrow off.' You say, 'I won't be here tomorrow. I'll be back the next day. See you then.'"

"Really? I can't imagine how that would go over." My bosses at the printing plant were brothers who took a very patronizing and controlling attitude toward their workers, all of whom were women.

"I guarantee you," Bob said. "If you've established yourself as a no-nonsense woman who keeps out of gossip and who does her job well, believe me, it won't be a problem."

He was right. While I rarely used this ploy, it always went smoothly when I told the bosses I would be taking a day off. I realized that he was indeed wise and that I was improving from his lessons. I was learning real world smarts, something that I would never have found in a university.

It wasn't long before seeking and receiving Bob's approval became a necessity for me. If I didn't get either, I tried harder and harder until I eventually got that happy nod of his head or the glow of pride in his eyes. And when he gave me that nod or glint of pride, I felt wonderful, as if I'd accomplished something amazing.

As time went on, I quickly rose in the ranks at the printing plant, going from packer to typesetter, to letterpress operator, to quality control and finally to the coveted front office position. I was solid in my "no gossip policy" and as a result, everyone admired and trusted me. I never dreamed I'd elicit such respect from people—and none of it would have been possible if it hadn't been for Bob.

The printing plant was housed in a small warehouse. All the various machines—the typesetter, gluer, quality control, presses and packing—were on the bottom floor. There was a small upstairs that looked out over the plant. The lunch area and our boss, Howard, had his office there along with lockers for the staff to store their things. He and his brother Dave owned the business.

One day I was feeling ill and there was nowhere to lie down for a quick rest. I asked Howard if I could lie on the floor in his office, as it was carpeted.

"Sure," he said, about to put his hand on my shoulder. I moved away quickly, remembering Bob's warnings, and his hand fell to his side. He reached into his pocket and handed me the key.

I went upstairs, opened his door and lay on the floor. There was nothing but solid concrete beneath the carpeting. I tried lying on my back, then on my stomach, but neither were comfortable. Then I turned onto my side, giving me a bug's view of the dust bunnies under Howard's desk. That's when I saw a small brochure laying on the floor, and I reached under the desk to pull it out. It was called *How To Manage Women*.

The advice contained in the brochure was enlightening. The basic rule it espoused was that if a man was unhappy at work, the boss had better see to his male worker's needs or the boss would get punched in the nose, or worse. This was accompanied by an illustration of a man in a suit (the boss) and a male worker (in overalls) threatening the boss with a closed fist. The next illustration showed the two men shaking hands, big smiles on their faces.

But for women employees, the message was different. The brochure advised that the boss didn't need do to anything if she was unhappy, because women cry and all they need is a pat on the head. The illustration for this point was a woman sitting at a table with great big tears flying out of her eyes and the boss handing her a tissue. She looks up in the next drawing with a smile and the boss gives her a patronizing pat on the back.

I got up and walked out into the lunch area. There, as if to illustrate that life is stranger than fiction, was Thelma sobbing that her printing press wouldn't work and she was behind in her work. Howard was standing over her, patting her on the shoulder. I was horrified.

I brought the brochure home with me that night to show to Bob. He read it with a mixture of anger and humor.

"Okay," he said. "What if this happened to you? What if you were unhappy at work and started to cry. What would you do?"

"Here's what I would do," I said, confidently. "If I had a problem, I'd go to Howard and very diplomatically tell him that *he* had a problem and that I expected him to fix it."

"Bravo!" Bob exclaimed. "That's the right answer."

"And I'll make a vow right now," I said. "I will never, ever let something at work make me cry. Never."

Bob hugged me. "That's my girl," he whispered in my ear.

The School of Bob was turning out to be much more useful than The School of Mrs. Trefzger.

CHAPTER 25

I FORGOT TO GET MARRIED

ONE EVENING OVER a dinner of pork chops, creamed corn, rice and
Wonder bread—Bob's favorites—he told me he quit his job as a delivery truck driver in order to pursue his dream of being a professional bowler.

"You've quit your job? To be a professional bowler? I don't even know
what that is," I said. Suddenly, I felt a shiver inside.

"It's always been my dream," he said. "A couple of good wins at a tournament and we'll be set for life." I was getting more and more nervous.

"But why couldn't you do that on the side? Like work a day job, then
bowl at night and on weekends?" I tried to look understanding, but I felt
frightened that we'd be broke soon.

"Of course you don't get it," he said with a slight menace in his voice, a
tone I hadn't heard for a while.

"Okay," I said, with a muster of hopefulness. "Explain it to me so I can
understand.

"I want to be a professional bowler," he said. "It takes a lot of practice
and dedication and I need to be able to practice every day, every evening
and all weekends."

Shit, I thought. I had just been reading one of my books about London,
along with a volume of Blake. I still burned inside with the desire to go
there. It was like a flame that only got hotter as I thought about it.

Bob and I had talked about dreams and aspirations in general. He had always agreed that having a dream or a goal was important although he'd never told me about his aspirations to be a professional bowler. But I understood his own strivings and ambitions for success, and that perhaps if he had a bigger, more pressing dream, then mine could wait.

"I promise you I'll win a lot of money, and that means we could save up and buy a house! Trust me."

I took a deep breath and tried to imagine having my own house. It was a foreign idea, but an attractive one. Having grown up with a mom who moved us at least fifty times, the idea of owning a home was a bit strange, but significant. It would mean I had arrived, a grown up and had attained one of the main ideals of the middle class. I began to think about places where we could buy a house, where we'd get furniture, how I'd plant a garden—the whole nine yards of the American dream.

But in the dark of night, I lay in bed, crying for my own dream, wondering how much longer it would be before I could move to London—with Bob of course—and become the writer I'd always wanted to be. I let my tears fall silently, with my head stuck in my pillow so my sobs wouldn't wake Bob.

With what seemed a bright, rosy but wholly uncertain future laying ahead for me, I continued to work at the printing plant, Bob bowled each day, every day, and we lived on the edge of financial disaster. Bob had proposed early on that he be in charge of our finances and I agreed. I felt I was already doing enough by bringing the money in and I trusted that he knew more about successfully handling money than I did. While it seemed we could never save any money, Bob always told me not to worry, that someday soon he'd win the big one and then we'd be off house-hunting. I continued to believe in him, my heart full of hope.

He bowled every night in a league at one bowling alley or another, and I usually accompanied him. I got to know every bowling alley in the greater Seattle area. Some of them, like Broadway Bowl near our apartment on Capitol Hill and Queen Anne Bowl were so old the pins were still wooden and were set by boys behind the lane. I enjoyed the old-fashioned places, but all of the alleys, old and new, were noisy, smoky and uncomfortable. Still, I came with him for a reason—to cheer him on towards his Big Win.

On weekends, he bowled in tournaments. Entering tournaments cost a lot of money, so when he lost, we often were in dire straits. To make up for that, he'd pot bowl during the day while I was at work, to win cash for groceries and gas. Pot bowling was a form of gambling. The players would put money in a hat or bowl or pot—whatever was on hand—and then whoever got the best out of three games won the pot. To Bob, it was like a part time job that traveled from bowling alley to bowling alley, and if he won, he had ready cash for any need.

I had entered an alternate reality, assuming a new identity of helpmeet, pseudo-wife, supporter and friend to Bob. He'd given me invaluable life lessons to make me a better person and to succeed in the world of work and I was indebted to him. But I still felt a tug.

If I ever looked a bit down-hearted or sad, he'd ask why.

"Nothing really. I want to go to London and write. I am just sort of missing that dream."

"What profit will your dreams bring?" he said irritably. "My dreams will bring us wealth, a home, a new car—all the things we need to be successful in life. Your dreams will bring us nothing. Or don't you want your own home?"

"Of course I do," I said, but did I? It seemed like I stood at the precipice of adolescence and adulthood and I was getting the impression that I was being selfish in wanting to succeed at my own dreams.

"Yes, I want my own home. I want you to be a success and I want you to achieve your dreams. And when all that comes to pass, then I'll work on my own. Of course I will support your dream totally, and maybe someday, you'll support mine." He took me in his arms and kissed my face.

"Trust me," he said. "It will all work out fine."

I became the sole breadwinner. Since he'd taught me well, my promotions at work brought in more income and in turn, that income supported his bowling fees. It was just that he never seemed to bring much money home from his bowling efforts, but I understood that things take time and solid perseverance.

Days slipped into weeks, weeks flowed into months and suddenly a year had gone by. My parents rented another house, this time in another suburb—a spread of shoddy new split-levels that soon sprouted moss on the roofs and mold in the sidings.

Bob bowled faithfully and I went with him every night, standing loyally by his side as he won some, lost more and always had a reason for why he didn't win. It was "too much oil on the lanes, the wrong shoes or the wrong ball."

"But I'm learning," he'd say brightly. "Next time will be the big win!"

Not for one second did I think that Bob would do anything other than achieve his dreams. With my support and encouragement, he would be a winner and our lives would soar to new, unimaginable heights.

But there was something missing and I knew exactly what it was.

As we were approaching a year and a half of living together, I felt a strange yearning. I couldn't stop thinking about the child I'd given away. Where was he? Was he alright? I never brought up my feelings to Bob on the subject, not that I felt he'd blow up, but because I saw no point in perseverating about it. I couldn't be sure if I was feeling guilty for giving Bob's child away or if I was just feeling restless. Whatever the case, I realized I wanted a child of my own.

We were sitting on the bed, watching the black and white television that sat on the top of the chest of drawers. It was the first night of the battle between the Oakland A's and the Cincinnati Reds. I waited until the game was over so that I wouldn't interrupt his viewing.

His favorite team, the Oakland "A's," won. I decided this would be a good moment. I turned to him and said, "I've been thinking about what it might be like if we had a baby of our own."

"Oh," he said, "one that you wouldn't give away?" That struck me as if he'd shot an arrow straight in my heart, but I persevered. "I'm sorry I gave up the baby, but I did what I thought was right at the time. How was I supposed to know we'd end up living together and being happy after all? I think about the baby every day. I want to have a child of our own, to keep and raise and love." The sound of excited TV sport news broadcaster played in the background.

Somewhat casually, he agreed we should try. "Sure," he said, "why not?" If I should have noticed a less than enthusiastic reply, I'd have put it down to baseball. I was more than excited and assumed he was too.

I became pregnant with our second child at the end of the World Series. In those days, home pregnancy tests were just out on the market and a pregnancy couldn't be officially confirmed until the end of the first six weeks. But I knew I was expecting almost immediately, tests or no tests. And I was filled with joy. Bob seemed pleased. This baby will be mine, ours and a grandchild for my parents.

I never discussed my first child with my parents, never expressed my sense of loss but I made the assumption that they would be happy. Although, they weren't happy about my relationship with Bob, sooner or later, I told myself, they'd get used to it.

This time, being pregnant didn't result in weight loss and anemia. I gained the medically acceptable weight. As time wore on, I couldn't eat enough tuna fish salad, peanut butter and Oreo cookies. In 1972, expectant moms didn't know they should worry about mercury in tuna, too much fat from peanut butter or high fructose syrup in packaged cookies.

The ladies I worked with at the printing plant were thrilled with my news. As my pregnancy progressed and my belly grew, they began to hint that Bob and I might want to get married. They were all from small towns east of Seattle and their sensibilities were perhaps more traditional than mine.

One day at lunch, they gathered around me and really pressed home their point. I was seven months pregnant by then and quite happy with the ways things were. But the ladies were determined.

Thelma said, "You want your baby to be legitimate, don't you?"

Marilyn said, "You'll feel so much better when you have provided a legal and religious foundation for your baby."

April and Debbie, Dottie and Christine all chimed in as well. "Don't you want to do the right thing for your baby?"

The right thing for my baby? I was not fond of ceremonies of any kind. To me, the idea of standing in front of someone who said words that magically made me married was absurd. Was marriage the "right thing" for my baby? I couldn't imagine how it would make a difference, but eventually I gave in. The ladies were thrilled. I wasn't sure how a person got married, but I thought I'd start by calling churches. "Hello," I'd say, "I need to get married and I wondered if you could do it. You probably need to know that I'm seven months pregnant and the father is black."

Apparently this wasn't the best approach. No one wanted to marry us, and several ministers hung up on me.

Maybe I should try a judge, I thought, *I hear they do marriages.* I called the courthouse in Seattle and sure enough, I found a judge who could marry us that coming Saturday, only a few days away.

Again, the ladies were thrilled to hear I was following their urgings. I thought I'd forgotten something and then realized I hadn't talked to Bob about it. It was only a few days away. I called home, but he wasn't there. I realized he was probably pot bowling at Rainier Lanes, so I called there and asked that they page him to the phone. When he answered, I asked "Are you busy this Saturday?"

"I've got a tournament at Robin Hood Lanes. Why?"

"Because I made an appointment for us to get married this Saturday, but it will be in the daytime so it shouldn't interfere with the tournament."

Bob was silent for a moment. "Really? You want to get married? We don't have any rings."

"The ladies at work think it would be a good thing to do. And we've both got rings. We'll just give them to each other."

"Hmm...all right. Do we need any one there? Like witnesses?"

"I don't think so." I said, and hung up the phone strangely exhilarated.

We went about our business for the remainder of the week. Both of us were busy and I didn't give it another thought. Bob didn't mention it at all. It had slipped from our minds.

Late Friday, the ladies at work wished me good luck as we all left for the weekend. I didn't think twice about the comment, and just replied, "You, too!" and was out the door.

Saturday came. Bob had gone to Rainier Lanes for a little pot bowling that morning. I took the opportunity to clean the apartment top to bottom. Then I cooked some dinner, put my feet up and started reading a book. Bob came home, we ate, and then we were off to Robin Hood Lanes for the tournament, which he lost.

On Monday morning, the ladies again gathered around me, looking expectant and excited.

Thelma said, "How did it go?"

Debbie and Marilyn and the rest crowded around me, their faces lit up with expectation and asked me the same thing. "How did it go?"

I was confused. "How did *what* go?"

"Your wedding? On Saturday morning? With that judge?"

"*Oh, shit!*" I said. "I completely forgot!"

I thought they were going to dismember me. But instead, they took over. They found a minister with the Unitarian Church who was free and willing to marry us the upcoming Saturday. They bought me a beautiful blue with white lace trim maternity wedding dress. They arranged for witnesses, then picked us up that Saturday, took us to the church and watched intently as Bob and I said our "I do's."

That evening, Bob was scheduled to bowl a midnight marathon at Leilani Lanes, so we took a nap, ate some hot dogs and then headed out where he would bowl all night long and I would sit and watch, occasionally nodding off. At four in the morning we headed home. He lost the tournament due to, he said, "too much oil on the lanes." I joked with myself that this was a short and novel honeymoon.

I never remembered the date of the wedding and we never celebrated an anniversary which as far as I was concerned was no big deal. The big deal was that I forgot to tell my parents. But I knew the moment my parents heard that I married Bob, it would be a very big deal indeed. So I simply didn't tell them.

John (left) and Isaiah (right)
playing basketball on the day
that they met. 1988

Isaiah (left) and John (right)
on the day they met. 1988

John, aged one year in his
grandmother's back yard.

Isaiah, aged one year, in
his family backyard.

John, aged 15

Isaiah, aged 18

Isaiah, aged 13

John, aged 13

CHAPTER 26

JEEZ, WE COULDN'T EVEN WHISPER IN MASS

THE WORKPLACE WAS different for women back then. The concept of maternity leave did not exist in the 1970's and a working, expectant mother had to leave her job around six weeks before the due date. She was considered a liability and distraction in the workplace. What if the baby made a sudden appearance in the break room? What if staff were so distracted by a growing belly that they didn't pay attention to their work? What if she burst into tears? The possibilities were endless.

While I would miss the ladies at work, I was not sorry to leave my job. It had become tiring and boring and I was eager to make everything ready at home for our little one. And while there was no "maternity leave" per se, a new mother could collect unemployment compensation for six months after the birth. This would allow me a half a year to be with my baby before I had to start working again. Unless, of course, Bob won the big one and I wouldn't have to go back to work at all.

Now at home, awaiting the arrival of my baby, I set about pulling a little nursery together in a corner of the living room. The women at work had given me a baby shower and from that I had lots of little baby clothes, a used crib and mattress with sheets and blankets, a case of baby food, Johnson & Johnson baby shampoo and soap, little booties and stuffed bears and boxes of formula. I knew at some point I'd need to learn what to do with all of it, but for the time being, I was just happy to be prepared for my little one.

It was unusually hot for the middle of May. The air was full of Seattle scents: the briny, fishy, creosote smell from the waterfront; the fragrance of lilacs and roses blooming in gardens; the aroma of pavement baking in the hot sun. Soon I would experience the smell of baby powder and dirty diapers.

"It's time to go," I said, clutching my enormous belly. I was experienced enough with labor and childbirth now to know when it was time. And it was time.

Bob was sitting at the kitchen table, reading a comic book. I snatched it out of his hands.

"I said it's time to go!"

"Oh shit!" He scrambled up from the chair, grabbed the bag I had readied at the door and whooshed me out.

When we got to the labor and delivery floor at the hospital, a nurse examined me, declared I had a ways to go and suggested we walk around. Bob was hungry so we took the elevator from the fifth floor down to the basement and found the cafeteria. He had a sandwich but I knew it was inadvisable for me to eat, so I just had water.

Then we walked back down the basement corridor and took the stairs to the first floor. A tour around the lobby and gift shop and then up another set of stairs to the second floor.

As soon as we emerged from the stair well, we heard my name being paged.

"Lisa Jones. Return to the maternity floor. Lisa Jones."

We rushed to the elevator and ascended to the fifth floor. A nurse rushed up to greet us.

"Where were you? We need to check you out."

"Oh, well you guys said to walk around so we went down to the cafeteria, then walked around the lobby…"

"We meant walk around this floor. Good heavens. Get your clothes off and let's see how things have progressed." She motioned Bob to take a seat in the waiting area and I followed the nurse.

I gave birth to my second son at the same hospital where my first baby was born. It was not without some worrisome complications, but my little baby boy was fine.

This time, the process of labor and delivery was much different. I was treated with respect and dignity because despite the fact that my husband was black, I was now married to the baby's father. Bob was pleased about his new son—he'd told me that he'd done a little "happy dance" in front of the nursery window while looking at his child.

On my second day post-partum, my mom and dad came to visit. They pulled chairs up to my bed and my father handed me a small bouquet of flowers. He looked a bit pained and I couldn't read my mother's face. Was she happy or horrified, pleased or perplexed? Everyone seemed a little uncomfortable, so as a diversion, I asked Bob to go get sandwiches from the cafeteria for lunch. As he left, my parents visibly relaxed.

My mother turned to me and asked, "How are you doing?"

I thought that my poor mom didn't know what to feel or what to say. There were too many emotions for all of us. The specter of the baby I'd given up and the happy arrival of our new baby seemed to swirl around me and my parents like a miniature hurricane.

"I feel good," I told her. "I probably haven't told you this, but I'm really excited that the hospital assigned a nursing student to me. After I get discharged, she'll come to the apartment for six weeks to see how things are going for me and the baby. She told me she would teach me how to swaddle the baby, bathe him, and prepare formula—all that stuff!" In those days, breastfeeding was frowned upon. Using formula to feed your baby was thought to be the safest and easiest method.

My mom looked pleased. 'That sounds wonderful. When do you go home?"

That was a tough question to answer.

When we'd left for the hospital, the electricity had been turned off because Bob hadn't paid the bill. We had agreed earlier in our relationship that it would be best for him to handle the money. At times, I wished I'd insisted on doing it as I would never have let the utilities to be cut off.

But at the hospital, I was too embarrassed to say anything to the nurses about the situation at home. If I had, they probably would have brought social services in to help but my humiliation kept me from asking for assistance. I thought that the only thing I could do was stay for one more day in post-partum in the hopes that Bob would win enough at pot bowling to get the lights turned back on.

I couldn't possibly have told my parents of the situation. Both of them would have exploded, pleased to have been given an excellent excuse to rage on about the poor choices I'd made.

As I mulled the matter over in my head, I noticed my mom was waiting for a reply.

"Oh, I think I'll be going home day after next."

"Well, that's good then," my dad said, pacing around my bed as if he couldn't wait to get out of the room.

"So," my mom said, "what is the baby's name?"

"John."

"John what?"

"Oh, you mean his full name? It's John Fitzpatrick J....oh my god, I forgot to tell you! We got married a few months ago."

My mother gave me a murderous look. She was understandably furious and my dad speechless. I attempted to smooth things over by reminding my parents about my distaste for ceremonies.

"Remember how I tried to get my diploma out of the hands of the principal at school so I wouldn't have to go to the graduation ceremony?"

"Yes I do," said my mom with an acid tone to her voice. "You didn't want to go, but your father and I wanted you to. Graduating from high school is a big thing. You'll remember that your father and I didn't get past the eighth grade because we were both so poor."

It was hard to imagine what being so poor was like. My mother told me many times that she had to leave school because she had no shoes to wear. She'd been wearing a pair that was so old they disintegrated. They had been too small from the start, leaving her feet deformed and painful. Her mother couldn't afford new shoes, she left school, borrowed an old pair of shoes from her younger brother and found work. As soon as she could afford to, she bought herself a new pair of shoes and returned the old pair back to her brother. As a result, she always bought the best shoes for me from Nordstrom.

I had been selfish trying to skip out on my graduation ceremony, not giving a moment's thought to how much it meant to my parents.

"I'm sorry, I really am. But getting married just wasn't a big deal. In fact, we forgot to go to the first appointment I'd set up with some judge. It was the ladies at work who stepped in and took care of everything for me."

As soon as the words escaped my mouth and I saw the look on my mother's face, I realized I was only digging myself further into a dark hole.

"I would have been happy to help, if you'd asked me," my mother said, her voice strained. I could tell it had genuinely hurt her. I felt terrible, so to make amends, I brightly said that I'd call on her to babysit.

Just then, Bob arrived with the sandwiches and the topic was dropped.

When we got home, with little baby John swaddled in a thin blanket and held in my arms, I was horrified. The apartment was an unholy mess. Comic books and clothes were strewn everywhere. There were unwashed dishes in the sink. I opened the fridge and it was completely dark and warm—the electricity was still off. Worse, there was no food in the fridge or anywhere else. Furious, I picked up the phone to call the light company, and discovered the line was dead—he hadn't paid the phone bill either. With our new little baby sleeping in my arms, I blew up.

"How on earth am I supposed to take care of a baby with no electricity, no phone, and the place looking like a pig sty? What have you been doing these past few days?" I placed little John in his new crib.

Bob's upper lip curled. I had come to know that look. It usually preceded bullying me or hitting me. "I've been pot bowling to get the money we need to pay those bills. Besides, it's your responsibility to make sure the apartment is clean."

"And how am I supposed to do that when I'm in the hospital recovering from giving birth?"

He was caught and he knew it. He looked sheepish and said, "I'm going to the bowling alley right now."

"Which one?"

"Probably Queen Anne. They have pot bowling on Friday's. If I win enough, I'll go straight down and pay those bills."

"Well, you'd better win because if you don't those business offices won't be open on the weekend and we'll have to wait until Monday. And I won't do that. I'll go to my parents if necessary."

He grabbed his bowling bag and left. Several hours later, the lights came on, the refrigerator engine started to hum and the electric alarm clock in the bedroom began to buzz. A few hours after that, the phone rang. It was Bob.

"Did the lights come back?" He sounded hopeful.

"They did, and obviously you paid the phone bill or this call wouldn't have come through. You must have killed it at pot bowling."

"I had to do what I had to do for my wife and my new little boy!" he said proudly, but somehow, that didn't ring quite true. Why couldn't he have done that before we came home? Better still, why did he let that happen at all? But I snuffed out those nagging thoughts because they only made things worse. Bob was clearly trying, and he'd promised to get those lights back on and he did. I just knew this would never happen again. We were going to be a successful couple and this was a mere detour in the road.

When he came home, he seemed truly apologetic. He emptied his pockets onto the dining table to show me how much cash he'd won. It looked like a lot, even after he'd paid the electricity and phone bills. He was excited. "Let's count it!"

Suddenly I was taken back many years to the brief time my dad had worked as a taxi driver. Every night he'd come home with a pocket full of coins - silver dollars, half dollars, quarters, dimes, nickels and pennies. I always got to count the money. I loved the weight of the silver dollars and half dollars. I'd line them up in straight rows, or make them into circles or pyramids. "Oh, yes – let's count it!" I said, in a burst of nostalgia. "I love to do that. I used to count the taxi money with my dad!"

"What's even better is I'm your new daddy, so you can count with me now," Bob answered. He put his arm around me and kissed my cheek.

As we sat in front of our collection of coins, his face beamed with tenderness toward me. Little John, safely swaddled, was napping in his crib and I turned to look at his sweet sleeping face. This was my family now. I loved my Big Bob and my Little John, more than I ever thought possible. Certainly, I never thought it would happen— that I'd ever have a husband and a baby, but here I was, happy and excited for our new lives together.

We counted his remaining winnings. It was enough to buy some groceries, formula and Pampers. My small and momentary twinge of doubt vanished. I thought *He's doing the best he can. It will get better. I just know it.*

It was the late spring of 1973 and I had six months to spend at home with my little baby. I firmly believed that it was only a matter of time before Bob won big at one of his tournaments and then I wouldn't have to go back to work at all. He was really good, everybody said so, and all he needed was a little luck on his side. But until then, we had to make some sacrifices. There were no new clothes for me now that the baby was born, since entry fees, bowling balls, bowling shoes and shirts all cost money— money that would one day pay off as long as I was patient and believed in him. And I had no problem with that; he won small pots often enough that I knew it was only a matter of time before he'd win the Big One. Everybody said so.

Until then, I was happy with every day I had with my baby. The first thing in the morning, I'd open the window near his crib and let the fresh air in. The warm sun shone through the open picture window and I loved the fragrance of spring flowers wafting up from the garden below our apartment.

John slept a lot, as newborns do. I would lay on the bed with him asleep on my chest and watch the Watergate hearings, which had just begun and were televised daily. The enormous scandal of the Nixon Administration was galvanizing, and like watching a train wreck in slow motion, I couldn't stop tuning in to the hearings as our government unraveled. I would whisper to my sleeping infant, *"This isn't how the world really is. It's a really good place. It's just a few people who do bad things."*

As I thought more about the corrupt Nixon administration, I could see that oppression doesn't exist without the tacit agreement of the oppressed, that somewhere along the line the public gave up or gave in to our oppressors. Our spirits broken, we accepted their corruption just as we accepted their domination over us. And if the personal was the political, then oppression began at home, behind closed doors, with no one to know what was really going on but the people who lived within.

That thought gave me a brief chill. But then John stirred again and the icy feeling up and down my spine gave way to the intense loving warmth I felt for my little boy. "It's going to be okay," I told him. *It's going to be okay,* I told myself. But deep inside, I wasn't so sure. My life had never felt so perfect, but it had never felt so false either. Something wasn't right, but I had no idea what was wrong.

As our government was imploding on national television over the months that followed, I created a happy, cozy routine for my baby and me. Every day, after Bob went off to bowl, I got John up, then bathed, clothed and fed him. I held him and danced him around the apartment to the music of the Spinners, Lou Rawls or the O'Jays. Sometimes, I read him poetry.

Before lunch, I would take him out for a walk in his stroller, sometimes up to Broadway to look in the shops, to the library for books and free magazines or to a nearby park to sit in the sun.

Sometimes when John and I were out walking, people would stop to look into the stroller and admire my baby. There were a few times, however, that weren't so pleasant.

One day as I was waiting for the light to change, an older woman walked up beside me and leaned down to peer into the stroller. Then she rose up with her back stiffened and looked at me. "Is that *your* baby?" she asked while peering down her nose at me.

"Yes, he is! Isn't he darling?" I said proudly. The woman looked me straight in the eyes, spat on the ground and walked away.

Another time, I was at a bus stop downtown carrying a three month old John, when a woman peered at him and then at me, and asked me if he was my baby.

"He is indeed!" I said. Buses were coming and going, inhaling and exhaling people, but my bus hadn't arrived yet.

"Do you know that means you have the blood of a nigger flowing through your veins? You have lain with the Devil and he is now in you and your nigger bastard child."

I was stunned and a little bit frightened. There, standing in front of me, was the face of ignorance, prejudice, and self-righteous rage. Someone like that could do anything—anything at all—and feel convinced that they were doing the right thing. Not just the right thing, but the necessary thing, to—in her mind—rid the world of darkness.

Where was my bus? Get me home, away from this woman who thinks she can spew hatred at me all she wants. What a bitch, what an ignorant, nasty bitch.

A young black man, standing near, overhead her terrible words and walked up to me. He was young and very big. He looked at the woman and said, "You talking to my mom? Did I just hear you talking about my little brother?" He stood up tall and puffed out his chest.

The woman looked up at him, told us both we were damned to go to hell, and scurried away, with her head down, like a rat.

I thanked the young man and he beamed at me. "No problem, mama. You don't have to put up with that kind of shit as long as Tyrone," and he pointed to himself, "is around." We both laughed and John began to wiggle and squirm.

At that moment my bus came and he helped me get on. "You take care now," he said as the bus door closed.

"Thanks, Tyrone! I may need you again and if I do, I hope you'll be right around the corner to protect me and my little one!"

I waved at him as the bus pulled away. Then I held John up to look in his eyes and said, "Wow. There's a whole lot of crazy and a whole lot of nice out there, huh?" With that, John spit up in my face.

As my mother had done when I was a child, Bob also brought music into my life. But rather than my mom's traditional jazz favorites, Bob introduced me to old black spirituals. To my surprise, I discovered that Sam Cooke had sung in a gospel group called the Soul Stirrers before he had recorded "You Send Me," the song that had riveted me when I was in the first grade, playing with Yolanda and watching American Bandstand.

Bob took me to many storefront churches, where the toilets rarely worked and there was no fresh air but where the singing was divine and the spirit was dancing in the aisles. Of course, I stood out since I was always the only white person in whatever church we went to. Sometimes the minister would ask if there was anyone present who needed to be saved, looking straight at me. I wasn't about to go up to the altar, have my head slapped to dislodge the devil, spit the evil out and then fall to the floor in a spasm of ecstasy, as others would do.

Instead I'd just say, "Oh, no thanks. I'm Catholic," hoping that would explain everything.

Regardless of the attempts to save my weary soul, I loved going to those little churches because of the music. Those voices were the true origins of the blues, jazz and rock 'n' roll—slave songs with hidden meanings, key words or phrases alluding to routes of escape for slaves, all couched in the language of the Old Testament. In the churches, the singing soared and the repetitive phrasings brought hypnotic happiness to the congregants. As the church reached a fever pitch of ecstasy, someone would jump up and speak in tongues, shouting unintelligible words to the sky. Then another person would jump up and "translate." The first time this happened it scared the crap out of me and I wanted to leave. But Bob explained what was happening and I calmed down.

"It's the spirit," he'd say. "The Holy Ghost coming down on people with lightning bolts of joy!"

"Jeez, we couldn't even whisper in Mass," I'd said, "let alone shout." What a diametrically opposed attitude toward the expression of faith.

Bob sang bass and sometimes he'd pull a few friends together to do quartet singing in one little church or another. And while his voice was quite good, he had little faith in his ability to sing and never felt free to just relax and let the spirit move him. Often he would refuse invitations to sing despite urgings from the congregants, his singing friends and me.

However, he would sing at home along with his records of old spiritual quartets: The Swan Silvertones, Dixie Hummingbirds, The Staple Singers, The Might Clouds of Joy, The Sensational Nightingales and The Pilgrim Jubilees. Most of the songs were *a cappella* and were utterly compelling in the searing soulfulness of their voices. Bob's bass voice was as good as any, even if he didn't believe it when I told him.

As the years went on, I would often listen to these records on my own, when Bob was gone bowling and John was out playing. There were times, especially when we were once again skirting the loss of our electricity or phone or both due to nonpayment, when these songs would directly affect my heart. Listening to those spirituals, I genuinely felt, if only for a brief moment, what it was like to be black, poor and hopeless.

For a few moments, I understood exactly what Maya Angelou meant when she wrote *I Know Why The Caged Bird Sings*. When I was feeling down, I sometimes felt the Holy Spirit—whatever that was—heating up inside me. I *did* know why caged birds sung. Bringing beauty like bird song into one's heart was the only way to stay sane and survive, especially when you couldn't change the one thing that brought so much oppression—the color of your skin.

But of course, I wasn't black or Latino or Asian. I was just a white girl feeling white guilt for the advances my European descendants enjoyed on the backs of African slaves. I often thought about what "white guilt" meant and wondered if there was some element of it in my relationship with Bob. That was a hard possibility to ponder. All I knew was that I, too, was feeling a sense of utter oppression and hopelessness. It seemed that no matter what I did, things would never change because I had no control over who I was or what I was doing.

But then again, wasn't that the idea? I'd turned myself over to Bob, so that he could take control of the life I couldn't control—my own.

CHAPTER 27

WOMEN WANTED

BOB WAS A mystery to me—one moment he was loving and protective, the next he was domineering and terrifying—but that baffling quality was a large part of his attraction. When he was loving and would envelope me in his large arms to hold me close to his broad chest, I felt completely safe. His large hands would enfold mine and I would always comment on the length of his fingers and how the palm sides of his hands were so much lighter than the top side.

"That's because us black folk didn't walk around with our hands palm side up when we were evolving in Africa," he explained one day. "We adapt to our surroundings. You're white all over because your ancestors came from Europe where the weather wasn't so hot. It's all adaptation."

"Then," I said, following his logic, "that just brings home the fact that race is irrelevant. We're all human and our looks come from adapting to the climate we lived in."

I was amazed by his intellect. He had told me that he skipped several grades in school and that when he was in high school, he was offered a scholarship to an elite boarding school run by nuns in upper Florida. His mother didn't want him to go and that was the end of that. I understood the anger and frustration he must have felt.

We often had long intellectual conversations. Generally, they were informative and expansive, as we shared our views of issues or imparted wisdom from both sides of our age and color differences.

But sometimes during these conversations, he would suddenly change and begin berating me, declaring that I was stupid and my opinions weren't worth discussing.

Those were the times when he became that other self, the one that frightened, upset and confused me. He would accuse me of ridiculous things, berate me for the way I looked or demean me in public. Never knowing which Bob he would be from moment to moment caused me to swing from fear to relief, from depression to joy. And the relief and joy were such a profound change from the fear and depression that they became all the more meaningful and valued.

What could have happened to him in his childhood to make him so unsettled, I wondered? I knew his mother had been savage, controlling and brutal with him. How could he possibly rise above the sad beginnings to his life? Convinced that the abuse he had suffered explained the abuse he inflicted, I was determined to help him reach a sense of security and safety, remembering what my mother once said—that the ones who are the hardest to love are the ones who need it the most. Loving Bob and bringing peace into his life would be my never-ending challenge—and it was a challenge I became convinced that only I could conquer.

I remembered spending that first night after bringing John home from the hospital, calmed that the electricity and phone were now working, but I got no sleep. Every time John stirred in his crib or cried out, I was up like a flash to take care of him. Bob slept soundly throughout the noise and clamor. I thought that this was how things were with a new baby. The mom struggles to get enough rest while the father sleeps soundly.

On the second night home from the hospital, as Bob was leaving for league bowling, I gathered up John and my bag full of baby things. I waited for Bob at the door, as I had done every night prior to his birth, to join him for a night at the bowling alley. He was carrying his purple bowling bag and was fumbling for the keys in his pocket.

He looked at me, the baby bag and his little son and said, "Where do you think you're going?" His voice was cold and his eyes frigid.

"I . . . I . . . always come with you for league." He said it with such coldness that I felt like I'd been struck with baseball sized hail.

We stood in the dark hallway, which was feeling darker and colder every second.

"Not with this baby you don't. You can't come with me anymore now that you've got him."

I was thunderstruck. While Bob was not overly involved in caring for his son, I had no doubt that he loved John. I figured that as an only child to a psychotic adoptive mom, he just didn't know what to do.

"Why not? I don't understand."

"It's not difficult, dummy. You can't come with me now that you have a baby. You will stay home."

With that, he opened the door and left.

I was so shocked and confused by what had just happened that as the door closed behind him, I stood there shaking so badly that I put John down in his crib so I wouldn't drop him. Then I sat down in the rocking chair and as the sun went down, I rocked slowly in the growing darkness.

I looked out the window at the glimmering lights of downtown Seattle. *Where am I? What am I doing here?* I simply didn't know if his actions were right or wrong, if Bob's treatment of me was normal or off the rails.

As the apartment grew darker and the lights of the city brighter, John started to fuss, so I picked him and we sat together in the chair. I rocked him back and forth, sang him little songs and recited a haiku I'd memorized for him:

> *Broken and broken*
> *Again by the sea*
> *The moon so easily mends.*

He fell asleep, his long eyelashes resting on the small pads of his cheeks. I put him back in his crib and went to bed as well.

I hadn't heard him come in, but Bob was there in the morning, looking sullen and irritated. As soon as I started scrambling his eggs, he started in on me.

"You can't do any of the things you used to do with me. You've got a baby now."

"Well, actually, he's our baby." I poured myself a cup of coffee and sat opposite him at the table. John was lying in his crib watching as a little mobile I'd made of colored paper slowly twirled over his bed.

"You wanted this," he barked at me. "You wanted this baby."

"And so did you. What is that supposed to mean anyway?"

"Things will never be the same," he said, looking petulant and angry.

"Of course they'll never be the same." I took a sip of the coffee. It was too hot and burned my lips. "We have a family now."

He slammed his big hands down on the table. Coffee spilled out of my cup. It had been months since I'd seen Bob's temper, and now, out of nowhere, he became the Bob that frightened me so, the Bob I thought I'd never see again.

"That was your decision, not mine."

My eyes narrowed and despite my growing fear—that feeling of my blood turning to ice in my veins—I fought back.

"What is the matter with you? Are you jealous of a little baby? Do you think I don't love you anymore simply because I have another person to love and take care of?"

His face hardened. I didn't know what was going to happen next. I walked over to John's crib and picked him up. Holding our baby in my arms, I said to Bob, "I'm *not* giving this one away."

"Who asked you to?"

"I'm just saying. You better shape up and accept the fact that we have a sweet little boy now. He needs you to be a good father to him, and that's what I expect you to be as well."

Wham! Bob slapped me hard and I fell backwards, hitting the floor, still holding John. He stood over me and sneered through clenched teeth, "Don't you ever speak to me like that again. Do you understand, bitch?"

I struggled up to my feet to face him, my cheek stinging, squeezing little John close to my chest to protect him.

"Oh yes," I said to Bob, looking him straight in the eye. "I think I understand you very well."

He slapped me again, and again I fell, tightly holding John. Before I could even get up, he grabbed the car keys and left, slamming the door behind him.

I sat on the floor for a long time, holding my baby, wondering what I was going to do. *Do I stay or do I go? And if I leave, where would I go? Is this how relationships and parenthood start? It is, after all, a huge change and an enormous responsibility. Perhaps it just takes time, lots of time, to adjust.*

I spent the rest of the day caring for John and wondering if Bob would ever return. I startled each time I heard a car door slam, each time I heard the front door open three floors below, and each time I sensed someone coming up the stairs.

As the day became night, I went into the bedroom and prepared John for bedtime. A last bottle of formula, a clean diaper and into his little P.J.'s and we were both ready for bed.

The apartment was dark and silent. John was asleep beside me in the bed. I was lying there, staring at the ceiling, trying to wake up from the nightmare life I had walked into so willingly and naively, when I heard the door open and close. Immediately, my heart began to race. He made no sound and my fear grew in intensity. All sort of crazy thoughts sprinted through my mind. *Was he loading a gun? Removing a hunting knife from his belt? Was I about to be murdered?*

While I was paralyzed with fear, I was also angry. I wanted to loudly demand that he tell me where'd he'd been all day, to berate him for worrying me so and to scream at him for causing me such anxiety. But I thought better of it. What good would it do? Whatever I did, it seemed I always lost.

He came into the bedroom and I sat up and faced him. Might as well look him in the eye, I thought, before he destroys me. But he sat on the side of the bed, took my hand and held it. I gently removed my hand from his, and lay back on the bed. I continued to look at the ceiling and reached for John with my other hand to assure that he was safely sleeping.

"I'm so sorry," Bob said softly. "I don't know what got into me. I didn't mean it." I remained silent, still staring at the ceiling. "Please believe me," he said. "Please. I am so sorry. It will never, ever happen again."

I turned to look him in the eye. The room was dimly lit from the street lights. Yet even in the relative dark, the whites of his eyes appeared to glow. That blue-gray light from the street illuminated his face and I studied it for signs of what he was really feeling. He looked sincere, his eyebrows raised in contrition. But I'd seen that look so many times before.

"Really?" I said. "Really? That's what you said before. I don't believe you."

He turned towards me and leaned in to kiss me on the cheek. "I mean it," he said. "I do. I don't know why I did that, but I'll never do it again. I promise."

"Are you jealous of our baby?" I asked him again, knowing the truth in my heart.

He hesitated. The room was silent but I could hear sirens outside, getting louder and then fading away. I heard cars passing on our street below. John was snoring softly.

"I'm not jealous," Bob said, breaking the silence. "But you don't do the things for me that you used to do."

"Like what?"

"Wash my back. Talk to me while I'm in the tub. Make sure I have what I need, like clean clothes." He stopped to think, as if he were reaching for ideas. "Now you fall asleep when we're watching TV."

I sat up again. In the darkness, I felt somewhat safe, reassured that if I couldn't see him well, he couldn't see me. "Are you serious?" I said. "You're a grown up. We have a child. What do you expect?"

"I *expect*," he said, his voice becoming strained, "things to be just the way they were."

My heart sunk. He had to be joking. Nothing else would explain the childishness of that remark. "But things are not the way they were. They never will be. We have a child now."

He looked stricken, as if the news that he was a father was devastating. I began to feel a little pity for him, realizing that having a child is an enormous sea change in life, especially for fathers. I swung my legs off the bed and sat next to him. He took my hand again.

"I'm not sure how to be a father," he said, his head hung low. "I lost mine so early. All I had was my mom."

And she had been a nightmare, using physical and emotional abuse to raise Bob. Did he expect me to use the same methods with our son? I had no intention of abusing my son, or of letting anyone else abuse him. John would be raised with love and compassion, with any correction to be meted out with care.

"You know," I said, "all you need to do is be loving and spend time with him. The rest of the stuff, like being a good example, will evolve." He looked wistful. "Does that make sense?" I asked.

"Yes. Yes, it makes sense."

The hour was late. "Move over," he said. "Put the baby between us and we'll all sleep as a family." He stood and got undressed as I scooted to the far side of the bed and moved John to the middle, then held up the blanket so he could get in.

Soon he was snoring loudly and John snored softly. But I couldn't sleep and continued to look at the ceiling until the street lights faded and morning light slowly lit the room.

Once again, life seemed to return to normal. I realized that in some ways, Bob was right. Taking the baby to a bowling alley every evening and weekend was not a good idea. The noise and cigarette smoke in a bowling alley was just not good for a baby. So I took to giving Bob pep talks before he left and then spent my evenings with my son. I knew that Bob needed to practice as much as he could if he was going to win the Big One. And once that happened, we'd be able to buy a house and live like normal married people. It was only a matter of time. In the meantime, even though I was practically a newlywed, I began to feel like a single mother.

When I worked at the printing plant before John was born, Bob came every payday to get my check. He paid the bills, gave me an allowance for grocery shopping and used the rest for bowling. There was little left for anything special or extra. I got John's clothes at Goodwill and economized as much as I could on food and necessities. We lived from paycheck to paycheck and always in the back of my mind was the worry that we would go broke, be evicted and have to live on the street.

When John was four months old, Bob got a job as a garbage collector for a small town just outside of Seattle. I didn't know he was looking for a job, or how he got it. It didn't matter. I was just ecstatic, since his bowling efforts were only taking money out of the house and bringing none in. Now my soon-to-expire unemployment income would be replaced with a real paycheck from a real job. However, the next month, Bob lost the job. He said the garbage collectors were joining a union and that one position had to be eliminated. Since he was the last hired, he was the first to go.

I had one month left to be on unemployment so reluctantly but diligently, I began to look for a job and for daycare. I couldn't let myself think about being away from John every day. But it was evident that Bob knew less than I did about caring for a baby, so I had to find some daycare. The thought was heartbreaking and intolerable, but I knew no other alternative. I'd find someone to watch John and Bob would be free to practice for his bowling tournaments during the day.

In those early days of feminism, many of the changes to bring equality to women had not yet occurred. The employment section of the newspaper still listed jobs as "Men Wanted" and "Women Wanted." The job opportunities for women were still limited to domestic help, secretary and teacher. There was no point in looking under the "Men Wanted," section, so I got out a pen and started circling any possible job a woman was trusted to handle.

There were several positions in "Women Wanted" that looked interesting. One was a secretarial position at Planned Parenthood. I called and got an appointment for an interview. Planned Parenthood? Slightly ironic, I thought. But a job is a job.

The clinic was on 16th and Yesler in Seattle's Central Area. I was greeted by an earnest looking young woman named Suki. She had me fill out on application and then took me on a tour of the clinic. My interview was more like a meet and greet with the bulk of my time spent being introduced to the staff. I met nurses, social workers, office assistants and the director. At the end, I was left in the director's office for a "chat."

She rose from her desk chair and shook my hand. "Donna," she said. "Donna Renton." I was delighted to detect an English accent.

She invited me to take a seat. Donna Renton was tall and rugged-looking, with an unruly head of pure white hair, reminding me of Margaret Rutherford in the 1950's Miss Marple movies.

As I took a chair, she said, "And your name is…"

"Lisa Jones."

"Well, Lisa, we are a big family here. We try to treat everyone the same, no matter what their job is. All of our clerical girls attend staff meetings and training sessions. We want everyone to learn about and understand human sexuality and reproduction."

There was a rumor circulating in the city that Planned Parenthood was actually performing abortions, and I asked Mrs. Renton about it.

"Donna. Please. Call me Donna."

"Okay, Donna, is it true that you do abortions here?"

"We call them 'terminations,' and no, we don't do them here. We refer women out for that. We counsel women, whether married or unmarried, about reproduction. We also provide prenatal services and postpartum support. Do you have a concern with the idea of abortion?"

I swallowed hard. I wasn't about to tell her about my shameful past. And it was indeed shameful. I'd been an unwed white girl who had a black man's child, and gave that child away. It didn't matter that I'd married him, it didn't matter that I had another child and was a good mother. What mattered was that I was considered a wanton, unclean woman who deserved to be shunned, even in the seemingly liberal world of Planned Parenthood.

If they knew the truth about me, they would shun me too, just like all the other agencies had done when I'd come to them for help.

"I wouldn't have one myself...I mean...I wouldn't have an abortion if faced with that choice. But I think women should be able to make their own choices legally."

She smiled. "How fast can you type?"

I was momentarily taken aback but recovered quickly. "I used to do 120 words per minute in business school, but I've been off work for a bit, so I'd say I can do 90."

"Lisa, I make quick decisions based primarily on instincts and my instincts are telling me that you are a fine, strong woman. Would you like the job?"

"Yes!" I said. *This was easier than I expected*, I thought. I couldn't wait to get home and share the good news with Bob.

"Then you're hired. See Melanie. She'll give you the details and have you fill out paperwork. Welcome to the Planned Parenthood family!"

Donna stood and gave me a hug.

Melanie, a bright young college grad with a degree in social work, was Mrs. Renton's assistant. She told me she hoped to work her way up to counselor. She was very pretty and extremely thin, with long blonde hair and no makeup on her blue eyes.

"Melanie," I asked, "Is Mrs. Rent...I mean Donna...is she from England?"

"Yes, she is. From London, I believe."

"Cool," I said. "*Wow!*" was more like it. Maybe I could have lunch with Donna at some point and talk about her hometown.

Melanie handed me W2 tax form. "After you fill this out, I'll tell you a little bit about the job and take you up to see your office."

My office? I thought. *Far out! I've never had an office before.* I finished the forms and handed them to her.

"You ready?"

"Yes. But for what?"

She laughed and said, "I'm going to show you around the clinic, take you to your new office and tell you about the job."

"Can you tell me about the job first?"

"Of course. You will be the secretary for our Training Department. There are four trainers and they work in the region which includes Washington, Idaho, Alaska, Montana and Oregon. They provide desensitization training for the social workers. They're a nice bunch."

"What does desensitization mean?" I felt like that might have been a naïve question but I really had no idea what it was. "I think I'll leave that up to Ralph to explain."

"Ralph?"

"Yes, Ralph McNeill. He's the director of training and he'll be your supervisor. So, are you ready for a look around?"

"Sure."

She showed me the clinical areas, the records room, lunch room, conference rooms and administrative offices. Along the way, she introduced me to the staff I hadn't already met, who were all young, eager social workers and nurses caught up in the new wave of feminism and the belief that women were in charge of their own lives and bodies. They seemed a positive and enthusiastic bunch indeed, and all extended a warm welcome to me.

"So Melanie," I said, "where's my office?"

"Oh, it's up the street in a different building."

"A different building? I don't understand."

"We've run out of space, so we leased some offices in a really nice office building up the street for the Training Department."

She led me out of the clinic and we started walking north on 16th, stopping to cross on Yesler. I was beginning to feel a tightness in my chest because this street was very familiar. We crossed Yesler and she pointed up the street.

"It's that building on the left, just past the trees. It's owned by an adoption agency, and we rent out the upstairs offices.

"Adoption agency? Which one?" I said, but I already knew the answer. "Medina Children's Agency. They do the hard adoptions, the children who are, you know, half black and half white. Have you heard of them?" "No," I lied. "Never heard of them. No need to." Shame and guilt rushed into me. How could I have told her the truth and expect that I'd still have this job? Yet, how could I deny the existence of my first baby, the one I'd held for such a short time and then allowed someone to take him away? It was a conflict of affirmation—could I acknowledge my first born son and remain confident that I'd have this job. I couldn't trust the answer to that question.

As we approached the building, I felt like I was walking through knee-high wet cement. By the time we reached the door, I started to sweat. But thankfully we didn't have to enter the Medina offices. There were stairs to the immediate right and I was beyond relieved when Melanie said, "Up you go!"

Melanie climbed the stairs, with me scurrying behind her. Once on the second floor, she pointed to the first room on the right.

"This," she said, "is your office." I looked inside. The far wall was taken up with a large document storage unit. Each shelf was stacked with different colored paper that I later learned were the various materials used by the trainers. To the left were a few filing cabinets and to the right, my desk—with a typing stand and an IBM Selectric typewriter. The walls were pink and there was a yellow poster with black flowers that said, "War is not healthy for children and other living things."

Melanie pointed to four other rooms. "These are the three trainer's offices, and then this big one is Ralph's. They're all out for a luncheon meeting but they'll be back soon. Perhaps you can meet them before you leave, but if not you certainly will when you start on....oh, when did Donna say you're going to start?"

"She didn't, but I'd like to start as soon as possible. I just need to line up daycare for my son, but that shouldn't be a problem." Since my mother had just quit her job as a bookkeeper in an elite floral shop, I thought it might be possible for her to take care of John for at least a couple of days per week.

"Oh cool. You have a baby? Good for you. How old is he?"

"Almost six months. I don't know how I'll get along without being with him every day."

"You'll be okay! You can have a family *and* a career!" Melanie beamed with pride at my moxie. *You don't know anything about me and my motivations,* I thought and then quickly admonished myself for being snotty. It was the mantra of women in the 1970's—you can have it all, but with the unspoken caveat that you will never get enough sleep for the next couple of decades and would be challenged daily to juggle the jobs of wife, mother, career woman, friend and daughter. I'm sure Gloria Steinem could do it, so I'd rise to the occasion too.

"I'll check with Donna if it's alright, but why don't you plan to come in next Monday?"

I was nervous and wanted out of the building. "That sounds good. See you then." I ran down the stairs, through the door and down the street to my car. I got in the car and sat there staring at the steering wheel. As I caught my breath, I wondered if things could get any weirder. *How am I supposed to work in the same building as the adoption agency I'd used? What if they see me and recognize me? What if they tell my boss that I was an unwed mother who gave birth to a black man's child? I'd lose my job, that's what. And I need this job.*

CHAPTER 28

WHAT HAVE I DONE?

I T'S HARD TO understand at times why odd coincidences and challenges come into one's life. First, I'd unknowingly moved into the same building where Bob lived. Then, a year later he saw my car on the first day of my job and slithered into my life again. And now, here I was, parked in my car in front of the building where I'd be working—just a short flight of stairs away from the adoption agency that marked the most painful experience of my life. I felt as if I were caught in a bizarre spider's web macraméd by a diabolical Earth Mother.

While I could have spent hours staring at the steering wheel and pondering the reason for inexplicable events, I decided I needed to just get on with things. Why I was offered a job housed in the same building as Medina Children's Agency was beyond absurd and a complete mystery. What in the world had brought me back to this very spot and for what reason? What mattered, however, was that I now had a job and I'd figure out how to deal with the challenge by simply keeping my head down and minding my own business.

Bob was thrilled that I gotten a job. He was eager to have a steady income that didn't involve him working at normal, everyday employment so he could continue working to become a professional bowler. I thought it best not to explain the inexplicable oddity of my new job's locale. Who'd believe it anyway? It was preposterous.

I spent the rest of that week preparing for the return to work. As I thought, my mother was pleased to be asked to watch John for me, offering to do so full time. This was a god-send, as finding day care was next to impossible, a pursuit that seemingly required an FBI investigation to make sure the daycare home was licensed, clean, had no complaints, was near-by and, most of all, affordable. Knowing my mother would have John was comforting and I felt a gratitude that was hard for me to express to her, but I tried.

I explained how to do his formula and what he didn't like to eat, his nap times and his favorite toy—a hand puppet we called Baby Beaver. I told her how grateful I was for her help.

"It's nothing," she said. "I'm not working just now anyway."

"Well, I want you to know how much I appreciate it."

"All right then," she said looking slightly embarrassed. She wasn't accustomed to gratitude from me and certainly not from my father. "Now what else do I need to know to take care of the baby?" She looked around at supplies that I'd brought in the baby bag.

"Just that I love you," I said, giving her a hug. She stood straight and emotionless. "Are you okay?" I asked.

She shrugged and looked down at the floor. "I'm okay. It's just been a long time since I've been hugged."

I felt instantly tongue-tied and so, in response, I hugged her again.

The following Monday, Bob drove me to work. I was so nervous I thought I might throw up, but I concealed it as best as I could.

"Good luck," he said, giving me a kiss on the cheek. "I'll be here to pick you up at 5:00, okay?"

I entered the building and quickly climbed the stairs. Melanie had come up from the clinic to greet me. The training staff was all there, sitting in their offices. Melanie introduced each to me.

Ralph McNeill, my new boss, was a short man with a neatly trimmed moustache and beard, a sort of Americanized Hercule Poirot. He shook my hand a little too long for my liking.

"Welcome! Welcome! Welcome! We are so glad to have you on the team. I want you to meet the other staff and get acquainted with your office and then I'll be spending some time with you later this morning to orient you to the department and to what we provide." He was nothing if not enthusiastic.

Susan Yoshita, short and bristling with energy, greeted me warmly. She explained that she was trained as an educator, but was also a nurse.

"I'm one of the trainers and we travel a lot. You may not see us for weeks at a time and I suspect you'll come to enjoy those quiet times," she said, giving me a wink.

Karen Epstein was of medium height, with thick, curly hair. She took my hand, looked deep into my eyes and said, "I'm so glad you're here. We need someone like you." When I looked a bit puzzled, she hastened to say, "That is, we need someone organized and efficient to keep us on track!"

Gerald Hilterman was tall and lanky. He greeted me warmly and explained that he'd retired from the CIA and was now working for Planned Parenthood as a diversion from being home alone and bored. I guess going from espionage to human sexuality was not a big leap.

Then Melanie spoke up. "So, I'm going to leave you in their able hands and let me know if you need anything." She was gone in a hurry, back to the clinic and her own job.

During that first day, I learned the tasks and expectations of my duties, including making appointments and travel arrangements for the trainers, how to keep the education materials up to date, typing memos and letters, filing, answering the phone—the usual office stuff.

After showing me around the offices and explaining where things were, Ralph invited me into his office and closed the door. He asked me to sit down, and then pulled his own chair uncomfortably close to mine. I moved my chair a bit away, and he again moved his chair to be closer. I felt rattled but figured this familiarity was part of the training department's zeitgeist.

"We do 'desensitization' work with Planned Parenthood counselors throughout Region IV."

I nodded and tried to look like I understood what he was saying, but it all sounded like a foreign language to me.

"Our counselors are expected to talk with clients about the intimate details of their sex lives," he said. "We provide a means to desensitize them from the details a client might disclose. It wouldn't do, for instance, for a counselor to gasp in horror if a client said they enjoyed using gerbils in their sexual life."

I swallowed hard and my eyes grew large with shock. "Gerbils?"

Ralph laughed. "Don't worry. You'll get the desensitization training too!"

I wasn't at all sure that I wanted this training. Combined with the Medina offices being downstairs, I was beginning to think I'd jumped too soon at an opportunity for a job. But then I reminded myself that there was a bigger goal in mind—that of supporting Bob in attaining *his* goals. I felt I was a strong woman and might be the only one on earth that could make a difference in his life. And if I was successful, what an accomplishment that would be! I would have brought happiness to my husband and molded a good father for my son.

I noticed Ralph was still talking.

"...and we have films from the Glide Foundation that we use. You've heard of the Glide Foundation?"

"Yes, I have heard of them," I answered, stumbling from my daydreaming back to the conversation.

Ralph sat back in his chair. "Well, tell me what you know."

"I know that Glide was once a church in San Francisco, but that it sort of changed in the Sixties into a social change sort of place."

"Ha!" Ralph laughed. "A social change sort of place indeed! Glide is almost too liberal for us, but not quite!" He looked at me for a response so I tried to appear curious but I was feeling like I just wanted to go home and change a diaper or something.

"Glide has done a set of videos on human sexuality that are our primary tools in desensitization. We have films about masturbation, sex between disabled people, lesbian sex, men-on-men sex, aging sex – you name it!"

I wondered if I should ask about sex with gerbils, but thought better of it. He continued, "The idea is to provide our counselors with so many intimate details of sex and all its variations, that when they face a client who describes—shall we say—unusual sexual practices, the counselor won't react in horror and will, in fact, provide service to the client without judgment. Does that make sense?"

I considered lying, and saying that it did, but instead I decided to be honest. "Well, no," I confessed. "It doesn't make much sense now, but I imagine it will as time goes on."

"Well put!" Ralph said, stroking his beard. "You will indeed be required to watch all the films and read all our materials. This'll be especially easy for you since we're gone so much. I'll show you how to set up the film projector and want you to feel free to read any of the books on our shelves, and of course, familiarize yourself thoroughly with our training handouts!"

This is more than a mere job, I thought. *This is an opportunity to learn something new, not necessarily a topic I'd have picked as an elective in college, but nonetheless, I was being given the chance to be involved in cutting-edge sexuality and women's rights issues. The experience might make me somewhat progressive and modern, a well-rounded woman.*

At the end of my first day, Bob picked me up as promised.

"So, how was it?" he asked as I settled into the car.

"Okay. Different. Nice people." I couldn't look him in the eyes, for fear he'd see that I wasn't being truthful, so I stared straight ahead and feigned nonchalance.

"That doesn't sound very enthusiastic."

"I'll be enthused later. Right now, I'm trying to adjust to being gone from John all day and learning a new job. It's a lot."

He pulled the car over and stopped. "You don't miss me too?"

I flinched, expecting him to hit me. He had taken to punching me hard in the chest, spontaneously, when we were in the car and I wanted to avert another assault. So I said what he wanted to hear. "Of course I missed you as well. More than anything."

Why am I doing this? Why am I lying to placate him for fear he might hit me?

"I missed you too!" Bob said with a wide smile and then he resumed driving. It wasn't unusual for him to be menacing and then instantly switch to innocuous civility. And when he did, the instant rush of fear and the equally instantaneous calm always left me unsettled. I never knew what his reactions, or mine, would be.

But that evening, everything was fine. We picked up John, drove home, and had a good dinner and then Bob went out to bowl and I took care of my little boy.

In the whirlwind of learning my job I discovered quickly that I had little time to think about the adoption offices downstairs. I read all of Planned Parenthood's training handouts—about chlamydia, warts, herpes, birth control, dryness, impotence. And in doing so, I began to feel like I was gaining a modicum of special knowledge about special things.

I watched all the films but, thankfully, didn't see any gerbils. With the first few films, I was shocked and somewhat sickened by the seeming ugliness of the people and mundanity of their sex lives, but slowly I came to understand. Ugly and mundane were the norm; images of Rock Hudson chasing Doris Day around a sofa were fantasy. In time, I came to understand that sex was merely a part of everyone's lives. It was like breathing.

Just before he left for a training session in Idaho, Ralph handed me a large book and suggested I read it while they were gone. The book was a collection of Victorian pornography. Naturally as soon as photography was invented, folks started taking pictures of sex. There were a lot of photos of fully dressed men with small, naked children; women and German Shepherds; women with women and men with men; and group sex. Every kind of sexual act I guess one could imagine was displayed by the rollicking Victorians.

When they returned from their trip several days later, Ralph pulled me aside and asked what I thought about the book. I tried to feign sophistication. I said, "While the subject matter was intriguing, the photographic skills of the time were a bit—would you say—limited? Everyone looked stilted but I'm sure they were enjoying themselves."

Ralph eyed me with an appraising expression. "You are learning quickly, Lisa. This must be what you were meant to do." Did he mean learn about sex?

"Well, thank you. I am indeed proud of my secretarial skills." By the look of disappointment on his face, I could see that wasn't what Ralph wanted to hear. He was beginning to creep me out.

I attended all of the monthly staff trainings. Despite the fact that the clerical staff was not clinical staff, we were strongly encouraged to participate in their trainings.

I learned about values clarification and role playing, avoiding sexually transmitted diseases and teenage sex. The two female trainers, Karen and Susan, took my education several steps further. After getting all the required permissions and clearances, Susan took me to a local hospital to watch three hysterectomies. Rather than feeling grossed out, the experience was astounding, leaving me with a short-lived desire to be an operating room nurse.

After work one evening, Karen took me to a private residence where a number of women gathered to learn about self-breast exams. This was new and heady stuff in 1974 and I began to swell with pride that I now had these experiences within me.

And then there was the break-in.

Coming upstairs one morning, I saw my typewriter cover on the hallway floor. *What on earth. . .* I thought. Then I entered my office. My typewriter had been knocked off the typewriter stand and lay broken on the floor. The case of handout materials was turned over and the papers scattered. I checked the other offices. Each had been ransacked. Desk drawers had been yanked open, the contents rifled through and tossed about. Books were swept from their shelves. I was breathless with shock and with the feeling that I'd been somehow violated.

A woman from the Medina offices came upstairs to tell me that there had been a break-in, that their offices had also been turned over and that she'd called the police.

I didn't recognize her face.

She said, "The police will want an accounting of what you think may be missing." She looked around and said, "It looks like your area wasn't ransacked as badly as ours. Would you like to come down and see?"

"Oh, heavens no!" I replied and she looked surprised. I couldn't possibly have gone down there and potentially be recognized. I tried to recover and stammered,

"I...I...think it will just upset me further. I'm sorry."

"No problem," she said. "I completely understand. Let me know if you need anything, okay?"

"Sure," I said. "Thank you."

Ralph, Karen, Gerald and Susan arrived within minutes of each other. I asked each of them to examine their offices to determine if anything had been stolen. All said they couldn't identify anything missing. It seemed that the break in might have had nothing to do with stealing. It was more malicious, almost political.

When I told Bob, however, he didn't seem upset about it. He calmly philosophized that these things happen and that since I was okay and no one was hurt, it just wasn't a big deal.

But it was a big deal to me. Bob didn't know Medina Children's Agency troubling connection to my past, much less that it was right downstairs. But the incident had brought me face-to-face with someone from Medina. It shattered my hope that I'd never be seen and possibly recognized by one of them. As a result, I held my secret even closer and tried hard to be invisible.

Only a few weeks after the burglary, I was alone in the building, working late. I had bid everyone good-bye in my office, and heard the last of the Medina staff locking up the front door and starting their cars.

I was enjoying the quiet while I finished up my work when I heard a noise downstairs. It was a thud or a bang coming from the Medina space. I had to think quickly about what to do. I thought I should check things out before I called the police. A dumb decision as I look back on it, but at the time it seemed sensible.

I grabbed a broom from the janitor's closet. I thought that if I were confronted by a burglar, I would beat him with the broom handle. With my breath held in frightened anticipation, I quietly went down the stairs.

I entered the Medina office space and silently listened. I thought I heard the sound again, coming from behind a door. *Okay*, I thought, *this is it.*

I tip-toed over to the door, listening closely. There was no sound from within. I reached out to turn the knob and quickly pulled the door open.

It was a small room and there was no one in it. But it was full of file cabinets, large, small and in-between. I stood very still and then it hit me. I'm alone in the file room of the adoption agency I'd used to relinquish my baby. Oh my God. What am I supposed to do?

I was aware that I stood in a space forbidden to me—which made it all the more overwhelming. Should I breach the secretiveness and privacy of adoption by searching for information about my child? What if they found out? And it wasn't just the privacy of the agency I'd be breaching—it would be the privacy of my own son and his parents. This was a monumental decision. Whatever decision I made I would have to live with for the rest of my days.

But all that didn't matter. Fate was presenting me with the chance to get prohibited information about my child.

I walked over to a small index card file cabinet. I opened it, closed my eyes and pulled out a card.

I nearly fainted.

Unbelievable as it was, on the very first card I pulled out, I saw my name, the name of the couple who had adopted my baby, their address, and occupations. The name "Isaiah" was written on the top of the card.

There I stood, looking at the 3 x 5 card that told me everything about where my baby was and who he was with. I sunk to the floor, still holding the card while waves of shock, joy, grief and disbelief washed over me.

It was quiet in the little room, in the building and beyond, as if the entire city was holding its collective breath. The only sound I could hear was my own shallow breathing. Somehow, I separated from myself. My spirit floated near the ceiling, looking down on the physical me. I was in a huge bubble, in my own universe of time and space, holding the moment still. It was if I'd returned to the original primeval earth. Before me was an unending line of ancestors, all celebrating the virtue of what I'd just found. But, in the here and now, the enormity of what I'd just done felt like an anvil tied to my head.

What have I done?

I suddenly remembered that Bob would be there soon to pick me up. I grabbed a piece of paper from the top of a file cabinet and quickly wrote down the information, returned the card to its drawer, left the Medina space and returned upstairs.

Soon, I heard a car honk and looked out the window. Bob had arrived to take me home. I switched off the lights, locked my door, ran downstairs and got into the car. I must have looked pale and shaken because Bob took one look at me and asked me if I was okay.

"I'm okay. I'm just tired, you know, from working late and all."

"Are you hungry?"

"No. I mean yes. Yes, I'm very hungry."

"How about barbeque at that place up the street?"

"That would be fine."

For the first time since Bob introduced me to the soul food at Home of Good Barbeque, the hot links and peach cobbler were tasteless and bland. My senses were in shock and even the hot sauce was dull.

How was I going to live with this ill-gotten knowledge?

CHAPTER 29

CAN'T BELIEVE MY OWN EYES

I FEARED THAT someone somehow would know what I'd done in that small room in the Medina office and that I might be arrested, so I kept to myself even more than before, head down and avoiding eye contact. My co-workers in the Training Department thought I might be depressed and frequently asked me if I was okay.

"I'm okay. Just tired," was my stock answer to anyone who asked. And I *was* tired. I lay awake every night, going over and over how this serendipity could have happened and what it meant. It was eating me alive, knowing where my firstborn lived, who adopted him and what they did for a living—and yet having to stay away, keep my own counsel and my secret locked away, pretending everything was the same as before. But of course it wasn't and it never would be. My firstborn son was no longer gone and out of reach; I knew exactly where to find him.

Was it a blessing or a curse knowing where he was and who he was? Should I try to forget what I knew? But how could I? In the small hours of the mornings or in the quiet of the ladies room at work, I cried silently. I had such conflicting emotions— fear, longing, and misery—but I had to work hard to conceal them from everyone, especially Bob.

Whenever I was able, I would furtively take out the little piece of paper that I'd written the secret information on and stare at it. My imagination would run wild. I read his name over and over: Isaiah. It sounded so odd to me. Isaiah. A Biblical name. What an additional irony. Had I kept him, I thought about naming him Seth—the third child of Adam and Eve—who I always assumed went on to populate the earth without all the drama left behind in Eden. I stared at his parents' names and their address, but who were they? Was he okay? Did I do the right thing? I'd drive myself to distraction and then tell myself to stop thinking about it. Then I'd fold up the little piece of paper and slip it back into my wallet, where I kept it close to me at all times.

Bob was still trying to hit The Big One and I was still encouraging him. But he was changing. I don't know if it was the frustration of not winning or if it was something else. But he was becoming more and more heartless toward me and our son. He was gone so much, without me and John, and I began to get the creeping feeling that he was lying to me.

Our landlady, Mrs. Tito, had asked Bob to manage the building; it was a great opportunity since it wouldn't take much work, and we'd get free rent. We thought that would be a great way to save more money. And I got to know all of the tenants. I hadn't realized it at the time but almost all the tenants were young women, starting their careers, looking for boyfriends, or going to college. I was the only one with a husband and a baby.

It was hot that summer of 1974. Everyone in our apartment building had their windows open to catch some cross ventilation. One hot day, Bob was next door visiting with Susan and her mother, who was a rather dour and eccentric woman. Susan was my age. She was petite and had long dark hair and fair skin. She struck me as a sweet girl, close to her mother, with no big plans for herself other than saving money to buy a big fancy lamp for their apartment.

Our phone rang and I answered it. It was Bob's friend Rosey on the line. Since the windows were open and Bob was right next door, I leaned out my window and looked into Susan's opened window to let Bob know he had a call. There he was standing near her doorway, kissing her and groping her behind. My blood instantly turned to ice.

"You've got a call," I said, my voice flat and emotionless. His hand fell from her butt and they both jerked around. Susan gasped and clapped her hand over her mouth. Bob just looked at me with a curious combination of disinterest and fury.

I ducked back into our apartment, went into the bedroom and sat on the edge of the bed. I heard Bob come in, pick up the phone and have a casual and jocular talk with Rosey, as if having his hand on Susan's ass and kissing her was no big deal. My thoughts raced. *How am I going to handle this?*

After he wished Rosey a good day and hung up, it was silent for a moment in the living room, as if he were standing still, thinking the same thought – *How am I going to handle this?*

He walked into the bedroom, stood in front of me and looked into my face. "What's the matter with you?" he snarled.

I tried a bold approach. "What do you mean 'what's the matter with me'?" *Was he completely out of his mind? I knew what I saw and couldn't imagine a response from Bob other than "I'm sorry. I made a mistake. Won't happen again."*

"I want to know what is wrong! You thought you saw me kissing Susan, didn't you?

I shouted, "You *were* kissing her. And fondling her butt."

He puffed up like a blow fish and his eyes bulged. "I figured that was what you thought. That's the kind of mind you have. Suspicious and hateful. Did it occur to you that I was merely comforting her? Her boyfriend dumped her. She was crying and needed comfort."

"Comfort, my ass," I said.

Wham. He slapped my face with such force that I fell off the bed to the floor.

"How dare you accuse me? Who do you think you are?"

"I'm your wife. Remember? I'm not your floozy neighbor. Who does *she* think she is?" My cheek stung badly and before I knew it, he pulled me up from the floor and hit the other cheek.

I was determined not to cry. But he went on bullying me, his voice belligerent and loud. On and on and on he went, close to my face, hissing that *I* was the floozy, the slut, the whore. That *I* was a terrible person to think that Susan would make a pass at him when he was only comforting her. That *I* had a dirty mind not him. That I was fooling around, not him. On and on and on until I finally gave in, because I couldn't take it anymore.

"Fine," I said. "Fine. Whatever you want me to believe. If you want me to think my eyes have deceived me, then fine. Just leave me alone."

But that wasn't enough for Bob. He had to win the big one.

"I demand an apology!" he said, his face still close to mine. "And when you've apologized to me, you are to go over to Susan's and tell her you're sorry for thinking she was flirting with me.

I couldn't believe it. "Are you joking?" I said.

He grabbed me by the throat and instantly I was swept back to the post office, to the time I first met him, when he confronted me on the street and choked me. He'd promised not to treat me that way again. But he had, over and over and still I stayed with him, worked for him, raised his child and babied him. What was wrong with me?

"You stupid bitch. You stupid whore. Susan is a decent woman, unlike you. She would never accuse me like you are."

I thought he had lost his mind. His hands tightened around my throat and I could barely breathe.

He threw me down onto the bed, got on top of me and pummeled me with his fists. Then he stopped, as if he'd been wound up and the spring had snapped. But his eyes were dark and evil again, and I was frightened for my life. If something happened to me, what would happen to my baby?

Bob followed closely behind as I walked down the hall and knocked on Susan's door. I was stinging with humiliation and my throat and face were throbbing with pain, but I knew if I didn't do as he said, that I'd be hurting even more.

She opened it slowly, and the moment she saw my face, her eyes went straight to the floor.

"Susan," I said, "I'm supposed to apologize to you for thinking I saw you kiss my husband and let him grope your ass. I guess I can't believe what my own eyes see. I guess I thought badly of you for what I thought I saw." I knew Bob was listening, so like a lobotomized cheerleader, I brightened my voice. "Can you ever forgive me for thinking so lowly of you?"

Susan looked shocked, as if I'd just belted out a Gregorian chant. Her eyes darted about and her hand gripped the door. She must have known Bob was nearby, but however insincere my tone may have been, she seemed immensely relieved to hear me bear the shame.

"Forgive you? Why...why...of course," she stuttered, raising her head to finally look me in the eye.

Her response threw me for a loop. I guess I must have been expecting her to reject my phony "apology," and offer me a sincere one in its place. Clearly, my words may have said I was the one who erred, but the tone of my voice and the look in my eyes made it clear—she had no right to be messing around with my husband.

Any woman with a shred of integrity would have got the point. Instead, as if she and Bob had cooked up this game together, she accepted my co-erced apology.

Now my mind and emotions were whipped into a frenzied maelstrom. Had I really misinterpreted what I thought I'd seen? Could I not trust my own eyes? My stinging face and throbbing throat told me one thing, but the seeds of doubting my own judgment and my own senses had been planted.

In the days that followed, I slipped into depression. I thought I'd been in bad situations before, but this one was growing in immensity. I thought I was smart. But I seemed to be stupid. I thought I could trust my own senses, but apparently I couldn't. I thought Bob was supposed to be "rais-ing" me but all I seemed to get were demerits and punishment. Is that what I deserved? Was he right and I deserved it?

I felt the tables turning. He was enslaving me and somewhere I believed I deserved it. After all, I *was* white.

I missed John terribly when I was at work, but when I was home I had to be careful I didn't show him too much affection. I felt like I had to walk a line between caring for John and making Bob feel the same amount of care and love. It was a replay of my childhood. I was used to being the pacifier, the one who got my parents to quit fighting by placating, making jokes, seeing to their wants and desires so they would quit yelling at each other. And here I was, doing it again.

The more I thought about my situation, the more I replayed my whole history with Bob in my head, which always returned to the baby I'd given up. Since finding out where he was, it took everything I had not to tell Bob—but I knew if I did, he'd only perceive it as one more male I was giving my thoughts and attentions to.

His irrational jealousy could appear out of nowhere. One time when Bob was taking a bath, he taught me just how important it was that his needs came first. He loved to have a long soak and I usually sat on the floor next to the tub and we'd talk about all sorts of things.

We were in the middle of a discussion about Watergate and the Vietnam War when I heard John crying in his crib. I got up to see about him.

"Where are you going?" Bob asked.

"The baby's crying. I'm going to see what's wrong." I left the bathroom and went to John. He needed a diaper change. After getting him into a clean Pampers, I laid him down, rocked him a little with my hand and he quickly fell back to sleep.

When I returned to the bathroom, Bob was out of the tub and drying himself.

"Here," I reached for the towel, "let me get your back." He pushed me aside and stomped into the bedroom.

"You pay more attention to him," he jerked his head towards John's crib, "than to me."

I stood holding the towel. I would have thought he was joking if I hadn't seen the look on his face. I thought I heard John cry again, and was suddenly frozen—go to John or listen to Bob? But it was only the muffled sounds of an ambulance. Bob pulled on a pair of pants with such force he was practically fighting them.

I tried to be gentle. "I thought we'd talked about this before. Remember? We have a baby now and we're taking care of him together." I realized that wasn't true. *I* was taking care of John. Bob was bowling. But I was determined to make him feel included.

Is this how fathers act? I wondered. I had no experience to draw on. My own father was emotionally distant, and very unhappy. And being unhappy, he had no time or interest in children. I learned early on to stay out of his way, and I also learned not to expect much from a father.

As for Bob, he didn't have much experience to draw on either. His father had died of a brain hemorrhage when Bob was seven. That's when his mother went off the rails, and took her insanity out on her little boy. Bob never stood a chance.

I understood the lack of loving parents in Bob's life and tried to cut him some slack. "It's just that now, I can't be in two places at once. If you both need me at the same time, at least for now I have to take care of John first. He's just a baby, and he'll be walking soon. Then we'll both be charging after him!" I tried to lighten things up a little to get him to laugh and see that all would be well in the end, but from the look on his face, I could tell it wasn't working.

"I'm no less important than I was before the baby was born," he shouted, throwing his towel at my feet for me to pick up.

And that's when I lost my temper.

"You need to grow up! You are a man, not a child, and it's my job to care for our baby."

Bob looked at me with something like confusion or surprise. I couldn't quite read his look and furrowed brows. I was concentrating on standing tall, balling up my fists, ready for a showdown.

"It's your job too. Perhaps if you'd pitch in you'd understand that it's simply not possible to be in two places at once, and that a grown man can take care of himself." I knew I was risking getting hit again, but it had to be said.

But he didn't hit me. He burst out laughing.

"You look so funny," he said. "Do you actually think I'm impressed with your stupid little show of... what would I call it? Defiance? Anger? You look like an idiot."

"How dare you laugh at me," I said. I tried desperately to hold on to my righteousness. I had a right to be irate and I had a right to be taken seriously, but I knew that by laughing at me, he completely disarmed me. "How dare you," I said through clenched teeth.

He just quietly put on a shirt and jacket and calmly announced he was leaving. He stood at the door and I went after him. His sudden change really threw me. I had no idea what was happening—was he leaving me? "Where're you going?" I asked him in a voice that betrayed my fears.

"I don't know." He knew he had the upper hand with me once again just by walking away.

"When will you be back?" I felt helpless, like a little girl again watching her daddy walk out the door, not knowing when or even if he'd return.

"When I feel like it." He slammed the door behind him.

Now I wasn't sure what was worse—being hit, or being left with growing anxiety and fear over what might come next.

I sat in the silence, remembering my parents' battles and what it felt like to never know what was coming next.

And then I started to giggle.

My parents and I were at the dining table, always the arena for their fights.

Every night, all three national news broadcasters presented the unedited gore and horror of the Vietnam War. I'm sure in households across the nation the news caused disagreements, arguments and debates. But at my house it caused outright battles.

"Those goddam gooks," my father would say. "Can't tell one from the other."

"That's precisely the point," my mother would counter. "Our soldiers can't tell a north Vietnamese from a south Vietnamese, so how do we know who to massacre?" My mother was deeply disturbed by the war and considered what was going on to be horrific.

"Who cares?" my dad shouted back. "They oughta line 'em all up against a wall and shoot 'em." The minute he said it, I could tell by the look on his face that my father regretted saying the words. Not because he didn't believe them, but because he knew they would start a huge fight. His eyes darted about and he reached for a cigarette, but my mom wasn't letting him off the hook.

"Now, there's an efficient way to end the war," she said sarcastically. "Just wipe them off the face of the earth. Oh, except Hitler tried that with the Jews, but there were just too many of them!"

The internal war of the Ulrichs continued unabated until my mother got up, picked up the bowl of mashed potatoes, walked over to my father and plopped the whole thing on his head. Then she smashed potatoes in his ears and removed his glasses to rub potatoes all over his face. Mr. Potato Dad!

My dad was so mad that I swore the potatoes on the top of his head were steaming.

That's where I stepped in.

"All right, you guys," I said. "If you line 'em all up against a wall and shoot them, then they'll be gone and you'll just have to find somebody else to fight with. Oh wait, you've got each other. Right?"

That brought an imperceptible smile to their faces and I knew what I had to do. Even though I also had strong feelings about the Vietnam War, and agreed with my mother, I wasn't about to side with either of them. It was my job to make a joke, or act silly to divert them so that their fights would end. But the Mashed Potatoes Incident was the first time I'd ever seen them get physical. It was time to put a stop to it before she served his face with gravy.

"I've got an idea," I said to my dad. "There's a bowl of salad, with Girard's dressing. You know how much Mom loves her salad."

With that, the scene went into slow motion. He got the bowl of salad, slowly walked over to my mom and plopped it on her head. She just sat there, unmoving and the tension grew unbearable. Suddenly she burst into laughter and my dad followed.

They just sat there at the table, laughing, the mashed potatoes still stuck to my dad's face and lettuce and tomatoes falling from my mother's hair. Before dessert, they cleaned each other's faces like happy lovers and I breathed a sigh of relief. Once again, disaster averted.

This is how I learned to placate and keep the peace—by being funny. I also learned to be hyper-vigilant, to constantly assess the mood in the house and adjust my behavior to help dispel any conflict. That proved a good training ground for life with Bob. It was second nature to me by then.

The memories of my parents' battles left me feeling rattled but strangely comforted. For all their fighting, I knew deep down that there was a lot of love and affection between my parents, so I assumed that the same was true of me and Bob.

But as the hours passed and the phone didn't ring and Bob didn't return, my fear and confusion returned. What if he never came back? Had he left me? Even worse, what if he did come back? What would he do? I watched the clock and listened to the silence as John slept soundly in his crib, my fear intensifying with every passing silent minute.

I got into bed and laid in the dark, fully clothed, listening to the sounds around me—car doors slamming, people laughing, a television blaring, the creaks of the building, doors opening and shutting—but none of the sounds were Bob coming back.

And then I heard his knees cracking. It was after 2:00 when Bob came home. I pretended to be asleep. He dropped his clothes on the floor, got into bed and was snoring within minutes. Only then did I feel safe enough to fall asleep.

CHAPTER 30

HIDE THE MAIL

REGARDED MY work as a source of solace. It was quiet there. I felt safe, but never dared to wonder why I needed to feel safe. Every day, I'd call my mom to see how John was doing, what he ate, and how long he napped. He was crawling around now, and her two dogs, Heidi and the newly adopted Samantha, followed him everywhere, like two furry nannies.

In the evenings, I would wait on the sidewalk in front of our building for my mom to arrive with John in the car. I could see him a block away and as soon as he saw me his little legs and arms would thrash wildly with joy. He was so obviously glad to see me that it made everything worthwhile.

I continued to hope that things would settle down for the three of us. And I knew that they would, just as soon as Bob made it. I still believed in Bob's dreams but I sensed that my enthusiasm was waning.

Sometimes, in the midst of daily living, I would take out the little piece of paper I kept hidden in my wallet and stare at what was written on it. His name was Isaiah. His address was nearby. His parents' names were Brian and Ginny Midkiff, and they were teachers. And their phone number was right there in front of me.

My feelings of guilt grew as I realized that by giving him up, I was depriving my second baby of his brother. Sometimes I told myself to stop looking for reasons to feel guilty and to just get on with it. But there were other times when I was so consumed with guilt and sorrow that I could barely function. My depression worsened and it was becoming more apparent at work.

At one point or another during those first months at work, each of my coworkers—Ralph and Susan, Gerald and Karen—individually took me aside to ask me if everything was okay. And it was always the same thing that was distracting me—the constancy of working right above the very place that had arranged for me to give up my baby boy. Since I couldn't possibly tell anyone what was really bothering me, I came up with normal-sounding problems to relate.

"I miss my baby."

"It's hard working, and being a mom and a wife."

"I'm worried that John doesn't eat enough."

"I'm concerned that he might get an ear infection, or pneumonia or shingles— anything."

All excuses were understandable to my work mates and I received heartfelt advice and support.

"There's a lot of research," said Susan, "about post-partum depression. I can get you something to read. It'll explain why you miss your baby so much."

Well, I thought, *I miss my baby because I love him more than anything on earth, but it's a sweet thought.*

"As feminists, we must figure out how to do it all—be a good mom and wife, plus have a fulfilling career," said Karen. I didn't have the heart to tell her that at the time feminism confused me, as she seemed so earnest and concerned about me.

Gerald, a lifelong bachelor, had nothing to offer other than, as he said, "a shoulder to cry on."

And I steered clear of Ralph, unless it was absolutely necessary to interact with him. He kept talking to me about sex, and sexually active adolescents and the role of liberal churches in releasing their parishioners from the bounds of propriety about sex. Everyone should talk about it, he said. Well, he sure did. He talked about it constantly. I found him creepy, so I didn't allow him to get me alone to offer advice or anything else, for that matter.

As before, Bob started coming to my job was to take my paycheck.

He would show up on payday, chat cordially with my co-workers, come to see me, get my check, have me sign it and leave. Everyone thought he was wonderful and often told me how lucky I was to be married to him. Eventually, he would no longer bother to have me sign them. He just forged my signature, cashed them and took the money. I was given an "allowance" that I could use for lunches and sundries. Otherwise I never saw my pay. Stupid? Yes. Naïve? Yes. Too trusting? Yes.

But it was very common in those days for women to defer financial matters to their husbands. I thought allowing Bob to handle our finances was a good idea. He understood money. I remember him flashing wads of money when I first met him. I was impressed. I thought it meant he knew how to get ahead and how to literally earn hundreds of dollars in cash—which seemed like so much money at the time. I felt protected. It seemed that having him oversee our finances was the best thing since I didn't have the experience or moxie to handle money. I only knew how to make it. But I quickly learned there was a fine line between protection and control.

As far back as I could remember money was the subject of nearly all my parent's fights. My mom always worked, as did my dad, but she handled the finances, paid the bills, bought the groceries and supposedly contributed to a savings account.

Since both my parents worked, I was considered a "latch-key kid." These were children who left for school in the morning and returned home from school in the afternoon to an empty house. When I was in elementary school, I was scared to be home alone, but as I got older, I watched American Bandstand religiously, danced by myself to the music and enjoyed the quiet before my parents got home.

But there was a little game my mom and I played. The game didn't have a name, but the rules were simple. When I got home, I was to retrieve the mail and immediately call my mom. She would have me read the return addresses on the envelopes and then would tell me which ones to hide and which ones to leave on the dining table. Her hiding place was always the top left drawer of her dresser, underneath her girdles.

As time went on, I learned that most of the envelopes that had windows on the address line of the envelopes were bills and that those were the ones that got hidden. Then packages started showing up and those, without question, got hidden in the back of her closet. As I added new packages, I noticed that most of them were still there, never opened.

When I made my daily call to my mom to read her the return addresses, she would say, "That one's OK. Hide that one. Hide that one. That one's OK."

Eventually I asked my mother what the hidden envelopes contained. She first told me it was none of my business, but when I was older, I insisted that she tell me during one of her daily envelope review calls.

"These are just bills for things I've bought that your dad knows nothing about and I don't want him to know about." I was confused.

"Like what?" I asked her.

"Oh...dresses, shoes, purses."

"But why wouldn't he want to know about that?"

"Because he's a cheapskate and never wants me to have anything."

"But you do have things!"

"Lisa, you need to mind your own business and leave these things to the grownups."

So I learned to just play the game and not ask any more questions. But one day when I was in high school, I forgot to hide the ones she'd asked me to hide. My dad came home from work, saw the mail and exploded. Perhaps he knew all along that she was buying things in secret. I don't know. I do know at dinner that night, holy hell broke loose. My father was furious with my mom. And my mom was furious with me.

Later she explained to me that she'd buy things, then unable to pay the bill, she'd borrow money from some finance company or other, then not be able to pay *that* bill. On and on she'd go, robbing Peter to pay Paul.

So that's what money came to mean to me—secrecy and fighting. As a result of her creative finance and the fights that it caused, I didn't want to control the money when I got married to Bob. Letting him have the control seemed a good solution and would, to my mind, prevent fighting—at least over money. I trusted him.

But maybe I shouldn't have. No matter how hard I worked or how much money I made, it seemed that we were always broke.

It took me a long time to recognize other irregularities as well.

We frequently had the power turned off or the phone disconnected. There was a period of three years, when John was two years old until he was five, that we had no phone at all. I came home from work one day to find my car gone. Bob said he'd sold it, but it wasn't registered to him and I never saw any money as a result of the supposed sale. I had no car for several years until he turned up one day in a dilapidated old green Chevy. It had a black vinyl top that was torn and the driver side door was held closed with a rope so that you had to enter from the passenger door. It frequently broke down.

It seemed that as I was earning more and more at work, we had less and less at home. I began to think that Bob was hiding things from me, just as my mom had hidden things from my dad. And if I was right, what was he doing with the money?

CHAPTER 31

MOTHERS AND MONSTERS

A S TIME WENT on, I began to mark my firstborn's birthdays in silence and sorrow. My secret grew with each year until I finally couldn't resist seeking him out. I was terrified to call or show my face at the door, but it wasn't long before I was stalking his home in the desperate hope that I would catch a glimpse of him.

My stalking began in increments. From my little piece of paper with the information where I'd written the illicit information I'd gotten that night at work, I knew that he lived in the Leschi neighborhood, an area of Tudor mansions and working class cottages. I drove by his house one day. The house was high on an embankment and was impossible to see clearly from the street. It looked small but it must have had an incredible view of Bellevue and Lake Washington.

But I didn't want to do anything to expose me or harm him. So I tried to keep away.

Yet obsession grew and grew until I was having dreams of my two little boys playing together. They ran in a field with grass so tall that I could barely see them. I could hear their laughter and watched as they tumbled and wrestled one little curly haired head after another popping up and then disappearing again in the grass. They would run up and throw their arms around me, panting, their little bodies hot and sweaty. The air was warm and thick with the smells of summer, the sun shining on the warm grass where we sat on an old quilt eating a picnic of bologna sandwiches, potato chips, Oreos and juice. We sang the songs I taught them—Moonshadow, Yellow Submarine and You Are My Sunshine. In these dreams we never left that field but just stayed until nightfall when we would lay on the quilt and count the stars.

I seemed to be slipping deeper into depression. My well-meaning coworkers constantly tried to counsel me, but I could only respond in vagaries—I didn't dare let them know what was really on my mind. After a year, I knew that as long as I worked there, I'd be torn up with memories of the son I'd lost. So I decided to find another job.

I left Planned Parenthood when John was eighteen months. I'd found a job as the secretary to the nursing director at a hospital on Capitol Hill. It was a much better job that offered health coverage for our whole family. I had a little office on the fourth floor of the hospital. There was a small window in one wall that opened into the large office of my boss. She and I used it to pass paperwork back and forth.

My boss, Margaret, was the Director of Nursing and while she was pleasant to me, she was a raging bull when it came to standing up for nurse's rights. She was a pioneer in developing nursing practice standards. I learned about healthcare and nursing issues from her and, for the first time, felt fully invested and involved in my job. Margaret often asked my opinions and allowed me to offer ideas and suggestions on how to make improvements in administrative organization. I got to know the head nurses on all of the floors as well as many patients. I especially liked to listen in on change of shift report, when patient information was passed from the current nursing shift to the oncoming shift. I not only got to learn about the patients, but learned fun charting terms like emesis, voiding and compliance. I was happy there and actually looked forward to going to work. Not only was I learning new things, but I felt that in supporting the Director of Nursing, I was truly involved in patient care.

The only drawback to my new job was that it was farther away from Leschi than the previous one, and with no car at that time, I had to end my shameful stalking of my little firstborn. But I didn't stop thinking about him or looking for him whenever I was in a crowd of people or in any public place. I'd only seen his face for a moment after he was born, but I knew I'd recognize him anytime, anywhere. I couldn't help but search faces wherever I went.

My mother was getting restive staying at home caring for John. She loved him, but she'd always worked and felt she needed to return to employment. She found a job as a bookkeeper for an interior design firm in downtown Seattle and was surrounded by beautiful fabrics and furnishings all day while the owner entertained her with catty stories about his clients.

Since she could no longer care for John while I worked, I found daycare for him in a lovely older home only a few blocks from my job. It worked out well to have him so close by and to know that he was well taken care of.

Although Bob never said anything about our first baby, I often wondered if he resented me for giving the baby up. Did he think about the baby? So far, his nascent role as a father to John was slowly evolving, and I wondered how the death of his adoptive dad affected his thoughts about what a father should be.

His adopted dad's name was Eddie. Bob told me that it was rumored in the neighborhood that Eddie was really Bob's biological father, but if it were true, Eddie never fessed up—maybe that's because Jeanette, Eddie's wife and Bob's adopted mom—had a temper that would have frightened a mafia kingpin. If Eddie had been screwing around and that's how baby Bob ended up in Jeanette's home, then it would certainly have explained a lot about how she treated Bob, who she called Bobby.

The house where Bobby grew up was on stilts, as were the other houses in the neighborhood, which was poor, predominately black and subject to flooding. Bobby played with his friends in the streets—rolling dice, spinning jacks and throwing balls. He claimed that his childhood was happy, but from what I heard, his childhood was anything but. And it seemed that things went from bad to worse when his father died.

When Bob was seven, Jeanette found Eddie slumped on the stairs that led to the second floor of their home. Bobby was outside playing marbles in the dirt street with his friends. Suddenly he heard sirens and looked up from his prized cat's eye to see an ambulance and the police race up and stop at his house. Bobby saw the ambulance men run into his home with a stretcher. He jumped up and ran into the house, his heart thumping against his little chest.

There was his father slumped on the stairs, his eyes open and staring and his face contorted into a terrible grimace. Bobby screamed out in horror and then his mother and the police shoved him out of the house without saying a word.

Bobby was terrified. Why did my dad have such a terrible look on his face? Why wouldn't they let me stay in the house? His thoughts raced and his heart pounded with terror. Even as he told me this story so many years later, Bob's hands would shake and there would be a look of fright in his eyes.

Eddie had died of an aneurysm but Jeanette told Bobby that the devil had taken him away, that the only dad Bobby ever knew was a bad man who deserved to die and that the grimace on his face was because he'd looked Lucifer straight in the eye and his face would stay frozen like that for all eternity. No one explained to Bobby that an aneurysm can happen to anyone, anytime. It must have seemed appropriate to them to use Eddie's sudden death as a lesson to Bobby: walk the road of righteousness or burn in eternity with sinners like his dad.

As was the custom in those days, a wake was held in the front room of the house, with the open casket sitting on a table, surrounded by candles. Bobby was not allowed to view his father and was instead told to stay in his room. He imagined all sort of horrors—that his dad had turned into a monster or a Cyclops or a zombie; that his dad would rise up from his casket, grab little Bobby and try to pull him back into the dead place; that his mom had actually killed his dad and didn't want Bobby to figure it out. He was overwrought with fear and loss.

After a few months had passed, Jeanette took seven-year-old Bobby to see his birth mother, Freddie Hill. Bob had been Freddie's thirteenth child and she had handed him over to the Jones family simply because she couldn't cope with so many children. Jeanette's motives for taking Bobby to his birth mother were unclear. Maybe she just wanted to be mean, or test his devotion to her. Or maybe she was hoping to give him back.

But if that was the plan, it failed before they'd even had a chance to knock on the door. When Freddie saw Jeanette come up her stairs holding Bobby's little hand, instead of opening her arms wide with joy as I would have done to see my lost child, she screamed "Get him out of here!"

"You shut your mouth!" Jeanette screamed back. She pushed little Bobby in front of her and then demanded that he make a decision.

"You gonna stay here with Miss Freddie?" Jeanette asked the little boy, who began to cry in confusion. She slapped his head and ordered him to stop.

"I don't want him. I don't want him. Get him out of here!" Freddie screamed even louder.

But Jeanette ignored Freddie and asked, more sternly this time, "You gonna stay with Miss Freddie? She's your mama, not me."

"Listen here, bitch," Freddie said over little Bobby's head, "I'm goin' tell you one more time—get him outta here!"

Jeanette let go of his hand, turned and went back down the stairs. Bobby followed behind her, his head cast down, kicking at rocks, to return to their house.

This story came out piece by piece over the first few years that I was with Bob.

When he'd tell me about it, I would get tears in my eyes but his face always remained passive and his eyes dry. It was if he were reading me the sports page. *Men don't allow themselves to express their feelings*, I told myself. *That's why he seems so detached.*

By the time I heard the whole story and put it all together, I realized how horrific and terrifying his experience was. I tried to imagine what it would feel like to have lost a father and then have your mother try to dump you on a woman who didn't want you. The desolation and sorrow must have been overwhelming for the seven year old Bobby.

My heart went out to him. Finally learning the extent of his sadness as a child, I believed that with lots of love and understanding, he could heal. I tried to be upbeat and supportive. I put little notes in his bowling bag telling him he was already a winner or greeted him with a fresh batch of homemade molasses cookies when he came home. I did whatever I could think of to make him feel safe, valuable and loved.

I wanted to feel hopeful for the three of us. As the mother and the wife, I would never stop trying to make Bob happy and heal the scars of his youth.

Even if he beat me now and then. He always asked for forgiveness and promised it would never happen again.

The last thing I would ever do was say, "Get him outta here." So each time Bob hung his head in shame, I instantly forgave him.

CHAPTER 32

WHITE MEN, BLACK TARGETS

IT WAS 1975, a new year for change and innovation. Bill Gates and Paul Allen founded Microsoft; the first episode of Saturday Night Live aired; the Vietnam War ended; and the price of a gallon of gas was 57 cents. And for Bob, John and I, it was another year in the quest to win the Big One and save money for a house of our own.

My parents returned to Sheridan, Wyoming for another year of construction work and asked Bob and I to house-sit for them.

I was elated. Even though it wasn't really ours, we would live rent free for a year and I was confident that we'd be able to save money so that on my parent's return, we'd have enough to put down on a house of our own. And John would have his own room.

I wasn't going to miss the apartment we'd been in the prior three years. All of the tenants, except us, were young women and I constantly feared a repeat of Bob's actions with Susan or one of the other seemingly cosmopolitan ladies of the building.

My mother was less stressed about this sojourn in Sheridan than she was the first time. Our move into their house went smoothly and I quickly set about decorating the smaller guest room for John. Not having money meant being extra creative with interior design.

I had several flat sheets with Sesame Street characters and I hung those on the walls, like wallpaper. I had a small book shelf that I painted cobalt blue to store his books and toys. His bed was a guest sofa bed that I kept open and piled with soft blankets and quilts. I left the rest of the house as it was, but kept it clean and tidy.

At dinner one night, I asked Bob, "How much do you think we'll be able to save while we're here?"

"Why don't you shut up about that?" he snapped. My stomach sank and I immediately lost my appetite. Where did that come from? I had been struggling with inexplicable dread during that time, and as it is with dread, didn't know where these feelings were coming from or why they were happening. The feelings would come out of nowhere and wash over me like a flood of glacial rivers. I just had a bad feeling— that's all I knew. I'd experienced feelings of dread most of my life. They just caught me off-guard and made me want to wilt, like a dying flower.

John was in his booster chair at the table, feeding himself scrambled eggs and grapes, smiling and giggling as toddlers do. I turned to look at him to anchor myself in the present. Then I turned back to Bob.

"What is your problem? I don't understand why you are so touchy about saving money. We *are* saving money, right? I mean, why wouldn't we? No rent to pay, plus you just started that legal messenger job."

"I told you to shut up." He yelled so loud that it startled John and he began to cry.

There were times when he treated me like this that I wondered how much his race played into the way he treated me, especially when it came to money or success. For so long I had learned to hide the fact that I'd had— and given up—a black baby, that the charming man I'd married beat me, and that I was so depressed I was nearly suicidal. How could the morass of lies that I had lived not include the fact that I married a black man? Of course everybody who met him knew that he was black, but there seemed to be a conspiracy of silence around the implications of our different races.

The naïveté of the 1960's was over and I needed to get real. After hearing stories from my mother about the way black musicians were treated, after losing my friendship with little Yolanda, after the Black Panthers invading my high school, could I honestly think that color didn't matter?

I had gotten glimpses of the rage borne of racism and slavery that lived within my husband. He told me stories of growing up in 1940's Tampa, Florida. Twice he'd been deliberately run over by white men in big automobiles, including one who jumped the curb and chased him with his car. He told me about this one night as we lay in bed.

"When the car hit me, I flew through the air and skidded to a stop on the other side of the street, hitting my head against the curb."

"Good Lord! Did you tell your mom? Did she call the police?" I asked.

"No."

"Why not?"

"She'd have givin' me a beating for being out playing when white men were around. And what do you think the police would have done? A white man hits a black kid with his car? They'd want to make sure the car was okay."

"That doesn't make any sense."

"It makes a lot of sense if you grow up black in the South. You ain't got no mother wit, so how would you know?"

I felt a change in his body language, as if he imperceptibly retreated into his blackness, leaving me unknowing, clueless and stupid in my whiteness.

It was a surprise to me when Bob took a legal messenger job. It was at XYZ Legal Messengers where, for a short while, one of his coworkers was Ted Bundy. The hours were scattered. Sometimes he would have to wait outside someone's home for hours. Sometimes, when a wife had her husband served with divorce papers, she might ask Bob to hang around until she felt safe for him to leave. He didn't get paid for the hours spent waiting or hovering; he was only paid for each service made. It was no career, but he told me he took the job in order to help out. So why was he being so snippy about it? Something wasn't right.

Sometimes he'd have to deliver legal papers to the hospital where I worked. Usually he'd have to go to the Personnel Department, get the signatures needed and then he'd drop by my office to chat for a minute or two.

But our funky green Chevy, with the driver's door held shut by a rope, finally broke down, and I was back to taking the bus to work with John. I'd walk him to his daycare and then run the three blocks to my office. Bob told me he was using a "company car" that they'd lent him until he could get one of his own. This was during the gas crises of the 1970's and one benefit of his job was that he could fill the car up at a special spot that had pumps for taxi cabs and delivery vehicles, and therefore didn't have to wait in the long lines at gas stations that appeared every time the fear of price hikes was raised.

One day I walked out of the hospital to run an errand and found the "company car" parked in the patient drop-off circle in front. There was a woman sitting inside it.

It was a warm day and the windows of the car were down. I didn't recognize her and that feeling of dread returned.

I walked up to the passenger side of the car.

"Hey! Who are you? Where's Bob?"

I could tell right away that she was taken aback and my radar was instantly switched on. "I'm his wife, by the way."

Her body stiffened and she looked terrified. Her eyes darted about and she didn't seem able to look me in the eyes.

"He's...he's...at Personnel, getting some papers signed." She immediately looked away, I imagine in the hopes that I'd disappear. But I didn't.

"And...who are you?"

"I'm...ah...I'm Sharon. The owner's daughter."

"Okay, Sharon. What are you doing with Bob on his job?"

"Oh, this is my car. He uses it to do his deliveries."

"Your car? I thought this was a 'company car.'" Little beads of sweat broke out on her forehead.

"Oh...I mean, yes...it *is* the company car. My dad lets me use it, and now he's letting Bob...I mean...Mr. Jones... use it."

"I'm sure it's okay if you call him Bob. After all, I do."

Just then, Bob approached the car and even from afar, I could see that evil look in his eyes. Clearly angered, he walked up to me, pulled me close and hissed in my ear, "What are you doing here?"

I pulled away from him. "I work here. Remember? What is *she* doing here?" Now he looked frightened, his eyes big and staring, like a meerkat on steroids. He ran around to the driver's side, jumped in and started the engine. I leaned in the open window, across Sharon and said, "I imagine you've got to get Sharon home. Or somewhere. Isn't that right, Sharon? You live somewhere, don't you?" With that, Bob let out the brake, stepped on the gas and raced off.

That night at dinner, Bob was contrite.

"I'm sorry," he said, his brown eyes liquid and sweet. "I was just caught off guard. I didn't mean to be so nasty."

I looked up from a plate of rice and beans.

"Why didn't you tell me about Sharon and the car? It makes me think you're hiding something."

"I'm not hiding anything!" His eyes started to change to that evil look, but then he instantly returned to being fluid and loving.

I reached out and touched his arm reassuringly.

"I'm sorry too. I didn't mean to be accusing. I just wondered who she is and why she was with you, that's all. No big deal."

He softened.

"She's the owners' daughter. Sometimes she comes with me because her dad is awful to her and she's having a hard time with her boyfriend."

I wondered why boyfriend problems made it necessary to hang out with my husband while he was working, but I let it pass. Bob had a knack for drawing people in who were struggling with some sort of personal problem, both men and women. But especially women. I tried to learn to live with it because he constantly assured me that these folks, especially the women, were just people who needed help. It seemed he always had someone he was "counseling."

My office was on the fourth floor of the hospital and my supervisor, the director of nursing, was next door. There was a window in the wall between us so we could pass things back and forth to each other. Sometimes she would leave it open during change-of-shift report and I could hear the stories of each patients' progress or decline or status quo. The night nurse manager would pass on information about hospital patients to the day shift nursing managers. I loved eavesdropping on these conversations because doing so made me feel like I was as involved in the care of the patients as the nurses were.

Directly across the hall from my office was the waiting room for the families of ICU/CCU patients and I often could hear soft sobbing coming from there. *Someday this will be me*, I thought. *I will be losing someone. Or perhaps it will be someone losing me. Either way, we come and go and in between we're to live, make a difference, love, improve, grow and gain insight into the human condition so that the next generation won't have to suffer so much. I hear those sobs from across the hall and my heart breaks for those families and loved ones.*

One morning, as I walked towards my office, I noticed that the waiting room was in disarray. There were blankets and pillows everywhere. Obviously a family had spent most of the night waiting to hear about their loved one. I knew housekeeping would be along, but I couldn't help myself. I went in and straightened the magazines. Then I went across the hall and opened my office door.

Report was already in progress in Margaret's office. She'd left the window open and as I took the cover off my typewriter, I eavesdropped as usual.

I heard the night nursing manager, Marcia, describing the arrival of a middle-aged man who'd had a heart attack. He'd collapsed at home and was brought by Medics to the emergency room. They quickly transferred him to CCU. His family—a wife and two young children—were in the waiting room across from my office for hours, hence the blankets and pillows. Apparently they'd arrived the previous evening, shortly after I'd left work.

"It's a shame he didn't make it," Marcia said.

"How old was he?" Margaret asked, while she and the nurse managers took notes.

"Fifty-three," Marcia said as she rifled through the patients charts. "He was a teacher and a musician."

"And he leaves a wife and two children?" Margaret asked. "Did they get a referral to social services?"

"They did. I recommended counseling for the children. Apparently, they're both adopted and I thought they'd need help getting over their loss."

Margaret's hand hovered over her notebook. "Good work, Marcia. And his name was…"

Marcia looked at her notes. "Ah….Midkiff. Brian Midkiff."

I slapped my hand over my mouth so that they wouldn't hear me gasp.

Margaret ran her finger down the patient list, found his name and checked it off.

"Okay," she said sitting back in her chair and stretching her legs, "who's next?"

I quietly closed the window, opened my desk drawer and took out my "Be Right Back" sign. I put it on my desk and left, quickly walking to the nearest ladies room, entered, shut, locked the door and broke down.

The obituary was in the paper several days later. Mr. Midkiff left his wife, Ginny, a five-year-old daughter, Millie—and a son Isaiah, seven years old.

Now I knew that little Isaiah was fatherless. I fought hard not to intervene, to let him know that he did indeed have a father. And a brother. But I kept it all to myself.

Time was growing close for my parent's return and as far as I knew, we'd saved no money. Bob said he was using the amount we would have paid for rent to enter more bowling competitions but he just wasn't winning. I began to panic.

"We've got to be out of here before they return," I said one Saturday morning as I took homemade biscuits out of the oven for our breakfast. Bob planned to leave for another tournament right after we finished eating.

"Why?" he asked as he poured honey on his hot biscuit. "Why do we have to be outta here as soon as they return? We can stay on for a while. We should stay as long as we need to. After all, we've got their grandson and they wouldn't let him be homeless."

But as it turned out, that was exactly what happened.

My mother fully expected us to be gone and the house in order when they came back from Wyoming, which was only fair. And her disappointment that we had not left was quite obvious and totally understandable.

"I'm going out this weekend to find us a place," I promised her. We were sitting in the kitchen drinking coffee. She was annoyed with me but distracted as John was racing around the house with his Big Wheel tricycle.

"I found a duplex we can rent. I'm going to see it on Saturday and if it's suitable, I'll pay the deposit and get a move-in date. Okay? I promise we'll be out of here."

The duplex was in a dubious part of town, but it had two little bedrooms and was affordable. I put down the deposit with the cash Bob had given me, and returned to my mom's with the good news.

"We'll move next Saturday. It's small but has everything we need." She was clearly happy, both to see us leave and to know I'd found a suitable place. During the rest of that week, I put our things in order, boxed them up and labeled them for the move. I spent the week picturing where things would go, how I'd decorate John's tiny room, where the little black and white TV would go for best reception and where I might hang my posters.

On that Saturday morning, I packed boxes and clothes into the trunk of the car he'd bought only weeks before. It was another jalopy, an old Chevy. At least the doors didn't need to be held shut by ropes. Bob helped but then went back to sleep in preparation for another tournament. My mom had agreed to keep John.

When I got to the duplex, the refrigerator and stove were gone. I was aghast and stomped to the pay phone across the street to call the landlord.

"Where are the appliances? I demanded.

"Oh," he said, "I had them removed."

"Why? I can't live in a place with no refrigerator or stove. I've got a baby for Pete's sake."

"You'll have to find your own appliances."

"Is that so? Those appliances were here when you showed me the place. And now you say I have to get my own? That seems like false and misleading advertising, don't you think? I mean, almost as if you'd done it on purpose."

"Look," he said. "Times are hard. They broke down and I can't replace them. I just don't have the money." I was furious and pulled the receiver away from my ear for a moment, to let the steam dissipate from my face.

"You know that lease I signed?"

"Yes, why?"

"Then you probably know where you can shove it. And I'll have my six foot, four inch, 250 pound husband come and get the cash deposit."

"No, no. You don't have to do that. I'll bring the deposit back right away. Just stay there and wait."

As I sat on the front steps waiting for the landlord to return the deposit, I desperately tried to think how I would break the news to my mom that we would not be moving that weekend. After the landlord dropped off my cash, I nervously returned to their house.

Bob had just gotten up and was getting ready to leave. He had his green bowling shirt on, with his name "Big Bobby Jones" stitched diagonally across the back.

"What's wrong?" My mom saw the look on my face and could tell I was upset.

"I don't know how to say this, but I tore up the lease and we're not moving today. The landlord had taken the appliances away and wasn't going to replace them."

At the same moment, Bob came up to my mom, rubbing his fingers together.

"Why are you doing that?" my mom snapped.

"Money! I'm going to win big money today.

That apparently was my mom's last nerve.

"Money? Money? What money? Why don't you work for a living like the rest of us? All you do is talk, talk, talk and never win. You're a loser."

Bob and my mom both turned to look at me. Clearly they were expecting me to agree with one or the other. Caught in turmoil and afraid to side with my mom for fear of Bob's reaction, I defended him.

"Don't talk to him like that! He's trying his best. It's hard out there to win when so many others are competing as well."

"Win? He wouldn't know the meaning of the word. He's a lazy bastard living off you and trying to live off me." She cocked her head at Bob and said, "Get outta here. Now!"

Just then, Bob's ride appeared in the driveway. He had arranged for a fellow bowler to take him to the tournament so I could use the car for the move—which I was supposed to do on my own, with little John, of course. Bob sprinted out the front door, got in his friend's car and sped away. I grabbed John and ran out to the already loaded car. I got John in his safety chair and drove away, kicking up dirt and rocks in my wake. I was sobbing and had no idea where to go.

CHAPTER 33

MOMENTARILY HOMELESS

I WAS DRIVING on the freeway. In the lane next to me, a guy in a station wagon was honking at me. I ignored him, but he persisted. Honk. Honk. Honk. When I finally looked over at him, he mouthed the words, "Can I help?" It was dangerous to try communicating on the freeway, but he looked earnest. But what on earth was he trying to tell me? I couldn't imagine why he would want to get my attention and offer to help.

Then I realized I was crying, crying so hard that I was leaning over the steering wheel, practically sobbing on the dashboard. The man in the station wagon honked again and motioned for me to change lanes and get off at the next exit. I nodded and put my signal on.

I got off at a downtown exit and pulled up to the nearest curb. The man pulled his station wagon up behind me and got out. John was sleeping in his car seat in back. I put the brake on and got out of my car as well. I wasn't sure what the man wanted. I felt as if part of me was in the car with John and another part was approaching a stranger with both trepidation and curiosity.

As he came nearer, I could see that he was an older man, with his gray hair showing underneath a brown trilby hat. Surely he must have been somebody's grandfather. His brows were furrowed as he came nearer.

"Miss, are you okay?"

I was hiccupping with sobs and wiping tears from my face

"Miss, are you able to talk?" I shook my head no.

"I couldn't help but notice you crying. You were driving a little errati-cally and I honked to get your attention. I noticed your baby in the back seat." He nodded toward the sleeping John. "I was worried that you might crash. I hope you don't mind my interfering."

He was tall and somewhat gaunt. His brown suit hung a bit loosely. Deep creases lined his face, but his eyes sparkled and he exuded confidence.

I looked around me and, like a slap in the face, I saw that I had pulled off the freeway practically in front of the Olive Towers. How things had changed in such a relatively short time. It seemed that hardly any time had passed at all since I'd moved into that building and discovered Bob there. And now, here I was, standing on the street homeless and sobbing in front of a complete stranger with one of Bob's children in the car and the other with his surrogate parents.

The sound of the cars passing by on the freeway reminded me of the sounds I heard then, in my studio apartment. I remembered someone had suggested that I pretend it was the sound of ocean waves coming in to shore. It never did work. It drove me mad then, and it was driving me mad again. I just wanted the noise to stop.

I found my voice. "No, I don't mind at all. I don't think you're interfer-ing. I appreciate your concern."

"Is there anything I can do for you?" I started to cry again.

"Oh, dear . . . . I'm so sorry. I didn't mean to upset you again." He seemed genuinely concerned and a look of worry continued to crease the clear, almost translucent skin on his face.

I started to back away from this kind stranger and towards my car. "I'm okay. Really. I've just had a terrible scene with my parents and my husband."

He smiled. "I see." He reached into his coat pocket, brought out a busi-ness card and handed it to me. I looked at it. It said, "Rev. Keith Hartung, United Lutheran First Church."

"Miss…"

"Mrs."

"Sorry. Yes, ma'am. If you find that you need help, please call me. Our church has a new program to help young mothers in need. I really want you to know that you have a place to turn to. We won't proselytize, I promise. We just want to help when you're ready to accept help."

I reached for the door handle. "Thank you. I certainly will contact you if I need to. Thank you so much." I got in the car, closed the door and locked it. John was still sleeping. The kind reverend started his car and slowly drove away, waving at me as he went by.

Why didn't I say something to him? Why didn't I tell him I had no place to live? Well … I thought … why should I? Just because he's got a card that says he's a reverend, doesn't mean it's true. Besides, I had long ago learned to keep my problems to myself. I didn't say anything to the nurses at the hospital after John was born about the electricity being cut off. I was too embarrassed. This time, I was too scared. I had no idea what I would do, but I'd figure it out on my own. I had my baby and our clothes. What else did I need? I had no idea where Bob was and, at that point, didn't care. But I looked at Rev. Hartung's card for a minute pondering my options and slipped it into my wallet, just in case.

In 1975 there were no women's shelters to turn to. The social and cultural revolution that started in the Sixties had not yet reached into the private darkness of what goes on behind closed doors. But I did remember hearing at work that the YWCA was starting a program for women in need. I pulled up to a phone booth, looked up the YWCA's number in the filthy directory hanging from a chain and called.

A young woman answered and when I told her why I was calling, she asked me to hold. When she came back on line, she apologized for keeping me waiting and then said, "We've just started this program and you're our first call! Oh! Sorry. I don't mean to sound excited when you're in distress, but we're so very pleased that you called and we can help."

She gave me the phone number of a volunteer who had offered her space for a woman in a bad situation, such as I was. Her name was Theresa.

I dialed her number from the same phone booth and when she answered I introduced myself, telling her I'd been referred by the YWCA.

"I'd be happy to have you come stay with me," Theresa said.

"I've got a two year old child as well. Still okay if we come for a few days?"

"No problem," Theresa said. She gave me her address which was not far from where I was.

She lived in an old house on Capitol Hill that had been converted into small apartments and studios. Her apartment was on the second floor.

Theresa was standing at the top of the stairs with her door open to greet John and me. She was short and wiry, as was her hair. She had reading glasses perched on her nose and a book dangling from her left hand. As she welcomed us into her small home, I breathed a sigh of relief.

It was a large apartment. Plants were hanging from macramé holders, political posters were taped to the walls and her small bookshelf, made of bricks and boards, held a myriad of books, from Mao's little red book to Herman Hesse's Siddhartha.

"Are you hungry?" she asked and I said we were quite hungry. We went into her small kitchen as John sat on the floor with his favorite books that I'd brought with me from the car. She took a can of tuna and a can of tomatoes from her cupboard and opened them, plopped the contents into a pot and cooked it until it boiled, then simmered it for a few minutes. Normally, I would have passed on a dinner of boiled tuna and tomatoes, but I was hungry. I remembered how my friend Mary snuck Thanksgiving dinner down to me as I was hiding in her basement. I told myself how lucky I was to have had such a good friend back then, and now a friendly stranger willing to help me and my son.

I gave John a bath in the shared bathroom across the hall from her apartment. It had a big old claw-foot tub that almost swallowed John. We both laughed while he splashed around, and he squealed and shrieked with such delight I forgot all about my situation. I tickled him and sang him silly little songs, then gave him a big cuddle while I dried him with a large towel.

Then we returned to Theresa's and slept on her living room floor.

In the morning, there was a knock on her door. Theresa opened it and I heard her talking in a low whisper to someone. Then she stepped into the hallway and shut the door.

When she returned, she looked stricken.

"What's wrong?" I asked her. She was pacing, wringing her hands, clearly upset.

"My neighbors have complained about the noise you and your little boy made in the bathroom last night." She spit the words out. "I can't believe how stupid they are! What's wrong with a little boy having fun splashing around in the tub with his mama by his side?"

I was sitting on the floor with John, watching him eat some Cheerios and toast. I shook my head. "Well, this is their home. It's your home too. But it's sort of communal living and I guess everyone needs to get along and respect each other". She came to a standstill and stared hard at the floor.

"They want John and I to leave, don't they?" I asked. I got up and started pulling our things together.

"No!" Theresa was clearly conflicted. "I want to help you."

She was a budding feminist who truly wanted to provide a haven for women in need, but I realized she wasn't in any position to really do much more to help.

"Don't worry. You've already helped. I really appreciate you letting us stay the night, and feeding us. It was very kind of you."

Theresa reached out and touched my arm. "But, where will you go?"

"I've.....I've got a cousin in North City. I'll see if I can stay with her. I'm sure she'll let me." I winked at her. "My cousin owes me a few favors, so I think it will be fine." I wanted Theresa to feel like I had things in hand.

"Thank you so much for taking care of us. I'll never forget your kindness."

Theresa helped us down the stairs. I got John settled in the car. Then I gave Theresa a hug and promised to keep her phone number in case I got in a jam again. As I drove away, I waved out the window at Theresa. I turned the corner and Theresa disappeared. I pulled over and started to cry again. *Now what am I going to do?*

I knew I had to keep working or I'd never be able to make it. I had very little cash—not enough to find shelter for John and me—only enough to get some food. I had never borrowed money from anyone in my life and didn't want to start unless things got critical.

I saw no other alternative but to live in the car until my next paycheck, which was two weeks away. I searched for a place in the neighborhood near my work, a lovely area of large older homes on tree-lined streets. I found a quiet spot on a residential corner and parked. The nearby street lamp provided enough light to see in the dark.

I'd never gone camping in my life and didn't intend too. I preferred indoor plumbing and 24-hour room service. But I wanted to make the best of a bad situation. So I told John we would pretend to be on a road trip. Each evening, as we sat in the car, I told John that if he closed his eyes and thought really hard, he could feel the car moving on the road. He could see the lights of each little town as we passed by; that the smells and sounds of new places were there to be enjoyed as long as he kept his eyes closed and concentrated.

I piled blankets on the floor in the back for John's bed and I slept on the seat just above him. John slept well, and was young enough to not find the situation questionable. I slept poorly, constantly berating myself for getting into this mess.

What kind of a mother was I?

For the next two weeks, John and I woke early. Every day, the dark skies of night would just be awakening too. The eastern horizon would become ever so slightly orange and then, as the sun continued to rise, the orange changed to pink, then yellow and soon, night had turned to day. A few people might pass by on their way to the bus but otherwise the street was empty. I longed for someone to stop by and have a cup of coffee, as if visiting a woman and her child in a car was as natural as pouring a bowl of cereal. I needed to feel normal, not isolated and desperate. Loneliness wrapped itself around me like a straitjacket.

I unfolded myself from the back seat and got John out of the car. We walked the few blocks to my work at the hospital. Since the craze of jogging at lunch had started, there were several areas for employees to shower. I would bring a few changes of clothes with me for the two of us and put them in a locker. We took showers and got dressed, then headed to the hospital cafeteria for breakfast.

The cafeteria opened at 5:00 am, and I'd get as much food as I could afford for us to eat. Afterwards, I walked John to his day care then returned to work trying to look as if I had just left my warm and cozy home and loving husband. I always greeted everyone with a perky "Good morning." I had to keep up a good face at work because I would have been horrified if anyone knew what was going on.

Meanwhile, I had no contact with Bob. I expected him to call me at work, or show up to see how we were doing, but he did neither. I knew he was probably at a bowling alley or staying with some woman but at that point, I didn't care.

I also thought my mom might call. She had left the bookkeeper job at the florist's and I had helped her get a job at the hospital, so it was only a matter of time before I'd run into her. She worked just across the street in another building on the campus. But she stayed away and I didn't run into her. Maybe she was feeling as embarrassed and stubborn as I was.

After two weeks, my paycheck arrived but Bob didn't come to get it. I was momentarily unsure what to do with it, as if it were some sort of foreign visa. At lunch, I went out and cashed it—the first time I'd had my own hard earned cash in my hands and not Bob's. I picked John up from day care and we walked to our car. John and I sat there for a long while that evening as I thought things through. He wanted me to play with his blocks and as he stacked the blue, red, yellow and green plastic blocks on the floor of the back seat, I realized that the money from this paycheck wouldn't be enough to put down first month's rent on an apartment. But it *would* be enough to get us a room for a night or two.

"Hey, sweetie!" I said to him, "Want to stay in a motel tonight?" He smiled at me. I could picture us lying in a real bed, watching television and having a delicious meal somewhere. At that point, even McDonald's sounded good.

Then I thought about Bob. He hadn't bothered to see if we were all right for two weeks. Was he being embarrassed and stubborn too? Was that a good reason for not checking on me and his little son? As if having to worry about finding a place to live wasn't enough for me to deal with, I realized that eventually I was going to have to figure out what to do about my marriage, as well.

My thoughts rolled around as if they were wet clothes tossing in a dryer. I couldn't decide what the best thing would be. I felt confused and was having trouble realizing that I was actually married and had a child to care for. It felt like my life had been caught up in a vicious whirlwind and that it had suddenly dumped me in an old beater car parked on a residential street corner. Night after night, I sat in that car watching my baby sleep, illuminated by the soft light of the street lamps, as I wondered where my sense of reality had gone.

Here I was sleeping in a car with a little toddler and no one to help us. Wasn't that what a husband was supposed to do? Where was he? So far, the marriage seemed to be all about him, and little about me and our child. I encouraged him, urged him to pursue his dreams of being a professional bowler and this is where I end up? Sleeping in a crap car? Not that I had held any ideals about married life, but it didn't take much to know that this wasn't it.

I started the car, drove to a payphone and called Rainier Lanes. I knew all the bowling alley phone numbers by heart.

"Rainier Lanes, Skip speaking."

"Skip, can you page Bob Jones for me?"

"Sure thing," and in the background I heard the intercom: "Bob Jones. Bobby Jones, telephone."

I could hear all the bowling alley noise in the background—pins falling on the alleys, bowlers whooping it up, glasses clinking, laughter, swearing, shouting. Then the phone was picked up and I heard his voice. "Hello."

I was in no mood to dance around with preliminary niceties. "Where have you been the last two weeks? Did you care where John and I were?

Did you miss us?" There was a short silence and I absurdly wondered if he was trying to remember who I was and what I was talking about.

"I've been here, mostly. At Rainier."

"Why?"

"You know they take of me here."

"Oh yeah. I know they take care of you. Lots of people do. But what about me and John? Did you wonder who took care of us these last weeks? You do remember us, right?"

"Don't be so stupid. I let you be for a while, that's all. You knew where I was. You could have called me here any time."

The sounds of the bowling alley receded and I knew he'd muffled the mouth piece with his hand so all the good folks at Rainier Lanes wouldn't overhear him berate his wife.

"Why should I have called you? Why didn't you come to my work to see about me? Do you know where John and I have been these last two weeks?"

"I figured you were staying at your mom's."

"After the way she treated us? No way. We've been sleeping in the car, showering at work and eating what I could afford, which isn't much." He was silent.

I continued on. "Where *were* you? Where did you stay? Who were you with?"

"I stayed at the bowling alley. They let me sleep in the back office and I ate at the café here," he said.

"Did they give you quarters for the pinball machines?"

"No. Why would they?"

"I just thought since they did everything else for you that maybe they fronted you some money so that you could play pinball. They're awfully generous with you."

"Do you have a problem with that?" he hissed into the phone.

"Yes I do. At least you had a roof over your head and decent food."

"Well, where are you now?"

"I'm in a phone booth. I'm getting ready to find John and me a motel somewhere since I got paid today."

He must have forgotten that payday had arrived, otherwise he'd have been at the hospital ready to take my check and cash it.

"Why don't you come pick me up here and we'll find a motel together, like maybe out near the airport."

I hesitated. I thought of swallowing what little pride I had left and asking my mom to help me. But that would mean giving up on my relationship with Bob and I was determined to have a better marriage than my parents and to do whatever I could to make a bad situation better. I wasn't ready to give up.

"All right," I said. "I'm on my way."

One more chance, I thought. *Only one more. And then what?*

Bob, John and I checked into a motel near the airport where we stayed for two weeks. I was relieved to have a real bed, a bathroom and television and tried to find some romance in being a vagabond. There was a bowling alley just down the highway, Lewis and Clark Lanes, and I dropped Bob there on my way to work so he could pot bowl for food money and to pay for the motel.

For the second time in a month, I took my next paycheck and set out to look for an apartment. I found a two bedroom second floor apartment in View Ridge, an area north of the University campus. The apartment was part of a group of apartment buildings that were built after World War II to house returning soldiers and their families. They were well-built, comfortable and had plenty of windows.

We bade farewell to the motel and moved in the next day. Since we had little belongings, moving was easy. I was overwhelmed with relief to be back in a place of our own, in a respectable, quiet neighborhood with a grocery store only two blocks away and the bus stop right outside our door. Although I was chronically exhausted, I was happy to be settled and eager to start building our lives together again.

But there were certain things that had to change in order for our marriage to continue.

One evening, after I put John to bed, I had a come-to-Jesus talk with Bob. I poured him a tall glass of Kool-Aid (his favorite drink) and made myself a cup to tea. Then I plunged in.

"I can't go on supporting the family while you bowl every day but still aren't bringing home anything to show for it. At this rate, we'll never be able to get a house and, frankly, I'm unhappy." There. I'd said it. I had been holding my breath. Now I let a sigh of relief escape.

Bob's face seemed passive. I couldn't read it. Was a hurricane about to break? I expected an explosion but I got agreement instead.

"You're right," he said. "I know that you do all the work and I feel less of a man because of it," he said.

"Really? You agree with me?" He nodded. "Then I have a plan to propose. Do you want to hear it?" I refilled his Kool-Aid.

"Okay. What is it?" He placed his elbows on the table and rested his chin on his hands, looking eager and hopeful, and his brown eyes shining with love.

"I think you should take care of John during the day while I'm at work. That will save us the cost of day care, which—by the way—is going to rise next month. Then I think you must get a job, something in the evening so I can take over watching John. If we do this for—I don't know—maybe six to twelve months, we should have enough saved to get a home."

His head kept nodding and he stared off into space for a moment. Then he sat back in his chair and leveled his gaze at me.

"That's what you want? A house and a new car?"

"Yes. That's what I want. I thought that's what you wanted too." It was a surprise to hear myself say that. Where did London and writing go? It didn't matter; I now had a child and a husband and they came first. My needs could wait.

"Don't you want that too? I mean, it's not unusual for a family to have a house and reliable transportation."

His eyes had hardened and he was now glaring at me. "You always did want to conform," he said, his voice turning from agreeable to challenging. "You want to be just like everybody else and lead your life like an automaton."

I had to think hard and fast before the conversation turned into a confrontation, or worse.

"Look, it's not a matter of conformity. It's a matter of taking care of our family properly, and not having it all fall on me." I stood to refill his glass of Kool-Aid but he waved me off so I took his glass to the kitchen to wash.

Then his demeanor changed again, back to the loving, caring husband he was supposed to be.

"I think it sounds like a great idea," he said loudly.

"So how do you want to go about doing this?" I asked, wiping my hands on a towel.

"Well, I'll start looking for an evening job."

I felt a surge of hope. "Maybe you can be a janitor at one of the bowling alleys. Or a late night delivery driver. I mean, whatever you can do to help."

"Yes, of course. Whatever I can do to help. I guess I'll just have to fit in my bowling when I can." His brow furrowed and he looked down at the floor and then up at the ceiling, his eyes widened as if inspired.

I felt momentarily brave. "You might just have to put it on hold for a bit while we get back on our feet—whatever it takes. I just will *not* live in a car again with our son sleeping on the floor."

"Okay. Okay. I got it. I'll make some calls tomorrow. I know a lot of people— someone will give me a job." He stood, stretched and yawned. His knees popped as he headed to the bedroom. "Now let's go to bed."

And so we did, and I slept soundly, hopeful that things might finally begin to change. But I never could have anticipated how profoundly they would change when a few weeks later Lynne came back into my life.

CHAPTER 34

COKES AND KOI'S

I HADN'T SEEN LYNNE for several years but deep inside me, in utter darkness and secrecy, I knew that I had never stopped loving her. Yet every time thoughts of her surfaced to the daylight, I ignored the feelings that arose within me and pushed them back into the darkness, where they simmered slowly.

I'd heard through Liz that Lynne had gone up to Alaska for nearly a year to work the fishing boats. Then she moved to Phoenix with a new girl-friend where she hoped to stop looking for love in all the wrong places and get settled. It didn't last long and once again she returned to Seattle. But we hadn't crossed paths since she'd been back.

Then one day, not long after Bob, John and I had settled in to the new apartment, I answered the phone at work and heard her voice, and the sound of it ran a thrill up and down my body.

"Oh my gosh," I said. "I've missed you so much. How did you know I was here?"

"You probably didn't know, but we have a mutual friend working in the X-ray department."

"Who's that?" I asked.

"Remember Barb?"

"Oh yeah. Barb. She works in X-ray?"

"She does. We were talking one day and I was telling her how much I missed you and she said she thought you were working at the same hospital, found your number and gave it to me! And here I am!"

We decided to have lunch together as often as possible. She worked at a sandwich shop and after her deliveries, she'd bring a sandwich for each of us and, if the weather was nice, we'd go up to the roof of the hospital to eat and chat.

She looked even more attractive than the last time I'd seen her. Clearly spending a year in Alaska had built some muscles in her small frame. Her hair was still thick and brown but now it was even shinier than before. Her cheeks were still ruddy, her eyes still an azure blue and her hands small but strong. When we first saw each other, after so long, she hugged me and held my face in her hands. Had we not been in my office, with people coming and going, I would have kissed her.

There were many things unspoken between us. I never discussed my marriage and she never asked. Yet I knew she sensed that something was wrong and in her extremely instinctive way, she let me know that she would always be there for me.

When we'd part, she would hug me long and hard, as if she didn't want to let me go. I knew I didn't want to let her go. The feelings I had for her when we were fourteen had only grown, albeit quietly and unacknowledged. I knew then, and I knew now, that I loved her so much I ached.

But it was a love I couldn't possibly pursue. I had a son now and he was my priority. I wondered how I could see her and not tempt myself with something so entirely forbidden that just thinking about it left me covered in goose bumps.

It didn't take Bob long to get a job delivering newspapers. He had to leave at midnight, go to the dispatch station to get his bundles and then drive his assigned route. The newspaper paid him by the route so he didn't have to go around collecting fees from each subscriber. It wasn't much money, but it was something.

Then one night before he left for work, he told me he had a brilliant idea.

"If I have *two* routes, I can make twice as much money!" He was pacing while he spoke, a clear indicator to me that he was either nervous, agitated or both.

I had just returned from putting John to bed. I plopped on the floor and wrapped my elbows around my knees.

"That's a brilliant idea? How are you going to do two jobs at once?"

"That's where you come in." He sat down on the floor next to me, more relaxed now that he'd shared his idea.

"Me? Are you joking?"

"No. Listen to me. We get up and you do the driving while I run up and down the street delivering the papers. I can do two routes that way and all you have to do is sit in the car and drive."

I couldn't believe what I was hearing. "All I have to do is sit in the car and drive? When do I get to sleep? What about John? I already have two full time jobs— one at the hospital and the other taking care of you and John. I think that's enough work for me."

I should have known he would explode. But I was safe on the floor; he couldn't knock me down.

"It's not going to hurt you to drive around in the middle of the night. You can take a nap at your lunch break if you're so tired. I'm just trying to do what you asked— which is to make more money so we can get that house and car that are so important."

"You were the one that first brought up a house of our own, if you'll remember." I instinctively glanced towards John's room. I didn't want him to wake up after I'd just gotten him settled.

Bob bit the corner of his lower lip. It was a gesture that I hated because he often got violent when he did it, as if he enjoyed hurting me. His nostrils flared. I knew it was coming and so, not wanting a scene, I gave in. "Alright. Alright. I'll try it, okay? For a week. We'll see how it works." Glancing again at John's bedroom, I said "We'll have to take John with us, of course."

"No we don't. Leave him at home. Nothing's going to happen to him."

"You're not serious? You think we should leave John here by himself? He's only two, for Christ sakes. Are you out of your mind?"

I could see the changes in Bob's face as he weighed the pros and cons of bullying me or letting it go. Would he fight me or concede that leaving John home alone in the middle of the night at the age of two wasn't only neglectful but unlawful. He must have realized the latter, because after a flicker of rage crossed his face, his expression softened and he gave in.

"You're right. Of course, we'll bring him along. I don't know what I was thinking." He struggled off the floor, his knees popping, then reached down to give me a helping hand up. He held me close to his chest and kissed the top of my head. Being held in his arms made everything right. It was a haven for me, a place where I could feel safe, if only for a moment.

The following Monday, I began getting to bed around 7:00, right after finishing up the dishes and getting John to bed. At 11:00, Bob would get me up. I'd get dressed and then fetch John as quietly as I could so he wouldn't wake up. I put his little sleeping body wrapped in blankets in the back of the car and we all drove off to dispatch to get the day's papers.

"We get the papers, then you drive out to where my route starts and it'll just roll from there," Bob instructed me.

"So, where does your route begin?"

He gave me the cross streets, and I gasped. His route was tantalizingly close to where my little boy Isaiah lived.

I could say that Seattle is a small town and that eventually you run into everyone you know. Or I could say that life is nothing but a random, capricious and meaningless series of events that lead to nowhere but death. I could say those things, but I don't believe them. I think that life has a plan, a rhythm and a purpose and that the seemingly mundane events that kept bringing me in proximity to my first born had a reason. I just didn't know what that reason was. I also didn't have time to think about it because working full time, being a mother and having to spend most of the early morning hours delivering newspapers kept me too tired to remember my name, let alone ponder universal questions.

As the months bled into each other, my exhaustion was profound yet I felt compelled to help Bob so that we could build a nest egg.

When we returned home around 4:00 am, I returned John to his bed and I would try to get an hour's sleep, but usually couldn't, knowing I'd soon need to start my day. I was beyond exhausted and, since I was now taking the bus to work, I learned to fold my arms, lower my head and sleep in my seat. But the wear and tear on me was too much and I began to eat more, as if food could replace sleep. I gained weight, which made Bob very angry with me. It was exhausting working two jobs, but I was willing to sacrifice and work hard to give my family a home. But when would that ever happen?

While I was working at the hospital during the day, John was in his dad's care and they developed an easy relationship. If the weather was nice, Bob took John to Woodland Park—a vast swathe of trails, hills, dales, softball and soccer fields, a mini golf course, a lake and a zoo. He let John run up and down the hills, so he could discharge the massive energy contained in his little body. Sometimes they went to the nearby zoo to see the elephants and eat hot dogs.

If it was raining, John would accompany his dad to bowling alleys. I wasn't thrilled about him being in a dark, smoky place all day, but at least we weren't paying for daycare and father and son were having fun together.

After six months of early morning risings and sleep deprivation, Bob announced he'd decided to quit delivering papers.

"You what?" I said

"I'm sick of it and I quit. Period. And I'm not going to worry about it, because now I have more time to bowl."

I thought, *Yeah. What really happened?* But then I realized that despite the return of money worries, I wouldn't have to get up every night and could instead get a good nights' sleep.

It was heaven to sleep through the night but it was weeks before I fully recovered. When I did, the truth hit me—there were no more second paychecks coming in. As grueling as that schedule was, we needed the money his job had brought in.

We were back to eating our poor food—a lot of beans and rice, canned creamed corn on grits, hot dogs and his favorite—fried Spam with Miracle

Whip on Wonder bread washed down with cherry Kool-Aid. But a meal of this sort didn't bother Bob. He was thrilled with a fried Spam sandwich. I wondered if he really had any incentive to make a living. He seemed satisfied to embrace of all things smacking of the poverty of his youth. Perhaps he didn't think he deserved anything better.

We were having dinner and he'd just made himself a second Spam sandwich when I ventured a suggestion.

"Maybe after you've had little time off you can look for another evening job?" His mouth full, he nodded in agreement.

"Sure, sweet pea," he mumbled. He swallowed. "I know it's not fair for you to be the sole support of our family."

I took a sip of my tea. "Really? That would be wonderful."

"I'll get something before you know it!" I reached to hold his hand, and he leaned over to give me a kiss. I was suffused with delight.

I was pleased that he wasted no time and soon found a job cleaning restaurants at night. He got paid a certain amount for each restaurant and though it wasn't a lot, it was enough for us to get by. It was a relief to have that extra income coming in again and soon I stopped feeling like the support of my family rested entirely on me. Maybe Bob really was changing.

It seemed that way at first. I'd put John to bed, wash up the dishes and clean the apartment and be in bed by ten, and by eleven Bob was kissing me and heading out the door. In the morning he'd be back in bed and I'd take off for work. Life was finally feeling normal.

But then one night, not long after he'd started cleaning the restaurants, Bob dropped the inevitable bombshell at dinner. He wanted me to go to work with him once again.

"We'll be able to make more money again. It'll be great, it'll be fun. We can turn the music up high and drink all the Cokes we want!"

"You've got to be kidding. I've only just caught up on sleep." I sipped some tea and eyed the Wonder Bread. I grabbed a piece and began slowly rolling it in my hand until it was reduced to a small ball. I could hear Bob droning in the background as I looked at the ball of Wonder Bread in my hand. *What would happen if this ball of bread transformed itself into a giant orb of gelatinous glue that grew bigger and bigger until it suffocated me?* Then I noticed Bob was still talking.

"This won't be like delivering papers," he said. "This will be much faster. Get in and get out. The restaurants are all on the waterfront close to each other. No long drives or anything like that." He tried hard to be convincing and stroked my arm in a gesture of comfort and collusion.

"I don't know how to do it," I said, popping the ball of Wonder Bread into my mouth and biting down.

"I'll show you how to do it. It's easy. You'll do the restrooms."

"The *men's* restroom?" Having never been in a men's restroom, I imagined that they stunk to high heaven with pee and that strange objects floated in the urinals, like maybe a cigarette butt with bright orange lipstick on the filter. "Yes, the men's restroom and the ladies. And you'll clean the dining areas. That mainly involves vacuuming. You have to be sure to pull out the chairs, vacuum under the table and put the chairs back. You can't knock anything over or mess with the place settings. So you have to be careful, but you'll learn!"

"And you?"

"I'll do the kitchens. They're the worst areas and I'm sure you don't want to deal with rats."

"*Rats?*" Rats often guest-starred in my nightmares.

"You'd be surprised what you find in the kitchens of even the best restaurants."

"I see." I gave this some thought, while Bob sat in silence waiting for me to say something. *So far, delivering papers didn't work out, even with my help. Should I believe that restaurants will be the mother lode for us? I knew they wouldn't. But I also knew that if I didn't go along with it, things were only going to get worse and I'd be blamed for it.*

I heaved a big sigh and said, "Well, I don't want John anywhere around rats, so I think I'll ask Cindy (our next door neighbor) if she can watch him while we're out cleaning."

"No you won't!" Bob's eyes flashed. Rage gathered like storm clouds in his face. But he immediately backed off. "Don't be silly. There are rats everywhere in this city. It's a port city, remember? Wharf rats big as dogs."

"Is that supposed to make me feel better?"

Bob laughed. There were times when Bob's laughter and smiling eyes warmed my heart and made me feel comforted, and this was one of those times. There was nothing the least bit threatening in his laughter; if anything, we were both humored by the image of wharf rats as our biggest problem.

"Of course not," he said, taking me in his arms. "I just want you to realize that you can't get away from rats in a city like Seattle. And they only hang out in the kitchens. If the cooks just picked up after themselves, there wouldn't be any rats at all. Trust me. John will be okay with us."

I closed my eyes for a moment, trying to envision this new set-up.

"Besides," Bob added, squeezing my waist. "This will help you lose weight." Bob was never satisfied with my weight. No matter how thin I was, to him I was still fat. When I did put on weight, I was an object of his derision and scorn. It seemed that either way, I never was what he wanted me to be.

"I don't need to lose weight. I eat just fine."

"I'm not talking about dieting. I'm talking about exercise. You'll feel much better if you get some exercise. Ever since you gave up the delivery driving, you've stopped going to the gym."

I'd stopped going because without the extra income, there was no money for gym membership. I knew Bob was being unkind and that he was wrong about my weight, but I was too tired to argue with him any longer.

"Alright. I'll give it a try. But if it's too much work for me, you've got to go on your own."

"Time to get up." Bob was shaking my shoulder to arouse me. I was so deep in sleep that he had to shake both my shoulders hard.

"Okay, okay," I mumbled. "Five more minutes. . ."

"GET UP NOW!" he yelled in my ear. "We've got to go."

Now wide awake, I arose full dressed to save time and gently got John out of bed. We ran down the stairs to the car, piled in and off we went racing downtown to the waterfront to start cleaning one of three restaurants.

Once inside, the operation went smoothly.

"You know where the vacuum, mop and bucket are, so get yourself started. I'm heading to the kitchen."

I placed John on a banquette and made sure his blanket was tucked in securely.

"Wanna pop?" Bob called out as he passed the cocktail lounge.

"No thanks. Maybe later." I always wanted to get the work done first before I relaxed with a Coke and listened to the music.

I learned that when they are empty, restaurants all smell the same. Cooking gas is the predominate aroma. The ones we cleaned on the waterfront also smelled of brine, creosote from the piers, and an undetermined fishy smell. Soon, I was swabbing out stone entrances with wax and wiping toilets with paper towels while Tony Bennett crooned in the background.

I had some favorite restaurants to clean and others that gave me the creeps. The Polynesia sat at the end of a waterfront pier. It was dark inside and there were unsavory stories about the place—murders, suicides, money laundering—that may or may not have been true. I just knew I hated it there. So I kept John with me in a basket I'd put together for him to lie in so I could be sure he was okay and carry him with me as I vacuumed the dining areas, while Bob rattled around in the kitchen, singing like one of the Temptations.

While the Polynesia was creepy, I enjoyed The Crab and The Clam which was further up the waterfront. There was an enormous wall aquarium just inside the door and I made friends with one of the fish, an orange koi. He would rush to the window to greet me every night. I longed to set him free, but he was a tropical fish and the waters of Elliott Bay were so cold that he'd die if I threw him in.

"I guess you have to stay in captivity for your own good," I'd tell him. "But you and I—we know the score, huh?" I wish I could tell my fish friend what captivity meant to me and how it made me feel. I imagined that if we could indeed converse, the fish would have more insight than I would. At least we could commiserate together.

As I vacuumed the dining areas, I'd often find the most interesting things on the floors. In the dark of these restaurants, people dropped things they didn't even know they'd dropped. The first time I found money, which was mostly coins, I gathered them up and placed them on the hostess desk.

Bob saw me from the kitchen and rushed up to me. "What are you doing?"

I looked up and saw his face, and it was clear that whatever I'd done, it was wrong.

"I found this money. And I'm putting it here so that the hostess or somebody will see it."

"Why?"

"Because it's their money. "

"No. It's yours. You keep it... Consider it a tip from a stranger."

And so I started putting the coins in my pocket. I found other things as well— umbrellas, scarves, mufflers, gloves, even jewelry. It felt like stealing to me, but if Bob said it was okay, then I was to accept that. Bob's beliefs and opinions drowned out my own. He knew what was right and I didn't.

After five years together, I no longer knew how to make my own decisions or have my own thoughts. Even when I did so, it was only a matter of time before Bob turned everything I did or said into something that he wanted. I was letting Bob tell me what to see and believe, what to think and feel, what to know and what to forget. I needed to love and be loved. Yet with each day, my sense of reality eroded, replaced by Bob's version of the world, by his judgments and decisions and by my own misguided willingness to place myself into his large, strong hands and trust that he wouldn't crumble me into a ball of Wonder Bread and toss me on the ground.

CHAPTER 35

UNEXPECTED OBITUARY

I T WAS THE spring of 1979. John had finished first grade. We left our apartment in north Seattle and rented a house in a suburb called Federal Way. We were finally going to live in a house, and even though it was in a suburb and was a rental, I felt that we were going forward.

It was an enormous house—a typical suburban split level, with five bedrooms and three bathrooms.

I still only had some rudimentary furniture, so some of the rooms were completely empty. We did manage to get a mattress for the floor and my mother had given me a few furnishings that she got at Value Village. She gave me some material—a large print fabric with a blue background with daisies and stars and I made a gigantic floor pillow for John to lay on when he watched T.V. Sometimes I'd lay next to him, with my head on the pillow too. We loved to watch *The Muppets, Mork and Mindy* and *Welcome Back Kotter.*

Moving away from the city gave Bob a perfect excuse to quit cleaning restaurants and once again, no longer needing to get up in the middle of the night, John and I returned to getting a full nights' rest.

Bob lost more than he won at the bowling tournaments but he kept trying. He would fervently assure me that next month, or next season, or next year things would be better.

"I only to need to win 'the big one' and we'll be set for life," he'd tell me while giving me a reassuring somewhat fatherly hug. I was never sure where or when "the big one" would be but I held onto my promise that I'd support his dream although my enthusiasm was eroding.

After he quit the job, he pared down his bowling for a few months and he began to bake. I had no idea he could make bread. I'd get off the bus in front of our house, walk in the door and smell the delicious aroma of fresh baked bread. That had to be the best smell in the world. I wondered if he was getting in touch with his feminine side.

He went from baking plain bread to cinnamon raisin bread. Then he tried his hand at other dishes. He made soups and Beef Wellington and whatever else struck his fancy.

One day as he was taking fresh baked dinner rolls from the oven, I said, "I think you've found your bliss!"

He set the baking pan down on the counter. 'What would that be?"

"Cooking! Baking! You've got a real talent and I think John and I shouldn't be the only people to enjoy your cooking."

"You've got to be joking," he said, carefully touching the rolls to test if they were done.

"I'm serious. You've got GI benefits from the Army. There's a great new culinary program at Seattle Community College. Why don't you see about your benefits and go to school?"

Despite my urgings, he did nothing to look into school. Not wanting to nag, I bought him used cookbooks to inspire him. He used them to make us wonderful dishes, but he wouldn't consider school.

"Why not?" I would say. "I don't get it. You could truly be an excellent chef and make a living doing something you love."

But he would ignore me. Perhaps, I thought, he wants a small life, a life with no expectations and few responsibilities. But I wanted a big life, full of learning, accomplishments and fun.

Meanwhile, I still saw Lynne. I wanted to keep the fact from Bob because I knew he wouldn't approve and he'd make me drop her. That was one thing I couldn't do.

We continued to have lunch together at least once every couple of weeks. Our relationship morphed into a deep friendship that cautiously and quietly skirted the edges of fervent love. Whenever I was able to see her, my blood tingled with passion.

If it wasn't raining, we went to the roof of the hospital and enjoyed a million dollar view of the city. Otherwise, we ate in the cafeteria.

We always sat close, shoulders touching, hearing each other's breath and just the barest touch of her body made my breathing irregular. Her blue eyes reflected the sky, her ruddy cheeks the earth. There was a depth in her eyes that seemed to me to be a vast and deepening well of ancient wisdom. She was an old soul.

Sometimes, Lynne and I would see each other nearly every day. But other times, there would be long intervals between our visits. She would meet some woman or other, fall in love, move in, enjoy a brief honeymoon, then it would be over. She was always a wanderer, coming into and out of women's lives. They all loved her and mourned when she left. But she always left. It seemed that nothing or no one could settle her.

When we hadn't had contact for a while I'd get a strong feeling that she wanted me to get in touch with her. I'd call her mom, Dorothy, and ask where Lynne was living nowadays. She'd give me a new address and phone number. When I'd call, Lynne would always say, "I wanted you to call; I need to talk with you. You are so perceptive with me. I love that!" Then we'd talk for hours.

As time went on, Lynne sounded increasingly sad and hopeless. I longed to hold her in my comforting arms and tell her everything would be okay. But then I'd have to get real. I had a son that I loved dearly and wanted to take care of. That had to be the priority. I sometimes told her that, and she always told me that she understood more than I could imagine. *More than I could imagine? What did she mean by that?* I was always afraid to ask, knowing that I'd get the answer that I longed for, but couldn't allow myself to hear.

There was a small cul de sac across the street from the house. Beyond that was a small angular piece of undeveloped land where the neighborhood kids would play. It had a nasty stink, hidden streams, climbing trees, muck, mud and salamanders. They called it The Swamp.

The summer of 1979 seemed a bit idyllic. Bob was enjoying a modest winning streak in the bowling alley. At the weekends, I would sit on the front deck of the house where I kept an eye on the kids playing in The Swamp. John would come home absolutely filthy. He'd take a shower, put on clean clothes, eat a sandwich and head back out to play soldiers and win the war. Life was good.

Autumn was rapidly approaching. John had started second grade in a small school near our house. This was my favorite time of the year—the peaty smell of leaves and sea salt in the air, the muted beauty of bare trees against a white-grey sky, and the taste of crisp red apples with sharp Cheddar cheese and plenty of cups of tea.

But at the start of that last week in September, I could feel in my bones that something was wrong. I didn't know what it was, but something was definitely wrong.

Towards the end of the month, those feelings got stronger. I began to feel those familiar signals: Lynne wanted me to call her. The message I was getting from her was unmistakable. It was on a Tuesday that the urge to call her was more pronounced. I kept thinking I'd save calling her for the weekend, when I'd have more time for a nice, long uninterrupted chat.

On Wednesday, I could barely stand it. I was so agitated I couldn't sit still or keep my thoughts straight. I kept getting up, as if I planned to go somewhere and then froze in confusion. Something was urgently nagging at me. I knew it had to do with Lynne. I could feel her emotions at times, as she could feel mine, especially when we were apart. I decided to call her that evening, but John came home from school and announced he had a big project due the next day and asked if I could help him. So I postponed the call again.

By Thursday, my agitation was unbearable. I talked to my boss, Ulla, about it. "I don't know what's wrong with me, but something definitely is off. I can barely stay still. I want to climb the walls. Honestly, I've never felt so agitated."

"You've seemed really off the past couple of days," she agreed. We were sitting in her tiny office in the basement of an old building that was part of the hospital campus. Her room was hot, close and stuffy but I barely noticed that day.

"Do you think I could take tomorrow off? I don't think I can work. Something is wrong and I guess I'm going to feel more and more agitated until I figure it out."

"Absolutely take tomorrow off. Have a nice relaxing long weekend and I'll bet you'll feel much better on Monday," Ulla said.

"Thanks," I said. "I appreciate it. I hope I can figure this out because it's miserable."

I went to bed that night with a mysteriously heavy heart. I slept fitfully, half awake, half asleep. And then something inexplicable happened. I felt arms around me. The arms lifted me up to a sitting position and then I felt the warmest, most loving embrace I'd ever felt in my life. I felt as if I were being infused with love. It was divine, nearly ecstatic. Then I was lowered back down to the bed. I felt a whisper in my head, so quiet I couldn't make it out. I stretched and rolled over. Bob, sleeping beside me, didn't stir and as I laid there, I wasn't sure if I'd had a dream or if I had indeed been woken for some sort of astral-affection. I decided to look at the clock and remember the time: 3:20 am. I planned to call Lynne's mom to get her current number on that Friday morning.

Three times I went to the phone and just as I was about to lift the receiver, I'd think, *Nah. Wait a while. It can wait. Lynne's mom is probably at work anyway. I'll call tonight.*

I got my bike out of the garage, hopped on and rode furiously up and down the twisted suburban streets of our neighborhood. It was a perfectly glorious day and as I rode, I felt the agitation slipping away. I spent hours exploring the little nooks and crannies of the areas that you don't see when you whizz by in a car or on a bus—mud puddles, dog houses, discarded McDonalds wrappers.

I felt so much better afterwards and that horrible urge to call Lynne had completely disappeared. I thought, *Whatever she wanted me for seems to have eased up. I'll call her next week for sure.*

The stellar autumn weather stayed gorgeous through the weekend. I had told Bob about the agitation and he agreed that I should just relax. So on Saturday I let the weekly house-cleaning go and only did two loads of wash. I sat out on the deck listening to the familiar blood-curdling screams coming from The Swamp. It sounded like the kids were playing War. I finished reading a book and started a new one. I made soup to go with the loaf of bread Bob had made and we had a lovely dinner together that night.

The next day was Sunday, which meant dinner at my parents. They'd bought a house with a half-acre backyard on the south end of Seattle, not too far from Federal Way. John and I had started making a habit of having Sunday dinners with my mom and dad, while Bob was bowling, which seemed to relax us all immensely.

I went to work Monday feeling better. All the agitation was gone. I couldn't explain to myself why I had felt so strange, but I was glad it was over.

That evening, after dinner, I sat at the table reading the newspaper. I was only half interested in the news and lazily flipped through the front page news, the editorials, business page, entertainment, and sports. But when I turned to the page with the obituaries, something caught my eye.

I screamed. And suddenly it felt like everything was in slow motion, and my scream would last forever. I couldn't breathe but somehow I was screaming. At that moment, my life changed forever.

"Oh my god! *Oh my god!* OH MY GOD!" I abruptly stood and the newspaper fell to the floor. Both John and Bob ran into the dining room.

"What's wrong? Mama, what's wrong? Why are you screaming?" my son asked, concern and fear on his face.

Bob took my shoulders and looked into my eyes. "Lisa. Lisa. Calm down. Calm down. What is wrong?"

I felt my head spinning, then the room started spinning and I fell to the floor.

There was something cold and wet on my face. Bob was kneeling next to me, wiping my cheeks and forehead with a washcloth. He got me up and sat me in a dining chair. "What on earth is wrong?" He looked frightened.

"She's dead. Oh my god. She's dead. No! This is a mistake. No. This is wrong. It's a mistake. It can't be!"

Bob shook me. "Who's dead?"

I picked up the paper, opened it and laid it out on the table. I pointed to an obituary and told Bob to read it.

"Faye Lynne McMillan. Born July 13, 1950. Died September 28, 1979. Age 29. Survived by mother Dorothy and step-father Ray. Also by sisters Sheryl and Nicolette. Service Saturday, September 30, 1979. Memorial donations to the American Lung Association." He sat silent after he read.

I got up, walked to the bathroom and started the shower. *I always take a shower at night. I always do. That way I don't have to do it in the morning and I can sleep a little longer. That's what I do.*

I got into the shower and cranked up the hot water until it was scalding hot. But suddenly Bob reached into the shower and turned the water off.

"C'mon. Get out." He wrapped me in a towel and sat me on the bed. The inside of my head popped like cap guns. Pop. Pop. Fireworks. Blinded by the light. Hysteria. Laugh? Cry? More fireworks. An earthquake. "There's an earthquake!" I screamed, but it was Bob shaking me.

"You need to calm down a little and think. Who can you call to find out what happened? Can you call her mother?"

"Oh, god, no. I couldn't talk to her. Not now." *Why hadn't I called last week? Why?*

"She was a smoker, right? Donations suggested to the American Lung Association? She probably had cancer." I knew Bob was trying, as best as he could, to empathize with me. He tenderly held me close.

"I should have known!" I screamed. "I should have known." And then I realized I *would* have known if only I'd called her. If only. If only.

"Lisa. Look at me. Who can you call?"

"Liz. I can call Liz." My voice was shaking so bad I wasn't sure if I'd actually spoken. It had been a very long time since I'd seen Liz. She too was in love with Lynne and had been as long as me. She realized that being in love with a girl made her gay. But when she told her parents that she was gay, her father said, "I'd rather see you pregnant." Poor Liz. She was so sweet and kind. I remembered how hurt she was at her father's comment.

"I'll see if she's in the phone book." Bob got the White Pages and began searching. "How's her last name spelled?" I told him and within moments, he found Liz's number. He dialed it and handed the phone to me. It rang a long time before I got an answer.

"Hello." It was Liz's voice, a voice I hadn't heard for such a long time. It was a low, sweet voice and the sound of it brought back such bittersweet memories. I could barely speak. "Liz? Liz? It's Lisa. I…I…Oh my god. What happened?"

Her voice was always solid and deep, but now it sounded weary, raspy and stressed.

"We tried to call you! The service was on Saturday. We tried all day Friday but we couldn't get an answer. Lisa…she killed herself."

I don't remember what happened after that. Bob told me later that I'd thrown the phone down and collapsed. He told me that he'd continued talking with Liz and that he'd have me call her back when I was able.

He lifted me to the bed and laid me down. When I came to, he was lying beside me, stroking my forehead. John was standing next to the bed, holding my hand.

Okay, I thought. *Okay. I've got to pull myself together. I don't want John seeing me like this. This is not good. At all.* I sat up and said I was better. I took the phone and dialed Liz's number again. She picked up right away.

"Lisa? Are you okay?"

"Oh Liz." I felt tears welling up and another scream gathering like a storm in my throat. "I can barely speak, Liz. I don't know what to say. How did it happen? What did she do? Are you okay? What about her mom and her sisters?"

Both of Liz's parents had committed suicide. I felt so badly for her that she now had to deal with a third suicide of someone she loved.

Liz tried to calm me. "I don't really know what happened. I just know that Lynne's girlfriend, Darlene, came knocking on our door, crying hysterically. She just sort of fell into my arms. My partner, Jo, brought her in and sat her down. But Darlene was incoherent."

My instantaneous thought was: *Who's Darlene?*

Liz said Darlene managed to tell them that the police had come to her door, asked her if she knew a Lynne McMillan, took her downtown to the morgue to identify the body, brought her back to her house and left.

"She came straight to our house," Liz said.

"But, I don't understand. What happened?"

"Do you remember how my dad killed himself?"

"Yes."

"Well, Lynne did the same thing. She drove up into the mountains, found a logging road, put a rag in the exhaust pipe with the engine still running, drunk a bunch of booze, took some pills and died."

My heart filled with sorrow. "Dear god, Liz. That's awful. Really awful."

"It made me furious with Lynne that she would chose the same way my dad did but I'm already over it." Liz was a strong person and didn't linger on the sad and awful in life. Perhaps that's how she coped.

"Look, do you want to come to our house and talk? We can look at pictures and laugh or cry—whatever we need to do. We can talk then. How does that sound? It will be our own personal wake, okay?"

I could see Liz's face as she spoke. She was the only person I knew who always searched for the bright side even when it seemed like it couldn't be any darker. We made a date to get together the following Sunday.

Before we rang off, I had a question I needed to ask. "Liz, this may seem odd, but do you know what time Lynne died?"

"Well, I saw the police report that Darlene brought with her. I think it said the time of death was around 3:20 in the morning."

For the rest of that week, I was a robot. I did and said what I was supposed to, went to work, came home, cooked, ate, cleaned, brushed my teeth, went to bed. I helped John with his homework and tried to have reasonable conversations with Bob without allowing my grief to show.

But inside my head, way inside, was a small woman who wouldn't stop screaming. I closed my eyes and willed her to go away, but the screaming just kept going on and on, day and night, night and day.

3:20 am. How could that be? I had to admit that even if it made no sense, Lynne had said good-bye to me in the last moments of her life.

CHAPTER 36

SURROUNDED BY GHOSTS

IT WAS A pleasant mustard-colored house that sat high above the street. There were fragrant rose bushes in the front yard and a garland of wisteria was draped along the roofline. It looked like a comfortable place to live.

"Nice looking place your friend has," Bob said as we got out of the car. Bob had insisted on coming with me even though I didn't want him to. And now that we were there, I figured I'd try one more time to get rid of him.

"Yes, it is nice, and you know, there's a bowling alley right around the corner. Are you sure you don't want to get in a few games while we chat? You know how boring it's going to be to listen to us."

"I'll bowl later," he said, "I want to stay by my wife's side." He smiled and put his arm around me and together we climbed the steep steps to Liz's door.

As soon as I knocked, Liz opened the door and threw her arms out for a hug.

"Oh, Lisa, she said. "It's been so long."

She looked the same as the last time I'd seen her. Her blonde hair was a bit longer and a bit darker but her eyes were still blue and her air of optimism had not diminished. I was immediately reminded of how safe I had always felt when I was with Liz, no matter what we were doing. She was always the one amongst us who kept a level head and always the one we turned to when we needed comforting or advice. Seeing her again after all this time made me realize all that I had missed by losing touch with her and I instantly felt at home in her house.

After I introduced Liz and Bob, she showed us to her living room. As we chatted briefly, I noticed that Bob was acting as if he was afraid of something. He sat so close to me on the sofa that you couldn't slide a piece of paper between us. I wanted him to just disappear and did my best to ignore him, despite him hogging my air space.

Liz introduced me to Jo, her girlfriend, and then walked into the kitchen. She soon returned with an enormous jar of homemade cookies. Jo stayed in the living room with us. She was tall and had short, graying hair. She couldn't look us in the eyes and seemed uncomfortable.

"I made these yesterday. They're my mom's recipe for chocolate chip cookies. I could just put my face in them!"

"Oh wow! I remember your mom's cookies. There was always a big jar of them in you guy's kitchen."

Liz offered us small plates, coffee cups and napkins.

"How do you like your coffee?" she asked as she headed into the kitchen. Bob said, "I don't."

I called out, "He doesn't drink coffee. Do you by chance have any Kool-Aid?"

From the kitchen, Liz yelled, "Kool-Aid? No. I don't have any Kool-Aid. Sorry."

"I'll have cream and sugar in mine, thanks," I said. I noticed there were several large photo albums on the coffee table. Jo seemed shy and overwhelmed, and kept busy corralling their beautiful white Samoyed dog, Mamie. Liz came back with a tray of mugs and placed it on the coffee table. Then she sat on the sofa and, after a quick glance at Bob, plastered herself next to me on my other side.

After several cups of coffee and a few too many cookies, Liz asked me if I was ready to look at the photo albums.

"Yes. Please. I'm ready."

Liz opened a large brown one and we slowly flipped through each page. We pointed out photos to each other, photos from so long ago that reminded us of our golden times together at the beach. We laughed and told embarrassing stories. Suddenly it was if Jo and Bob had completely disappeared. A thought kept banging in my head. *This is where I belong. Right here. Nowhere else.*

But we could only reminisce so long before the other reason for my visit couldn't be avoided any longer.

Liz closed the photo album and looked at me. "You didn't know Lynne was suicidal?"

"No. How could I have known?"

"Don't you remember that one party we had at her house? I think we were all about sixteen."

"I'm not sure which one you mean," I said.

"Dorothy and Ray were out of town and Lynne was having a party that Saturday."

"Oh yeah....I sort of remember....Wait! Wasn't that the night she shoved her hand through the kitchen window and then raked her wrist across the shards?"

"That's the one."

"We were all drunk," I said. "Oh, my god, how could I have been so stupid? I didn't want to think that she'd slit her wrist on purpose. I remember she was lying on the kitchen floor, bleeding everywhere and no one knew what to do because we'd all been drinking. Oh yes. I remember now. How could I have forgotten?"

"Do you remember what she said?"

I closed my eyes. It was as if I had gone back in time and was floating above the scene.

"I was sitting on the kitchen floor, holding her head in my lap and pressing cold washcloths on her wrist. People were screaming and running around. Some of us were furious, some were scared and I—now I remember—I was heartbroken. Yes, heartbroken." I remembered clearly that the thought of losing Lynne, especially to suicide, was unbearable.

Liz reached over and took my hand. I was perilously close to falling apart and she clearly understood that.

My voice was barely audible. "Yes, I remember. I think I must have blotted it out. I remember what she said. I held her head and asked her why. 'Why did you do this? What are you trying to do?' And she looked in my eyes and said, 'I just want to be free.' She said it over and over again. And I kept asking, 'Free? Free from what?' And then her sister Sheryl arrived."

"Yes," said Liz. "I had called Sheryl and she rushed over. We got Lynne into Sheryl's car. The rest of us piled in your car and we drove Lynne to the hospital. We were all yelling at each other trying to come up with a plausible story about why her wrist was in tatters without giving ourselves away."

"Giving yourselves away from what?" Bob asked.

Liz and I both looked at him and said simultaneously, "We had been drinking!"

Liz continued. "We were minors. And we knew it was against the law to try to kill yourself. We didn't want any of us, especially Lynne, to go to jail. And we didn't want to get busted for drinking."

"I'd forgotten how drunk Lynne was that night," I said, shaking my head slowly and valiantly fighting back tears.

"Lisa, maybe you knew this and just forgot because it's so sad. But Lynne tried many times to kill herself. She just hurt too much. The world hurt her. She couldn't find a place or a person to make her happy."

"But why did she give up? What about this Darlene? Weren't they happy?" I wanted to find a rationalization, a perfectly good reason that this happened. But more than anything, I wanted to be told it was just a bad, bad joke and that Lynne would pop out of hiding and yell, "Gotcha!"

"They had been happy," Liz said, "but Darlene said that lately they'd been fighting. She said just a few weeks ago she found Lynne out in their garage, sitting in the car with the engine running."

The full weight of it struck me in the chest, taking my breath away. *Why hadn't I called her? Why?*

Liz offered me another cup of coffee. She returned from the kitchen with two mugs, one for me, the other for her. She looked at Bob and said, "You sure I can't get you something?" He shook his head no.

"Dorothy can't handle taking care of Lynne's ashes and asked me to do it."

"She was cremated? My god. I missed the funeral and now there won't be a grave I can go visit?" *This can't be real,* I told myself.

"Dorothy and I both know that Lynne would want her ashes scattered in the Sound. I'm going to rent a little boat next week at the marina. Would you like to go with me to say a final goodbye to Lynne?"

"Yes. Yes, I would very much."

"Well why don't you give me your phone number? I'll call you when I've got the boat arranged and we'll meet at the dock. How does that sound?"

"That sounds good," I said and I wrote down my work phone number for her.

Bob was digging me in the ribs with his elbow. I turned to him and said, "What? What do you want?"

"It's time to go." He abruptly stood up and turned to Liz.

"Liz, it's been a real pleasure," he said, as charming as ever. "Nice to meet you, Jo." He extended his hand to Jo for a shake then turned to me and said, "Get your coat."

Liz walked us to the door. Bob walked ahead and started down the stairs. I turned to give Liz a hug. She grabbed me and held me close. She wouldn't let me go. She just held me and held me.

"Come on. Let's get going." Bob was now down on the street, unlocking the car.

"Okay. You'll call me?" I whispered in her ear.

"I'll call you. I promise." She gave me one last squeeze and then let me go.

I got in the car and Bob drove away. It was a long drive back to Federal Way and we sat in silence for quite a while. But when we got on the freeway, Bob said, "You know, its fine with me if you want to visit your lesbian friends. I think, in fact, you should feel free to do so."

Puzzled, I looked at him and said, "What are you talking about?"

"I'm talking about your cozy little good-bye. That woman did not want to let you go. So, I will say again. You are more than welcome to visit your lesbian friends."

"Okay." I wondered where this was going.

"But if you do," and he slowly turned to look at me, "if you do, you'll never see your son again. Never. Do I make myself clear?"

Bob had made threats before. He made it clear to me many times that he would kill me if I tried to leave him. I was afraid to call his bluff. But he'd never threatened John before. My heart froze and I knew that I'd just seen Liz for the last time.

I hid my sorrow as best I could, and got on with work and soon I began to earn promotions. But when I looked at the future, I sank into a deep depression. Lynne was gone, and with it, my safety net. I knew that if I ever needed her, she would have helped John and me without question. I would have been safe with her. But now that safe harbor was gone.

Sometimes, when I was alone and it was the middle of the night, I'd get out of bed, quietly pick up my purse and tiptoe down the hall to the kitchen. I'd take my wallet out of my purse, and slide out the slip of paper Lynne had given me so many years ago. I would hold the note to my heart and recite by memory:

> ... *"Do it if you have to, you above all others can,*
> *because you have the realization of life,*
> *a gift God gives only few."*

In the fall of 1979, the board that governed the hospital where I worked decided to provide scholarships for employees. I was offered a one-year grant to take whatever classes I was interested in. I felt like this was some small vindication since I'd given up the government grant to the University of Washington so long ago. I had little to no proficiency in math so I used my scholarship to take night classes in algebra at a nearby community college.

The days were short and the nights long. There was little break in the low grey cloud cover that made the Pacific Northwest foggy, misty, mysterious and melancholy. As I navigated the sprawling night campus, I thought I saw Lynne everywhere—in the shadows, standing under a street light, entering the library, having a coffee in the student cafeteria—as if she were just waiting for me to notice her. But I was only staring at strangers.

And during the day I seemed to see Isaiah everywhere. I thought I saw him at the hospital, peeking around a corner and running away laughing; walking down the street with his mother, holding her hand and skipping; or standing near a bus stop downtown, there one minute and then lost in a swirl of people getting on and off the buses the next.

I was surrounded by ghosts. My friends were gone; and what few friends I still had, Bob had managed to keep away. And now Lynne was nothing more than ashes floating on the Sound. And what of my dreams? Those, too, seemed to have died one by one. Going to London seemed as impossible as flying to the other side of the Milky Way—so far that I'd never get there. With each of my losses I began to die bit by bit.

And bit by bit, I felt as if I was disappearing into timelessness.

CHAPTER 37

I GUESS I'LL NEED A PASSPORT

I HAD NEVER experienced such sorrow. Lynne came to me night after night in my dreams and I woke every morning with a feeling that her spirit was looking down on me and my grief. How could she be gone? My mind and heart couldn't handle it. Her loss was beyond my comprehension. Yet I had to go on.

Every June I observed Isaiah's birthday silently and secretively. I missed him even though I didn't know him. It felt strange to observe the birthday of someone who I didn't know and who didn't know me, but I was compelled. After all, I may have given him up for adoption but he was still my biological child. Usually I would mark the occasion in my head—write a notation in my journal or just say a little prayer, a greeting to the skies hoping a cloud would carry my thoughts to him. I clung to the special secret I had about him and hoped one day we'd meet.

I had gotten another promotion and was now working in the alcohol and drug treatment service. The offices were housed in an old brick apartment building across the street from the hospital. It was a U-shaped building built around a welcoming courtyard.

One day, I was leading a meeting in a room that overlooked the courtyard. Halfway into the meeting, I looked out the window, and saw John sitting on a bench reading a comic book. I thought, *Wait a minute. What on earth is John doing here? He's supposed to be in school.*

Then I realized it was Isaiah. I jumped up and ran out of the room, through the reception area and outside. But he was nowhere to be seen. Had I imagined it? Somehow, within those few seconds, Isaiah had disappeared. I returned to the meeting to find everyone regarding me oddly, but I offered no explanations for my sudden departure and continued with the meeting.

But my thoughts were in turmoil. I knew I wasn't imagining it; I'd clearly seen a boy, and that boy had been a dead ringer for my son. Seeing him made me realize how all those other boys I'd thought were Isaiah, were not. This time, seeing the real one, there was no doubt about it. Why was he in the courtyard? The offices on the second and third floors were the mental health service. Had he been seeing someone there? He was nine years old at the time. Perhaps he was going to grief counseling after the loss of his dad?

After that sighting, I became even more obsessed. I knew where he lived, and wondered if he was going to the junior high school that was only five blocks away from my work. How could I find out if he did indeed attend that school there without tipping my hand or breaking the secrecy I had to keep?

The library, I thought. The downtown library had the annuals of all the schools in Seattle going back decades.

One day on my lunch hour I took the bus to the library. It was pouring rain. I'd forgotten my umbrella and darted from overhang to overhang trying to stay dry. I felt furtive and suspect.

The librarian I talked with asked me to wait a few minutes, disappeared into the hidden repositories of books, and returned with the annual I'd requested. I took it to a table and sat down. Before I opened it, I told myself that I wouldn't be disappointed if Isaiah's picture wasn't in there. After all, I was making a supposition based entirely on nothing but my own hopes.

Outside the rain continued to chuck down. The sky was an angry slate grey and deep indigo blue, casting a pall of dreariness through the library windows.

I opened the annual and flipped through the pages. There were pictures of sports and drama productions, a jazz chorale and the journalism production team that produced the annual. Then I browsed the class pictures. I figured Isaiah might be in the seventh grade and found that section. Slowly, I turned the pages, starting with the "A's" and ending at the "L's." There he was—the boy in the courtyard. My heart momentarily stopped. *There he was.* My child. He was ten years old and looked just like his brother John and his father Bob. Seeing his face on the page, a whirlwind of emotions blew through me—happiness, sorrow, pride and shame. I approached the librarian's desk.

"Hello, ma'am, can you make a copy of this page for me?" I felt so guilty, as if I'd just asked her to make a copy of Hustler magazine.

"Sure. It will only take a second." She left the desk to go to the copy machine.

When she returned, she handed me the copy. "Thank you," I said. "Thank you so much."

I looked at my watch and realized I would need to run for my bus in order to get back to work on time. I folded the copy, put it deep inside my purse and made a dash outside, irrationally hoping that I could stay dry if I maneuvered between rain drops. A ridiculous notion, but it helped me to concentrate on getting back to work and to put aside for the moment the marvelous vision of my son's face.

I was sinking in secrets. I didn't tell a soul about Isaiah and no one had any idea how hard Lynne's death had hit me. And they sure didn't know about my situation at home, which was rapidly becoming full of sorrow and loss. I was feeling crushed under the weight of the secrets I kept, but I had no idea what to do. While I could hide my secrets, it was getting harder and harder to hide the fact that I was falling apart.

My coworker, Vera, pulled me aside one day and said, "You don't seem like yourself. Are you okay?"

I wanted to burst forth with my fears and sorrows, take all the secrets within me and throw them at her feet. I knew she'd understand. Instead, I said, "Yeah, I'm okay."

But Vera knew me better than that. "I don't think you're okay at all. You don't smile anymore. Your voice is flat. Your face looks vacant. You move as slowly as molasses in January. Something is wrong. This isn't you. Maybe you should see a therapist or something."

I felt like she'd just hit me hard in the solar plexus. I had no idea that my affect had changed so much. I thought I was doing an excellent job of hiding my feelings and turmoil.

"Oh, yeah, maybe I should see someone. I'll give that a think. Thanks for telling me." I patted her on the shoulder.

Ronald Reagan was in his second term as president. MTV and VH1 had debuted on television. A gallon of gas was just over a dollar. John was moving into second grade and I continued to earn promotions at work.

Bob carried on being either sweet and loving or cruel and bullying. I had grown accustomed to focusing on the sweet and loving side, and excusing the cruelty and bullying. In addition to being my husband, lover and friend, he continued to be a father figure for me and I depended on his advice and guidance, even though they might be delivered in an overbearing way. It didn't matter how it was delivered, I trusted and needed his guidance. It was pathetic, I knew that. But I didn't know what I would do without him.

He won at bowling infrequently but he did bring in a bit of money working as a janitor at the local bowling alley and sports complex at night. At least that was what he said he did. I always had some suspicions that he might be doing as little as possible. I could easily see him drinking a lot of free Coke and playing the pinball machines all night. There were dark rumors that the Mafia owned the complex and I sometimes wondered if Bob was doing favors for them. It was a ridiculous notion that I berated myself for thinking, until one evening when our car was set on fire.

Bob had gone out bowling and I was fast asleep. It was nearly midnight when the phone rang. It was Bob and he was out of breath.

"Someone set the car on fire!" He sounded frightened.

"What? Good Lord, are you okay?"

"I'm okay."

"Are the police coming? Did you call the fire department?"

"The fire's out. No need to bother them."

A chill went up my spine. "What do you mean 'not bother them'? Who did this? Why don't you want the police involved?"

"The fire is out," he said, now sounding irritated. "Someone ran out from the bowling alley with a fire extinguisher and put it out."

"Can you drive it?"

"Yeah, the damage was to the drivers' seat."

"Really?" Even though it was late at night and I was tired and getting ready for bed, I knew something wasn't jiving with his story.

"What in the hell is going on here?"

"Just never mind," he growled at me. "I'm on my way home. I just didn't want you to be shocked when you saw the car, that's all." He hung up and I prepared myself for a scene.

Soon he pulled into the driveway. I ran down the stairs and out the door, still wondering if he was really okay or if his irrational attitude was just his attempt to downplay how serious it really was.

He got out of the car, brushed past me and went up the stairs and into the house. I looked at the car.

The fire had burned the driver's seat down to the springs and the seat back was gutted.

I went back in the house and confronted Bob. He was in the bedroom, taking off his shoes.

"Who did this?"

"I don't know and it doesn't matter. Don't worry about it."

"What do you mean 'don't worry about it'? Someone set fire to our car. Why shouldn't I worry about it?"

He stood up to unbutton his shirt and looked at me with scorn.

"Because I said so. Leave it be. The car runs and that's all that matters."

Was there a point in belaboring his insistence that car arson was nothing to worry about?"

I stuffed pillows and towels into the burnt hole in the seat so I could drive to work without the springs poking my butt. I stretched an old sweater over the seat back and tied the sweater arms together in the back to secure it in place. Bob wouldn't discuss the fire, who set it or why, leaving me to imagine the rumors about the Mafia were true.

In 1987, the hospital ran into its first budgetary crisis. Every department was ordered to eliminate at least one position. I was still working in the alcohol and drug treatment program as the administrative manager. There were four clinical managers. I suggested to the medical director that if I could teach the clinical managers how to do budgets, supervise support staff, and manage space projects to extend services or add facilities then my own position could be eliminated. And if my position was eliminated, I would qualify for unemployment. How nice, I thought, to maybe not work for a couple of months before looking for another job. So, getting rid of my position seemed the sensible thing to do.

The medical director, Lily, agreed. She had been my boss for three years and while I loved the work, I had difficulties working with her and would not be saddened to leave. I trained the clinical managers, tied up loose ends and prepared to go.

Towards my last day in that position, I had an appointment with Human Resources to discuss my leaving. I sat across the table from someone I'd known a long time, someone who—like me—moved up the ranks into managerial positions. "I'm sorry to see you going," Jim said. "You've been an asset to this place."

"Thanks, Jim. Perhaps I'll find something else here but to be honest, I think I'll enjoy a little time off." The truth was that the only time off I'd taken in nearly twelve years was for medical reasons. I'd never been on a real vacation.

"So do you understand the severance you will receive?" he said.

I sat back in the chair and crossed my leg. "Severance? I'm not sure what you mean by that. I know that I'll get my vacation time cashed out."

"Didn't anyone tell you?"

"Ah. . . no."

"Your severance includes all your vacation time, plus two weeks' pay for every year you've worked here."

I sat up straight. "You've got to be joking."

"No. I'm not kidding. So, I've done a little calculations and it looks like your total payout will be around $14,000."

I got a rush of chills up and down my body. I could barely speak. "Fourteen thousand dollars?" I stammered.

"Yup! The check will be ready at the end of this week." He reached out to shake my hand. "Good luck. I know you'll land on your feet."

I returned to my office looking dazed. My coworker, Jenny, asked me if I was okay.

"I'm good," I told her. "I just found out that I'll get a check for $14,000 at the end of the week as my severance package. I had no idea."

Jenny looked overjoyed. "Do you know what this means?"

"No, not really. I'm still just taking it in."

Maureen, one of the clinical managers, smiled broadly. "It means you can go to London! You'll have enough money to go to London!"

Everyone who knew me knew that going to London was my dream. I couldn't believe what she'd just said. "Seriously?"

"Seriously. You'll have more than enough to go to London." I couldn't really let myself think that might be possible.

"Of course, you'll need to check with Bob, but I'll bet he'll be just fine with it." I couldn't predict what he'd say, but I knew that if Bob said no, my co-workers would know what kind of a controlling and domineering husband he was and that was the last thing he wanted anyone to know.

That evening, I told Bob about the severance. We were sitting on the bed talking, as I slipped off my work shoes.

He was understandably thrilled to hear about the money. He said we could pay off some bills, get a new washer, and even get a new TV.

"Well, and guess what Jenny said today at work?"

"What did she say?" I could tell he was suddenly feeling expansive.

"She said that I should take some of this money and finally go to London!"

"She said what?"

"That I should go to London. And everyone agreed—they even said you'd want me to go."

There, I'd said it.

He was silent for a moment. Then he said, "I think you should go. As soon as possible.

"Are you serious?"

"Yes, I'm serious.

I burst into tears. After so many years of dreaming of London, I was actually going to go there! It was unfathomable and I wasn't fooling myself. I realized that Bob had agreed with it—not because he genuinely wanted me to be happy, but because he wanted to live up to the image he'd created among my coworkers.

John, who had been watching TV, heard me crying and ran down the hall to see what was wrong. "I'm going to London!" I told him.

"You are? Mama, that's what you've always wanted!" He started to jump up and down in his excitement for me.

The next day, when I arrived at work, everyone looked at me as if to collectively say, "Well...?"

"I guess I'll need a passport," I said, "cos I'm going to London!"

CHAPTER 38

THE THAMES IS BROWN

SOON LEARNED THAT planning for a trip was half the fun. Bob wanted me to take someone with me, so I asked my work friend, Shirley. Shirley was an enthusiastic person, blonde and full of energy. Short but incredibly strong, she had been state hurdling champion in high school. I once watched her chase a purse snatcher near our work. I'd never seen anyone run like that; she sort of lowered herself to the ground and then ran as if her legs were the wheels of a Corvette. There was no question that she could take of herself and maybe that's why Bob wanted her to come along. She, too, had never travelled overseas and was ecstatic to be asked to accompany me.

"The first thing we need to do," I told her, "is to get our pictures done and apply for our passports."

"Cool!" Shirley was nearly jumping up and down with excitement.

Together we got our passport pictures taken, bought some travel clothes, a camera and luggage.

As we spread the London A-Z map on the living floor and consulted travel guides, the reality of this dream-come-true hit me and I was momentarily hysterical. Laughing and crying at the same time for the same reason—I was going to visit my personal Mecca!

John looked through the tourist guides with us and helped find a hotel just off the Bayswater Road. He made me promise to keep a journal to record every single detail of the trip and to bring him back a T-shirt.

The soonest we could leave Seattle was on November 18. It was a less than perfect time; a storm of historical proportions had hit England just the month before, killing people and knocking down trees and power everywhere. Then a fire hit the Tube at King's Cross, leaving everything smelling like smoke and covered in soot.

But these misfortunes were not in the forefront of my mind. After longing to go there since I was a child, I was finally going to London.

November 19, 1987

Dear John,

    Shirley and I are finally settled into our hotel. Our flight was really long—about eight hours but we weren't tired when we landed. We got a bus that took us to the Marble Arch, one of London's main intersections. From there, we walked back west to our hotel in Bayswater. To get to our room we had to climb up some stairs, then down stairs, and then take a sharp left to climb more stairs. Eventually we arrived at the door to our tiny twin-bedded room. The room is so narrow that I can stand with my arms outstretched and touch both walls!

There was a tall window at the end of the room with a deep sill. After a full day of walking, we sat in that window sill and watch life flow by on Queensborough Terrace below.

On that first night, I awoke with a start and thought *Oh my god! Am I really here?* I got up and quietly went to the window, pulled the curtain aside and opened it. A small whiff of night air floated through. Below a Bentley whispered by on the wrong side of the road. The aroma of Middle Eastern cuisine, mingled with the smell of McDonalds, soot and car emissions, wafted up. I saw people walking into the Boots drugstore on the corner. I heard the Tube rumble below and a million different languages and dialects from the pedestrians passing by, like some sort of symphony that had been orchestrated to greet me. There was a street sweeper singing out loud with his Walkman. Sure enough, I really was in London.

"I think we should plot out a route to take for each day we're here," Shirley suggested the next morning, as she unfolded the London A-Z map. "And here," she shoved a piece of paper at me, "keep this with you."

"What is it?"

"I figured out the exchange rate and applied that to the money we have. See here," and she pointed to little round drawings, "I tried to draw the various coins we have and then equate those to our money."

I thought Shirley might be a little obsessive until I remembered that she had a degree in Accounting.

"Okay, then. Thanks for this." I folded the paper and slipped it into my pocket. "So do we want to do some tourist stuff today?"

We each had a cup of tea that we'd brought up from the breakfast room, and Shirley took a sip of hers.

"What kind of tourist stuff?"

"Tower of London? Buckingham Palace? Harrods? Piccadilly Circus?" I asked, overwhelmed at the possibilities before us.

Shirley had finished blow drying her curly blonde hair and was now bouncing around like Shirley Temple on Ritalin.

"We should do whatever we want! How about no plans at all? How about we just wander around and see what we see?"

What a concept. Just let the day unfold and see what it turned into. I never could have done this with Bob.

20 November 1987

Dear John,

Shirley and I walked and walked and walked today, covering a large swathe of the Borough of Westminster. The mornings have been foggy and the night air nippy. There are the most fabulous Christmas decorations everywhere. London is adorned with holiday jewels. In Knightsbridge, Harrods is ablaze with lights both inside and out. Elaborate illuminations are stretched across Oxford, Regent, and Old Bond Streets. We rode the Tube only once because as we descended into the station, the smell of sulphur smoke and grease from the fire at Kings Cross station was overwhelming and we left. From now on we will rely on above-ground double-decker buses and our own two feet to get around.

And guess what? Remember that book I love so much, 84 Charing Cross Road? Well, Shirl and I found where it used to be, just up the street from Piccadilly Circus. It's not a bookstore anymore. It's a record store. But they have the old sign of Marks and Company (the bookstore's name) hanging in back of their store, above the cash register. I took a picture that you'll see when we get home! And I asked Shirley to take a picture of me standing under the sign. The guys in the store said they have thousands of tourists come every week to do the same thing!

For the first time in my life, I felt truly at home. This was where I belonged. Perhaps it was from studying the map for so long, but I seemed to know where to go, what corner to turn, and what direction to head. In wandering the city, we came upon so many unexpected delights that I confirmed what I have thought all along—London is magic.

Immigrants were being absorbed into London's heart and soul. We heard comments about it frequently. The man who drove the bus from Heathrow expressed his viewpoint, somewhat wistfully. "I'll probably be the only Englishman you meet on your stay," he said.

I was sitting opposite from him, asking questions as we sped by—"Is that Holland Park?" "Did we already pass Shepherds Bush?" "Shouldn't Kensington be on the right?"

"Wow." He momentarily took his eyes from the road to look at me. "Have you lived here before?"

"No." He looked confused so Shirley piped up. "She's just spent her entire life studying the map."

"Well," he said, "you should apply for The Knowledge. You'd make a good cab driver."

"Don't tempt me," I laughed. "But, are you serious? Do you really feel like you're the only Englishman in England?"

He looked around, as if checking to see that no Nigerians or Pakistanis were nearby.

"Yeah, I do. I don't know where London is going, but it's definitely leaving me behind."

There were now so many folks from faraway places living in England that their presence was reshaping the face of London. In Kensington Gardens, we strolled down the Broad Walk and thought we were in Abu Dhabi. Men in flowing robes, women covered head to foot in veils. Teenagers gathered, speaking in foreign tongues. We found the English in the far northwest corner of the Gardens, huddled from encroaching immigrants, clinging to their singular ways.

From our window, I observed London life flow by. There was a small private school just below us and I watched a Bentley pull up. A man in a white robe tied with an embroidered belt dropped his two daughters at the door, his proud beaming smile an aura that stayed in his stead. His girls were dressed in the school uniform—red and white checkered dresses over white blouses with Peter Pan collars, shiny black shoes and straw hats with red ribbon above the brim while he was obviously in his native garb.

22 November 1987

Dear John.

Today in Mayfair we peered through the glass door of a private club and saw a black maid in full uniform, carrying a silver tray with two brandy snifters up a spiral staircase. We couldn't believe our eyes! A black maid! In a black uniform with crisp white apron and little hat!

In Knightsbridge, our tea at Harrods was served by a woman from Haiti.

> *In the Food Halls we marveled at the holiday decoration in the*
> *Pasta Department where a second-generation Italian man fashioned a*
> *Christmas tree with red, green and yellow strands of linguini hanging*
> *from a wooden bar.*
>   *We saw Buckingham Palace and Speakers' Corner. Yesterday we*
> *took a tour of the Tower of London, enjoying The White Tower, St.*
> *John's Chapel and the Crown Jewels, where the uniformed Beefeater*
> *guard urged everyone to keep moving by saying, "Move your laigs lie-*
> *dies." I shall now be attempting to speak Cockney and confuse everyone*
> *when I get back!*

As we wandered about, timing and serendipity were with us: we entered Westminster Abbey just as a service was starting so we stayed to observe the rituals and hear the magnificent music of this unexpected treat.

Seeking shelter from a sudden downpour, we ducked into a small theater in Soho only to find we'd come just before a performance was about to start. I hadn't noticed what was on the marquee. We just ran in, bought the last two tickets and saw Agatha Christie's play, The Mousetrap, which at that point had been playing in St. Martin's Theater for thirty-five years. If I had purposely wanted to see that play I probably wouldn't have been able to get tickets. As it was, I felt London was giving me lovely surprises at every turn.

We stopped in a crowded pub in Mayfair and were soon approached by two young men who asked if they could share our table. Normally I would have freaked out if strange men wanted to talk with me, but I was in London and Bob was in Seattle. So I said, "Sure. Bring your pints over and join us."

The pub was small and hot, even as the arctic night air swirled small ground fog outside the door. Shirley was having a warm beer. I had Coke.

"Ah, Yanks," one of them said as he and his friend settled in at our table. He was very tall and thin, wore a khaki colored jacket with a white turtleneck.

"Hullo, ladies, I'm Colin and this is my mate, Patrick. What part of the States are you ladies from?"

"Seattle," Shirley told them.

The other young man, Patrick, was shorter with curly brown hair. He said, 'What brings you all the way across the planet to London?"

Shirley pointed to me. "She loves London! She's always wanted to come here, huh?" She turned to me for confirmation.

"Yes it's true." Colin saw that I had my worn A-Z map with me and I said "Show me where you live."

Colin unfolded the map and pointed to Clerkenwell. Patrick looked over the map, shaking his head. "For the life of me," he said, "I don't know why maps show the Thames as blue. Let's be honest. It should be brown. A deep murky smelly brown."

"I hope you don't think it rude of me, but why would you 'always' want to come London?" asked Colin. "It's a filthy, noisy, stink of a city. We're overrun with foreigners and we true English are disappearing."

"You know, our bus driver from Heathrow said basically the same thing," I said. "But I don't understand. People from other countries, races, ethnicities have always come to London and been integrated. Right?"

"That's true to some extent," Patrick said. "But not without fighting and rampant discrimination. It's the reason nationalism has grown so much and I dare say some Londoners are downright xenophobic."

"Well, to answer your question about why I would want to come to London, my answer is that I don't know. Perhaps it's the history or the literature or something completely undefinable." Colin and Patrick raised their pints. "Well, then let's drink to you! Welcome to London!"

The next afternoon, we took a step off Oxford Street to find ourselves on Carnaby Street, where those Swinging Londoners of the Sixties bought their gear. But now the street held nothing but cheesy souvenir shops run by Turkish men.

I paid more attention as we walked and slowly I noticed that there were people of many ethnicities and backgrounds, and they were Londoners too. That was the wonderful thing about the city—everyone belonged and they all defined the essence of the greatest city in the world.

As Empire builders, the English were accustomed to the immigration of those they oppressed. But now, refugees fleeing civil wars and ethnic cleansing had brought desperate people who pried open the doors to London with their withered hands. I pictured a huge tidal swell of people of every color one could imagine, from every part of the globe, swimming from the North Sea up the tides that became the Thames.

Whether the natives liked it or not, London opened its arms to everyone. It enveloped me in its arms in a great hug and, like Liz on the steps of her home, didn't want to let me go.

Our time in London flew by and we only saw a minute fraction of the city. It left me longing for more even before we had to leave.

But time was up and I had to go. "I'll be back," I told my city. "I don't know when, but I'll be back."

And that promise came to fruition sooner than I'd anticipated.

CHAPTER 39

THE ROPES BROKE

I RETURNED FROM LONDON a changed woman. The changes in me were so much more than having finally been to the place of my dreams. For the first time in many years, I felt accomplished and confident. I no longer needed to be envious of the friends and co-workers who had already been there. Now I, too, could talk of taking international trips, experiencing long flights, and navigating my way through the confusing city of London that was, in essence, an overgrowth of disparate villages. I knew that I wanted to go back but I had no idea how or when that could happen. Perhaps that was the root of my subsequent problems; despite the inner joy I felt, there was an equal and opposite feeling running through me.

Shirley and I had become close friends after our trip to London. We spent a lot of time together and I was happy to have a friend that Bob approved of. But, despite a new friend and the trip to London, I felt like I was somehow losing myself.

It was Shirley who first noticed that something wrong with me.

We were at my house and she was helping me fold laundry in our bedroom. I lifted up a towel from the basket and folded it in half, then half again, and in half a third time until the towel was an unwieldy mountain of absorbent cotton.

Suddenly she snatched the towel from my hands and said, "What is *wrong* with you?"

I stared at the towel in her hands, while her words moved slowly through my mind. "What do you mean?" I finally asked.

"Look at you. It's like you aren't even alive." I had never seen Shirley's face so serious and worried.

"Huh?"

"This has been going on for a while and I haven't said anything. But it's just getting worse. You've changed. You don't even laugh anymore. We used to laugh all the time, but now it's like you're just a shadow."

I realized my arms were dangling lifelessly at my side and my shoulders were slumped as if I had osteoporosis. I sat on the bed and looked around the room. Everything seemed to be been drained of color and dimension. It was as if my gaze took color away, making everything flat and gray. When I shifted my gaze, I imagined the color returning to whatever I'd been looking at. Shirley was right. Something was wrong with me.

She sat beside me. "I've noticed this since we got back from our trip. You seem like you don't care if you live or die."

That struck me like a slap on my face. I felt a slow icy realization come over me. "I...I...guess I don't care either way. I could live. I could die. It just doesn't matter." I was speaking to the wall, unable to look at my friend. She stood up and grabbed me by the shoulders.

"That's not right! You aren't supposed to feel like that. What would Bob do if you died?"

Bob? I thought about it for a second. A feeling of profound emptiness began to well up inside me. It was the first time I noticed that I felt miserable, as if I'd lost any reason for living. It was an unsettling revelation. I didn't care at all about what Bob would do if I died.

"You know, I really don't care."

Shirley still had her hands on my shoulders. I looked at her as if she were my mother and I an admonished child.

"Okay, you don't care about Bob. But what about John?"

I burst into tears. "Oh my god!" I said. "What's wrong with me? I've become so miserable that I didn't even think about my own son. John is everything to me. I couldn't die and leave him alone."

"I think you should see your doctor," Shirley said. "You seem so unhappy. It's like you can barely talk. You're walking so slow and humped over like you have no energy."

"You're right. I *don't* have any energy."

"Well I want you to see a doctor and get some help."

My tears abated. "Okay," I said. "I'll call my doc in the morning to get an appointment. But I don't know what to say. Do I just call up and say I feel dead inside?"

"Depressed. You just tell him you're depressed and need to get some help."

In those days, being depressed carried a social stigma. Depression was viewed more as a woman's issue, or a bad attitude, rather than a clinical condition and those who took medication for it were considered mentally ill. No one talked about being in therapy. It was a secret that no one with depression wanted people to know they had. It was considered weakness, or laziness, or just a sign that whoever had it belonged in the lowest level of society. Depression was nothing to talk about in public.

But I knew Shirley was right. The thought that I was one of those people who needed help felt like a punch in the gut. But maybe that was one punch that I actually needed.

I called my doctor on Monday and got a referral to the mental health service. I got an appointment for the next day. I must have sounded desperate. The only bad part was that I'd just accepted a promotion to a management position in the same department—the mental health service. Awkward to say the least.

"Do I really have to take pills?" I'd been referred to a psychiatrist, Dr. Meister, and was sitting in his office. It was lined with books. Piles of papers, books, and charts were everywhere—on the floor, his desk, even piled high in the non-working fireplace. *Thank god I'm not here for claustrophobia or OCD*, I thought, as I gingerly stepped among the stacks of paper to sit in the only chair that wasn't serving as a file cabinet. As I passed by, I noticed an open drawer of his desk. Lying inside was a case of pancake makeup, flesh-colored foundation thicker than Elmer's Glue, the sort of thing used in high school drama classes. *"Okay,"* I thought. *"That's weird."*

I imagined that if he opened his closest, we'd be buried in an avalanche of paper, professional journals and medical charts.

He stroked his graying beard. "You won't have to be on them for too long—just until you're feeling yourself again."

"Okay. How will I know when I'm feeling better?"

"What do you mean?" He stopped playing with his facial hair to look at me straight on.

"I mean I've felt like this for so long, I've forgotten what I felt like when I wasn't depressed."

He gave a short laugh, as if to cajole me. "Oh, you'll know. You'll remember how it felt before you were depressed. Trust me."

I didn't trust him. This is a psychiatrist who wears pancake make-up, for Pete's sake, but I followed his instructions and took the anti-depressant as prescribed.

But after six weeks, I still didn't feel any better, so I returned to the psychiatrist.

"Really? You're not feeling any better?" Dr. Meister had applied too much makeup that day and in the dry heat of his office, it had begun to crackle.

"No. And I'm so worried all the time. I'm so…I don't know…nervous."

"What do you mean by 'nervous'?'

"I don't know. Sometimes on the bus home, I think the bottom of the bus is going to fall out and I'll drop to the freeway, skidding to a stop in the express lane." He burst into laughter, but I didn't see the humor at all. Then he regained his composure.

"We'll try a different drug then. Paxil is a new drug that seems to be working well for a lot of patients, especially those who have concurrent depression and anxiety."

"Okay. I'll try Paxil."

But that didn't work, either. In fact, it made things worse. Then I tried Prozac and that made me feel terrible. I finally settled on Zoloft and after a bit, it seemed to work.

But just as the doctor said, as soon as I began to feel better he had me stop taking it.

Within a week, I plunged into blackness. I called Dr. Meister.

"I'm not doing well since I quit the Zoloft." I felt as if I were on a diabolical roller coaster, sitting backwards, watching where I'd come from and not knowing where I was going. He agreed to put me back on Zoloft.

And through it all, I felt like a fraud. Here I was, working in the mental health service, and I was apparently as crazy as our clients. When I was at work, I tried hard to conceal how I felt but I imagined some of the clinical staff might have noticed something. If anyone had noticed, though, no one said a word, and Shirley proved to be a true friend by keeping my secret as if it were her own.

One day at lunch, I told her how I was feeling. "I'm just not advancing here. I'm still ambivalent about things."

"Like what?" Shirley and I were sharing a big salad—we were on the Fit For Life diet and running after work each evening in my never ending quest for thinness.

"Bob, for one. Work, for another. Getting back to London, if ever. Everything." I hadn't told her about Isaiah and so couldn't wade into those waters.

"Well perhaps you should see a psychologist. Someone you can talk to, someone who can guide you. You know—a professional friend, sort of." Shirley could see that I was looking cautiously at her suggestion.

"You know, I've seen a psychologist already. It was long ago, after I had given up…" I suddenly realized I was about to inadvertently reveal my secret of Isaiah.

"Given up what?"

"Oh, nothing really. Just given up on life. It was after I left home."

Shirley finished her half of the salad, put down her fork and looked me straight in the eye. "Why would you come close to giving up on life when you'd just graduated high school?"

"Shirl, really, it doesn't matter right now. But I started going to group therapy with a psychologist—get this, his name was Dr. Bob. It wasn't a good experience so I guess I'm leery of people who call themselves therapists."

Shirley had begun to laugh a little. "So, why don't you find someone else? Like maybe a woman?"

I started therapy with a psychologist recommended by my family doctor. Dr. Smalls was in private practice with an office near my work. It was easy to walk there for my weekly lunch time appointment.

I was reticent to talk about what was really bothering me. The mental health community was a small one, and even though the psychologist I saw wasn't affiliated with my work, I still worried that word could get back to my colleagues. And far worse, even though Bob knew I was getting therapy, I didn't want him to know anything about what I discussed in my treatment. I knew it was supposed to be confidential, but he had proven over and over again that he could find out anything about me if he wanted. And knowing that, I feared that anything I revealed to the psychologist about my true thoughts or feelings would somehow get back to him. So I used subterfuge by steering my sessions with her towards anything but my marriage. I knew that at least part of my depression was the imminent eighteenth birthday of my first born child and the pressing perplexity of whether I'd meet him or not.

Living a lie was almost second nature to me at this point. No one at work would have believed the life I lived at home. At work, people saw me as vivacious, poised and talented. They all thought I was lucky to be married to Big Bob, and they enjoyed visiting with him when he came to pick up my paycheck just as he had always done.

We were driving home after he'd picked me up at work one day when I broached the subject of spending some money on something I deemed essential.

"You know, I'd really like to get a hand-held Dictaphone for work. I really need it to record meetings before I forget the details but, you know, the boss won't let me have one. She says its non-essential."

Bob had driven onto the freeway and briefly turned his head to look at me.

"So?"

"Well, I'm sure we still have money from my severance and I'd like to use some to get a Dictaphone."

His brow furrowed and he looked uncomfortable. "Sure," he said, 'Sure you can get one. Right after I win the Big One."

There it was again. Week after week I brought home the paycheck; how much longer was I going to patiently wait for him to win the Big One? I was beginning to think that it might never, ever happen and I would forever be the sole breadwinner in our family. And that wasn't what I'd signed up for.

"Well, when will that be?" I asked him in a snappy tone. "It hasn't happened so far. I've spent the last decade or so supporting you so that you could live out your dream and I've seen nothing in return."

I wasn't sure how I had arrived at such a low point. After all, I'd been to London. But I was still working hard yet had nothing to show for it. I was still living in a rental house and still waiting for Bob to contribute to our finances. I knew that when Shirley exposed my unhappiness to me that I didn't care about anything.

"I promise you it will happen soon. I've got that new ball and those new shoes and they work much better on the oil being used on the alleys these days. It's only a matter of time. I've got that trip to Orlando for that huge tournament and need what money we have left for that."

"What trip to Orlando?"

"I'm sure I told you. I'm going with a couple of guys from league. The first prize is $100,000. You could buy a dozen Dictaphones with that!"

"I only want one. And how is it you have the money to go to Orlando?"

"Oh, I've got a sponsor."

"Who?"

"A guy from league."

"And he'll expect a return on his investment when you win, right?" Bob's eyes began to dart around. I assumed he was looking for cops.

"Well, yeah. He'll want a small percentage of my winnings."

"How much of a percentage?"

"Do you want me to go into this knowing my wife supports me or thinking that you don't?"

"I really don't give a shit anymore." Such impudence would usually have gotten me a slap, but he did nothing. Perhaps he was in shock.

We pulled into the driveway of our house. John was outside shooting hoops with his Swamp buddies. He ran across the street to give me a hug. Bob went inside and plopped on the sofa. I went into the kitchen and made eggs and rice for dinner, a quick meal I often resorted to when I was particularly tired. And at that moment, I felt like I had been struggling up Mt. Everest for a very long time. My climbing ropes were just about worn and soon I would tumble into an icy crevasse too exhausted to call for help.

It's an odd feeling—odd and strange and other-worldly—to realize that you no longer care if you live or die. There was a void within me that once had been filled with happiness and interest in life. I went over and over in my mind that I had been a terrible mother and that John would be better off without me. If I left him on this planet to go to another, it was fine with me.

I went to my family doctor and asked for a prescription of Valium. "Just temporary work-related stress," I told him.

That weekend, I cleaned the house as usual, then settled to watch my favorite Saturday afternoon British shows on PBS. I went to the bathroom and looked at my reflection in the mirror. I saw nothing there. It was if I didn't exist. I returned to the sofa and took all the pills at once. I fell into a comatose state and while I don't remember much of that event, I do know that I spent two days curled up on the sofa and that at one point, Bob lifted one of my eyelids and shined a flashlight into my eye.

I didn't respond and he left to go bowling, leaving me there to sleep it off.

I awoke on Monday morning, just in time to go to work.

I made other stupid attempts at suicide. I was confused. I guess I didn't really want to die and I knew I was crying out for help, but the thought of John eventually being grown and gone made living seem useless.

I swallowed a bottle of Ipecac and immediately started throwing up. I spent several days in the hospital after that attempt. This was the hospital where I worked.

Everyone thought I was so happy and accomplished. I couldn't tell these people why I was throwing up. I had unnecessary tests and endoscopies to determine the problem. Of course there was no problem in my stomach. The problem was in my heart and soul.

Thoughts of Lynne were with me constantly. She came to me in my dreams. She would float into my consciousness and then, just as I tried to move closer to her, she'd float away. These dreams were galling and frustrating. I would awake from them feeling sad and hopeless.

I missed Lynne desperately. Sometimes I would drive into town and over to the beach to sit on a bench on the bulkhead and sob. I didn't want to dwell on the sadness in Lynne's life or my own, but depression skewed my positive thoughts and healthy dreams turning them into a meaningless bog.

And I missed my living friends. Bob had cut me off from them and his threat of taking John away from me if I tried to see my friends again paralyzed me; I didn't dare take the risk. They had no idea what had happened to me. I'd stopped calling or returning their calls years before. They probably thought I'd dropped off the face of the earth or that I'd moved to London.

How could they have known that I was living so close by, but disappearing piece by piece into an abyss with seemingly no way out?

But as the year was coming to a close, I kept at therapy, concentrating on my childhood and I finally got on the right regimen of psychotropics. June 9—Isaiah's eighteenth birthday—was close at hand. I was determined to be better by the time I met Isaiah. *If* I met Isaiah.

Chapter 40

Have I Just Made an Enormous Mistake?

I T WAS 1988. It had been eighteen years since Isaiah was born and fifteen years since I'd discovered the information about where he lived, where he went to school, and who his parents were. And for all those fifteen years, I'd kept that information quiet and never told a soul. But in June, Isaiah would be eighteen and legally free to search for his birth parents and I would be free to contact him. Of course, he might reach out to me, before I reached out to him.

My concern wasn't just with my having a relationship with Isaiah. I also wanted him to have a relationship with John and Bob. The knowledge that Isaiah had been without a father since the age of seven often stabbed at my heart. Ever since coming across his father's obituary as I had, I constantly worried that his mother was struggling to raise Isaiah and his adopted sister, Millie, on her own. Knowing how hard that must be, I was tempted so many times to call her.

But I never did—until a few months before Isaiah's eighteenth birthday.

I waited for the weekend, when Bob would be out bowling and John out hanging with his friends.

I sat on our bed, sitting cross-legged and propped up by pillows. I took the phone and dialed her number. After a couple of rings, a woman answered and I asked if she was Ginny Midkiff.

"Yes." I heard a slight hesitancy, as if she thought I was trying to sell her something, but at the same time I wondered if she'd been expecting this call. "Who is this?"

"Well, I have a lot to tell you and hope you have a few minutes. My name is Lisa and I'm…I'm…your son's biological mother." It was a blunt and quick statement that brought a long silence on her end of the phone.

Finally, she said, "How did you get my number?"

"Well, do you have a few minutes?" I hadn't anticipated how emotional this was and I began shaking all over.

"I didn't have a few minutes before, but now I do. Please tell me what is going on here." Her voice sounded firm and angry. *Oh crap, I thought, have I just made an enormous mistake?*

Slowly I told her my story—finding out I was pregnant, deciding I would relinquish my child for adoption, marrying the father after all, having another son, working at Planned Parenthood—and how I discovered the information about who had adopted Isaiah.

Again there was a long silence on her end and then I spoke up.

"Ginny, I want you to know that I don't intend to try to be his mother or usurp your authority or be something I'm not. I gave him life but you raised him. In no way do I want to take that from you or diminish it in any way. But I'd like you to know that he has a biological father and brother. And me, of course."

There was a long pause on the other end of the phone and then I added, "Do you still have some time to talk?"

I heard her let out a long breath. "Yes. Yes I do," she answered softly.

I shifted in the bed and the pillows fell away from behind my back. I could hear the faint sound of the television on her end. It sounded like a basketball game.

"Will you tell me about Isaiah?"

For the next hour, Ginny told me all about Isaiah: his schooling, friends, activities, interests, hopes and dreams. As she talked, I was compelled to comment, "So does his brother," or "John does the same thing." Though they had yet to meet, it sounded like John and Isaiah shared many characteristics and traits. As we talked, I could feel the tension leave my neck and shoulders and my arms right down to my fingers. From the sound of her voice, I could tell that she had relaxed as well. We went from being strangers and potential enemies, locked in a battle for the heart of Isaiah, to being two mothers talking about their sons.

I told her about John and a bit about myself and a smaller amount about Bob. Isaiah had not had a father for eleven years and I thought Bob should be eased in.

Ginny agreed. Then our conversation turned to the matter at hand.

"Ginny," I said, "I don't know why I was led to that file room at work and I don't know why I found that information card first thing. I've never known if it was a blessing or a curse, because I have to tell you, it's been tempting over the years to just show up knocking at your door."

I heard Ginny gasp.

"Oh, I would never have done that," I reassured her, laughing to lighten the mood. "Never. But you do understand how hard it's been to keep this all to myself?"

"I do," she said. "I knew this day would come. Not that you would call me, but that Isaiah would want to find his birth mother. I've been preparing for it. But I have to ask you to make me a promise."

"Of course. What do you want me to promise?"

Ginny took a breath. "He graduates high school in a few weeks. He's been accepted at Washington State University." She paused. "He wants to be a veterinarian." I could hear a smile in her voice.

"Really? A vet?"

"He's always loved animals and he decided that by being a vet he could be with them and take care of their ills."

I was impressed. "Wow. Good for him. I imagine he'll make a very good vet."

"So, here's the promise I want you to make. After he graduates in a week, I'll be driving him to Pullman to get registered. I'll get him settled, buy whatever he needs and then we'll head home. It's very important to me that he goes to college and getting him ready to start school is my priority."

"Understandably!" Once again my pillows had slipped. I thought I heard Bob drive up. "Ginny, do you mind holding for a sec?"

"No, not at all." I laid the receiver down and walked to the front bedroom to look out. His car wasn't in the driveway and I let out a small breath of relief. I wasn't ready to tell him about this situation. I wanted to do so in my own time, at the right time. And this wasn't it. Perhaps I was afraid that if he knew that I was talking to Ginny, he'd grab the phone from me and hang it up—once again taking control of my decisions. I couldn't let that happen.

I returned to the bedroom, arranged my pillows and picked up the receiver.

"Where were we?"

"We were talking about Isaiah going to college."

"Right."

"So Lisa, if you can promise me you'll stay away until after I've gotten him set up at WSU, I promise that I'll tell him about you and his brother and father."

"You have my promise. Believe me, I've lived with this for a long time. I can wait a little longer. And I think when you tell him about us, that you should leave it entirely up to him. Don't you agree?"

"Oh absolutely, and thank you for saying that. I was worried about what your expectations would be."

"Basically my expectations are to find him well and happy. And after talking with you, I now know that he is well and happy. Of course I want to meet him and maybe encourage a relationship with his brother. But just talking to you has set my mind at ease."

I paused for a moment, listened to cars pass on the street, readjusted my pillow, and turned on the lamp as it was getting dark.

"Listen, Ginny. After you tell him, let's leave it up to him whether to call us or not, or wait for a while or not call at all. It's up to him. I truly don't want to rock the boat. You've done a lot of work raising Isaiah and Millie—it's Millie right?"

"Yes, Millie. We adopted her about a year after Isaiah. And I'm concerned about her. Millie will probably never meet her birth mother. No one knows where she is. So I do want to be sensitive to Millie's feelings about it."   "Of course," I said. "So, can we agree to that? You tell him about us and then it is entirely up to him in terms of a next step, or none at all."

"Absolutely."

We made our promises and agreements. We understood each other, one mother talking to the other, exchanging anecdotes about their sons. After three hours on the phone, I realized that she was a strong woman doing her best to raise two children on her own. Meeting Isaiah could go either way or not happen at all, but at least Ginny and I got to know each other.

After I hung up the phone, I sat in silence for a few minutes, then I became hysterical, laughing and crying at the same time. Relieved. Happy. Excited. Sad. I had done it. I was going to see my first born son sometime soon—at least, I hoped I would. But either way, he would know that we existed and that we wanted to meet him. And that felt like a miracle.

Now it was time to bring John and Bob in on my secret. For all those years I had never told Bob that I knew where our son was—and for all those years I had never told John that he had a brother. Bob had controlled every aspect of my life but this one piece, and I was not about to give up control now that I was so close to meeting my son. I was the one in control of this life-altering event and I was going to do what I thought was best. And I thought it was best to tell Bob first. He returned home soon after I ended my conversation with Ginny.

He bounded up the stairs, a big smile on his face. "Guess what?" he said.

"What?" I couldn't imagine what might make him so enthused. "Uh.... you won?" I said tentatively.

"I won three hundred dollars!"

"Well that's lovely. I'm really happy for you." I tried to look enthusiastic, but was distracted by what I was about to say. "And I've got something to tell you."

"Why can't you be more excited by my win?" He pouted, then turned away, trying to ignore me. I might need a touch more finessing but I wouldn't be deterred. He sat down at the kitchen table and I tried to be attentive.

"It really is great that you won! I'm proud of you. So, you must be hungry?"

"No, Billy bought me a Herfy Burger on the way home. So what do you need to talk about?"

I sat down next to him. "Remember when I worked at Planned Parenthood?"

"Yeah," he said. "Why?"

"Did you know that on the first floor there was an adoption agency?"

"No," he said. "Why?"

I drew in a big breath. "It's the adoption agency I used when I had the baby adopted."

"Okay." He began to rap his fingers on the table and his left leg started to bounce.

"Pay attention please. I'm trying to tell you something important."

He looked up from the table and into my eyes. "I'm listening."

I told him the story of how I found out about Isaiah. Not knowing how he'd take it, I spoke haltingly just in case I might need to stop mid-sentence to avoid a possible backlash from him.

"You know where he is?" He yelled "You've known since the 70's? You kept it to yourself all this time? Why?" Bob's brows came together and his nostrils flared. I saw surprise turn to anger in his face *Here it comes*, I thought. *He's going to explode. Keep calm, but stay firm.* "Yes," I said, not weakening. "I kept it to myself. I couldn't see any point in telling you at the time. There was so much going on in our lives, remember? We were working all the time. John was a baby. It just seemed the prudent thing to do." He backed off.

"Why are you telling me now?"

"Because he'll turn eighteen soon and will be able to search for his birth parents."

"I don't get it." Bob got up and poured himself some cold water from the pitcher in the fridge.

"I've talked with his mom. Today. I spent three hours on the phone with her."

"Good lord! What were you thinking? Are you out of your mind?"

"She was upset at first. But then she realized I wasn't trying to snatch him away from her, and we ended up having a good conversation."

"I think that was a stupid, stupid, stupid thing to do." He looked at me with disgust in his face but I was ready for that reaction, so I continued.

"I've been keeping this secret for fifteen years now. I can't and I won't hold it in any longer. Besides, I don't want to take him from her. I just want him to know he has this other family that he might want to meet."

"Well," he said walking into the living room to plop in front of the television, "it's your decision. You'll have to live with the consequences. It's on you. If you get hurt, don't come running to me." His upper lip curled, a gesture he often used to indicate his immense disapproval.

"You know, he's your son too."

"No he's not. You took that privilege away from me."

"Oh, okay. So here it comes. I thought you'd forgiven me. At least you said you had."

"It doesn't matter. He's got his own life and doesn't need you busting in on it."

I was not to be deterred. Meeting my son could be the single most important event of my life—and in the life of John.

"Here's the deal," I told Bob. "I'm going to meet him whether you like it or not. He was silent.

At fifteen, John was no longer a little boy. He was tall and strong. But no matter how big he got he would always be my sweet little boy and I wanted to protect him. And as I thought about how young he still was, I realized that I wasn't much older than he was when I met Bob. I had thought I was so grown up back then, when I was so eager to get away from my parents. But now, thinking of John, I realized I had been just a child myself when I met and married Bob. At times I could see myself in John. He was bright and full of promise, as I once had been. He had a future that I wanted to be rosy and accomplished. He needed to travel the world and learn where his place was, and not be held back by his father.

I was about to tell John my secret. How would he handle it? What would it do to his world? John and his friends went to the mall that Saturday to see a movie and flirt with girls. They had walked home from the mall. When he came up the stairs, I gave him a big hug. He smelled like fresh air and clouds as he squirmed from my grip.

"John," I told him "I need to talk with you about something. Something good."

"Sure thing, Mom. Right now?" He had immediately gone to the refrigerator. He poured himself a glass of milk and grabbed some homemade molasses cookies.

He sat at the table, already eating a cookie and spilling a little milk. "Don't worry, Mom. I'll clean it up."

"Spilt milk doesn't matter just now." A curious look passed across his face, as if he was wondering why suddenly making a mess didn't matter.

"So, what's up, mom?"

I took a deep breath. "I've got something to tell you, sweetie. You know, you've grown up as an only child."

"Yeah."

"So did I."

"Well, duh. What are you getting at, Mom?"

"I remember asking my mom one time—I might have been about eight—if I had a brother or sister somewhere. I hoped that maybe they'd had another child and maybe forgot about him or her. I thought if I asked, my mom would suddenly remember and say that I did indeed have a brother or sister and that it was high time that we got him or her back home."

"Okay. But I don't get this."

"You will," I said, touching his arm. "Just listen." I watched him stuff more cookies in his mouth.

I related to John the story of his brother. I had no idea how he would take it.

He might have been furious that I'd given his brother away. He might have been indifferent. But he was neither.

"Mom, you're saying I have a big brother and that he lives in Seattle and will be eighteen soon?"

"Yup, that's what I'm saying."

"What's his name?"

"Isaiah. Isaiah Midkiff."

"When can I meet him? Will it be soon?" John was jumping up and down with excitement.

"Calm down, sweetie! I hope we can meet him soon, after he graduates from high school. I've already talked with his mom and we decided she'd tell Isaiah about us and then it would be up to him if he wanted to meet us or not."

"You talked with his mom? How does that work? *You're* his mom."

He got up to get more cookies and milk and I briefly thought to tell him he'd had enough, but let it go.

"Isaiah has two moms, which might be a horrifying thought for most folks. But sweetie I'm not his mom in the sense of raising him. I gave birth to him, but then he was adopted and Ginny did all the work of raising him."

"Wow," John said, shaking his head. "Wow. Wow. Wow."

"I know. It's a lot to take in. But now you know you have a brother! How cool is that?"

"Oh, it's way cool! I can't wait!" John got up to get more cookies.

"Okay," I said. "Now you've had enough!"

Bringing Isaiah into our lives was a huge risk and I knew it. He might not want anything to do with us. I would respect and accept it if that were the outcome. It was also possible Isaiah might not be the sort of young man I'd want John to associate with. I doubted that, but it was something I had to consider. And Isaiah might be angry and hurt. He might hate us. I wanted to be mentally and emotionally ready and consider all the possibilities. Any way I looked at it, meeting him would bring a sea change that would affect all of us for the rest of our lives. Would we sink or would we swim? I had no idea, but I was about to find out.

Chapter 41

The Secret's Out

THE SCHOOL YEAR ended and Isaiah turned eighteen. I had kept my promise to Ginny that I wouldn't try to contact him until this birthday. Now I hoped she would keep her promise.

I sent her a card with a photo of John in it. The picture was one I had taken that prior Christmas in a clothing store near the Pike Place Market. I'd used my zoom lens from across the store so that John wouldn't notice I was taking his picture. Having seen Isaiah that one day at work and seeing his photos in his school annual, I knew that he and John could be mistaken for twins. They both had the same twinkly eyes and broad smile, curly hair and budding moustaches. If Ginny knew how much alike they looked, I just knew that she'd want Isaiah to meet his only brother.

I waited a few days and then I called her. I sat comfortably at the rickety old desk we had in the kitchen. Above it was a calendar with Isaiah's birthday highlighted in yellow. I fiddled with the phone cord as I dialed her number.

She answered so quickly that I wondered if she had been expecting my call.

"Ginny, this is Lisa. Isaiah's birth mother? Is this a good time to talk?"

"Yes," she said. "This is a good time."

"Well, how have you been? How is Isaiah? Did you get my card?"

She laughed and that was a good sign. "Yes, I got the card and the picture and I just can't believe how much alike the two of them look!"

"Pretty amazing, huh? So tell me, did Isaiah get all through graduation? And did you? I mean, graduating from high school is a big deal for the moms, isn't it?"

"Yes, it sure is. I feel like I can breathe now. I think I've been holding my breath for a long time but yes, Isaiah is now graduated from high school. It all went very well. I'm happy. He's happy. And we leave this weekend to drive to Pullman and register him for the fall."

She asked me about John and I updated her on his schooling and his interests which had moved from Hot Wheels to girls. I asked her if Isaiah had a girlfriend.

"No, not now. He had a couple in high school but no one serious. Does John have someone serious?"

"I hope not!"

I had stopped twisting the phone cord and had taken up a pen, twisting it in my fingers and then doodling on a piece of paper.

We talked more about our two boys and all the while I was thinking, *Eighteen years. Eighteen years and now this is really happening. God Lord, how things have moved and changed since that day eighteen years ago when I let that nurse take my newborn baby from my arms.*

And it was fifteen years since I'd discovered the information about him and his family in the file room of the Medina Adoption Agency. I'd been living this secret for so long that I could hardly believe it had all come down to this day, this phone call and, I hoped, this reunion.

My mind had wandered off into the realm of so many possibilities that I had also wandered from our conversation.

"I'm sorry, Ginny. What did you say?"

"I said we will drive to Pullman on Saturday and return the same day."

"Wow. That's ambitious. How many miles is it from here to there?"

"A lot!" she said. "I'm going to let him drive there, and then I'll drive home. I want to get it done in one day so we don't have to stay over."

There was a small silence suddenly growing between us. I wasn't sure what to say that wouldn't sound pushy or demanding. She must have sensed that.

"And I promise, on the way back, I will tell him all about you and your family."

I started to cry. "Thank you so much. I really don't know how I can thank you. I know that it will be up to him if he calls or wants to meet us, but you have been so generous with me."

"No. It's you who has been generous with me! You didn't know me but you gave your child to me to raise and love. I've always told Isaiah that his birth mother loved him so much that she let him live with me and his father. It was a brave thing you did."

Now I was really crying. And, she started crying too. We cried, then stopped, then burst into laughter.

"Well, I don't know about you," I said, "but I'm really tired of crying."

"Yeah, I am too!"

"So let's not cry anymore and instead concentrate on our two boys and hope that they'll find brotherhood to their liking." I knew I was jumping the gun, but I wanted to be as positive as I could.

I looked down and noticed that I'd drawn flowers all over the little piece of paper and I smiled. I always drew flowers when I was my happiest, and I couldn't imagine a happier moment than meeting my long lost son.

Now I just needed to count the days until the weekend and hold close the hope that Isaiah would call.

On that Saturday, I pictured Isaiah with Ginny driving across the brown wheat fields and endless farmland of eastern Washington to register for college. It was June and the nights were longer now. I paced around the house, trying to keep busy so I wouldn't think about Isaiah but that was a foolish effort. Isaiah was all I could think about—Isaiah, his brother John and his birth father Bob.

It was starting to get dark and my heart began pounding. *No*, I told myself, *he won't call today. Maybe tomorrow or just later sometime. But he will call at some point. I just know it. Just probably not today.*

Toward the end of that day, as the skies were darkening, I made myself a cup of tea and sat down at the kitchen table to work on a crossword puzzle when the phone rang.

I jumped up and dashed into the kitchen, snatched the receiver off the phone and breathlessly said, "Hello."

"Hello. I'm Officer Brokaw with the King County Sherriff's Office Benevolent Society and I…"

"Not interested. Sorry." And I hung up. Then I felt bad for hanging up on an officer of the law.

A short while later, the phone rang again. Would it be him this time?

"Hello," I said anxiously.

"Hi, Mrs. Jones. This is Denaee. Is Johnny home?"

"Johnny?" I never called him that. I was beginning to get irritated. Why wasn't Denaee the real caller I was waiting for? And who was Denaee anyway?

"Well, Denaee, John isn't home just now. Would you like to leave a message?"

"Oh no, that's okay. I'll see him in Algebra next week."

I sat at the kitchen table and considered having a shot of the cooking sherry that had to be somewhere in the kitchen cabinets.

And then the phone rang again. I waited a moment, bracing myself for another unwanted caller. Then I took up the receiver.

"Hello," I said tentatively.

There was a short silence on the other end and then I heard a deep voice say, "Hi. This is Isaiah."

There was another short silence as I tried to retain some semblance of composure. I didn't want to cry and I didn't want to sound like an idiot.

"This is Lisa." I had to stop momentarily because I felt tears of joy starting to well up. "I'm so glad you called."

"I am too. My mom told me about you on our way home and I wanted to call as soon as we got back."

"I'm so glad you did." I was tongue-tied and couldn't think of anything sensible to say, so I blurted out, "Ah...um...how was your trip?"

"It was good. My mom drove back and she showed me the picture of my brother and I'm so glad she was driving because if I had been, I'd have driven right off the road!"

There was a little voice inside me screaming, *You are talking to the son you gave up eighteen years ago. Is this real? Is it really happening?*

Then I returned to the present and heard Isaiah saying...."maybe tomorrow."

"Tomorrow?"

"Yeah. I could come to your house or you can come to mine. I mean, if you want to meet."

Are you kidding? "Oh, yes! I want to meet you and so does your brother. And your birth father as well. Tomorrow would be fine. Perhaps we should come to your house first. What do you think?"

"I have a birth father?" I realized that I'd been so focused on having John and Isaiah meet that I'd put Bob aside.

"Yes, you do have a birth father. His name is Bob and he could come tomorrow as well if you like."

"I would like that a lot."

He gave me his address and directions on how to get to his house. I didn't stop him or tell him that I already knew his address because I wasn't sure if Ginny had told him that part yet. I didn't want him to think I'd been stalking him for the last fifteen years, even if that was the case.

We agreed to come by at 1:00.

"I can't wait to meet you guys!" Isaiah said, the excitement in his voice palpable.

"Me neither!" Then we hung up.

I fell into the kitchen chair shaking, laughing and crying at the same time. I had just spoken with my first child. It was incredible. No, it was more than that. It was *beyond* incredible. For the moment, my depression lifted and I could see that life was really very good and that patience was a virtue that had just paid off for me.

Soon John came home from a baseball game. As he was walking up the steps, I said, "Guess who we're meeting tomorrow?"

He ran up the stairs and said, "My brother? Are we going to meet my brother?" He threw his arms around me and twirled me around.

"Yes! Yes! We're going to his house at 1:00 tomorrow to meet him. Can you believe it?"

What a trite question to ask. I couldn't believe this was happening to me. How could John truly believe it was happening to him?

"Mom, I can't wait! What did he sound like? What did he say?" John had poured himself a glass of milk and quickly made a peanut butter sandwich.

"He sounded like you. Honestly. He has a deep voice, like your dad, but his inflections sounded like you. And he laughs like you. That's so odd, isn't it? You guys weren't raised together, but there are similarities between you. He's really excited to meet you—more excited than meeting me, I think, since he already has a mom. But now he knows he's got a brother and that's pretty thrilling for him."

"He's just as excited to meet you, mom."

"I'm sure he is," I said, but there was still a part of me that wondered. "I've just kept this secret to myself for so long. Sometimes I would watch you playing by yourself in your room and think, 'He should be playing with his brother right now.' But all in good time and the time is now here."

We were joyous. "How about I beat you at a game of rummy?" I suggested. "It'll make the rest of the night go faster."

"Sure. Only it's going to be the other way around. I'll be beating you. Just so you know."

He got a deck of cards, shuffled and dealt them. It was a deck that Leilani Lanes gave away. The card backs had their name and their logo of a bowling ball racing towards a pineapple tree. I got an odd satisfaction playing with those cards, as I thought about all the time I spent in bowling alleys with Bob, all the time I spent worrying about John and all the time I spent keeping my secret. It was an ironic symbol to have the logo from the bowling alley fanning us each time we shuffled the cards. I pointed it out to John.

"All things come around again, don't they mom?" For being only fifteen, John often displayed a mature understanding of life that was beyond his years.

"They indeed come around again. I don't understand why things happen the way they do but I've always believed that good will prevail and that justice comes to those who wait. And guess what? Our waiting is over. How are we even going to sleep tonight?"

"Well," John said, "I could just wreck you at rummy. You won't be able to hold your cards you'll be so whipped. Then all I'll have to do is tuck you in!"

"Very funny, little man. We'll see about that."

Just then, Bob arrived home from another Saturday at the bowling alley. Before I could speak, John jumped up and excitedly told Bob about Isaiah.

Bob looked at me. "Oh, so you guys are meeting him tomorrow?"

"Yes we are! Isn't it incredible? You will come with us, right?"

Bob looked uncomfortable. I couldn't read his face, something I was usually able to do with no problem. Years of his abuse had taught me to pick up on the slightest cue. But today I saw a myriad of emotions in his eyes. I thought he might cry, or maybe laugh. It was hard to tell.

"No. I think it should be just you and John. I don't want to overwhelm Isaiah. Having me along might be too much all at once."

I had to admit that not only was he right, but that I was relieved. I didn't want him there. It might be too much for Isaiah, but I also felt that I wanted John and me to spend time with him first.

"Okay. I understand and I think you're right. We don't want to scare him away, do we?" I got up and threw my arms around Bob. He held me tight and kissed me on my forehead. One of the best things about him was his hugs. Even when he was bullying me, hugging him was always a source of comfort. I knew that he loved me in his own way, despite how horrible he could be. *Everything will be better soon*, I told myself. *Soon our family will be together and everything will be fine. Just fine."*

How foolish I was to believe that even this monumental event might change everything for the better.

CHAPTER 42

HE LOOKS JUST LIKE ME

I TURNED ONTO Isaiah's street, just as I had so many times over the years, but this time, I pulled up to the curb and set the brake. "I imagine most folks enter off the alley," I said to John, "Because it's flat. No stairs. There's a lot of stairs here, huh?"

"Alley? How do you know there's an alley?" John asked, and then a sly smile crossed over his face.

"Never mind, mom, I think I already know." He reached over and gave my hand a squeeze.

"Doesn't matter really, does it? We're here and that's all that matters."

"Shall we start the ascent?" John and I got out of the car and climbed the steep stairs to the front door. The concrete stairs were uneven, skewed one way or the other, probably the result of one of the earthquakes we'd had in Seattle over the years. Once at the top of the stairs we turned and looked at the view of the lake and mountains beyond. While the house looked modest, the view was priceless.

John and I stood at the front door. I was so anxious and eager that I wasn't sure how to act. I'd played this moment over in mind endlessly and now that it was here, I felt completely at a loss.

I lifted the knocker and just as I was about to let it bang, the door opened.

It was dark in the foyer, but there he was—tall, slender and looking just like John. Isaiah invited us in. What is the etiquette for the occasion of meeting your son?

I thrust out my hand for him to shake and blurted out "I'm Lisa. You can call me Lisa. I mean, I don't want to confuse the issue. Because you should call me Lisa and that won't hurt your...."

John interrupted me. "Mom, it's okay." Then he hugged his brother and we all went in.

I looked around. "Where's your mom?"

"She thought it might be best if she weren't here for this first meeting," Isaiah said.

"Really?"

"Yeah, it's okay. She said she'd meet you all later."

I was shaking like an addict on her way to detox. I'd worn my best work dress and had John put on some clean clothes. Isaiah was wearing a blue shirt with short sleeves.

He took us into the living room and introduced us to his sister Millie, who was sitting on the sofa. Above her hung a wool tapestry of an African woman. Millie was seventeen and would be entering her last year at high school. She was very pretty and sweet.

Directly across was a fireplace and on the mantle framed photos of Isaiah and Millie with their father, Al. There were more pictures on the walls and a small bookshelf, but I began to feel like the room was reeling and shifted my focus to the kids.

All three of them sat on the sofa. I took a seat on a nearby chair. I felt uncomfortable and was frantic. *What should I say? What should I do?*

I was worried about saying the wrong thing or embarrassing myself in some way. If I let myself go, I thought I might just explode or melt or something equally ridiculous. Then I remembered I'd brought my camera because I wasn't sure how this meeting would go, and if I never saw Isaiah again, at least I'd have photos.

"Do you guys mind if I take some pictures?"

Isaiah said, "Sure. Do you want us to stand in front of the fireplace?"
"No, no," I said. "Just stay where you are on the sofa. That's fine."

I moved around the room, taking photos from different angles. Meanwhile, John and Isaiah started up a conversation. I couldn't hear most of it, but I heard a few "Yeah, man" and "Me too's." I stopped taking pictures. *Isaiah and John are trying to get to know each other,* I told myself. *Let them be.*

Millie suggested that we all go out to the street behind their house. "There's a basketball hoop there," she said. "These two guys are so tall they could probably just stand on the ground and put the ball in the basket!"

John jumped up from the sofa and said to Isaiah, "There's no point in trying to beat me, cuz I can't be beat."

Isaiah said, "Oh yeah? We'll see about that." We all marched outside, walked through someone's backyard and emerged on the next street. Millie, although young, had the sense to realize that everyone was nervous. Shooting hoops was a superb idea.

They played for about an hour, back and forth, sweating, jumping and laughing.

I took more photos and then sat on the curb and watched this dream playing out before me, this dream that had finally come true. It was almost too much to take in. I remembered how I used to try to picture his little face before he was born, how I wondered who he was and what he might become. I drifted back to his birth and the brief moment that I held him, when I saw his little face, not knowing his future nor mine. And now here are my two sons playing basketball together. It was beyond all my wildest hopes.

John took the ball, burst to the side then shot the ball into the basket. "Damn! You're good!" Isaiah said to his brother.

As I watched them play, more thoughts raced through my mind. There they were, brothers who had just met each other, playing basketball—an instant and universal game for disparate boys to bond, however briefly.

I couldn't help but wonder what would have happened if I hadn't given Isaiah up. All those years my two sons were unaware of each other. What had they missed out on? It was now near the end of the 1980's. The times had changed. If I'd had Isaiah today, I thought, I would have kept him. Now mixed raced children were not considered the end of life as we knew it in the 1960's.

If I'd known I would marry his father, what would I have done? I let the "what if's" race through my mind until I heard Isaiah yell.

"See? I told you! You can't beat me!" and that brought me back to reality.

We returned to Isaiah's house three hours later. I'd offered to take them somewhere to eat, but they all said they weren't hungry. I wasn't either. Perhaps we were all too excited. But when I looked at my watch, I said. "Wow. It's been three hours. Maybe we should go so your mom can return to her house!"

Immediately everyone got up and grouped around the front door. *This is where I pull myself together.* I said, "Isaiah, meeting you has been wonderful for John and me. I hope it was for you too."

"Definitely," he said, and then he reached over and gave a little brotherly punch on John's shoulder.

"You may have won me at hoops today," John said, "but next time you watch out. I'll kick your behind!"

Would there be a next time? "Do you have our phone number?" I asked Isaiah and then said, "Oh, of course you do! You called us, didn't you?"

"You know your mom and I talked and maybe she told you. This is all up to you now. If you want to see us again, you call us. If you don't want to see us again, it's okay. At least we've met each other!"

"Oh, you'll hear from me." Isaiah beamed.

I gave him a hug and felt my brains rattling around in my head. It was more than I could have ever hoped for. I had held him so briefly so long ago. Thinking of the past and the here and now made me just shake my head in disbelief. Now, I'd just given him a hug and he hugged me back. In the words of my youth, the experience was a trip.

"Isaiah, I have to tell you something."

"Okay."

I held him at arm's length.

"When I was being discharged from the hospital, I told the nurse that I wanted to see my baby. You. It was against the rules, she said, but after some persuading from me, she brought you. I held you in my arms..." My voice started to break. John and Isaiah both looked horrified that I might start to cry. I got hold of my emotions and continued.

"Okay....I held you in my arms and gave you a little kiss on the forehead. Then I told you that I'd see you again. And now here we are. It's... it's...pretty amazing."

"Definitely," Isaiah said. "That's kinda cool."

I nodded my head and said, "Yeah. It's way cool."

As we pulled into our driveway, Bob came out of the house. "You've got a call," he said. "I'm not sure who it is, but I asked him to hold." I reached into the car to grab my purse.

"Did you ask who it was?"

"No. Just get up here and take this call." I wondered why he seemed so grumpy.

I ran up the stairs and into the kitchen. The phone receiver was laying on the counter. I snatched it up. "Hello."

"Hi, this is Isaiah."

"Well, hi there yourself. What's up?"

"Can I come out to your house?"

"Of course you can. When would like to come?"

"Now, please." His voice was so soft, yet eager, that it sounded almost like a little boy's asking for one more big push on the swing.

I had to hold on to the kitchen counter to keep from falling down in a dead faint. My little boy wanted to see me again! I held the receiver to my chest and turned to Bob who was sitting at the kitchen table playing Solitaire. I knew he was aware who was on the phone. After all, if he'd ever suspected the male on the other end of the line was anyone but Isaiah, he never would have told me of the call.

"Your oldest son wants to come for a visit right now," I told him, my voice almost cracking into a joyous sob. "Are you ready for this?"

His head was down, and he heaved a big sigh. "Sure," he said finally, and I could tell that he was almost as nervous as I was. He just wasn't going to let his nerves show.

I got back on the phone and gave Isaiah the directions to our house. We were at least twenty-five miles from his home so I knew it would take them a while.

"Okay then. See you soon. Call if you get lost, okay?"

John overheard me on the phone and said, "Is that Isaiah? He's coming out here now?"

"He's coming out here now!" We hugged again in excitement, and then I said, "Maybe you should straighten up your room a little."

John reluctantly shuffled off to his room.

"At least hang up your clothes, please," I called after him.

After I had hung up, I stood behind Bob and rubbed his shoulders. "I know this might be sort of hard for you. But he wants to meet you. He wants to see where we live. I told him to call when he wanted to see us again—*if* he wanted to see us again— and look what he did. He's coming out here right now."

Bob was a big man and his shoulders were wide. I could feel knots in his muscles and tried to massage them out. He stopped me and said, "Why don't we get some pizza or something so we can eat together? I'll go to Godfather's and get a couple of our special Canadian ham, sausage and pineapple with extra cheese. Sound good?"

"Sounds wonderful." He put on his coat and pulled on his knit cap but then hesitated, as if he had suddenly forgotten where the pizza place was. I could see that he was in the grip of confusion, fear and joy so I gave him a huge hug and told him it would be fine.

"Well, we'll see how this goes." He turned to leave but I stopped him at the head of the stairs to give him another hug.

"Yes, yes we will," I said. "We'll see how it goes!"

Bob left to get the pizza while I tidied the house. I put plates, forks and knives on the dining table along with some glasses for drinks. Then I noticed the glasses were streaky so I washed them, dried them and inspected them for any signs of lipstick, fingerprints or something ghastly like dried eggs. I realized I was fussing and told myself to get a grip.

I paced back and forth *"Hurry up! Hurry up!"* I could see the street from the window over the kitchen sink and watched obsessively, hoping that Bob would get home before Isaiah arrived.

Then finally, Bob pulled up in our old battered car, turned up the driveway and into the garage. He ran up the stairs with the pizzas, panting for breath. I quickly took the boxes and placed them on the table. Then I gave an appraising glance at everything but nothing looked right. I started to take the plates away, stacking the silverware on top.

"What are you doing?" Bob asked. "And where's John?"

"John is in the shower and I don't like the way the table looks. I think I'll put the pizzas on some serving plates. No wait! I'll slice them up and they'll be all ready and then I'll...."

"Hold it. What has gotten into you?" Bob took the plates from my hands and returned them to the table. "The pizza is already sliced. You need to calm down."

"But I want everything to be beautiful and perfect. I don't want him thinking we're slobs."

Bob laughed. "He isn't coming here to see if you've dusted recently. He's coming to meet us and spend some time with his other family."

"You're right. I know you're right. I just need to take a couple of deep breaths and take it down a notch or two, right?" I consciously lowered my shoulders, which had been riding just below my ears, and slowed my breath from panting to somewhat normal.

"Now you're talking." Just then, John emerged from his room. He had put on clean clothes and looked more than presentable. Then I gave Bob an assessment, looking at him from top to bottom. His tennis shoes were untied. His shirt was partially tucked in. He still had on his coat and knit cap, and I could barely see his eyes through the dirt fog on his glasses.

"You need to clean your glasses, take off that cap, tuck in your shirt and tie your shoes," I told him and he dutifully did.

Just then, we heard a car pull into our driveway. John ran down the stairs, followed closely by me. At that moment, I realized the possible permutations of our budding relationships were many. Our lives were changing forever and there was no turning back. Not that I wanted to.

I looked back and Bob was still standing in the kitchen.

"Come on," I urged him.

"I'll be right there." He needed time. I understood that.

"Well, come down when you're ready, okay?"

John had opened the door and burst outside and I followed.

There in our driveway was an old VW van. The body was orange with a tan top. There were bumper stickers on it that let everyone know the owner of the car was a liberal-leaning, equality-believing, justice-for-all hippie. Ginny climbed out from the passenger side. It was the first time we'd clapped eyes on each other. I ran up and threw my arms around her.

"You must be Ginny! I'm so glad to meet you! I'm Lisa and this is John. Welcome! I hope you're hungry."

"I sure am!" Isaiah got out of the car and gave John some sort of handshake; I didn't know what it meant, but assumed it had something to do with hip-hop.

Suddenly Isaiah stopped and looked up at the house with an expression of fear and curiosity. Bob came through the door and the moment he saw Isaiah, he burst into tears. That was the last reaction I'd expected.

We all stood there, watching Bob until I said, "What's wrong?"

Bob's hand was shaking as he reached for a handkerchief in his pocket.

"He looks just like me when I was his age. Just like me!"

Clearly, Isaiah was uncomfortable with this unexpected display of emotion, so I touched his shoulder and said, "We've got pizza!"

John ran ahead past his dad. Isaiah followed but stopped when he got to Bob. He put his hand out for a shake, but Bob grabbed him in a big bear hug. "It's good to meet you, son," Bob said. Then he inexplicably said, "I didn't know. I didn't know."

"Good to meet you, too," Isaiah said, as he eased out of Bob's arms. I hung back with Ginny, letting the males go ahead.

Ginny waited beside her van. She stood straight, her chin jutted out slightly giving her a determined look, her eyes bright blue and short hair a fiery red. She was slightly shorter than me. Everything about her seemed to say that she was a bracing, strong woman.

"I wasn't expecting to meet you today. I felt bad that you left your house for our visit with Isaiah so I'm doubly glad to see you now!" I gave her another hug.

She hugged me back and said, "I just thought your first time seeing Isaiah should just be you guys. I didn't mind being gone at all. I took the dogs for a long run at the Arboretum."

"Well, it was very thoughtful of you. Shall we go in?" and I led her up the stairs into the house.

Bob, Isaiah and John had already torn into the pizza. My effort at some sort of civilized meal had flown out the door. They were eating the pizza straight from the boxes, ignoring the plates, forks, and napkins I'd been so worried about.

I gestured to a dining chair and invited Ginny to sit down. I sat next to her and we both grabbed a slice of pizza. Then we ate together, our first meal as what I hoped would be a blended family. We were all swimming in unknown waters, lacking the vocabulary to express ourselves.

But it didn't matter. We made small talk as we ate and let the obvious and understandable discomfort melt away at its own pace. One thing I had learned—you can't force emotion or love or understanding. You just remain patient and let things unfold gently over time.

Yet I couldn't help thinking that this could all tumble around me, that the extremes of my marriage—cruelty, horror, fear, abuse—might reveal itself and cause Isaiah to be afraid to be with us. If that happened, how would I be able to go on?

CHAPTER 43

GODZILLA AND POPCORN

THINGS UNFOLDED RATHER quickly. Isaiah wanted to stay the night at our house. I was so overwhelmed with joy that he wanted to stay with us that I blurted out, "Yes, of course you can stay!"

"Is that okay, mom?" Isaiah asked Ginny and I immediately realized that in my excitement, I had unwittingly overstepped my bounds. Ginny needed to make that call, not me.

"If it's okay with Lisa and Bob, it's fine with me," she answered to my relief. "I mean, it's summer and there's no school tomorrow, right?"

I looked at Bob and he nodded. I turned to Ginny. "It's just fine with us. John, okay with you?"

"Of course!"

What's happening here? I asked myself. *We've just met today and he already wants to stay with us. Is it possible that I'm dreaming?*

I tried to think practically. We may have to set some rules right away. As much as I wanted Isaiah in our lives, I didn't want him to think our house was a refuge, a place to come when he might be mad with Ginny or rebelling against a decision she might make that he didn't like. I tried to think with my mind, not my heart and it was hard to do. These were uncharted waters that we'd sailed into and they came with no manual, rule book or life vest.

I brushed my worries aside, though, as Ginny and I conferred about logistics. "I have to go to work tomorrow, and I leave very early," I said. "Bob could probably take Isaiah home later, couldn't you?" I turned toward him, and had never seen him looking so puzzled and so pleased. For the first time since I'd known him, Bob didn't seem as if he were losing control, or in control. He was observing, and not calculating. He was just smiling and nodding like a happy parent, and I felt a rush of love for him.

"No problem." He seemed to be thinking, like me, that this was all a dream. I wanted to say to Isaiah, "I hope you like bowling alleys," but stifled the urge. I knew that when Bob took Isaiah home the next day, he'd have John with him and would want to stop at his favorite bowling alley, BowlWorld, to show off his boys. And I prayed that wouldn't scare off Isaiah once he got a taste of that world!

It was getting late. We decided Isaiah and John could rent a movie and Bob left to take them to the video store. "No gum," I said. "And no candy."

They dutifully agreed, while I knew they'd just ignore me.

Meanwhile, Ginny and I sat at the table and talked.

"How do you feel about this?" I asked her.

"I have mixed feelings," she said.

"Me too!" I said, relieved that I could voice them.

"It's just a lot to take in. I knew this day was coming, as I know you did. But it's still hard." Ginny's eyes looked a bit teary and I instantly felt her pain and confusion. "Ginny, remember I told you that I had no intention of demanding that I'm now the mother and you're not?" She nodded and reached for my hand.

"Yes, of course I remember. And I don't feel that you're lying to me."

"I'm not at all. You are Isaiah's mother and I respect that. You raised him—you clothed and fed him, you took care of him when he was sick, you made sure he would go to college. You have done all the jobs that a mother does that I couldn't do for Isaiah. That makes *you* his mother. I'm just not sure what I am to him."

She let go of my hand. "What do you mean?" Ginny looked earnestly at me.

"Oh, I just mean that if you were to introduce me to someone, how would you refer to me?"

"'This is Lisa, Isaiah's birth mother'."

"Oh, that sounds good! I could only think of introducing myself as 'The Womb,' and that sounds kind of icky."

Ginny burst into laughter. "Oh yes, 'birth mother' is much better!"

Then I felt serious. "Listen, Ginny, you and I are walking into unknown and uncharted territory. Should we agree to talk often with each other, just to see how we are feeling and sort of monitor things?"

She once again reached for my hand. "I think that's a great idea. And you're right. We've never done this before. We both told Isaiah that it was up to him after we met if he wanted to stay in contact. And apparently he does. Perhaps we should set some rules. There needs to be a basic understanding that while Isaiah can decide if he wants to continue seeing you guys, you and I are still the bosses."

"I couldn't agree more," and I gave her hand a squeeze.

Just then, Bob returned with the boys. They had chosen two movies and asked if I could make popcorn.

"Coming right up!" I said, looking over to Bob. He looked tired. The intense emotion of the day had worn him out. But his eyes sparkled with happiness and I was glad for that.

Ginny stood and spoke to Isaiah. "I expect you to be respectful and do as you're told. Do you understand?"

Isaiah looked at his mom with love and patience. "Yes. I understand." He gave her a big hug.

Ginny gathered her purse and sweater. "You guys want to walk me out to the car?"

"Why don't you take some pizza home for Millie; she might like some. And maybe she might want to come for a visit?"

"Thanks for the offer, but no. Millie is currently trying to be vegetarian and probably wouldn't eat any pizza. And I'll ask her about a visit. But as I said, we have to tread lightly with her because she'll probably never meet her birth mother."

We all stood outside and talked. Isaiah and John were looking antsy and I asked Bob to take them back into the house and get the video set up. Ginny and I hugged for a long time. I was grateful to have her be so cooperative.

Then she got in her bumper-stickered VW van, backed out of our driveway and drove away, waving out her window.

The boys settled into the living room. John put a blanket and some pillows on the floor for them to lie on. In addition to the movie—"Godzilla versus Mothra"—we had a Nintendo so they could also entertain themselves with Super Mario Brothers.

I made a big bowl of buttered popcorn and hot chocolate, admonished them both not to spill and then gave each a kiss on the forehead before I went down the hall to our bedroom.

My mind was reeling. I had met my first-born son that morning and by the end of the day, he was staying the night in our house. I couldn't believe that he'd been a newborn when I'd first kissed his little forehead eighteen years before. And now I got to kiss his grown up forehead as I said good night.

Bob was already asleep and snoring when I came to our room. He was one of those people who could fall asleep the moment his head hit the pillow. I was a lifelong insomniac and my inability to sleep morphed over the years—now I couldn't fall asleep until I heard Bob snoring. Then I felt safe to sleep myself.

I got into bed and lay there, listening to the sounds coming from the living room. I could hear Godzilla roaring. I could smell the popcorn and chocolate. I could see the flickering shadows of the movie on the hallway wall. And then, in absolute joy and peace, I finally fell asleep.

I woke early, before my alarm went off, slipped into my robe and walked quietly down the hall. There they were, sprawled on the floor, sleeping in the debris of popcorn kernels and gum wrappers. *Hmm...I thought I said no gum. Oh well.*

Gum didn't matter. Debris didn't matter. What mattered was that I had left my secret, self-imposed prison and was now free to welcome Isaiah into my life and share my joy with everyone I knew.

But then I realized—I hadn't told my parents.

Chapter 44

May I Introduce You?

The following week at work, I started telling a few of my coworkers about being reunited with my son. At first, it was hard to talk about it. I'd kept this secret for so long. But with each succeeding person, telling my story got easier. None of them had ever suspected that I'd relinquished a baby and all were surprised and happy for me.

However, I remembered the lesson learned when I forgot to tell my parents I'd gotten married. I needed to tell them that Isaiah had entered our lives, before they found out some other way, like dropping by to find him sitting on our couch. And Isaiah needed to know about them.

The opportunity to tell him came when he called during the week to arrange to visit us that weekend.

"I think I may have not mentioned yet, but you do have grandparents—my mom and dad. Would you like to meet them when you visit this weekend?"

"Grandparents? Really? My mom's parents are on the East Coast and I have only seen them once. I would love to meet my grandparents!"

"Good. I'll let them know. And you need a ride on Saturday?"

"Yes, if you don't mind."

"Not at all. We'll stop by their house on the way back."

On Friday, I dropped by my parents' place on the way home from work. I walked in the back door and called out, "Hey! Anyone here?"

I found my mom in the kitchen making soup and my dad, having just showered after returning from work, was sitting in the living room reading the paper.

"Are you staying for dinner?" my mom asked.

"No thanks. I just stopped by to tell you something. So could you both sit down for a minute?"

My mother instantly looked alarmed.

"It's nothing bad, okay?" I told her. "Nothing to be upset about. In fact, it's good news." Or so I hoped it would be. After all, when I'd told her the news of my pregnancy all those years before, she dealt with it by insisting it was a kidney infection.

A fleeting and momentary urge came over me to tell them that they would soon meet my kidney infection, but I stifled it.

My dad got up from his chair, grunting with the growing arthritis in his knees, and joined my mom and me at the kitchen table. "What's this about?" he said.

"Well, I'm not sure how to say this…" My mom heaved a big sigh.

"You're not pregnant, are you?"

I suppose that was her worst fear, which was ironic, given the pain I'd lived with all those years, keeping my knowledge of Isaiah to myself, not to mention the hell I'd been living through with Bob. I assumed that neither of them knew the truth about the life I was leading. I figured they were as fooled as everyone else since they never said anything, asked any questions or invited me to confide. And I didn't feel safe confiding to them or anyone else, on the off chance Bob would hear of it and make me suffer for breaking those closely held secrets of our marriage—the secrets that made it possible for him to continue his cruelties.

"I'm not pregnant, but you are close." I took a deep breath and continued. "Last weekend, I met my firstborn child."

"What are you talking about?" My mother looked distressed and began fidgeting with the salt shaker.

I knew that her defense mechanisms went into overdrive and I endeavored to be patient and kind.

"Mom, let's not pretend you don't know what I'm talking about, okay?"

I got up to pour myself some coffee from their never-empty pot of the dark, bitter liquid. Like my mother, I always added sugar and cream and as I stirred, just like her, I dinged the spoon on the inside of the cup.

Returning to the table, I told them the entire story about Isaiah.

Afterwards, my dad propped his elbows on the table and leaned forward. "When can we see him?" I was surprised by his eagerness, but then I really had no idea how he felt about so many things. I knew that when they were in Hawaii, he made a few unfortunate racial comments to his crew after my mom told him I was pregnant by a black man. But that was a long time ago. Perhaps the years had softened him. Or perhaps loving John had softened him.

My mother recovered. "Yes, yes, when can we meet him?"

"I thought I'd bring him by tomorrow."

"Tomorrow? Saturday? This Saturday?" My mom started to cry and when I looked at my dad, his eyes were tearing up.

Good heavens, I thought. *Did they really care all along? Had this been a loss for them as well? They never said anything, never offered anything all those years ago. If their reticence to express their feelings had broken through long ago and I felt they cared, I might have kept my baby.* The thought cut straight through my heart.

I was looking into my mug, watching the cream I'd just added to my coffee swirl as the lyric from a Carly Simon song swirled in my head.

"I had some dreams, they were clouds in my coffee, clouds in my coffee."

I roused myself as I heard my mother saying "What time tomorrow?"

"Oh, it'll probably be around noon. Is that okay for you?"

"Of course," my mom said. "I'll bake a pie. Does he like pie?"

"I imagine he does. And your homemade chocolate cream pie is heaven!" The events surrounding the introduction of Isaiah into his new family were surreal. I felt as if I'd dropped out of a cloud and landed on earth, bringing the strange twists of fate and coincidence with me. How were people supposed to react? I saw my parents do what most folks would do—get on with daily living while quietly and privately absorbing the incredible changes about to occur.

As I prepared to leave, my father had returned to his paper in the living room, his legs crossed and one foot dangling, and my mom was chopping more vegetables for the soup pot.

John and I picked him up at his house around 11:30. Ginny was there and we chatted for a moment on her front porch.

"So far, this seems to be going well," she said. "Don't you think? He's really excited to meet your parents."

"They're excited too. In fact, I think they're more than excited. I think they're blown away. All those years we never talked about him. I think they just worked hard to put it out of their minds. So for them, it's like an emotional explosion, I guess."

I paused for a moment while I looked back, seeing a myriad of roads taken and not taken lying crisscrossed behind me. Ahead I saw a huge open door opening upon a mystery. I saw where'd I'd been and the aftermath of the decisions I'd made. Before me, I saw unknown challenges and potential happiness.

"You know, I feel like I've walked out of a jail. Perhaps for my parents they feel like they've just regained their eyesight after years of blindness. Scratch that—way too dramatic, but you know what I mean?"

Ginny laughed. "Yeah, I know what you mean. My parents were less than pleased when I married Brian. I didn't hear from them for a year." *Hmm...their loss*, I thought.

Isaiah came out with his duffel bag and announced he was ready.

"Bye mom!" He kissed Ginny on the cheek, and then gave me a hug.

On the way to meet my parents, I asked him how he was feeling about it all.

"Well, I never thought I had a brother or grandparents or another dad," he said.

"It's a lot to take in, isn't it?"

"It's fucking awesome!" He looked stricken. "Oh my gosh, I'm so sorry I said that. I just was...you know...excited. I've always wanted a brother!"

"It's okay, Isaiah. I've heard the word before. Of course, not from you but it really is okay. Don't worry about it. And I think John has always wanted a brother too."

I took the exit off the freeway and sped along the surface road to the traffic light where I turned left to get to my parents'.

"We're almost there, just another turn, and another, and—here we are!" I pulled into the driveway and honked the horn.

My parents' had actually bought a house. Their peripatetic years were over. The house had a semi-circular driveway in the front, with tall firs standing between the road and the driveway. The house was a typical rambler. My dad had painted the exterior a pale yellow a few years before, when they first moved there. Every spring, he always planted marigolds along the edges of the house. The back yard was enormous. There were three apple trees that John loved to climb when he was young.

Beyond them were my dad's rose bushes. It was his constant challenge and disappointment that he was never quite successful in coaxing the black spot off the leaves or get the blooms to open without aphids. But he tried. Beyond their backyard was an undeveloped parcel of land overtaken by wild blackberries and several families of grouse.

My mom and dad came out the front door as Isaiah was getting out of the car. They were overwhelmed with emotion. My dad nearly tripped off the front steps. My mom was drying her hands on her apron, the red and white gingham one that I'd made in the eighth grade. It always pleased me to see her wear it even though it was poorly made.

I don't think either of them knew what to say or do, so I stepped in.

"Isaiah, this is your grandmother and grandfather. Mom, Dad, this is Isaiah— your oldest grandson."

"Isaiah," my mom said, taking his hands, "it is a pleasure to meet you." My dad reached out to shake Isaiah's hand, but Isaiah intercepted it and gave my dad a hug instead. Then he hugged my mom and she started to cry. Then I started to cry. Then my dad and Isaiah got teary eyed. *Oh crap*, I thought, *do something!*

"Well, we can't just stand outside weeping. Let's go in and have coffee and pie. You did make pie, right?" I said to my mom.

"I made two! A chocolate cream pie and an apple pie!" She was clearly pleased to have hungry pie freaks to feed.

"My favorites!" Isaiah said. He was six foot five and my mom was five foot one. He towered over her. He put his arm around her shoulder and she led him inside. My dad, John and I followed.

As soon as we entered the house, Isaiah noticed the piano in the living room.

"Can I play it?" he asked my mom.

Her eyes lit up like she was on fire. "*You* play the piano?"

"I try to. I've never had lessons. I just pick out tunes."

My mother was clearly about to collapse. "*I* learned on my own too. I can't believe you play the piano!" I had no idea that the music gene had traveled from my mom and landed on Isaiah.

Isaiah pulled out the piano bench and sat down. My mom said, 'Play something for me, won't you?"

"Okay, I will. But then you need to play something for me, okay? Mostly I play things that I've made up."

"You mean composed?"

"Right, composed!" My mom sat down next to him at the piano and Isaiah began to play a tune he had floating around in his head. It was a soft tune, a bit ethereal and slightly new age. I looked around the room to see my dad and John sitting on the long brightly covered sofa, captivated by Isaiah's music.

"That's really impressive, Isaiah!" My mom was in her element with her newly found grandson sitting at the piano with her.

"Now you play something!" Isaiah said.

My mom took over the keyboard and played some of her old standards— Darktown Strutters Ball. Black and White Rag. Sleepy Time Gal. Bill Bailey. Her small hands flew over the keys with the fast rhythms of ragtime and traditional jazz.

Isaiah was enthralled, as was my dad. John and I watched our two musical family members chatting excitedly and intimately on the piano bench.

I went into the kitchen to make a pot of coffee, and called out, "Who wants pie? There's apple and chocolate cream."

"Apple pie with cheddar cheese," my father said.

"I'll have the same," said my mom.

"Can I have some of both?" Isaiah asked.

"Only a very small, nearly invisible slice of *my* chocolate pie for my brother and a great big one for me," said John.

For the remainder of the afternoon, we sat around the kitchen table, talking and eating pie. Isaiah had a lot of questions for my mom and dad—so many that only a fraction could be shared at the time.

But who cared that the questions couldn't all be answered at once? There'd be plenty more time for all us to be together, much more time for Isaiah to get to know my parents, I figured, as the evening came to a close and I herded the boys back into the car.

"You'll have plenty of time to get to know each other," I promised Isaiah.

But I was wrong.

CHAPTER 45

PUT HIM IN THE ROSE BUSHES

IT IS SAID that a person marries his or her parent and I believe it's true because in marrying Bob, I married my father. Why would an otherwise intelligent woman marry an abusive man if it were not a subconsciously driven replication of her childhood relationship with her father?

My father was a stranger to me. He shared nothing of his personal history, his outlook on life or his dreams and aspirations. What little I knew of my father came from angry stories my mother told me. The anger in her narrations either came from some sort of righteous indignation on his behalf because his childhood had been abysmal or from her own dissatisfaction with being his wife.

My father had a very low opinion of women, and he took that out on my mother and me. His constant verbal assaults and criticism left me feeling useless, disrespected and undeserving. He worked to undermine any happiness my mother and I might have. As I grew older I couldn't understand why my mother stayed with him. But in time I understood that she, too, had married her father—a man taken from her so early that he was merely a fantasy. Losing her father when she was so young left within her a sense of abandonment that she then replicated by marrying a man so emotionally distant that he might as well have been dead. She stayed in that emptiness for forty-seven years. But with advancing years and the introduction of a new grandson, my father changed. He seemed to be kinder, more patient and more interested in me and my abandoned dreams of being a writer in London.

As I was leaving their house one Sunday, shortly after Isaiah had left for college in Pullman, he came after me as I was getting into my car.

"Hey! Wait a second," he yelled at me as he ran out of the house.

Oh, great, I thought. *Now what have I done?*

He was out of breath and panting when he got to my car.

"I wanted to ask you about your writing. Are you doing anything with your writing?"

I couldn't believe what I was hearing and was momentarily too stunned to speak. I'd had no idea he was even aware of my dream to be a writer or that I'd done any writing at all. "Are you? Are you writing?" he asked.

"No, not really."

"Well you should," he said. "You should be writing. You're a good writer and I'd like to see you write something."

That was the last time we talked.

Five days later, he had a heart attack in the parking lot of Costco, was revived by medics, rushed to a nearby hospital and prepped for emergency insertion of a pacemaker. But he didn't make it.

The only people at his funeral were friends of my mothers' and mine and Barry. Barry had gotten married, had a son, divorced and never stopped drinking beer. I hadn't seen him in quite a while. He truly loved my father and was grief-stricken at his passing. My mom, on the other hand, seemed weirdly nonchalant.

After the service, the funeral director told my mom that his ashes would be ready in two weeks. I asked her to call me when she got the ashes so we could figure out what to do with them.

When six weeks passed and I hadn't heard from her about the ashes, I called.

"Oh, the ashes," she said. "Yeah, I picked them up weeks ago."

"You were supposed to call me when you did, remember? Where are they now?"

"In the back seat of the car." My mouth fell open.

"You've been driving around for weeks with his ashes in the backseat? I'm coming right over."

It was a cold, gray windy November day. I left work and drove to their house.

She was in the kitchen chopping celery when I arrived.

I got the box out of her car and was surprised at how heavy it was. The wind kicked up a bit, sending a chill down my spine. I returned to the warmth of the kitchen.

"So, mom, what do you want to do with these? I mean, you can't just drive around with them."

"I don't know. You could scatter them in his goddamn rose bushes for all I care."

The wind was cold and sharp and the sky so low with gray clouds that the air had that same silence following a snowfall, that sense of time stopping and of being closer to the earth.

I set the box down on the leaf-strewn grass in front of his meager roses. He was never able to coax truly splendid blooms from them. I had no idea what to do, so I got a shovel from the garage and dug a hole in the ground between the roses. Then I returned to the house.

My mother was still in the kitchen, grinding beans by hand for a pot of coffee. "Did you want to participate in this at all?" I asked her.

"Oh, I guess." She threw on a coat and tied a scarf around her head. "C'mon," she said and we went outside.

The grass was wet and I held on to her so she wouldn't lose her balance.

As we stood over the hole I had dug, I felt like a wretched maiden looking down from a Gothic tower. The sense of surrealism whipped around my ankles as I opened the box and let the ashes fall. To my horror, the wind picked up most of them and carried them away. I quickly covered the hole so that the remaining ashes would stay amongst the roses.

As we both stood there, looking at the ground, I felt that something more was needed. I was thinking a recitation of the 23rd Psalm might be appropriate:

The Lord is my shepherd; I shall not want.
He maketh me to lie down in green pastures:
He leadeth me beside the still waters.
He restoreth my soul:

Or maybe one Our Father, three Hail Marys' and one Glory Be.
I turned to my mom.

"Ah, did you want to say anything?"

"Yeah," she said still looking at the ground. "Forty-seven years is a long goddamn time!" Then she turned and walked back to the house.

I was horrified. How could she be so callous and uncaring? I just stood there, looking at the roses. The wind was so cold and dusk was coming, making the sky grayer, darker, and eerier.

Is this how his life ends? Is this how she really feels? And if she does really feel this way, why did she stay with him for so long? But these were obvious questions. What was the heart of the matter? Having had no father, she chose to live her life with a ghost, with a man who was like emotional ether, just barely giving her the love and security she needed so badly. For her I guessed that was enough.

I went in and found her finishing the pot of coffee. She turned to look at me and said, "Want some?"

I sensed a difference in the house that I hadn't noticed before. The tension was gone. The unhappiness had vaporized. His clothes, pills, cigarettes were gone. There was no trace of him. And the grimace she always had on her face, the result of grinding her teeth with tension, was gone. I realized I hardly recognized her.

I sat down. "Yeah, I'll have a cup. Thanks."

My father was completely gone. His loss was sad, but it didn't affect me much as he'd never played any sort of role in my life. Now I was left with this other "father," this man I'd married who said he'd teach me about the world. And he did. He taught me how to succeed but also how to believe I deserved the abuse he leveled at me. I found myself wondering, "How soon will he die? How soon will I be released?"

And that's when it hit me. I had been so determined that John and Isaiah would be free of Bob's anger, that Bob wouldn't define for them what their relationship with each other would be, that I hadn't realized how much I deserved that same freedom. I'd stood up to Bob when it most mattered—when it came to bringing Isaiah back into our lives. Maybe now it was time to take the bull by the horns and put that same determination to greater good—to getting Bob out of our lives before I found myself standing over his ashes without a shred of pity.

CHAPTER 46

WHERE IS MY CHILD?

ISAIAH WAS NOW in college and John was in his junior year in high school. He had big hopes for a basketball career and was being scouted by minor league teams. But something was wrong. I had felt it for a long time – a feeling of dread that I couldn't identify or assign to any cause. I just knew that something was not right.

John had gotten so tall and thin. He was fast as lightning on the basketball court. But I was a bit worried he played too much basketball—he was already a junior and had to start thinking about college, though I was also worried I could never afford to send him. Then one afternoon as I was washing the dishes, he burst into the house after school, shouting happily, "Mom! Mom! I've been scouted!"

I had no idea what that meant, but it must have been a good thing because he was deliriously happy.

"Scouted?" I asked him, drying my hands on my apron and giving my son a big hug. He smelled like fresh outdoor air, just like when he was a little boy and we would play outside in the autumn leaves.

He quickly hugged me back then began to jump up and down with joy. "It means I may get a scholarship to a university. Can you believe it?"

"Well it's absolutely wonderful! It's what you wanted, isn't it? Wait'll we tell your dad." It was a delicious irony—that my son would be offered a sport scholarship when so many years past I too had been offered a chance for a college degree but let it go. This time my son would be the one to go to college with all the encouragement Bob and I could give.

Immediately, John became subdued. He stopped jumping about and shouting. His smile faded and his head dropped.

"What's the matter, sweetie?" I asked him.

"He won't let me, mom. He won't. He doesn't want me to succeed at anything. He tells me all the time how worthless I am."

"What?" I felt like I'd just had a boulder hit my stomach. Could it be that Bob was being as demoralizing with John as my mother was with me? "I don't understand what you mean."

"Mom, you're always at work. Or you bring work home. Or you're tired and go to sleep early. You don't know what goes on when you aren't here." He shook his head in resignation.

"What on earth are you talking about, sweetie?" I had to grab a kitchen chair and sit down.

"He tells me I'm evil, but I think *he's* the evil one. Sometimes I think he's jealous of me."

I sat there, dumbfounded, my mouth hanging open in disbelief. How could I have been so oblivious to whatever it was that Bob had been doing to John to make him talk like this? Did John think I had turned a blind eye on purpose? Did he think that I even knew?

"Oh my god, John, please believe me. I had no idea—" but he cut me off.

"Mom, don't worry, I know you didn't know. The look on your face tells me that. Don't cry, please. You just don't know what goes on when you're not here."

"My god, John. I…I…don't know what to say. Or think. Or do. I'm gutted. Did you talk with Isaiah about this?"

"Not in so many words, but he's onto Bob. Bob hasn't fooled him one bit."

Isaiah was on to Bob, but not me? Was I that blinded by fear or self-absorption or my constant promises to myself that things would get better?

I was always waiting for progress in our lives, but there was never any improvement. I felt like I was sliding down a mine shaft. What I was hearing had turned my blood to ice and I began to shake.

"Sweetie, how long has this been going on?" Waves of guilt washed over me. How could I have been so utterly blind and insensitive? I had been mistreated by Bob for years, but my son? If John was suffering Bob's abuse right under my nose, how could I have not known?

"Mom, it's been going on a long time. Right now, I've got a basketball scout offering me a scholarship. The head of the drama department wants me to audition for a part in West Side Story. He says I look Puerto Rican. But I'm afraid to do it. I'm afraid Bob won't let me and he'll make a scene and embarrass me and then I'll lose all my friends."

I had noticed that he'd recently begun referring to his dad as Bob. Was it because he no longer considered him his dad, but his tormenter?

"I'm going to have a long talk with your dad tonight."

His eyes popped open. He looked terrified. "Mom, please don't talk with him about it. Please. It'll just make things worse."

"Dear god," I said, looking straight into John's eyes, "*What* has he been doing to you?"

"The same things he does to you, Mom." The thought of Bob leveling his special brand of intimidation, humiliation, abuse and discouragement on John horrified me.

Just then, we heard the car come up the driveway, the engine switch off and the car door open and shut. My blood turned cold. John immediately went to his room. I followed after him, and gave him a kiss and hug.

"Don't worry sweetie. I'll handle this. It will all be better!" I put a patently fake smile on my face and headed down the hall to my room.

Bob came up the stairs. I heard him throw his keys on the table, pull out a chair, and start shuffling cards for a game of solitaire, a habit that had become obsessive as he went out of his way to avoid actually interacting with us when he was home. Suddenly, there was silence, except for the cracking of his knees as he walked down the hall to our room. When I looked up, there he was in the doorway. He had that look on his face, the look I'd seen so many times before and seeing it now, just after my conversation with John, caused my anxiety to grow. I thought he somehow knew John and I had been talking, what we'd been talking about and how he and I had both concluded that Bob was a monster, although the conclusion was not spoken aloud.

I tried to soft-pedal it. "Hey honey! How was bowling tonight?"

"Okay. Why?" He took off his coat and dropped it on the floor. Then he sat on the edge of the bed to remove his shoes and socks.

"Oh, I was just hoping that things went as well today for you as it did for John."

"What is that supposed to mean?" He turned to glare at me. I was nervous, but determined to allow John to have a decent chance in life.

"Well, what I mean is that John told me that he's been scouted for a basketball scholarship. I'm so proud of him! Aren't you?"

Bob stood, turned and directed his steely eyes on me. "He doesn't deserve it, and I've told him so. I've also told his teachers and the coach."

Why would he do that? Why would he actively sabotage John's chances in life? A more horrifying thought came over me. What else, Bob? What else have you done to our son?

"Are you joking? Of course he deserves it. He absolutely deserves any good thing that comes in his life. How could he not deserve it?"

"You know what, you dumb bitch? You're just as stupid and worthless as he is." He pulled me off the bed and threw me against a wall. My foot twisted back and I knew at once that my little toe had broken. I shrieked in pain. He slapped his hand over my mouth and hissed at me to shut up.

"I'm warning you right now. Don't talk to him or anyone else about this. Do you understand? Do you?" He took me by the shoulders and threw me against the dresser. I fell to the floor with a thud. The pain in my toe was excruciating. I howled as my foot was again bent back.

Bob pushed me onto the bed. "Go to sleep. Now! I'll take care of this." He started down the hall to John's room. I tried to follow him but the pain of my broken toe slowed me. I stood in the shadow and watched as he passed by John's room, sat back down at the kitchen table to shuffle his cards and play solitaire.

Before I returned to our room, I quietly checked to see that John's door was firmly shut. *God,* I thought, *I hope John didn't hear any of this.* I went to the bathroom and took a Tylenol for the pain. There was no point in seeing a doctor about my toe. I'd just bind it with an Ace bandage. I got into bed and lay awake for a long, long time still listening to the shuffling cards. I was in terrible pain, the toe throbbing and horrifying thoughts flooding my head. But as long as I could hear the shuffling of the cards, I knew that Bob wasn't hurting John, and that he wasn't coming for me. The Tylenol began to hit me and I fell asleep.

When I woke up, I looked at the clock. It was four a.m. and Bob was lying next to me, snoring like a diesel engine. I got up quietly, unsteady and my toe hurting, and went down the hall to see about John. I opened his door and looked in.

He wasn't there. His room looked like a tornado hit it. Most of his clothes were missing from his closet.

I looked for him in the kitchen, the bathroom, even downstairs in the laundry room and in the garage. He was nowhere. *Where is my child?*

I jerked Bob awake. "Where's John? He's nowhere in the house. It's 4:30 for god's sake. Where *is* he?"

Bob opened one eye, looked at me and said, "I killed him."

CHAPTER 47

BREAKING FREE, MAYBE

I DIDN'T KNOW what happened but I came to on the floor. Had I fainted or had he knocked me unconscious? He towered over me as if he were a Godzilla and I a mere mortal. "I killed the dogs too."

I struggled to get up, felt bile rising in my throat and covered my mouth in case I vomited. *What more must I take*, I thought, *before everything I ever thought I knew in this world explodes into nothingness?* My son was gone. I was overwhelmed with fury, shock and terror. How had my life gotten to this point?

"Really? You killed my son? And the dogs?" I stood before him defiantly, my hands on my hips and my chin jutting out. "Then you might as well kill me too. Now, right now! Get it over with!"

He broke into laughter. "Do you really think I'd kill my son and my dogs?"

"Frankly, I don't know what to think." Just then the dogs ran upstairs and down the hall to sit dutifully at our feet. They'd been in the back yard.

"Okay, the dogs are accounted for. *Where in hell is John?* If you don't tell me where he is, I'll call the police. Do you understand?"

With growing horror, I realized that I should've called the police long, long ago. It was time to bring in the authorities, time to expose Bob for what he really was—a cruel and demented monster—and stop keeping secrets.

He grabbed me by the throat, a move that by now was expected. He slammed me up against the wall and with sickening clarity I remembered nearly twenty years past, when I thought he'd kill me, choking me in a Chinatown alley. Nothing had changed, I thought. Absolutely nothing. His promises and apologies were as worthless as he was.

I struggled to speak. "Go ahead. I dare you, you worthless coward! Get it over with. Snap my neck, I dare you!" I tried to kick him but he raised his knee to me and shoved it in my belly. I doubled over and he lost his grip on my neck.

I stood up and faced him. *"Where is my son, you fucking asshole?"*

Rather than answer, he sat on the bed and patted the space next to him—an invite to sit.

"I'm not sitting with you. Are you kidding? Tell me where my son is or I swear to God, I'll kill you."

He looked up at me. His expression had completely changed. He now appeared contrite, his brown eyes searching my eyes for some sort of understanding, as if I could possibly comprehend the venom in his heart.

"John's left home. He took off in the middle of the night."

"Why?"

"Because he's a loser."

"Bullshit! You're the loser. *Where in the hell is my son?*" I could feel my face turn red, my breathing labored, my armpits sweating and hives popping up on my body.

He slapped me, sending me reeling into the open closet. I landed on a pile of shoes. My toe bent back a second time and I howled with the pain.

Jesus Christ, I thought. I'm sitting on a pile of shoes, with a broken toe. With clear vision, I saw that I had sunk so low that I couldn't tell truth from fiction, that I'd kept secrets far too long and that I'd exposed my son to the evil that was Bob. I was finally pushed over the edge.

"You've been abusing me for years and I let you. But you've abused my son as well?" I accused him. "How could you? Godddammit, how could you? You are a monster...an abusive monster...a demon!"

Bob looked down at me, with a patronizing smile but something deeply unnerving smoldering in his eyes. Then he smiled.

"Did you know I put a curse on you the day we met?"

"Give me a break"

"I put a curse on you—a Santeria curse—and it will never go away."

I shook my head, sitting on my shoes, my toe hurting and my world crumbling.

"I don't believe in curses. I'm a Catholic, remember? I believe in forgiveness and love."

Then he changed again, his eyes sweet and soulful.

"I know you're worried," he said. "But John and I had a long talk last night. He's fine. He just needs to get away."

"He just needs to get away? What is that supposed to mean? He's seventeen years old, not some old professor taking a sabbatical. And what do you mean by a long talk? Was it the sort of talk where you tell him about everything he's done wrong and how you're the greatest person in the world? Was it *that* talk?"

Bob's demeanor changed again and he was pissed at me once more. "You've always taken his side. Always. That's why he's so worthless now."

"I don't take sides, you idiot. We're his parents. There are no sides."

His gaze momentarily turned darker. He raised his fist, but then put it down and returned to the nice, caring, understanding look.

"He's not doing well in school. He thinks he's being offered a sports scholarship but his grades aren't good enough. He doesn't deserve it."

"Really? What he deserves is an understanding and supportive father who will step in and see that his grades improve."

I struggled to get up from the pile of shoes, my toe screaming in pain.

"As I said, you've *always* taken his side." He began to bite his lower lip and doing so made his expression look terrifying.

Dawn was breaking and a thin light began to appear through the windows.

I managed to scramble to my feet and put on my clothes. "I'm going out to find my son. You can do whatever you damn well please." I had let his tyranny rule way too long. He couldn't threaten me with violence anymore because I no longer cared. I'd lost my son. Once again, a son was taken away from me, just as the social workers carried Isaiah in their arms out of the hospital and to the home of strangers. I was emboldened, saying things I'd never dared to before.

"Oh, and about being a loser....when was the last time you won anything at bowling?" His eyes flashed with anger and he moved towards me. He was so big and so tall it seemed his enormous presence could block out the sun. "If you're thinking of choking me, remember—I'm the only one in this family making a living. You don't want me to show up at work with bruises on my neck, do you?"

He dropped to the bed. He put his head in his hands, sitting there on the edge of the bed, looking like a reprobate beggar—his coat torn, his shoes dirty, his face unshaven, his glasses held together with tape. It was like I was seeing him for the first time, really seeing him for what he was, rather than what I thought he should be or wanted him to be. At that moment, I realized that he was not only a loser but he was no damn good and never would be.

My toe throbbing with pain, I went out that day and walked all through the neighborhood looking for John, stopping at his friends' houses, the Swamp, and the track field at his school. He was nowhere.

I'd never been separated from my son, ever. I was sick with worry. Yet, incomprehensibly, I didn't call the police or his school. I had grown so isolated, living with an omnipotent monster who had twisted my own sense of reality that it seemed impossible someone from the outside world could help.

I wracked my brain to think of where John may have gone. I had to assure myself that he was okay and would soon call me. I got up, went into the bathroom and looked at my image in the mirror.

"Who the hell are you?" I asked the mirror. I stared at myself long and hard. A tidal wave of regret flooded me. I saw that I had to rise and become a warrior. I kept staring at my image, picturing myself as Boudicca, avenging queen of the Celtic Iceni people in ancient Briton and thought about how she pillaged Roman Britain after her daughters were raped. She knew furiously how to stand up and be a woman and a mother. It was more than high time I did the same. I could only hope that it wasn't too late.

The next day, I thought about looking some more, but there was no place else to look. I would just have to wait for John to come home on his own. I went to work as dutifully as I always did. But now I was a zombie. My body was manifesting the stress, anxiety and depression in my life. The hives were still on my neck. I began to sweat profusely under my arms. I could barely breathe because my asthma had kicked into overdrive. I was falling to pieces. Day after day, night after night it went on, spiraling down into absolute blackness.

I told my mom that John had left. She was confused, then angry. "Why did you let that happen to him?" she demanded.

"God, I wish I knew," I said.

And still there was no word from John.

I tried to reconcile the Bob that forced my son away and the other Bob—the one who could be kind, helpful, caring, and even funny. He was indeed a monster, but not entirely. Perhaps his mother's treatment had twisted his mind. Perhaps there was a little boy inside of him, terrified that his adopted mother would abandon him on the steps of his birth mother. Perhaps it seemed that no woman wanted him, that he was a motherless child with no escape or hope. And perhaps that left him with a deep seated need to control any woman who crossed his path.

So many years had passed. So much had changed and yet remained the same. I thought meeting Isaiah would change him, would bring light and happiness to us all. I was wrong. But none of that mattered anymore. My son was gone and I didn't know where he was. Week followed week, month followed month and it was nearing six months since I'd seen John.

I finally became so ill from the stress at work and home that my physician told me I had to quit my job. He said it was killing me.

Bob saw an opportunity and took it. As long as I was incapacitated with this anguish, he could really control me. Suddenly, he feigned interest in my well-being. He solicitously went to my doctor appointments and nodded in agreement when my physician told me to leave my job.

"Oh sure," I said to Bob after we left the doctor's office and returned to a quiet, empty house. "I'm supposed to quit my job? I'm the only one working. I supply our livelihood and always have. How are we supposed to get by without my income?"

"Don't worry about it," Bob said, putting his arm around my shoulder. I shoved it away.

"Don't worry about it? Are you joking? You don't work. You were supposed to win the Big One at bowling and you never have. You've driven my son from the house and you tell me not to worry?" I broke down, crying inconsolably. Bob tried to comfort me, but I pushed him away again.

"C'mon Babygirl. It's going to be alright."

"No it's not. It will never be okay. And don't call me Babygirl ever again."

My heart was racing. I could hear it pounding in my ears. I started to gasp for breath. Bob must have realized that this was no joke and didn't want to take a chance. As I was bent over trying to get a breath, he called 911. The medics came, carried me out of the house on a stretcher and took me to the nearest hospital.

The staff in the emergency room must have quickly determined that I was not having a heart attack. I was having a panic attack. They admitted me to the psychiatric unit, where I spent three days trying to sort out my future with social workers and nurses.

After I was discharged, I called my job and gave my notice. I finally had to admit that I could not function at work and that trying to do so might be the end of me. In the corners of my mind, I told myself over and over that I would find John and that we'd leave, just take off somewhere away from the horror and towards a small light of hope. And I couldn't do that if I were sick.

But despite the fact that I was quitting under doctor's orders, the hospital fought my application for unemployment insurance, so we went for over four months without any income, except for what Bob won pot bowling. It was as if the past two decades hadn't happened, as if we were still homeless, living in a motel on the pocket change Bob won.

My life would continue to spin around in circles, repeating the same mistakes, the same calamities and the same losses until I found the courage to bring everything to a screeching halt.

But how would I do so?

CHAPTER 48

INDEPENDENCE DAY

I T HAD BEEN a year since my dad had died and my mother finally decided to sell the house. I used my unemployed time to help her get ready to put the house on the market. But I had an ulterior motive. I hoped that John might turn up at her house one day. Every time the phone rang, every time a car drove by or I thought I heard a knock on the door, I startled—praying that it was John.

There was so much stuff to go through, years of objects that my parents had accumulated. I enjoyed spending time with her sorting through things.

"How about you go out in the garage and tackle the stacks of National Geographics?" my mom said. "And those nine lawn mowers he was supposed to fix. I'll start in the bedroom. How does that sound?"

"It sounds great. I've wanted to clean out the mess in the garage for years!"

Over the months of April and May, we cleaned out years of accumulated things that were no longer needed and probably never needed. I was so pleased that she culled her kitchen things. How many electric woks does a person need? She had two and never used either of them. They went into the "yard sale" pile.

When we took breaks, we'd have coffee and look through old pictures. I picked up a picture of a handsome young man who looked like a strong farm boy. The picture, taken in a photo booth, looked like vintage 1930's. "Who's this?" I asked my mom.

"Oh, that was Frank. He was a boyfriend. He lived outside of town on his family's farm."

"I knew it! A farm boy!" I held the small picture at arm's length and regarded him with a judging eye. "Why didn't you marry him?"

"Good question. If I had I'd probably be living on the same farm. My hands would be like leather and my face unrecognizable from all the wrinkles. I wanted to come to Seattle more than I wanted to marry him, or anyone for that matter. Besides, if I'd married him, there wouldn't be you."

Near the end of May, I put an ad in the paper for our yard sale. People swamped the place looking over things. Over the course of that day, we sold everything. Then she put the house on the market. It sold within a week and the week after that she moved to a small studio not far from the house and got busy living her new life.

One day, after I'd returned from a long walk, I sat at staring off into the sky on the front deck when the phone rang. I was tired and had a cramp in my leg. I walked slowly to the phone and picked it up.

"Hello?"

"Mom?"

"Oh dear god! John? Is that you? Where are you? Are you okay?" My hand flailed behind me to find something to sit on.

"I'm okay, mom. I've been staying with friends. I left my high school and started going to one that's a little further away."

"You've stayed in school?"

"Well, I've tried."

"John, do you know how much I've missed you? How worried I've been?"

"Listen, mom. I called for a reason. I called to tell you something and then it's up to you."

I stood at the kitchen sink, looking out the window and watching the road ahead, as I always did, to make sure Bob wasn't on the way home.

"What is it? What do you need to tell me?"

"Mom, this is going to sound kinda hard, but here it is. If you don't leave Bob, you will no longer have a son. You will no longer be my mother. It's that simple. You've got to leave."

I felt like the air had been sucked out of the room.

"Mom? Did you hear me?"

"Yes, sweetie. I heard you."

"What are you going to do?" What indeed was I going to do? I was so depressed I could hardly move, but something deep inside me was starting to stir.

"I've quit my job. Where would I go?"

"Do what I've been doing. Live with friends. Live in the woods if you have to. Just leave and you and I will figure it out."

Bob was driving down the road with his blinker on, ready to turn into our driveway.

"I've got to go."

"Why, mom? Is he there?"

"He's coming up the drive. Sweetie, where are you?" He gave me a vague idea of where he was staying. But he was adamant with his message.

"Mom, I've said what I have to say. I'll talk to you later. Just think about what I've said and do it. Get the hell out of there or you aren't my mom anymore."

He hung up just as Bob was climbing the stairs. I replaced the receiver quietly and started putting water in the kettle for tea. My hands were shaking and I felt unsteady as I turned the burner on. I got down my tea cup and put a bag of English Breakfast in it. Bob gave me a quick peck on the cheek and asked if I'd gone on my walk yet.

"No, I haven't. I'm just about to go, right after I have my tea." It was a lie, but a good excuse to get out of the house while he was there.

"Okay. Want me to come with you?"

"No."

"Okay. Then I'm going to take a bath."

The kettle went off and I poured my tea. As I drank it, I pretended to be working on a crossword puzzle. He disappeared down the hall to start his bath. I finished my tea, tied up my shoes and left.

As I walked, I thought about everything I'd lost. My job. My son. My health. My self-respect. Any vestige of confidence. And Isaiah was in Pullman, so far away.

I looked down, watching gravel jump out from under my shoe as I walked on it. I had gone several miles when I suddenly halted. I stopped looking down at the dirt, lifted my head high and looked up at the sky. It was warm and there were no clouds. The sky was absolutely blue. I noticed the smells of late summer—wild blackberries growing on the banks of the small lake nearby, the scent of freshly mown grass, and flowers—all kinds of flowers. I could taste the sweat that rolled down my forehead to my chin. The taste mixed with the lingering loveliness of the tea. And I heard a small distant voice in my head. It said, *How much longer will you play this charade? It's a charade. Do you hear me? How much longer?* It was getting louder and louder until I clapped my hands over my ears to make it stop.

I sat on a log near the road and watched cars go by while I tried to think clearly about what I was going to do, how and when I would leave. There was no question about it now. It was only a matter of logistics.

When I got home, Bob was asleep. I sat in the kitchen and thought about what I would take with me. I orchestrated it in my mind. My clothes. My paintings. All the little drawings John had made that I kept in a box. My books.

At the time, I was driving my mother's old station wagon. I visualized putting the back seat down and stuffing my things inside. I thought I might even be able to get the mahogany secretary that my mom had given to me into the back.

And then I waited. And while I waited I rehearsed it over and over in my mind. I knew exactly how I would do it and when.

Bob was leaving for Las Vegas in a week. Once again, he was going to a bowling tournament. Once again he was going to win the Big One. And once again, he had borrowed money from some poor sucker to pay his way, with the promise of sharing the winnings upon his return.

I drove him to the airport that morning and dropped him off. He called that afternoon to let me know that he'd arrived.

"You better win this time," I told him and then I hung up.

The next day was Independence Day. Every year, all the neighbors pitched in to buy fireworks and they'd set them off in the street. The noise always made the dogs nervous. They'd glue themselves to me, panting and panicky. This year, I truly knew how they felt.

It was getting dark. People were gathering in the street near the Swamp. As soon as the sun went down, they began setting off firecrackers. The noise was deafening and the dogs were pacing and whining. People were shouting and laughing with wild abandon.

Then the phone rang.

"Hello." I stood in the dark kitchen, looking up the street like I always did.

There was a short silence and then I heard, "I'm having chest pains."

It was Bob and his voice sounded small as if trying to cajole me into falling for more lies.

"You're having chest pains? Why are you calling me? You're in Vegas. Call 911."

"I can't bowl. I don't feel well. I don't think I can do it."

And finally, something snapped inside me. It took a long time. It took losing my son and having him threaten to disown me to finally get it.

The fireworks outside were constant and getting louder. With each explosion, the kitchen briefly lit up with red, white and blue colors.

My feelings spilled out of me and into the phone.

"I'm leaving you."

"What do you mean?"

"I mean I'm leaving you. I've had it with you. You're not having chest pains. There is nothing wrong with you except that you're a loser."

I hung up the phone. I no longer felt pity. I no longer felt myself tied up with white guilt. And more important, I no longer loved him.

The phone rang again almost immediately. I snatched up the receiver.

"Didn't you hear me the first time? I'm leaving you."

"You can't leave me."

"Yes I can. You've driven John away from home. You've bilked people out of their money. You've promised me for twenty-three years that you were going to win the Big One and finally provide for your family. But all you've done is lose."

"You can't leave me. I'm having chest pains."

"Then call 911. Why do you keep calling me?" It was as if I was talking to a body bag, as if I were punching it as hard as I could, as if I only cared about one thing—tearing the bag apart and watching its contents spew on the floor.

"I've got a gambling problem. I need help."

Oh, now I get it, I thought. On top of everything else, now he's a gambler? Great. So that's it. He's gambled away what little money he'd managed to con someone out of. Could it have been that all this time his obsession with bowling was just a form of gambling?

"You have a gambling problem? Is that why we never have any money, no matter how many promotions and raises I get? You're a gambler? Well, then you're right where you belong. I'll bet there's a lot of Gamblers Anonymous meetings in Vegas. Go to one. But I'm telling you now, and you'd better believe me, I'm gone."

I hung up again. And again he called, but I didn't answer. In the darkness of the house, lit only by the fireworks outside, I calmly packed my things, just as I had rehearsed in my mind. I packed my clothes in an old suitcase, took down my paintings and tied them with a string, packed my books in grocery bags and took them down to the car.

Neighbors were everywhere, milling in the street, shouting and celebrating. The air smelled of smoke and beer and I don't think anyone noticed me.

I looked into the back of the car and realized I had room for the mahogany secretary. I went back upstairs and took the top part off with a screwdriver, then carried first the bottom and then the top section outside. In rearranging my belongings, I managed to get both pieces into the car.

But there was one problem. The dogs were in a state of panic from the noise.

So I did some more rearranging and managed to get them into the front seat.

As I was scanning the house to see if I needed anything more, the phone rang again. I decided to answer it.

"What do you want?" I was losing patience. Now that the dam had broken, the pent-up anger flooded out of me.

"How can you do this to me?" he asked.

"Still having chest pains?"

"No."

"Okay then. How can I do this to you? Let's see. I've endured twenty-three years of your abuse. God knows what you've done to John but whatever it was, he's gone and I don't know where he is. You have never cared for anyone but yourself. You are more than likely an adulterer, and I know you're a loser and a thief. Do you want me to go on?"

"No." He sounded oddly distant and unemotional. I wasn't sure if he really cared about anything other than saving whatever 'reputation' he thought he had. The thought that I might tell the truth about him frightened him more than anything else. As long as he kept John and me silent, too frightened to tell anyone about the war zone we lived in, he controlled us. Once we spoke out, his control completely disappeared and he returned, powerless and unimportant, to the dust that first formed him.

"Well, can we talk when I get back?"

"No." I hung up, went down the stairs, got in the car and carefully backed out of the driveway. The celebration continued, with more fireworks lighting up the sky but they got dimmer and the noise began to fade as I carefully drove down the street and away from my life of horror.

I didn't know where to go, so I went to my moms' little studio. It was late and she was asleep. I used my key to let myself into the building and then, with a quiet knock, into her studio.

She startled awake. "Lisa, is that you?

"Yes. I'm sorry I woke you."

"What time is it?" She sat up and looked at her clock. "It's 3:30. What on earth are you doing here?"

"I've left Bob." The words sounded so strange and foreign, totally beyond comprehension. I was shaking with anxiety, fear and doubt. It was if I'd said, "Oh. I've cut my feet off and thought I'd bleed to death here. Hope you don't mind."

"I've left him, Mom. And I'll never go back." I knew that my voice was shaky but I rattled on. "I've left him for good. I don't know what I'm going to do, but I'm never going back to that house or to him. I'm finally done, mom. I'm free!"

She was aghast. "Really? You really left him?" She sat on the side of the bed and turned her bedside lamp on. In the light I could see her sleepiness disappear. Her hair was a mess, but I imagine I looked like warmed over death. "God, what a relief! I never *could* stand him and he was mean to John."

That was news to me, and I started to demand a reason from her for keeping those feelings to herself all those years. But, on second thought, it just didn't matter.

"Can I stay here for a few days until I figure out what to do?"

"Of course you can. You can stay here as long as you want."

"I've got the dogs. They're a mess from the fireworks. I know that you can't keep them here permanently, but could we let them in for the moment?"

"Of course." I went back out to the car, let them out, and brought them into my mother's studio. They were panting and I got them two bowls of water.

I'd declared my own Independence Day. I could hear fireworks going off in the distance. The noise was muffled and soon died out completely.

As I lay on the floor wrapped in a quilt, with the dogs arranged around me, I pictured myself launched into the air, lighting up the night sky with my own brilliant independence.

But first I had to figure out how I was going to move beyond the tight grip of terror I'd been kept in so long. It wasn't going to be easy.

CHAPTER 49

WAS BLIND BUT NOW I SEE

IN THE MORNING the phone rang again. My mom said, "I'll answer it." I heard her say, "Yes, she's here," and I began to shake.

"You told him I'm here? Good lord, what are you thinking…?"

"Take the phone," she said. "It's not Bob. It's John!"

I was trembling. I sat at the kitchen table and my mom brought me a cup of coffee. I took the phone from her.

"John, sweetie, how did you know I was here?"

"Mom, I'm so proud of you. You finally did it! I called this morning and since there was no answer, I thought I'd try at Grandmas' and here you are!"

"Where are you? Please, I need to see you. I've missed you so much."

"I'll come by later and we'll talk."

"Okay, but first you need to talk with Grandma. She's been worried sick about you."

I handed the phone back to my mom and heard her say, "Goddamn it John. Where the hell are you? I've been out of my mind with worry…"

I got up and went into the bathroom, leaving her alone to lovingly admonish John and tell him how much she cared for him.

I looked at myself in her mirror and once again examined it. I saw resolve in my chin, hope in my eyes and a slight smile. *Isaiah will be proud*, I thought. *I know John is.*

At the moment my life laid like burnt crumbs in a toaster but I had done it. I had finally left Bob and there was no turning back.

I had three dollars to my name when I declared my independence. I was grateful that my mom took me in, but I knew I couldn't sleep on the floor of her tiny studio for long. The next morning I decided to ask her for help.

She awoke before me and was rattling around her tiny kitchen, making coffee and toast. She had her old chenille robe on. It was so ancient that the color couldn't quite be determined and the swirling chenille patterns were all but worn away. I remembered buying it for a Christmas gift for her when I was still in high school.

I got off the floor and sat on her loveseat, which was too short for me to sleep on. The dogs milled around the small space.

"Mom, I need to talk with you. I'm broke. I don't even know if and where we have a bank account, and I imagine if there is one, it doesn't have much in it. I've been on some job interviews and I'm pretty sure this one place is going to hire me. But in the meantime, would you consider loaning me some money so that I can get an apartment?"

"Of course I will." She set a cup of coffee down on the table for me.

"Really?"

"Yes, really." She was smiling. "I'll help you with whatever you need." I realized I'd been holding my breath, waiting for her answer and I was so relieved that I burst into tears.

"Let's have breakfast and then head out to find you a place to live." I could see that my mother was happy to help me. Because she was no longer browbeaten by my father, she had a new lease on life. And since she sold the house and had a nest egg, she was able and willing to help me build my own new life.

"I'd love to but can we wait until John comes?" I said.

He arrived about an hour later. I threw my arms around him and cried into his shoulder. My mother tried to punch him in the shoulder, but he quickly moved away.

Instead she got a big hug.

After we had breakfast, we got in her car and drove to the place in Seattle I loved most—Alki Beach. I found a small studio apartment in the lower level of an old house. My mom paid the deposit and first month's rent. Then we went to a furniture warehouse and bought a sofa bed, a chair, a television and bookshelves.

I moved in on July 11th, just one week after I left Bob.

I started a new job in the travel industry on the 13th. It was a much less responsible job than the one I'd left at the hospital, and it paid poorly. Still, it was a job. It was enough to pay the rent, buy food and gas. I started paying my mom back at $25.00 with each paycheck. And since the job caused no mental distraction, I had the energy to fix up my new apartment.

Isaiah had walked the line between his adoptive family and his birth family. He was back from Pullman and declared he was done with college. Ginny wasn't very happy about it. She and I discussed if there was anything to be done to change his mind, but she ultimately decided to let it be.

Isaiah arrived back in town just as I was moving into my new place. He was surprised but not shocked. I asked him to come over and help me put my new bookshelves together. I had decided that I would tell him about why I left only if he asked. I still wanted to give him a chance, if he wanted, to have a relationship with Bob and didn't want to taint his opinions.

We were sitting on the floor, surrounded by pressboard shelves, funny little nuts and bolts and instructions in five different languages, none of which made any sense to us. I thought some motivation might be necessary.

"After we put the bookshelves together," I said, "let's go for a burger or fish and chips, or something and then maybe a ride up to Snoqualmie Pass. How does that sound?"

His eyes lit up. "Sounds good! I'm hungry. Let's get this thing done!" He had brought a boom box so I could listen to a tape he'd made of his music. It was the perfect remedy for soothing our tempers after too many failed attempts to put it together.

"Maybe I should just pile my books on the floor," I said, feeling defeated. "No way," he said. And soon, after tightening the bolts and hammering a few pegs into place, the bookshelves were standing upright waiting to store my books. We cleaned up the debris and headed out for food and the mountains.

I threw myself into activities that I couldn't do while I was married. I signed up for a writing class at the University—an exciting and ironic thing for me to do. I was finally at the University, although not on the four year scholarship offered me so many years ago. Nevertheless I was happily taking a three quarter certificate program in creative non-fiction.

I joined a women's chorus and was swept up in a busy schedule of rehearsals and performances. And I decided to find my old friends that I'd been kept away from for so long.

Mary was married to a park ranger, living in the Grand Canyon at Roaring Springs. Mona was also married and working at a bank. Deego was a bit of a recluse, but I coaxed her out for dinner at my place. Beethoven was divorced, living in southern California and raising a daughter.

It was fulfilling to find that I had the kind of friends that I could just call after twenty years and feel like we'd just talked the day before.

The last friend I looked up was Liz. I was nervous about connecting with her. Even though I had left Bob, I still felt the fear of reprisals from him if I visited my "lesbian friends."

Liz was a nurse working at a state institution and was so pleased to hear my voice that she broke into tears. The last time we'd talked had been when Lynne died, and after I'd allowed Bob to threaten me with not seeing John if I continued to talk with her, I hadn't anticipated her joy at hearing from me.

She invited me to dinner that following Saturday. She made soup and baked brie. I brought a bottle of wine. We talked until 3:00 in the morning. We cried. We laughed. And she made me feel so at home and so loved, that when I left there was a glowing trail of happiness behind me.

The holidays were approaching which meant that the chorus was booked with performances. I was busy with that, as well as writing assignments from my class at the university.

I bought a small Christmas tree for my apartment. My mom gave me all of her old ornaments since there was no room in her studio for a tree. I invited her, Isaiah and John, and Liz to my place for warm cider and tree decorating. It was the first time in my adult life that I entertained at a holiday. And while it was all on a small scale, it was the happiest holiday I'd had since I was a child.

We cleared space to put the tree, opened the boxes of ornaments and sat around discussing how to tackle the job at hand. Liz brought Christmas music and that, mingled with the fragrance of the apple-cinnamon cider I had simmering on the stove, filled my little place with warmth, joy and family love.

I served roast beef with Yorkshire pudding and mince pie. While I was never a good cook, I followed the recipes to the letter and the dinner was pretty good. It gave me satisfaction to serve real brown gravy that hadn't first been green or red or hadn't had a full bottle of Worcester sauce poured in to make it brown.

We all sat around my gate-leg table to eat. John looked at the Yorkshire pudding and said, 'What's that stuff?"

"It's like an edible bowl that holds gravy," I told him. "Just try it."

Isaiah had already tucked in, saying he'd never had Yorkshire pudding before.

"This is The Bomb!" he said with his mouth full.

To the sounds of *Chestnuts Roasting On An Open Fire*, and over the light of the candle stick I'd used to decorate the table, my eyes met Liz's and something happened. Something good, but puzzling. It was like an electric jolt exploded between us.

After we finished eating and pushed ourselves away from the table, sighing and groaning, we opened gifts with abandon and the floor was soon littered with torn wrapping paper and ribbons. Some of the wrapping paper was made with glitter and the shine twinkled like little stars on the carpet.

I asked John and Isaiah if they wanted to stay the night.

"Can we rent videos?" John asked.

"Can you make us popcorn?"

"Yes, to both questions." Then I stopped and thought a moment. "Did you guys want to try to talk to your father and wish him a merry Christmas?"

"No," they both said in unison.

We walked up the street to the video store and I bought a jar of popcorn at the grocery to make on the stove, with real butter.

Liz offered to take my mom home and as they were leaving, I grabbed Liz's arm and said, "Call me, okay?"

"I was already planning to do just that," she said with a wink. She took my mom by the arm and I gave them both a kiss on the cheek. When my lips touched Liz's skin, I felt a sizzle of passion like I'd never experienced before.

After they left, I spread a couple of blankets and pillows on the floor, and popped in a video. I lay on the sofa and all three of us watched *Terminator 2: Judgment Day*. I fell asleep before it ended but I could hear John and Isaiah talking and laughing. Then it was silent.

I was the first to wake up the following morning. There they lay, on the floor right in front of me. Popcorn kernels, gum wrappers (I was pretty sure I'd said no gum) and comic books were strewn about them. They were both snoring loudly. I got up and quietly made a cup of tea. I sat on the upholstered chair in the corner of the room, tucked my feet under me, and watched them sleep as I sipped my tea.

I thought about Christmas of 1970 when I was pregnant with Isaiah—hungry, tired and very scared. In the ensuing twenty-two years, amazing and terrifying things happened. But, now here I was, living free and with my two sons asleep on the floor just like the first day we met Isaiah.

It was cold outside. A smattering of snow had fallen, enough to freak out the citizens of my city. But I felt quite warm, sitting in my chair, my sons sleeping, my mom doing well and strange but sweet thoughts of Liz swirling in my head.

The words of a song circled in my head—not a holiday tune but one of the spirituals I learned from Bob's gospel records:

Amazing Grace, how sweet the sound,
That saved a wretch like me.
I once was lost but now am found,
Was blind, but now I see.

EPILOGUE

Summer 2014

I DIVORCED BOB six months after I left him in 1993. For eighteen years neither John, Isaiah nor I had any contact with Bob. But late one night, John received a phone call from a nurse in a hospital south of the city limits. She had found John on Facebook and wondered if he knew Bob Jones.

"Yes, I do," John replied. "Why?"

"Are you related?" the nurse asked.

"Yes, he's my father. Why?"

"Mr. Jones is in the hospital and we need a family member to help him make decisions about his continuing care, if he wants heroic measures, you know—that sort of thing."

John called me with the news. I felt myself immediately move into the fear and anxiety I lived with for so long. When I went to bed that night, I had a nightmare that a viper with Bob's head was crawling through the bedroom window and I woke screaming.

In the morning, John and I drove to the hospital. Since neither of us had seen Bob for so long, we were nervous, scared and full of trepidations. But we both knew that we couldn't let him die alone. And though I knew he would never apologize to me for all that he had done, I also knew that John wanted so badly to hear his father say he was sorry.

Bob was lying in bed, his big feet sticking out from the sheets, very thin and with sores on his legs. As we walked in, he was telling the doctor, "Just shoot me. Just shoot me. I don't want no measures. Just shoot me."

We conferred with the physician, Dr. Ramamurti. He was from India, young, quite earnest and clearly frustrated.

"He won't eat or drink. He won't do any physical therapy. He just keeps telling us to shoot him. And that is why we needed to find some family to help with decisions. Obviously, we can't shoot him."

Seeing him after so long was difficult. The source of my pain and nightmares, the father of my sons, lay in his hospital bed thin, old and helpless.

John and I conferred with Dr. Ramamurti, but neither of us could make a decision about end of life procedures. But we took advantage of this brief encounter with Bob to settle a few things.

John talked with Bob as I waited in the hallway. I paced, hoping things would go well for John. Bob apologized to John, saying he hadn't been a good father.

In the hallway, John told me that Bob had offered an apology.

"Did you forgive him?" I said.

"Yes," John said, tears forming in his eyes.

"Good. Good for you. Good for him." I gave John a long hug.

To my complete amazement, John brought his daughters to meet their grandfather a few days later. Despite the way Bob treated him, John still wanted his dad to approve of him. The girls were so sweet to him, and the youngest even got Bob to eat his lunch by feeding it to him. Bob was enchanted with his granddaughters and that made John so very proud.

A few days later, he was moved to a nursing home. I talked with the nursing director and the attending physician. They told us that Bob was in total organ failure, had advanced diabetes and heart disease. They wanted a decision from us about the course of care left for Bob. Did we want more attempts to improve his conditions or just apply palliative care and let him go naturally?

How utterly ironic, I thought. *John and I are being asked if we want to prolong the life of the person who caused us such misery. How many times over the years did I wish he was dead just to escape the torment John and I endured?*

"I think we need to talk with him," I said. "I divorced him eighteen years ago. I can't make that decision." John felt the same way.

We entered Bob's room. The physician leaned down close to Bob's ear and said, "Mr. Jones. Your family is here. We want to know what you'd like us to do. We can prolong your time here with treatments or just provide you with pain relief and let nature take its' course."

"It's up to you," Bob said, lifting his head to look directly at John and me.

"No, it's not up to us," I said. "You need to make the decision." John glanced at me and gave me a small nod of his head. I quietly left the room and stood outside in the hallway. I could hear John talking in a low voice to his father.

I don't want it to be like this, I thought. *It doesn't matter how he treated us. He's still a human being who is about to die. I don't want to look back on this and have regrets. And I don't want him to die without forgiveness.*

Soon, John came out of the room. "Are you alright?" I asked him.

"Yeah, I'm okay, but he won't make the decision."

"I'm going to talk with him." I went back into his room. It had grown dark outside and there was only a small light on above his bed.

The television, hanging from the wall opposite his bed, was tuned to a game show. I picked up the remote and said, "You don't want to watch this, do you?"

He shook his head.

"Well, let's see if I can find something better." I flipped through the channels until I found a football game. "That's more like it, eh?"

He nodded his head.

I took a chair and sat down right next to his head. Bob stared at the ceiling as I said, "I want you to know that I forgive you. I forgive you for everything you've done to John and me."

But he wouldn't look at me. His eyes were fixed on the wall above the television. He had a smile on his face.

"Do you remember the time we were playing four-square in that park near the Center and some English group came along and played with us?" he said.

"Yes, I remember. It was Jethro Tull. They had a concert that night and were wasting time until it started. They wanted to know what we were doing, and after we explained, they asked if they could join us."

This was before John was born. I wondered if that was his only pleasant memory of our years together. Not the day John was born, or the day we married, or the day we met Isaiah—just playing four-square in a park with Jethro Tull?

His gaze returned to the wall above the television, but this time his eyes were wide with fear.

I tried to imagine what he was seeing.

"Do you see a light?" I asked. "If you do, you need to follow the light. Look for the light, and when you see it, follow it. Trust it. And, you'll be fine. The light will take you home."

I took his hand—the hand that had slapped and punch and caressed me—and whispered, "I loved you. But you kept John and me from accomplishing things. You brought sorrow and fear to us, and very little love. But I forgive you. I want you to know that."

He still stared at the wall, and I quietly backed out of the room.

John had been waiting. I came up to him and said, "Do you want to go back in and be with him for a while?"

"No. I just want to get out of here. This place is giving me the creeps."

"Me too. Let's go."

I had just drifted off to sleep when my phone rang. It was an aide from the nursing home.

Her voice was sweet and consoling. "I have some bad news for you, Mrs. Jones. Mr. Jones has passed away. I'm so sorry. I know this is a difficult, sad time and you'll need a while to absorb the news."

"Do you know what happened?"

"We think he had a heart attack, finally. His body just shut down. He was such a sweet man, Mrs. Jones."

"Well, how wonderful. But I haven't been Mrs. Jones for a long time."

"Oh gosh," she said. "I didn't know. I'm really sorry. This must be so hard for you."

"You know, I'm really okay. Really. Please don't worry about me. Now, did I leave the phone number for the funeral home, or do I need to call them?"

"I'm sure that can wait until you're really ready to make those arrangements."

She sounded so sweet and concerned. I hated to dissuade her from her compassion, but I also couldn't listen to it much longer.

"I really am fine. Since I divorced him a long time ago my grief is— shall we say—tempered."

"Oh, I see. Yes, of course." I told her I'd call the funeral home and arrange to have his remains picked up and taken for cremation.

Then I called John. "Hi, sweetie," I said. "I know it's late, but I think you know why I'm calling."

"He's dead?"

"Yes. He's dead. Do you want me to come over right now?"

"No, I'm fine. I've been expecting it and I know you have expected it too. Are you alright?"

"I'm fine. You sure you you're okay?"

"Yes. I'm really okay."

I was sitting in the dark on the edge of my bed. The faces of my sons floated before me. I saw their sweet little baby faces change and grow into the young men they now were.

But when I tried to picture Bob, tried to remember how he looked when I first met him, I only saw the shadow of an old man who died with nothing in the world except, at the last moment, John and I. I saw us hovering over him, trying hard to care for him and even harder to wish him well on his journey to a happier place.

My mother had ten good years after my father died. She traveled, played piano with a band of senior citizens and enjoyed getting to know Isaiah. But when I found her in her apartment existing on salsa and chips, I decided it was time for her to go to a nursing home.

The cancer she'd fought years before had returned and metastasized to her lungs and colon. She was taken to a hospital by ambulance and after x-rays and blood tests the attending physician told me that she had one to two months to live. She made the decision to withhold food and water which would hasten her death. She also made the decision not to have a funeral and told me where she wanted her ashes scattered.

I took time away from work and sat with her every day. She was on palliative pain medications and slept most of the time. But when she woke, we talked—about music, John and Isaiah, my dad and Montana.

I invited some of her musician friends to come by and bring their instruments. She asked them to play some of her old favorites—Bill Bailey, Stardust, and a medley of Louis Armstrong tunes. It was cramped in her room, but they managed to play a few tunes, bringing an appreciative audience of staff, visitors and patients to her door.

During the first week of February, she was admitted to hospice and in the early morning hours of the next day, she slipped away.

In April, when the weather was better, we went to Lake Quinault on a mountainous peninsula west of the city to scatter her ashes in the lake as she had requested. As we walked down the sloping grounds toward the crystal clear lake, I noticed a gazebo near the shore. My mom had always wanted a gazebo and my dad always promised to make her one, but never did.

"Let's go sit in the gazebo first," I said to Isaiah and John.

I had forgotten some of the words to Sleepy Time Gal, the song she used to sing to me when I was a little girl before my bedtime, but I faked it—just as my mom would have done. We bellowed out *Hello Dolly* and *Georgia* as tears filled our eyes.

Then we walked to the shoreline and scattered her ashes in the lake. They floated on the top of the water before gathering enough moisture to sink.

Over-arching these events was Liz. The spark that sizzled between us at that Christmas party in my little studio quickly grew into a blaze. We fell in love with each other and I moved into her house on Valentine's Day 1993. We've been there ever since.

I was finally able to live outside the closet that I'd kept myself in since I was fourteen. I told Liz that I wasn't going to live a lie anymore. We began a journey of social justice activism that took us to many cities around the country. I would never have imagined how fulfilling it was picketing a church in Salem, Oregon, marching in a rally for strawberry workers in Watsonville, California, commemorating the 25th anniversary of the Stonewall riots in New York City or joining the Gay Pride parade in San Juan, Puerto Rico.

As our years progressed, our relationship was strengthened by surviving together the sorrows and grief that would certainly have ended other relationships.

We found each other and have grown in love and friendship each day since. John and Isaiah are both glad to see me so happy.

Our state approved marriage equality on the November ballot, and on December 12, 2012 Liz and I happily got married.

We have two sons and three grandchildren who we adore. I've been to London eight times now; two of those trips solo. I've walked miles and miles there, wandering around, learning the streets and structures, and making the city mine.

As I write this, Isaiah is forty-five years old. He has a son, my first grandchild, Sam, who is thirteen. Last year, Isaiah married a wonderful woman named Coral. Ginny is still a woman with unbridled energy and we have a very special relationship of deep understanding and respect.

John is forty-two and has two daughters, Lily and Rose. He is engaged to a lovely woman, Adele.

When I think back and remember where I've come from, the joys far outweigh the sadness. I lost Isaiah, but found him. I lost John, but he returned. I lost my first love long, long before but found, in Liz, my true love—the person I will always cherish and spend the rest of my life with.

At some point, as we age and have the benefit of hindsight, we look back and usually see more good than bad, more affection than loneliness and more joy than sorrow. That's how I see it now.

And I get older I realize–as John Lennon said—that all I needed was love. That's all anyone needs and that's what we all deserve.

ABOUT THE AUTHOR

L ISA RICHESSON IS a wife, mother, grandmother, and friend. She's lived in Seattle, Washington all her life. She's been a contributor to an anthology about the mental health system and has published travel essays on London and book reviews in a number of journals. She and her wife live in Ballard. This is her first book.

Made in the USA
San Bernardino, CA
11 May 2016